PROPERTY RIGHTS AND SOCIAL JUSTICE

Property Rights and Social Justice analyses 'progressive property' in action by examining the role of constitutional property rights guarantees in mediating private ownership and social justice. It combines insights from property theory with enlightening doctrinal analysis of the interaction between property rights and social justice in the constitutional and broader legal context. It does so through the prism of the Irish Constitution's property guarantees, which uniquely in the English-speaking, common law world both protect property rights and require their regulation by the State to secure social justice. Through this analysis, the book grounds key debates in contemporary property theory in fresh, illuminating doctrinal examples, and enhances global debates about the constitutional protection of property rights. It argues that primacy is perhaps inevitably afforded to political determinations about the appropriate mediation of property rights and social justice, meaning that the political impact of constitutionalisation needs to be disentangled from its strict legal effects.

RACHAEL WALSH is an Assistant Professor in Law at Trinity College Dublin, Ireland. Her research is focused on the interface between public and private law in the context of property, with publications in the *Modern Law Review*, the *Law Quarterly Review*, the *International Journal of Constitutional Law*, the *European Constitutional Law Review*, and the *Canadian Journal of Law and Jurisprudence*, and leading international edited collections. She is also a co-author of the current edition of the leading treatise on constitutional law in Ireland, *Kelly: The Irish Constitution* (2018).

CAMBRIDGE STUDIES IN CONSTITUTIONAL LAW

The aim of this series is to produce leading monographs in constitutional law. All areas of constitutional law and public law fall within the ambit of the series, including human rights and civil liberties law, administrative law, as well as constitutional theory and the history of constitutional law. A wide variety of scholarly approaches is encouraged, with the governing criterion being simply that the work is of interest to an international audience. Thus, works concerned with only one jurisdiction will be included in the series as appropriate, while, at the same time, the series will include works which are explicitly comparative or theoretical – or both. The series editor likewise welcomes proposals that work at the intersection of constitutional and international law, or that seek to bridge the gaps between civil law systems, the US, and the common law jurisdictions of the Commonwealth.

Books in the Series

Property Rights and Social Justice: Progressive Property in Action, Rachael Walsh

Carl Schmitt's Early Legal-Theoretical Writings: Statute and Judgment and the Value of the State and the Significance of the Individual, Lars Vinx and Samuel Garrett Zeitlin

Remedies for Human Rights Violations: A Two-Track Approach to Supranational and National Law, Kent Roach

(*Continued after the Index*)

PROPERTY RIGHTS AND SOCIAL JUSTICE

Progressive Property in Action

RACHAEL WALSH
Trinity College Dublin

CAMBRIDGE
UNIVERSITY PRESS

CAMBRIDGE
UNIVERSITY PRESS

University Printing House, Cambridge CB2 8BS, United Kingdom

One Liberty Plaza, 20th Floor, New York, NY 10006, USA

477 Williamstown Road, Port Melbourne, VIC 3207, Australia

314–321, 3rd Floor, Plot 3, Splendor Forum, Jasola District Centre, New Delhi – 110025, India

79 Anson Road, #06–04/06, Singapore 079906

Cambridge University Press is part of the University of Cambridge.

It furthers the University's mission by disseminating knowledge in the pursuit of education, learning, and research at the highest international levels of excellence.

www.cambridge.org
Information on this title: www.cambridge.org/9781108426930
DOI: 10.1017/9781108551373

First published 2021

A catalogue record for this publication is available from the British Library.

Library of Congress Cataloging-in-Publication Data
Names: Walsh, Rachael, author.
Title: Property rights and social justice : progressive property in action / Rachael Walsh, Assistant Professor, School of Law, Trinity College Dublin.
Description: [New York] : Cambridge University Press, [2021] | Series: Cambridge studies in constitutional law | Includes bibliographical references and index.
Identifiers: LCCN 2020055295 (print) | LCCN 2020055296 (ebook) | ISBN 9781108426930 (hardback) | ISBN 9781108446907 (paperback) | ISBN 9781108551373 (epub)
Subjects: LCSH: Right of property–Ireland. | Social justice–Ireland.
Classification: LCC KDK215 .W35 2021 (print) | LCC KDK215 (ebook) | DDC 346.41704/32–dc23
LC record available at https://lccn.loc.gov/2020055295
LC ebook record available at https://lccn.loc.gov/2020055296

ISBN 978-1-108-42693-0 Hardback

For Neil Taaffe, and my parents, Michael and Linda Walsh

CONTENTS

ACKNOWLEDGEMENTS

I had the benefit of support and insights from many individuals in writing this book, which I am very glad to acknowledge here.

Three constitutional law scholars fundamentally shaped my approach to this topic, and to constitutional law in general. First, Frank Michelman encouraged my interest in constitutional property law through supervising my master's thesis at Harvard Law School and through his inspiring 'Constitutions and Property' reading group. I could not have asked for a better, more thoughtful grounding in the area. Second, Oran Doyle supervised my PhD thesis and imparted the importance and value of both critical, theoretically grounded reflection and accurate doctrinal analysis in constitutional scholarship. Oran has been a great support throughout my academic career. Finally, the late Andre van der Walt examined my PhD thesis and characteristically went above and beyond the ordinary expectations of that role. He became an invaluable mentor to me and generously connected me with an exciting global network of constitutional property scholars. These included a group of early career constitutional property scholars who came together to establish an exciting and supportive space for testing new ideas, the Property Frontiers Research Network.

My outstanding colleagues at Trinity College Dublin create a very supportive environment for research and have provided valuable feedback on several draft chapters of this book through staff seminars and meetings of the Private Law Discussion Group. Oran Doyle and Sarah Hamill kindly provided detailed comments on multiple chapters. My former colleague at King's College London, Eloise Scotford (now of UCL), provided helpful advice and guidance at the outset of this project that influenced my overall approach.

My co-authors on the fifth edition of *Kelly: The Irish Constitution* (Bloomsbury, 2018), Gerard Hogan, Gerry Whyte, and David Kenny, all generously shared their insights and expertise about Irish constitutional law. As work on that book overlapped with the early stages of this project, those insights are likely reflected here in many ways.

I had the benefit of outstanding research assistance, at the early stage of this project, from Nora Ní Loinsigh, and throughout its completion in 2019–20 from Daniel Gilligan, for which I am sincerely grateful.

My editorial team at Cambridge University Press, Finola O'Sullivan and Marianne Nield, were extremely supportive throughout the writing process. I am very grateful for their efficiency and encouragement, and for their championing of the project.

Aspects of this work were presented at various international conferences and benefited greatly from feedback from colleagues at those events, notably the Notre Dame/Oxford Constitutional Roundtable in London (February 2018); the 'Rethinking Expropriation Law' colloquiums in Cape Town (December 2016), The Hague (June 2015), Rome (September 2014), and Groningen (September 2013); the Society of Legal Studies Conference, University College Dublin (September 2017); the SARCPL International Conference in Property Law, University of Stellenbosch (July 2017); the Moral Values in Private Law Conference at King's College London (June 2014); the Young Property Lawyers Forum, KU Leuven (November 2013); and the Young Property Lawyers Forum, University of Stellenbosch (October 2012). I am indebted to all the participants at those events for their insights and reflections on my work.

Some paragraphs in Chapter 3 are taken from 'Land Law, Property Ideologies and the British–Irish Relationship' (2018) 47 *Common Law World Review* 7, and I am grateful to the publishers for permission to reproduce those paragraphs here. I am also sincerely grateful to my co-author on that article, Lorna Fox-O'Mahony, as the collaborative process of writing that article and sharing ideas about progressive property helped me to clarify and fine-tune my broader approach in this book.

Some paragraphs in Chapter 7 are taken from 'Reviewing Expropriations: The Search for "External Guidance"', in B. Hoops et al. (eds.), *Rethinking Public Interest in Expropriation Law I: Public Interest in Expropriation* (The Netherlands and South Africa: Eleven Publishing and Juta Publishing, 2015), p. 125, and again I am grateful to the publishers for permission to reproduce those paragraphs.

Finally, this book would not have been possible without the support, forbearance, and good humour of my husband Neil and our children Rory and Kate, who were all unavoidably close to the writing process due to the COVID-19 lockdown. My heartfelt thanks are also owed to my parents, Michael and Linda, who have provided unstinting support to all my academic endeavours.

1

Progressive Property in Action:

Widening the Doctrinal Lens

1.1 Introduction

Property theory spans a wide range of overlapping issues, including addressing private ownership's moral justification,[1] its core features and scope as a matter of private law,[2] and its status as a matter of public law,[3] often without distinguishing sharply between the applicability of the concepts and arguments developed at the level of theory in these various contexts.[4] The complex relationship between property rights and social justice is a theme that cross-cuts these issues.

Duguit famously described property as a social function rather than a subjective right,[5] an approach that proved particularly influential in

[1] See, e.g., J. Waldron, *The Right to Private Property* (Oxford: Oxford University Press, 1991) and S. M. Munzer, *A Theory of Property* (Cambridge: Cambridge University Press, 1990).

[2] See, e.g., J. Penner, *The Idea of Property in Law* (Oxford: Oxford University Press, 1997); E. J. Weinrib, *The Idea of Private Law* (Oxford: Oxford University Press, 2012) and A. Ripstein, *Private Wrongs* (Cambridge, MA: Harvard University Press, 2016).

[3] See, e.g., L. S. Underkuffler, *The Idea of Property: Its Meaning and Power* (Oxford: Oxford University Press, 2003).

[4] See, e.g., J. W. Harris, *Property and Justice* (Oxford: Oxford University Press, 2002), H. Dagan, *Property: Values and Institutions* (Oxford: Oxford University Press, 2011), addressing issues of both legal structure and justification, G. S. Alexander, *Property and Human Flourishing* (Oxford: Oxford University Press, 2018), A. J. van der Walt, *Property in the Margins* (Oxford: Hart, 2008), P. Gerhart, *Property Law and Social Morality* (Cambridge: Cambridge University Press, 2013); J. W. Singer, *Entitlement: The Paradoxes of Property* (New Haven: Yale University Press, 2000), J. Purdy, *The Meaning of Property: Freedom, Community and the Legal Imagination* (New Haven: Yale University Press, 2010), all expounding property theories that are applied to both private law and public law issues.

[5] L. Duguit, 'Les transformations générales du droit privé depuis le Code Napoléon' (Paris: Félix Alcan, 1912), reproduced and translated in J. H. Wigmore, E. Borchard, F. Pollock, L. B. Register and E. Bruncken, *Progress of Continental Law in the Nineteenth Century* (Boston: Little, Brown and Company, 1918), p. 65, p. 74. For useful overviews, see M. C. Mirow, 'The Social-Obligation Norm of Property: Duguit, Hayem, and Others' (2010) 22 *Florida Journal of International Law* 191, L. van Vliet and A. Parise, 'The Development of

civilian jurisdictions.[6] Honoré identified ownership as having a 'social aspect' that was recognised '[e]ven in the most individualistic ages of Rome and the United States'.[7] For Honoré, ownership's 'social aspect' was reflected in the susceptibility of property rights to limitation, for example through taxation or expropriation procedures. That 'social aspect' has come to be widely accepted by property scholars of all schools of thought.[8] It is also central to both judicial decision-making and legislative law-making – as Gray puts it, '. . .all modern jurisdictions are actively and inevitably engaged in defining (and redefining) the social boundaries of the institution of property.'[9]

Scholarly debate has shifted to the parameters of the 'social aspect' or 'social function' of ownership.[10] It has also turned to consider the appropriate legal means of giving effect to that 'social aspect' or 'social function'. Considering these debates, Baron distinguishes two broad 'camps' in property theory: 'progressive property' theorists and

the Social Function of Ownership: Exploring the Pioneering Efforts of Otto van Gierke and Léon Duguit' in G. Muller et al., eds., *Transformative Property Law* (Cape Town: Juta, 2018) p. 265.

6 See, e.g., A. dos Santos Cunha, 'The Social Function of Property in Brazilian Law' (2011) 80 *Fordham Law Review* 1171; M. C. Mirow, 'Origins of the Social Function of Property in Chile' (2011) 80 *Fordham Law Review* 1183; C. Crawford, 'The Social Function of Property and the Human Capacity to Flourish' (2011) 80 *Fordham Law Review* 1089; T. T. Ankerson and T. Ruppert, 'Tierra y Libertad: The Social Function Doctrine and Land Reform in Latin America' (2006) 19 *Tulane Environmental Law Journal* 69; N. M. Davidson, 'Sketches for a Hamiltonian Vernacular as a Social Function of Property' (2011) 80 *Fordham Law Review* 1053 and D. Bonilla, 'Liberalism and Property in Colombia: Property as a Right and Property as a Social Function' (2011) 80 *Fordham Law Review* 1135. Van Vliet and Parise note a degree of impact in the UK and the US: 'The Development of the Social Function', (n 5), pp. 270–71.

7 A. M. Honoré, 'Ownership', in A. G. Guest (ed.), *Oxford Essays in Jurisprudence* (First Series) (Oxford: Oxford University Press, 1961), p. 107, pp. 144–45. See also Kevin Gray, arguing '[t]here remain today few true property absolutists': K. Gray, 'Land Law and Human Rights' in L. Tee (ed.), *Land Law: Issues, Debates, Policy* (Devon: Willan Publishing, 2002), p. 211, pp. 222–23.

8 See E. Rosser, 'Destabilizing Property' (2015) 48 *Connecticut Law Review* 397, 402; S. Hamill, 'Community, Property, and Human Rights: The Failure of Property-as-Respect' (2017) 27 *Journal of Law and Social Policy* 7, 13 (available at: https://digitalcommons.osgoode.yorku.ca/cgi/viewcontent.cgi?article=1264&context=jlsp) and A. J. van der Walt, 'The Protection of Private Property Under the Irish Constitution: A Comparative and Theoretical Perspective' in E. Carolan and O. Doyle (eds.), *The Irish Constitution: Governance and Values* (Dublin: Thomson Roundhall, 2008), pp. 398, 399.

9 Gray, 'Land Law and Human Rights' (n 7), p. 245.

10 See, e.g., Crawford, 'The Social Function of Property' (n 6), 1134 describing property's social function as 'hotly disputed', and Ankerson and Ruppert, 'Tierra y Libertad' (n 6), 120, noting '. . .its contours remain obscure and its character evolutionary.'

'information theorists'.[11] Whereas progressive property theorists accept a significant degree of contextual decision-making in property law in light of owners' social obligations, information theorists prioritise rule-based enforcement of owners' rights to exclude as a more efficient means of ensuring simplicity and predictability in property law. Progressive property and information theorists also diverge on the appropriate division of institutional responsibility for the mediation of property rights and social justice. Progressive property scholars ascribe a larger role to judges in adapting property rights to the needs of social justice on an evolving basis; information theorists argue that such adaptation, where necessary, should be predominantly via legislative reform.

This scholarly debate about means and about the relative priority of judicial and legislative decision-making in mediating property rights and social justice has so far largely occurred at the level of theory, with limited connection to legal doctrine.[12] Doctrinal analysis can undoubtedly pay insufficient attention to theory – in particular, to ideas and intuitions about the value of private ownership that influence judicial decision-making, often unconsciously and almost always implicitly.[13] As Alexander and Peñalver put it, '…at the base of every single property debate are competing theories of property – different understandings of what private property is, why we have it, and what its proper limitations are.'[14] Those debates influence adjudication and as such appropriately inform doctrinal analysis. However, property theory can also benefit from attending more closely to legal doctrine as a means of grounding and testing theoretical arguments.[15] Particularly where property theory aims to improve the law for some purpose or for the benefit of some cohort of people, that theory should be assessed in part by reference to its impact on legal doctrine and outcomes. This is particularly important in

11 J. Baron, 'The Contested Commitments of Property' (2010) 61 *Hastings Law Journal* 917.

12 For example, Ankerson and Ruppert note '…a marked paucity of English-language literature' on the social function doctrine: Ankerson and Ruppert, 'Tierra y Libertad' (n 6), 119.

13 On this point, see K. Gray and S. F. Gray, 'The Idea of Property in Land' in S. Bright and J. Dewar (eds.), *Land Law Themes and Perspectives* (Oxford: Oxford University Press, 1998), p. 15.

14 G. S. Alexander and E. M. Peñalver, *An Introduction to Property Theory* (Cambridge: Cambridge University Press, 2012), p. xi.

15 On doctrinal legal research see, e.g., T. Hutchinson and N. Duncan, 'Defining and Describing What We Do: Doctrinal Legal Research' (2012) *Deakin Law Review* 83 and C. McCrudden, 'Legal Research and the Social Sciences' (2006) 122 *Law Quarterly Review* 632.

the context of constitutional property law, which necessarily involves judges in distributive matters usually left to the elected branches of government.[16] As Alvaro points out, empowering judges to strike down legislation based on constitutional property rights raises the possibility of divergence between judges and legislative majorities on the extent to which property rights are appropriately subordinated to democratic will.[17]

At its most basic, constitutional property law concerns '. . .the regulation of state actions that have a direct or indirect impact on private property rights'.[18] It can involve legislative interferences with property rights, but also administrative action or even on occasion the application of private law rules.[19] Guarantees for individual property rights in both domestic constitutions and international conventions and treaties are increasingly in the spotlight,[20] responding to the rapid expansion that has occurred in regulatory control of private ownership.[21] Underkuffler points to constitutional property rights as having '. . .immediate and powerful relevance to the vast majority of citizens', as well as the '. . .potential ability to bankrupt government.'[22] However, the function of property rights guarantees is often ambiguous, at least beyond paradigm cases such as compulsory acquisition of land.[23] The individual and

16 F. I. Michelman, 'Liberties, Fair Values, and Constitutional Method' (1992) 59 *University of Chicago Law Review* 91, 99.

17 A. Alvaro, 'Why Property Rights Were Excluded From the Canadian Charter of Rights and Freedoms' (1991) 24 *Canadian Journal of Political Science* 309.

18 A. J. van der Walt and R. Walsh, 'Comparative Constitutional Property Law' in L. Smith and M. Graziadei (eds.), *Research Handbook on Comparative Property Law* (Oxford: Elgar Publishing, 2017), p. 193.

19 Ibid.

20 On property rights as human rights, see T. Allen, *The Right to Property in Commonwealth Constitutions* (Cambridge: Cambridge University Press, 2000); T. Allen, *Property and the Human Rights Act* (Oxford: Hart Publishing, 2005); T. Allen, 'Liberalism, Social Democracy and the Value of Property under the European Convention on Human Rights' (2010) 59 *International and Comparative Law Quarterly* 1055; Gray, 'Land Law and Human Rights' (n 7), p. 211 and R. Cruft, 'Are Property Rights Ever Basic Human Rights?' (2010) 12 *British Journal of Politics and International Relations* 142.

21 On the impact of the expansion of the regulatory state on property rights, see K. Gray, 'Can Environmental Regulation Constitute a Taking of Property at Common Law?' (2007) 24 *Environmental and Planning Law Journal* 161 and C. Serkin, '*Penn Central* Take Two' (2016) 92 *Notre Dame Law Review* 913, 941.

22 L. S. Underkuffler, 'Property and Change: The Constitutional Conundrum' (2015) 91 *Texas Law Review* 2015, 2028.

23 For analysis of the function of constitutional property clauses see, e.g., F. I. Michelman, 'The Property Clause Question' (2012) 19 *Constellations* 152; T. Allen, 'The Right to

social values that influence the application of such guarantees are complex and at various times overlapping or conflicting.[24] That complexity is heightened by the fact that in common law jurisdictions, constitutional or human rights guarantees interact with private law protection of property rights. Van der Walt argues, '[a]s a rule the tension between constitutionalism and democracy or between the constitutional guarantee of private property and the need for social restructuring and affirmative action geared towards greater social equality becomes the central point for discussion of most theories of property.'[25] Legal responses to that tension cannot be effectively analysed by property scholars absent a perspective that places ownership's 'social aspect' at its centre and that carefully considers both theory and doctrine. A better understanding of the function and impact of constitutional property rights can be gained by analysing how legal decision-making about such rights is influenced, often under the surface, by ideas of the merits of private ownership and social justice.

A core aim of this book is to highlight some of the advantages of such an approach by exploring how progressive property, which foregrounds questions about the appropriate mediation of property rights and social justice, could be developed through fresh doctrinal analysis. By analysing the legal interpretation and application of the Irish Constitution's property rights guarantees, which in many respects illuminate how progressive property theory can manifest in constitutional property rights adjudication, the book reveals pitfalls and opportunities for the progressive property research agenda. It aims to contribute to both comparative constitutional property scholarship and property theory: Irish constitutional property law is illuminated by being considered through the prism of progressive property theory; that theory in turn is grounded by

Property', in T. Ginsburg and R. Dixon (eds.), *Comparative Constitutional Law* (Oxford: Edward Elgar Publishing, 2011), p. 504; J. Nedelsky, 'Should Property be Constitutionalized? A Relational and Comparative Approach' in G. E. van Maanen and A. J. van der Walt (eds.), *Property Law on the Threshold of the Twenty-first Century* (Antwerp: Maklu, 1996), p. 417; B. Bryce, 'Property as a Natural Right and as a Conventional Right in Constitutional Law' (2007) 29 *Loyola of Los Angeles International and Comparative Law Review* 201; G. S. Alexander, 'Constitutionalising Property: Two Experiences, Two Dilemmas' in J. McLean (ed.), *Property and the Constitution* (Oxford: Hart Publishing, 1999), p. 88.

24 G. S. Alexander, 'Property's Ends: The Publicness of Private Law Values' (2014) 99 *Iowa Law Review* 1257; Alexander, 'Constitutionalising Property' (n 23).

25 A. J. van der Walt, 'Comparative Notes on the Constitutional Protection of Property Rights' (1993) 19 *Recht en kritiek* 39, 40.

being analysed in the context of a constitutional property law framework that broadly fits the progressive property mould. The analysis embraces the broad tenets of progressive property (considered further in the next chapter), but highlights challenges presented by such an approach in constitutional property rights adjudication. As such, it offers a friendly critique of progressive property focused on identifying new directions for scholarship within that school of thought.

Section 1.2 of this chapter develops the rationale for a renewed focus on doctrine and outcomes in progressive property scholarship and signposts some of the insights that such an approach yields. Section 1.3 establishes the foundations of Irish constitutional property law upon which the analysis in subsequent chapters builds and highlights why the Irish example provides a particularly illuminating example of progressive property 'in action'. Section 1.4 outlines the structure of the rest of the book.

1.2 Widening the Doctrinal Lens

1.2.1 The Status of Doctrinal Analysis in Progressive Property

Rosser points out that both progressive property theorists and information theorists care about how their arguments map onto doctrine.[26] He identifies two ways progressive property has deployed doctrinal analysis to advance its arguments: first, to demonstrate the potential for greater social inclusion; second, to highlight legal exceptions to owners' exclusion rights that advance other social values. As he puts it, '...progressive scholars have offered new interpretations of existing doctrine and traditions in property law as a way of creating space for property law to better serve human values.'[27] Alexander characterises this as a central aim of progressive property theory, arguing, '[u]sing property to help the lives of marginalized people is, after all, what makes progressive property *progressive*.'[28] To that end, doctrinal analysis is a necessary element of progressive property's research agenda.

Rosser criticises progressive property for working *with* the existing property law framework through doctrinal analysis rather than seeking to disrupt it. A different concern about progressive property's treatment of

26 Rosser, 'Destabilizing Property' (n 8), 402.
27 Ibid., 434.
28 Alexander, *Property and Human Flourishing* (n 4), p. 320.

legal doctrine, to which this book responds, is its narrow focus. Overall, progressive property's arguments have not been tested or grounded through comprehensive doctrinal analysis, whether domestic or comparative.[29] As Lovett points out, the debate between information and progressive theorists has largely centred around a small set of US property law decisions.[30] There has also been occasional consideration of select German and South African examples.[31]

However, two trends in progressive property scholarship point to a renewal of interest in doctrinal analysis. Some progressive property scholars in the US have engaged in comparative analysis that considers relevant constitutional property law examples from other jurisdictions.[32] At the same time, non-US property scholars are developing independent, doctrinally grounded progressive property approaches to particular

[29] For criticism of the narrow range of examples employed by 'progressive property', see e.g.: J. A. Lovett, 'Progressive Property in Action: The Land Reform (Scotland) Act 2003' (2011) 89 *Nebraska Law Review* 739, 740; E. Rosser, 'The Ambition and Transformative Potential of Progressive Property' (2013) 101 *California Law Review* 107, 111.

[30] Lovett, ibid., 740. As Lovett notes, the decision of the New Jersey Supreme Court in *State* v. *Shack* 58 N. J. 297, 277 A.2d 369 (1971) is a recurring example in progressive property. Other decisions that he identifies as receiving attention include *Jacque* v. *Steenberg* v. *Homes, Inc.* 563 N.W.2d 154 (Wis. 1997); *Matthews* v. *Bay Head Improvement Ass'n* 471 A.2d 355 (N. J. 1984); *Raleigh Ave. Beach Ass'n* v. *Atlantis Beach Club*, 879 A.2d 112 (N. J. 2005); *Preseault* v. *United States*, 100 F.3d 1525 (Fed. Cir. 1996), and the decisions of the US Supreme Court on whether certain regulatory interventions go so far as to trigger the Takings Clause of the Fifth Amendment of the US Constitution (so-called 'regulatory takings' jurisprudence).

[31] From South Africa, *Modderklip East Squatters* v. *Modderklip Boerdery (Pty) Ltd* (2004 3 All SA 169 (SCA), 2005 5 SA 3 (CC)) has received attention. See, e.g., G. S. Alexander, *The Global Debate Over Constitutional Property: Lessons for American Takings Jurisprudence* (Oxford: Oxford University Press, 2012); G. S. Alexander, 'The Social Obligation Norm in American Property Law' (2009) 94 *Cornell Law Review* 745; G. S. Alexander and E. M. Peñalver, 'The Properties of Community' (2009) Ten *Theoretical Perspectives on Law* 127. German decisions that receive comparative attention include *The Hamburg Flood Control Case* (1968) BVerfGE 24, 367 (389); *The Co-Determination Case* (1979) BVerfGE 50, 290 (339); *The Small Garden Plot Case* (1979) BVerfGE 52,1. See Alexander, 'Constitutionalising Property' (n 23); G. S. Alexander, 'Property as a Fundamental Constitutional Right? The German Example' (2003) 88 *Cornell Law Review* 733; Alexander, *Property and Human Flourishing*, (n 4), pp. 218–29; R. Lubens, 'The Social Obligation of Property Ownership: A Comparison of German and US Law' (2007) 24 *Arizona Journal of International Law & Comparative Law* 289 and A. J. van der Walt, *Constitutional Property Law*, 3rd ed. (Cape Town: Juta Publishing, 2011).

[32] See notably Alexander, *Global Debate Over Constitutional Property* (n 31); Alexander, 'The Social Obligation Norm' (n 31) and Alexander and Peñalver, 'The Properties of Community' (n 31).

property law problems.[33] This book builds on these nascent trends in progressive property scholarship by bringing the theory and doctrine of constitutional property law together '…as part of a shared project to understand the working of law in action.'[34] It combines insights from property theory with fresh, illuminating doctrinal analysis of the interaction between constitutional property rights and social justice in Irish constitutional property law.[35] Like other emerging non-US progressive property scholarship, the approach adopted is problem-focused and locally-focused.[36] Specifically, it considers the insights that can be drawn from judicial responses to constitutional property law's core dilemmas formulated in the context of a framework that broadly fits the progressive property model. In doing so, it responds to Ran Hirschl's injunction that comparative constitutional law should move beyond 'the usual suspects'.[37]

1.2.2 Benefits of a Wider Lens

Van der Walt advocates more 'marginality thinking' in property law, in part on the basis that '…it forces one to look for the paradox and the contradiction rather than for broad theory and grand narrative, for diversity rather than uniformity, for dissent rather than consensus, for conflict and chaos rather than consent and order.'[38] Davidson captures the challenges of mediating property rights and social justice as follows:

> Every society must confront certain recurring points of tension inherent in private property. These include the balance between individual

[33] See, e.g., Gray and Gray, 'The Idea of Property in Land' (n 13); Gray, 'Land Law and Human Rights' (n 7); A. J. van der Walt, *Property in the Margins* (Oxford: Hart, 2008); S. Blandy, S. Bright, and S. Nield, 'The Dynamics of Enduring Property Relationships in Land' (2018) 81 *Modern Law Review* 85 and L. Fox, *Conceptualising Home* (Oxford: Hart, 2007). Rob van Gestel and Hans-Wolfgang Micklitz note that doctrinal legal research is more firmly rooted in European scholarship than in US scholarship: R. van Gestel and H. W. Micklitz, 'Why Methods Matter in European Legal Scholarship' (2014) 20 *European Law Journal* 292, 294.

[34] G. Davies, 'The Relationship between Empirical Legal Studies and Doctrinal Legal Studies', (2020) Erasmus Law Review doi: 10.5553/ELR.000141.

[35] In this way, it combines elements of what Siems labels traditional and contextual legal research: M. M. Siems, 'Legal Originality' (2008) 28 *Oxford Journal of Legal Studies* 147, 148.

[36] On the merits of a problem-focused, locally attuned approach to comparative property law scholarship, see R. Walsh and L. Fox-O'Mahony (2018) 'Land Law, Property Ideologies, and the British-Irish Relationship' 47 *Common Law World Review* 7.

[37] R. Hirschl, Comparative Matters: The Renaissance of Comparative Constitutional Law (Oxford: OUP, 2014), p. 192, 205–23.

[38] van der Walt, *Property in the Margins* (n 33), p. 245.

> freedom, collective responsibility, and limitations on harm, as well as incentives for productive activity, recognition of personal connection to property, and others. Society confronts these tensions through the resolution of individual disputes, with legal institutions that inherently draw on the values and imperatives of a given historical context. As a result, there is no singular social function – there cannot be – and no possibility of a transcendent, unified theory of what that function should be.[39]

The analysis in subsequent chapters is guided by these perspectives, working on the basis that 'broad theory' and 'grand narrative' are unlikely to capture the full range of influences in constitutional property law. Rather, this book shows that a fuller understanding can be gained from exploring how 'the paradox and the contradiction' that constitutional property law embodies is manifested in the doctrine and outcomes generated by constitutional property rights adjudication, and from striving to better understand the drivers of incoherence and unpredictability where such doctrinal patterns emerge.[40]

This demands a local perspective, involving: '…close attention to jurisdictional differences, and to broader social, economic and cultural considerations not always apparent from the face of constitutional texts, legislative provisions, or even judicial decisions'.[41] As Davidson puts it, '[t]here may be some continuity and stability in the institutional arrangements instantiated through property, but as with material resources and local conditions in architecture, the process of contestation leaves a vernacular residue on those structures that reveal starkly localised resolutions.'[42] Such localised responses are informative from a comparative perspective, since most jurisdictions with constitutional property rights encounter the same legal problems in their application.[43] Accordingly, this book aims to contribute to both comparative constitutional property law and property theory by analysing the distinctive Irish response to the difficult doctrinal questions raised by constitutional property rights. That analysis is informed by, and attends to, the evolving legal, political, and cultural contexts in which constitutional property rights adjudication

39 Davidson, 'Sketches for a Hamiltonian Vernacular' (n 6), 1058.

40 In this respect, the approach adopted loosely reflects what Robert K. Merton famously described as a theory of 'the middle range' that '…captures the twin concern with empirical inquiry and theoretical relevance.' R. K. Merton, *Social Theory and Social Structure* (New York: Free Press, 1968), p. 59. For application of this approach to comparative analysis of land law, see also Walsh and Fox-O'Mahony, 'Land Law, Property Ideologies, and the British-Irish Relationship' (n 36).

41 van der Walt and Walsh, 'Comparative Constitutional Property Law' (n 18), p. 214.

42 Davidson, 'Sketches for a Hamiltonian Vernacular' (n 6), 1058.

43 van der Walt and Walsh, 'Comparative Constitutional Property Law' (n 18), p. 193.

takes place.[44] It is also informed by the theoretical ideas about private ownership that are identifiable influences in the text of the Irish Constitution and in the instincts that judges bring to bear in constitutional property rights adjudication, which are unearthed from constitutional property doctrine and outcomes in the chapters that follow.[45]

As is discussed further in the next chapter, much faith has been placed by the progressive property school of thought in concepts such as social justice, social obligation, community, and human flourishing in seeking to reconcile legal protection of property rights with the regulatory freedom necessary to ensure a fair and proper functioning democratic society.[46] In doing so, progressive property theory has faced criticism for failing to pay sufficient attention to the 'means' of property law as distinct from its ends, in particular to how such complex, value-laden concepts might be interpreted judicially, and through such interpretation impact on the predictability, stability, and efficiency of property law.[47] This book shows that an important step for progressive property in responding to such criticism is to analyse the doctrinal impact of progressive property theory in jurisdictions where its ideas have a formal legal foothold. Such analysis provides a means of uncovering patterns of predictability in the application of the fairness-based standards favoured in progressive property theory.[48]

[44] As Michael Diamond puts it, '[t]he content of the term [property] depends on the culture in which it is employed and, within any particular culture, very often upon the period in which the concept is being discussed': M. Diamond, 'The Meaning and Nature of Property: Homeownership and Shared Equity in the Context of Poverty' (2009) 29 *St. Louis University Public Law Review* 85, 86. See also Alexander, *Global Debate Over Constitutional Property*, (n 31), p. 245.

[45] In this respect, the book responds to Harris' injunction that, '. . .the underlying justice reasons ought to be unearthed, much more often than they are when, in legal reasoning "ownership" is invoked as a principle.' Harris, *Property and Justice* (n 4), p. 368.

[46] See, e.g., J. W. Signer, *Entitlement: The Paradoxes of Property* (New Haven: Yale University Press, 2000); J. W. Singer, 'Property as the Law of Democracy' (2014) 63 *Duke Law Journal* 1287; G. S. Alexander, 'Ownership and Obligation: The Human Flourishing Theory of Property' (2013) 43 *Hong Kong Law Journal* 451; G. S. Alexander, E. M. Peñalver, J. W. Singer, L. S. Underkuffler, 'A Statement of Progressive Property' (2009) 94 *Cornell Law Review* 743.

[47] H. E. Smith, 'Mind the Gap: The Indirect Relation between Ends and Means in American Property Law' (2009) 94 *Cornell Law Review* 959.

[48] J. W. Singer, 'The Rule of Reason in Property Law' (2013) 46 *UC Davis Law Review* 1369, 1389, M. Poirier, 'The Virtue of Vagueness in Takings Doctrine' (2003) 24 *Cardozo Law Review* 93, 175.

Perhaps more fundamentally, doctrinal analysis is vital if progressive property is to develop as an effective legal framework for enhancing equality and inclusion, which is identified as its fundamental goal.[49] As Lovett points out, '...the failure of property law scholars to discover new property rule making and decision making in action can freeze the imaginative capability of theoretical scholarship.'[50] Fresh doctrinal analysis has the potential to uncover spaces and levers within property law systems for realising progressive ends. It can also highlight aspects of progressive property theory that may prove difficult to implement in practice. These insights from doctrine can in turn guide the progressive property research agenda. This book responds to '...the palpable shortage of new subjects in property law analysis' identified by Lovett[51] by offering a comprehensive analysis of Irish constitutional property law. In doing so, it treats attention to local, contextual factors and histories as a vital aspect of comparative property scholarship, particularly where a progressive approach is adopted.[52] As Davidson puts it, '[a]n emphasis on the *social* in property's function, by definition, makes clear that what society may require of an owner is always grounded in a particular culture and specific social, economic, and political conditions.'[53]

The Irish case-study reveals through its doctrine and outcomes, '...an ongoing process of legal and political negotiation towards a middle-ground position: respect for private property rights, appropriately delimited by social justice considerations.'[54] It demonstrates that socially responsive constitutional protection of property rights is achievable, but

[49] See Rosser, 'Destabilizing Property' (n 8), 428, arguing, '...arguably, at the heart of progressive property scholarship is the idea that those without title but with a history of enjoying particular forms of property have some sort of right to such property.' See also Alexander, *Property and Human Flourishing* (n 4), p. 320.

[50] Lovett, 'Progressive Property in Action' (n 29), 741. Similarly Blandy et al. argue, '...building an understanding of property in land from resources such as judgments and empirical data results in law that can be better designed to reflect property as it is understood and practiced, composed of complex, contextual relationships between people and place': Blandy S., Nield S., and Bright S., 'Real Property on the Ground: The Law of People and Place' in H. Dagan and B. Zipursky (eds.), *Research Handbook on Private Law Theory* (Cheltenham: Edward Elgar, 2020), p. 237, at p. 253.

[51] Ibid.

[52] Walsh and Fox-O'Mahony, 'Land Law, Property Ideologies and the British–Irish Relationship' (n 36).

[53] Davidson, 'Sketches for a Hamiltonian Vernacular' (n 6), 1057. See also Alexander, *The Global Debate* (n 31), p. 245.

[54] Walsh and Fox-O'Mahony, 'Land Law, Property Ideologies, and the British–Irish Relationship' (n 36), 26.

that a degree of unpredictability concerning the scope of constitutionally protected property rights is inevitable. However, the outcomes in Irish constitutional property law have been such that unpredictability is largely confined to its margins, showing that a predominantly contextual approach can be adopted in constitutional property rights adjudication without fundamental destabilising effects.[55]

1.3 Foundational Principles

1.3.1 Property in the Irish Constitution

Stern helpfully highlights a range of potential usages of the term 'property': to refer to a thing that is owned; to refer to individual rights pertaining to a thing; to refer to a thing's status as 'owned'; to refer to property law as a whole. However, he notes that in the US context, '[c]onstitutional usage is more precise', focused on property rights.[56] That more precise usage is also identifiable in the Irish Constitution's private property provisions, where the language used consistently refers to 'property rights'. Accordingly, this book focuses on how Irish judges reconcile the demands of such constitutional rights with the requirements of social justice and the common good.

The Irish Constitution, adopted in 1937, protects individual (as opposed to State[57] or institutional[58]) property rights in two provisions.[59] Article 40.3.2° secures such rights alongside other personal rights against 'unjust attack'. It provides: '[t]he State shall, in particular, by its laws protect as best it may from unjust attack and, in the case of injustice done, vindicate the life, person, good name, and property rights of every citizen.' Article 43 states:

55 On the significance of analysing outcomes to identify predictability in the application of contextual standards, see J. W. Singer, 'Justifying Regulatory Takings' (2015) 41 *Ohio Northern University Law Review* 601.

56 J. Y. Stern, 'Property's Constitution' (2013) 101 *California Law Review* 277, 286.

57 The State's property rights are dealt with in Article 10 of the Irish Constitution.

58 The property rights of religious institutions are expressly protected in Articles 44.2.5° and 44.2.6°.

59 Article 40.5 guarantees the right to inviolability of the dwelling, which is touched on but not analysed in detail in this book. For detailed analysis, see G. W. Hogan, G. F. Whyte, D. Kenny and R. Walsh, *Kelly: The Irish Constitution*, 5th ed. (Dublin: Bloomsbury Professional, 2018), pp. 2019–60, and R. Walsh, 'Reviewing Expropriations: The Search for "External Guidance"' in B. Hoops, E. J. Marais, H. Mostert, J. A. M. A. Sluysmans and L. C. A. Verstappen (eds.), *Rethinking Public Interest in Expropriation Law I* (The Hague and Cape Town: Eleven Publishing and Juta Publishing, 2015), p. 125.

> 1 1° The State acknowledges that man, in virtue of his rational being, has the natural right, antecedent to positive law, to the private ownership of external goods.
>
> 2° The State accordingly guarantees to pass no law attempting to abolish the right of private ownership or the general right to transfer, bequeath, and inherit property.
>
> 2 1° The State recognises, however, that the exercise of the rights mentioned in the foregoing provisions of this Article ought, in civil society, to be regulated by the principles of social justice.
>
> 2° The State, accordingly, may as occasion requires delimit by law the exercise of the said rights with a view to reconciling their exercise with the exigencies of the common good.

These constitutional provisions have 'progressive property' overtones in identifying property rights as appropriately delimited by social justice and the common good. They interact with Ireland's common law system, in particular its private law protection for property rights. As is considered further in Chapters 3 and 4, they involve so-called double-protection for property, securing both the institution of private ownership and individual property rights.[60]

The property rights guarantees in the Irish Constitution have generated a large body of case-law on a range of issues central to global debates in constitutional property law and theory, for example: what values are vindicated through the protection of property as a human right and how should those values be balanced; what types of valuable interests should be protected for constitutional purposes; what reasons should justify regulatory interferences with private ownership; what standards should be applied by judges when reviewing restrictions imposed on the exercise of property rights; when should deprivations of property rights be constitutionally permissible; and when should compensation be required to be paid to adversely affected owners.[61] These doctrinal problems all raise the foundational question of the appropriate allocation of institutional responsibility for laws and decisions with distributive implications.[62] As

[60] On the question of 'double-protection' in comparative perspective, see A. J. van der Walt, 'Double Property Guarantees: A Structural and Comparative Analysis' (1998) 14 *South African Journal on Human Rights* 560.

[61] For comparative discussion of the core questions in constitutional property law, see van der Walt and Walsh, 'Comparative Constitutional Property Law' (n 18); van der Walt, *Constitutional Property Law* (n 31); Allen, 'The Right to Property' (n 23).

[62] Michelman, 'Liberties, Fair Values, and Constitutional Method' (n 16).

the analysis in the subsequent chapters will show, the predominant response of Irish judges to this question has been to defer to judgments about the appropriate mediation of property rights and social justice reflected in legislative and/or administrative decisions. At the same time, they have been influenced by the classic liberal understanding of ownership underpinning the common law. Accordingly, Irish constitutional property law shows that property theories that are presented and contested in binary terms do not translate into constitutional property law in such terms. Rather, judges are influenced, incompletely and inconsistently, by a range of arguments, ideas, and intuitions about property rights on the one hand and social justice on the other hand, which feed implicitly, and sometimes unconsciously, into constitutional property rights adjudication.

The contentious constitutional property law questions highlighted above are analysed in subsequent chapters by exploring how they have been addressed in Irish law. Those legal responses are considered in light of relevant progressive property scholarship. As will be seen, that analysis does not always yield clarity, or an easy or stable settlement of tensions between property rights and social justice.[63] However, by extrapolating the reasons for judicial decisions addressing those tensions (which are not generally expressed openly and explicitly), and by assessing the emerging legal principles through the prism of progressive property theory, the analysis builds a comprehensive picture of how progressive property ideas may be reflected in legal doctrine and the outcomes in terms of property rights protection that such an approach may yield. The aim is not '...to unveil uniform principles falling into distinct categories'[64], nor to resist incoherence and ambiguity where it emerges – constitutional property rights decisions that do not easily fit the progressive property model are considered, as well as those that do. The aim is also not to suggest that Irish constitutional property law provides a gold-standard example of progressive property in action that should be replicated in other jurisdictions. Rather, the focus is on analysing the response of Irish judges to the key questions in constitutional property law to expose tensions in the mediation of property rights and social justice that resist easy or predictable resolution even where progressive property ideas have a clear constitutional foothold.

[63] As Chris McCrudden puts it, '[i]f legal academic work shows anything, it shows that an applicable legal norm on anything but the most banal question is likely to be complex, nuanced and contested.' McCrudden, 'Legal Research and the Social Sciences' (n 15), 648.

[64] S. Bartie, 'The Lingering Core of Legal Scholarship' (2010) 30 *Legal Studies* 345, 348.

1.3.2 Constitutional Foundations

This book focuses on the relationship between property rights and social justice in the Irish constitutional framework and does not purport to provide a comprehensive analysis of Irish constitutional law in general.[65] However, a few basic terms and principles are important for understanding the analysis of legal decisions in subsequent chapters. The Irish Constitution was adopted by the people in 1937, replacing the 1922 Constitution of the Irish Free State (Ireland's first post-independence Constitution).[66] Doyle summarises the basic governance structure established by the 1937 Constitution as '…an attempt to continue some traditions of Westminster government, notably the model of responsible government (whereby the Government is not directly elected by the people but is rather elected by and accountable to Parliament), while distinguishing Ireland in other ways.'[67] According to Article 15.2 of the Constitution, law is exclusively made in Ireland by the Oireachtas, which is comprised of the lower and upper houses of parliament (Dáil Éireann and Seanad Éireann respectively) and the President. In practice, the lawmaking process is generally dominated by the executive, led by the Taoiseach (Prime Minister).[68] Legislation that is approved by Dáil Éireann and Seanad Éireann must be signed into law by the President.[69]

Once enacted, laws are subject to constitutional review, with the High Court, the Court of Appeal, and the Supreme Court having jurisdiction over constitutional issues.[70] Judges are not elected in the Irish legal system, but rather are nominated by the Government.[71] An unusual

[65] For an excellent concise overview of Irish constitutional law, see O. Doyle, *The Constitution of Ireland: A Contextual Analysis* (Oxford: Hart, 2018).

[66] On the 1922 Constitution, see L. Cahillane, *Drafting the Irish Free State Constitution* (Manchester: Manchester University Press, 2016).

[67] Doyle, *The Constitution of Ireland* (n 64), 1. See further Chapter 3 on the relationship between the government and the Oireachtas.

[68] On this point, see ibid., pp. 19–20. On the legislative procedure, see Hogan, Whyte, Kenny and Walsh, *Kelly* (n 58), pp. 431–34.

[69] On the constitutional functions of the President, see Hogan, Whyte, Kenny and Walsh, *Kelly* (n 58), pp. 252–75, Doyle, *The Constitution of Ireland* (n 64), pp. 72–80.

[70] For comparative analysis of key features of this process in Ireland, see P. Passaglia, 'Irish Judicial Review of Legislation: A Comparative Perspective' in G. F. Ferrari and J. O'Dowd (eds.), *Seventy-five Years of the Constitution of Ireland* (Dublin: Clarus Press, 2014), p. 17.

[71] The Government acts on the advice of the Judicial Appointments Advisory Board. On judicial appointments in Ireland, see D. Kenny, 'Merit, Diversity, and Interpretive Communities: The (Non-Party) Politics Of Judicial Appointments And Constitutional Adjudication' in L. Cahillane, T. Hickey and J. Gallen (eds.), *Politics, Judges, and the Irish Constitution* (Manchester: Manchester University Press, 2017), p. 136 and on planned reforms, see L.S. Cahillane, 'Why Judicial Appointments Reform is Necessary',

feature of Irish constitutional law is the scope for pre-enactment judicial review of bills as well as judicial review of the constitutionality of enacted law. Article 26 sets out a procedure for the President, on the advice of the Council of State, to refer a bill to the Supreme Court for a judgment on its constitutionality prior to signing it into law.[72] In such cases, the Attorney General and appointed counsel advance arguments for and against the constitutionality of the bill. The decision of the Supreme Court on such a review is final: if the constitutionality of a bill is upheld, it is immune from subsequent constitutional challenge. Article 26 references are rare – there have been 15 in total, and none since 2005. Four of the leading Supreme Court decisions in Irish constitutional property law arose through Article 26 references rather than through individual challenges to enacted laws.[73] Consequently, a high proportion of exercises of the power of referral for abstract review have been in the property rights context.

The legislature in enacting laws and administrators applying such laws are presumed to have acted constitutionally unless the contrary is proven in evidence.[74] Therefore, where an interpretation of legislation is open that is compatible with the Constitution, that interpretation will be adopted by the courts.[75] Article 15.4 provides that the Oireachtas shall not enact unconstitutional laws and deems any such laws invalid. The effect of a judicial finding of unconstitutionality is ordinarily invalidation of the relevant legislation or administrative decision or act.[76] While the Irish courts do have jurisdiction to award damages for breach of

Constitution Project @UCC, 16 December 2019, available at http://constitutionproject.ie/?p=713.

72 See Hogan, Whyte, Kenny and Walsh, *Kelly* (n 58), pp. 477–93. The composition and functions of the Council of State are set out in Articles 31 and 32 of the Constitution.

73 *Re Article 26 and the Housing (Private Rented Dwellings) Bill 1981* [1983] IR 181; *Re Article 26 and the Employment Equality Bill 1996* [1997] 2 IR 321; *Re Article 26 and Part V of the Planning and Development Bill 1999* [2000] 2 IR 321 and *Re Article 26 and the Health (Amendment) (No. 2) Bill 2004* [2005] 1 IR 105.

74 *East Donegal Co-operative Ltd* v. *Attorney General* [1970] IR 317. For detailed analysis of the presumption of constitutionality in Irish law, see Hogan, Whyte, Kenny and Walsh, *Kelly* (n 58), pp. 984–1025.

75 See, e.g., *The State (Quinn)* v. *Ryan* [1965] IR 70 and *East Donegal Co-operative Ltd* (n 73).

76 The Supreme Court has begun to experiment with suspended declarations of unconstitutionality, although not in the context of constitutional property law thus far. For analysis of trends in invalidation on grounds of unconstitutionality in Irish law, see G. W. Hogan, D. Kenny and R. Walsh, 'An Anthology of Declarations of Unconstitutionality' (2015) 54 *Irish Jurist* 1 and Hogan, Whyte, Kenny and Walsh, *Kelly* (n 58), pp. 1051–83.

constitutional rights,[77] the doctrine considered in this book concerns constitutional challenges to legislation or administrative decisions resulting in either a particular interpretation being adopted by the courts to ensure coherence with the Constitution through applying the presumption of constitutionality, or in the legislation or decision being invalidated on grounds of unconstitutionality.

1.4 Outline

Chapter 2 analyses progressive property theory in more detail and considers the property values that are captured in progressive property's pluralistic approach. In doing so, it establishes a framework for the reader to assess the immanent, evolving influence of property theory in the doctrine and outcomes of Irish constitutional property law that are analysed in subsequent chapters.

Chapter 3 addresses the nature of the property rights guarantees in the Irish Constitution, their drafting history, and their relationship as developed through judicial interpretation. It analyses the origins of the progressive framing of constitutional property rights in the Irish context, as well as of the dual protection of the *institution* of private ownership and *individual* property rights. It argues that the drafters intended a division of labour whereby the courts would protect property rights while the interpretation and application of the 'social aspect' of ownership would primarily be a matter for the legislature. Subsequent chapters build on this insight by showing how that division of labour has largely been respected by judges in constitutional property rights adjudication.

Chapter 4 turns to the reach of the constitutional property rights guarantees, considering the rights that they entail and the range of circumstances in which they are engaged. This raises complex, contested questions concerning the meaning of ownership, including whether it should be understood in interpersonal terms or in terms of individual relationships with 'things', and whether it involves 'a bundle of rights' that can be packaged in various ways or entails core or essential powers for owners. The analysis in Chapter 4 of the circumstances in which constitutional property rights are engaged shows that the legal impact of these ideas is more complex and involves significantly more overlap

[77] Hogan, Whyte, Kenny and Walsh, *Kelly* (n 58), pp. 1535–42.

between competing perspectives than their dichotomous presentation at the level of theory suggests.

Chapter 5 analyses the standards of review that the Irish courts use in constitutional property rights adjudication. It focuses on the proportionality principle, which is an important point of convergence between many jurisdictions with constitutional property rights guarantees.[78] It does not purport to provide a comprehensive analysis of the wide range of theoretical and doctrinal issues raised by the proportionality principle, but rather focuses on the distinctive questions that arise where it is deployed by judges in constitutional property rights adjudication. It further considers the impact of the text of the Irish Constitution's property rights clauses on the formulation and application of standards of review.

Chapter 6 turns to the foundational question of fairness that judges are required to address in resolving constitutional challenges grounded in constitutional property rights, considering the range of factors that Irish judges employ in determining whether there has been an 'unjust attack' on such rights in contravention of the State's duty under Article 40.3.2°. That analysis brings us to the heart of the mediation of property rights and social justice through constitutional property rights adjudication. The overall picture that emerges is of judicial deference to the decisions of the elected branches of government concerning that mediation. Where judges have doubts about the fairness of interferences with property rights by the State, such doubts are often smuggled into decisions under the cover of 'non-property' principles like the rule of law, retrospectivity, fair procedures, and rationality, rather than through direct judicial engagement with the tension between property rights and social justice.

Chapter 7 analyses the protection of owners' security of possession in Irish constitutional property law. In particular, it considers the question of whether a 'public purpose' requirement for deprivations of property rights or restrictions on the exercise of property flows from the progressively framed delimiting principles in Article 43.2 of the Constitution, and if so, what that entails. It draws lessons from Irish constitutional property law for progressive property's attempts to address the 'public purpose' question in ways that both preserve the State's ability to acquire

[78] See, e.g., T. Allen, 'Property as a Fundamental Right in India, Europe and South Africa' (2007) 15 *Asia Pacific Law Review* 193, 193, arguing '. . .the constitutional law of many states also includes a test of proportionality, by which the impact on the property owner must not be unreasonable'.

or abrogate property rights in the public interest and protect owners' and their communities against unfair exploitation.

Chapter 8 expounds the nature and degree of constitutional protection for owners' security of value in the Irish context by analysing the compensation principles that have been developed in respect of deprivations of property rights or restrictions on the exercise of property rights. This analysis demonstrates how constitutional property law can combine rule-based and contextual judicial decision making to generate relatively predictable legal principles. Chapter 8 raises again the theme of judicial deference to the elected branches of government concerning the mediation of property rights and social justice by analysing how Irish judges have carved out space for statutory exceptions to default compensation entitlements rooted in the Constitution.

Finally, Chapter 9 concludes by synthesising the broad picture that emerges from Irish constitutional property law about the mediation of property rights and social justice and the emerging lessons and insights for the progressive property school of thought.

2

Understanding Progressive Property:

Traits, Themes, and Values

2.1 Introduction

Chapter 1 presented the rationale for locally focused analysis of constitutional property law that attends to how property theory influences legal doctrine and outcomes. It also introduced the debate between progressive property theorists and information property theorists concerning the appropriate means of mediating property rights and social justice. This chapter builds on these themes through deeper analysis of the progressive property school of thought and the plural values that progressive property identifies as secured through the legal protection of property rights. The aim here is not to evaluate the merits of the various approaches to justifying and delimiting property rights that are considered, nor to comprehensively analyse all of their features. Rather, this chapter explains the values that animate progressive property theory in order to assist the reader in considering their doctrinal impact in subsequent chapters.

Much of the property theory that is considered is centred on the private law of property. However, the values that are in issue may also influence constitutional property law. Moreover, in some cases, the theories are applied by their proponents to both private law and public law issues concerning property.[1] Consequently, the distinction between public and private law, although not insignificant in this context,[2] is

[1] See G. S. Alexander, *Property and Human Flourishing* (Oxford: Oxford University Press, 2018), Peter M. Gerhart, *Property Law and Social Morality* (Cambridge: Cambridge University Press, 2014).

[2] On the significance of the distinction, see R. Walsh, 'Property, Human Flourishing, and St Thomas Aquinas: Assessing a Contemporary Revival' (2018) 31 *Canadian Journal of Law and Jurisprudence* 197. See also Alexander, ibid., p. xvii, arguing '[a]lthough I certainly do not hold that any rigid categorical separation between the public and private realms is tenable, I do consider that the distinction between public and private law is a meaningful convention.'

certainly not strict or firm, and property values can have influence in both contexts.[3]

Section 2.2 examines the progressive property school of thought in more detail. Since progressive property adopts a pluralistic understanding of the values secured through legal protection for property rights, Section 2.3 considers those values from the perspective of progressive property to situate that approach in the wider landscape of property theory. It analyses information theory and the relevance of owners' expectations, the relationship between property rights, personality and personhood, and some of the connections that are drawn between property rights and autonomy. Section 2.4 concludes.

This analysis signposts ideas about property rights and social justice that are discernible influences in the doctrine and outcomes in Irish constitutional property law that are the focus of this book. The Irish Constitution protects property rights but expressly subjects the exercise of such rights to delimitation by the State to secure 'the exigencies of the common good' and 'the principles of social justice', setting up a striking double commitment to both property rights and social justice that reflects many of the values and debates involved in progressive property theory. As in progressive property theory, a plurality of property values will be seen to influence Irish constitutional property law, often implicitly and partially, and sometimes inconsistently.

For example, Locke's contention that individual effort and contribution to the value of an external thing should generate a claim to protection has partially influenced the range of circumstances in which the Constitution's protection for property rights is deemed by the courts to be engaged.[4] As will be analysed in Chapter 4, some valuable economic interests accruing to individuals *without* labour are protected.[5] In other cases, the courts treat the absence of individual labour as decisive in rejecting a claim to constitutional protection for a particular valuable

[3] H. Dagan, 'The Public Dimension of Private Property' (2013) *King's Law Journal* 260 and G. S. Alexander, 'Property's Ends: The Publicness of Private Law Values' (2014) 99 *Iowa Law Review* 1257, *Property and Human Flourishing* (n 1), p. 63.

[4] See discussion below at (n 137)–(n 144).

[5] See, e.g., *Re Article 26 and the Health (Amendment) (No. 2) Bill, 2004* [2005] 1 IR 105, where the Supreme Court upheld the argument that the applicants had property rights entitling them to recover fees paid for health services they were legally entitled to receive for free, emphasising the importance of private ownership to individual personality and humanity.

interest.[6] Where individual effort of some kind is identifiable but where the activity is characterised by the courts as speculative (such as, for instance, land development), the value accruing through that activity is not strongly protected.[7]

Similarly, the Irish courts accept that ensuring security of legally formed expectations is a function of the protection of private property rights, but they do not afford absolute protection to owners' expectations.[8] For example, Chapter 5 will show that the simple fact of loss of value does not give rise to a constitutional claim in all cases.[9] This will be reinforced by Chapter 8's analysis of security of value, which explains that full compensation is presumptively required where owners are deprived of their property[10] but that statutory exceptions to that presumptive compensation requirement to secure the common good and social justice may be constitutionally permissible.[11]

As will be analysed in Chapter 7, the Irish courts have acknowledged the existence of a relationship between private ownership and individual personality.[12] However, the courts have not guaranteed a strong right to security of possession.[13] Relatedly, the Irish Supreme Court has recognised a connection between property rights and democracy, including the relatively greater importance of legal protection for property rights for vulnerable individuals.[14] However, it has only done so in one decision, which it has not yet applied in other cases. This chapter aims to assist the reader in understanding the theoretical underpinnings of these doctrinal patterns, which are explored in detail in subsequent chapters.

[6] See, e.g., *Maher* v. *Minister for Agriculture* [2000] 2 IR 139.

[7] See *Re Article 26 and Part V of the Planning and Development Bill, 1999* [2002] 2 IR 321, where the Supreme Court rejected the argument that compensation for compulsory acquisition of private property had to reflect the value added to the land by a grant of planning permission.

[8] For example, the Supreme Court's decision in *Re Article 26 and the Health (Amendment) (No 2) Bill 2004* (n 5) reflects a strong enforcement of legally established expectations concerning property.

[9] See, e.g., *PMPS* v. *Attorney General* [1983] IR 355 and *Hempenstall* v. *Minister for the Environment* [1994] 2 IR 20.

[10] *Rafferty* v. *Minister for Agriculture* [2014] IESC 61.

[11] Ibid.

[12] See *Buckley* v. *Attorney General* [1950] 1 IR 67 at 82 and *Re Article 26 and the Health (Amendment) (No. 2) Bill, 2004* (n 5) at 201–02.

[13] See, e.g., *Clinton* v. *An Bord Pleanála* [2005] IEHC 84, [2007] 4 IR 701.

[14] *Re Article 26 and the Health (Amendment) (No. 2) Bill, 2004* (n 5).

2.2 The Progressive Property School of Thought

2.2.1 *Surveying Progressive Property Theory*

Progressive property is alive to what Freyfogle terms '. . .the landscape repercussions of property rights.'[15] It maintains that ownership does not mean absolute freedom within a bounded sphere or over particular things, because the protection of the property rights of some necessarily involves the exclusion of others from available material resources, thereby disempowering certain individuals within society.[16] Overall, such theories are concerned with the social vision that underpins property as an institution and with the character of the social relationships that it facilitates.[17]

At the core of the progressive property school of thought is a statement by Alexander, Peñalver, Singer, and Underkuffler that was published in 2009 to counteract the prevailing dominance of law-and-economics analysis in property law.[18] The 'Statement of Progressive Property' articulated a number of core principles: that property should be recognised as an idea and an institution, rather than simply being understood as a guarantee of individual control over resources; that attention should be paid to the social relations shaped by property and to the values it serves; and that those values should be recognised as 'plural and incommensurable' and as capable of generating individual obligations relevant to judgments about the interests that should be recognised in law as property entitlements.

The values in question include life, human flourishing, the protection of physical security, the ability to acquire knowledge and make choices, control over one's life, wealth, happiness, '. . .and other aspects of individual and social well-being.'[19] The pursuit of these values through property is said to implicate '. . .moral and political conceptions of just social relationships, just distribution, and democracy,' and to require

[15] E. Freyfogle, 'Property and Liberty' (2010) 34 *Harvard Environmental Law Review* 75, 116.

[16] C. K. Odinet, 'Of Progressive Property and Public Debt' (2016) 51 *Wake Forest Law Review* 1101, 1148.

[17] G. S. Alexander, 'Pluralism and Property' (2012) 80 *Fordham Law Review* 101, 107–08, J. Baron, 'The Contested Commitments of Property' (2010) 61 *Hastings Law Journal* 917, 924.

[18] G. S. Alexander, E. M. Peñalver, J. W. Singer, and L. S. Underkuffler, 'A Statement of Progressive Property' (2009) 94 *Cornell Law Review* 743.

[19] Ibid.

virtue.[20] Rational choices amongst values based on reasoned, contextual deliberation are required, drawing upon '. . .critical judgment, tradition, experience, and discernment.' Finally, given the necessarily empowering effect of possession of property, progressive property theory argues that property law should facilitate all individuals in acquiring the resources needed for full social and political participation, and more broadly should '. . .establish the framework for a kind of social life appropriate to a free and democratic society.'[21] Mulvaney resists the suggestion that the 2009 Statement marked a decisively 'new' turn in property theory, instead characterising those developments '. . .as seeking to give existing progressive conceptions of property new traction in legal scholarship and to encourage continuing work that delineates and clarifies the content of these conceptions in the present day.'[22] Certainly the signatories of the Statement all developed aspects of its principles in earlier work.[23]

Scholarship by non-signatories displays features that also reflect a progressive approach to property, although as Bray notes, the degree of consensus among those accounts is 'an open issue'.[24] Since the Statement was published, some scholars have directly built on its principles in developing theories of property[25] and analysing particular property problems.[26] Other scholars have been claimed for the progressive property school of thought without necessarily explicitly committing themselves to it. For example, Freyfogle advocates a human flourishing approach to property and has been characterised as part of the progressive property school of thought.[27] Nedelsky's work on property has

[20] Ibid.

[21] Ibid., 744.

[22] T. M. Mulvaney, 'Progressive Property Moving Forward' (2014) 102 *California Law Review* 295, 354.

[23] See, e.g., E. M. Peñalver, 'Property as Entrance' (2005) 91 *Virginia Law Review* 1889; J. W. Singer, *Entitlement: The Paradoxes of Property* (New Haven: Yale University Press, 2000); G. S. Alexander, 'Critical Land Law' in S. Bright and J. Dewar (eds.) *Land Law: Themes and Perspectives* (Oxford: Oxford University Press, 1998), p. 52 and L. S. Underkuffler, *The Idea of Property: Its Meaning and Power* (Oxford: Oxford University Press, 2003).

[24] Z. Bray, 'The New Progressive Property and the Low Income Housing Conflict' (2012) *Brigham Young University Law Review* 1109, 1116.

[25] See, e.g., Mulvaney, 'Progressive Property Moving Forward' (n 22) and Gerhart, *Property Law and Social Morality* (n 1).

[26] See, e.g., Bray, 'The New Progressive Property' (n 24); Odinet, 'Of Progressive Property' (n 16) and J. A. Lovett, 'Progressive Property in Action: The Land Reform (Scotland) Act 2003' (2011) 89 *Nebraska Law Review* 739.

[27] Bray, 'The New Progressive Property' (n 24), 1112.

similarly been identified as progressive.[28] The freedom and autonomy focused property theories developed by Purdy and Dagan prompted their characterisation as 'social obligation theorists',[29] although Purdy and Dagan disagree with some aspects of the Statement of Progressive Property.[30] Davidson's work also displays a progressive orientation.[31] Approaches to property law focused on sharing[32] and inclusion[33] are also broadly aligned to the progressive property agenda.

The influence of progressive property theory is identifiable beyond US property law scholarship. In the South African context, van der Walt's work has a strongly progressive tenor,[34] although he expressed reservations about some of the ambiguities of progressive property theory as articulated in US scholarship.[35] In the UK, Gray's work has been claimed for the progressive property school of thought.[36] In addition, there is a close affiliation between the progressive property school of thought and Fox-O'Mahony's scholarship,[37] and the recent work of Blandy, Bright,

[28] Mulvaney, 'Progressive Property Moving Forward' (n 22), 358.

[29] See, e.g., Alexander, 'Pluralism and Property' (n 17). See also Bray, 'The New Progressive Property' (n 24), 1112 and E. Rosser, 'Destabilizing Property' (2015) 48 *Connecticut Law Review* 397, 412.

[30] See H. Dagan, 'The Social Responsibility of Ownership' (2007) 92 *Cornell Law Review* 1125 and J. Purdy, 'A Few Questions about the Social Obligation Norm' (2009) 94 *Cornell Law Review* 949.

[31] See N. M. Davidson, 'Property and Identity: Vulnerability and Insecurity in the Housing Crisis' (2012) 47 *Harvard Civil Rights-Civil Liberties Law Review* 119; N. M. Davidson, 'Standardization and Pluralism in Property Law', (2008) 61 *Vanderbilt Law Review* 159 and N. M. Davidson and R. Dyal-Chand, 'Property in Crisis' (2010) 78 *Fordham Law Review* 1607.

[32] See most notably R. Dyal-Chand, 'Sharing the Cathedral' (2013) 46 *Connecticut Law Review* 647. For an Irish 'sharing' perspective, see L. Fox-O'Mahony, 'Property, Sharing and Identity: Applying Andre van der Walt's Theory of Property and Social Justice in Northern Ireland' in G. Muller et al. eds., *Transformative Property Law* (Cape Town: Juta, 2018) p. 173.

[33] D. B. Kelly, 'The Right to Include' (2014) 63 *Emory Law Journal* 857, Peñalver, 'Property as Entrance' (n 23).

[34] See, e.g., A. J. van der Walt, *Property in the Margins* (Oxford: Hart, 2009).

[35] A. J. van der Walt, 'The Modest Systemic Status of Property' (2014) 1 *Journal of Law, Property and Society* 15, most notably 56–7.

[36] See Bray, 'The New Progressive Property' (n 24), 1121, 1123.

[37] See, e.g., L. Fox-O'Mahony, *Conceptualising Home: Theories, Laws and Policies* (Oxford: Hart, 2007), 'Property Outsiders and the Hidden Politics of Doctrinalism' (2014) 67 *Current Legal Problems* 409, 'Property, Sharing and Identity' (n 32), N. Cobb and L. Fox-O'Mahony, 'Living Outside the System: The (Im)morality of Urban Squatting after the Land Registration Act 2002' (2007) 27 *Legal Studies* 236.

and Nield on enduring property relations.[38] A notable contrast between the US approach to progressive property and its manifestations in other jurisdictions has been a greater focus on progressive property in action outside the US, with scholars paying close attention to progressive property ideas in analysing local legal responses to particular property problems, for example the security of tenants against eviction,[39] rights of access to countryside for leisure purposes,[40] and protections against repossession for mortgagors.[41]

This account is not in any way exhaustive and doubtless the appropriate classification of these and other scholars could be debated at length.[42] The aim here is simply to describe the progressive property school of thought as encompassing a core membership and a periphery of closely related work that displays at least some agreement with the claims made in the Statement. Even amongst the signatories of the Statement, progressive property is, as Bray puts it, 'a broad and diverse doctrine'.[43] Beyond the signatories, it is best understood as what Rosser describes as '. . .more an orientation than a fully defined set of values or intellectual commitments.'[44]

Alexander identifies three shared characteristics of progressive property theories: '(1) their shared goal of human flourishing, (2) their understanding of property as based on a pluralistic value foundation that includes but is far from limited to preference-satisfaction, and (3) their commitment to improving the lives of those who live on the margins of society.'[45] Rosser further suggests deprioritising the right to exclude and

38 S. Blandy, S. Bright and S. Nield, 'The Dynamics of Enduring Property Relationships in Land' (2018) 81 *Modern Law Review* 85.

39 See, e.g., Van der Walt, *Property in the Margins* (n 34).

40 See, e.g., K. Gray, 'Land Law and Human Rights' in *Land Law: Issues, Debates, Policy*, Louise Tee (ed.) (Willan Publishing, 2002) 211, 'Can Environmental Regulation Constitute a Taking of Property at Common Law?' (2007) 24 *Environmental and Planning Law Journal* 161.

41 See, e.g., Fox-O'Mahony, *Conceptualising Home* (n 37), Nield et al., 'Enduring Property Relationships' (n 36).

42 For example, Mulvaney identifies Jane B. Baron, Zachary Bray, Nestor Davidson, Rashmi Dyal-Chand, Eric Freyfogle, John A. Lovett, Ezra Rosser, Susan Bright, Hanoch Dagan, Benjamin Davy, Jennifer Nedelsky, Lorna Fox O'Mahony, Richard Shay, and Andre van der Walt as writing in a progressive vein on property issues: T. M. Mulvaney, 'Legislative Exactions and Progressive Property' (2016) 14 *Harvard Environmental Law Review* 137.

43 Bray, 'The New Progressive Property' (n 24), 1109.

44 E. Rosser, 'The Ambition and Transformative Potential of Progressive Property' (2013) 101 *California Law Review* 107, 115.

45 Alexander, *Property and Human Flourishing* (n 1), p. 320.

recognising public claims over private property as core themes of progressive property.[46] Bray identifies a number of 'common traits' of 'new progressive property': 'its deeply communitarian nature; its resistance to absolutist or libertarian theories of private property; its doubts about a predominant law-and-economics focus in property law, and its embrace of a wider array of values.'[47] The primary focus in this book is on analysing the doctrinal impact of these 'common traits' through the prism of Irish constitutional property law. Accordingly, scholarship with a progressive property orientation is explored in subsequent chapters where relevant to the contentious doctrinal issues that are analysed. The next parts of this section set out in more detail some of the contributions to progressive property theory that are particularly significant in that analysis.

2.2.2 *Human Flourishing in Progressive Property Theory*

Progressive property justifies and delimits private property rights by reference to the broader project of securing human flourishing. Freyfogle emphasises the pluralistic nature of human flourishing, which he argues is '. . .deeply laced with moral and prudential choices'.[48] He contends that private ownership can both aid and hinder human flourishing depending on how human flourishing is defined in different ways and in different contexts. Adopting a similarly pluralistic approach, Alexander argues for an understanding of property rights based on an Aristotelian conception of human flourishing according to which life within a community of social relations is necessary, as well as '. . .the capacity to make meaningful choices among alternative life horizons, to discern the salient differences among them, and to deliberate deeply about what is valuable within those available alternatives.'[49]

[46] Rosser, 'Ambition and Transformative Potential' (n 44), 145.

[47] Bray, 'The New Progressive Property' (n 24), 1117–19.

[48] E. T. Freyfogle, 'Private Ownership and Human Flourishing – An Exploratory Overview' (2013) 2 *Stellenbosch L Rev* 430, 435.

[49] G. S. Alexander, 'The Social-Obligation Norm in American Property Law' (2009) 94 *Cornell Law Review* 745, 761–62. He contrasts this understanding of social obligation in property law with the 'strikingly thin' traditional liberal restriction on owners committing nuisance, 753. For full elaboration of this approach, see *Property and Human Flourishing* (n 1), 'Property's Ends' (n 3), 1260, 'Governance Property' (2012) 160 *University of Pennsylvania Law Review* 1853, 'Intergenerational Communities' (2014) 8 *Law Ethics Human Rights* 21, 24–5. He applies this understanding of property rights primarily, but not exclusively, to private law, addressing public law issues like expropriation: see

Alexander's pluralistic vision of human flourishing involves a number of core values: autonomy, personal security/privacy, personhood, self-determination, community, and equality. He contends that all individuals are equally entitled to flourish and to access the material resources that such flourishing requires. Accordingly, he argues for a social obligation norm in property law founded upon reciprocal recognition of the entitlement to flourish. As he puts it, '...in recognition of my obligation to support and sustain the very society that makes my flourishing possible, my ownership is inherently limited by that same obligation.'[50] That obligation is limited to what is required to facilitate human flourishing. Developing this theory, he distinguishes between 'general obligations', concerning '...goods that are constitutive of the requisite material background for flourishing' that are imposed on all members of society (for example through general taxation measures), and 'specific obligations' that burden and benefit specific groups of individuals because of their positions.[51] 'Specific obligations' can be satisfied in a variety of ways, including potentially imposing negative and/or positive obligations on owners.

Also writing from a human flourishing perspective, Peñalver argues that collective decisions about land use should be made where such decisions are likely to be more morally correct than individual decisions.[52] Such decisions should induce and encourage owners to act virtuously of their own accord, as well as helping '...to clarify social obligations and coordinate collective virtuous actions.'[53] However, Peñalver acknowledges the significance of autonomy to human flourishing and suggests that determining the appropriate distribution of decision-making power is 'a difficult puzzle' requiring a broader perspective than economic analysis.[54]

Writing together, Alexander and Peñalver have further developed these ideas.[55] Their theory envisages plural modes of human flourishing,

Alexander, *Property and Human Flourishing* (n 1) p. xvii, describing his theory as in the first instance one of private law.

50 Alexander, *Property and Human Flourishing* (n 1), p, 59. He holds that ownership is not always required; it depends on the capability or capabilities at stake.

51 Ibid., pp. 55–56.

52 E. M. Peñalver, 'Land Virtues' (2009) 94 *Cornell Law Review* 821. See also Peñalver, 'Property as Entrance' (n 23).

53 Peñalver, 'Land Virtues' (n 52), 871–72.

54 Ibid., 874.

55 G. S. Alexander and E. M. Peñalver, 'Properties of Community' (2009) *Ten Theoretical Inquiries in Law* 127, 134. For application of this approach see, e.g., C. Crawford, 'The Social Function of Property and the Human Capacity to Flourish' (2011) 80 *Fordham*

and stresses the need for individuals to have the capacity to choose and deliberate carefully upon their options in life. They draw on the capabilities approach developed by Sen and Nussbaum, according to which a well-lived life is one that conforms to certain objectively valuable patterns, or 'functionings'.[56] Alexander and Peñalver argue that property institutions and distributions, particularly the rights involved in ownership in different contexts, should be judged on whether and to what extent they facilitate individuals in living well. Furthermore, the mutual recognition amongst individuals of the value of human flourishing requires that those with the means to flourish share their resources with those who would otherwise lack the necessary material resources. At the same time, discrete groups should not be subject to repeated and disproportionate demands for sacrifice in the interests of the community.[57]

2.2.3 *The 'Democratic Model' of Property*

The Statement of Progressive Property committed to the idea that all individuals should have the resources required for full participation in the political process, and that the democratic system should be shaped and developed to secure equality for all. This commitment reflects most directly Singer's approach to property, which focuses on its relationship with a fair and equal democratic society. Like Alexander, Singer proceeds from the basic premise that '*owners have obligations as well as rights*'.[58] Those obligations are owed to other owners, as well as to non-owners, and they require owners to share their property with non-owners and to use their property in a manner that is compatible with facilitating the entry of non-owners into the property system.[59] For Singer, the dialectic between individual and collective interests is in determining the meaning and scope of property rights rather than in identifying permissible limitations of such rights.

Law Review 1089. Alexander builds upon his work with Peñalver in *Property and Human Flourishing* (n 1).

56 Alexander and Peñalver, 'Properties of Community' (n 55), 136. For more on the relationship between Sen's thinking, property, and freedom, see J. Purdy, 'A Freedom-Promoting Approach to Property: A Renewed Tradition for New Debates' (2005) 72 *University of Chicago Law Review* 1237.

57 See also Dagan, 'The Social Responsibility of Ownership' (n 30) on the importance of preventing unfair burdening.

58 Singer, *Entitlement* (n 23), p. 16.

59 Ibid, p. 18.

Singer traces in his own work, and in the work of Alexander, Peñalver, Underkuffler, and Purdy, a 'democratic model of property' that aims at '. . .understanding the role that property and property law play in a free and democratic society that treats each person with equal concern and respect.'[60] It requires attention to be paid to the effects of the exercise of legal rights on others in society and to the qualitative character of the social relations that result from such impacts.[61] In this regard, property owners have what Singer terms 'an obligation of attentiveness'.[62] Any given set of property rules or institutions cannot be endorsed without considering their likely or existing systemic effect. Furthermore, the democratic model is pluralistic, accepting that property promotes various values, including autonomy and mobility, and stability and change.

The 'democratic model' reflects and builds upon property theory that connects private ownership with the health of a democratic society, in particular the proper functioning of political processes. From this perspective, private property is valued as a means of empowering individuals to participate effectively in the public sphere. As Waldron puts it, '[i]f a man owns the resources he needs, then he depends for his use of them on the say-so of no one but himself, and so material necessity is unlikely to be transformed into moral or political dependence.'[63] Some (undefined) level of secure possession of property is regarded as necessary to ensure free-thinking and acting individuals. In this way, property rights are understood to give individuals what Michelman terms 'social and political competence'.[64] On this basis, Sunstein identifies 'a strong democratic justification' for private ownership.[65]

[60] J. W. Singer, 'Democratic Estates: Property Law in a Free and Democratic Society' (2009) *Cornell L Rev* 1009, 1047.

[61] Ibid.

[62] Ibid., 1048.

[63] M. J. Radin, *Reinterpreting Property* (Chicago: University of Chicago Press, 1993), p. 301.

[64] F. I. Michelman, 'Property as a Constitutional Right (1981) 38 *Washington & Lee Law Review* 1097, 1102. Elsewhere he suggests that property is '. . .an indispensable ingredient in the constitution of the individual as a participant in the life of the society, including not least the society's processes for collectively regulating the conditions of an ineluctably social existence' – 'Mr Justice Brennan: A Property Teacher's Appreciation' (1980) 15 *Harvard Civil Rights and Civil Liberties Law Review* 296, 304. Similarly, Laura Underkuffler notes, '[i]t is through the places that we live that we have social networks, economic means, and (generally) any hope of political influence. . .In short, the ability to possess physical property and the ability to participate in the political process are linked deeply and irrevocably.' L. S. Underkuffler, 'Kelo's Moral Failure' (2007) 15 *William & Mary Bill of Rights Journal* 377, 383–84.

[65] C. Sunstein, *Designing Democracy – What Constitutions Do* (Oxford: OUP, 2001), p. 223.

These connections between property rights, political independence, and the enhancement of democratic societies can be further related to the idea of 'property as propriety', which overlaps with progressive property theory in conceiving of property as a means of preserving proper social order and social justice.[66] As Rose put it, the purpose of property is '. . .to accord to each person or entity what is "proper" or "appropriate" to him or her. . .And what is "proper" or appropriate, on this vision of property, is that which is needed to keep good order in the commonwealth or body politic.'[67] The understanding of 'property as propriety' is particularly identifiable in American civic-republican theories that treat property rights as a source of social and political empowerment.[68]

2.2.4 Bridging the Gap between Progressive Property and Law and Economics

As noted above, a key aim of the Statement of Progressive Property was to respond to the perceived dominance of law and economics in the property law domain and to encourage more property scholarship to adopt a pluralistic understanding of the values secured by protecting property rights. This resulted in polarisation in the literature, with for example Gerhart characterising property theory as 'significantly dichotomous'.[69] In fact progressive property recognises the importance of efficiency, and of stable legal protection for owners' expectations concerning the possession, use, and value of property.[70] The heart of the substantive disagreement with information theorists concerns whether property law should be assessed and developed solely by reference to

[66] Freyfogle suggests that the 'propriety' approach evolved to emphasise social justice and owners' responsibilities: E. Freyfogle, 'Property Law in a Time of Transformation: The Record of the United States' (2014) 131 *South African Law Journal* 883, 904.

[67] C. M. Rose, *Property and Persuasion* (Boulder, CO: Westview Press, 1994), p. 58. See also Singer, 'Democratic Estates' (n 60), 1035.

[68] W. H. Simon, "Social-Republican Property" (1991) 38 *UCLA Law Review* 1335, 1340, G. S. Alexander, 'Time and Property in the American Republican Legal Culture' (1991) 66 *NYU Law Review* 273, 284. See also D. R. McCoy, *The Elusive Republic: Political Economy in Jeffersonian America* (University of North Carolina Press, 1980), p. 68, J. Williams, 'The Rhetoric of Property' (1998) 183 *Iowa Law Review* 277, 317.

[69] Gerhart, *Property Law and Social Morality* (n 1), p. 10.

[70] See, e.g., J. W. Singer, 'Property as the Law of Democracy' (2014) 63 *Duke Law Journal* 1287, 1289, arguing '[u]nder any rubric or conception, property suggests a stable basis of expectation with respect to control of valued things'.

efficiency and preference-satisfaction, and if not, how the relative significance of other values should be understood.[71]

Bray identifies 'the possibility of a useful synthesis between the law-and-economics approach and many norms and values that have often been defined as incompatible with it' as a key contribution of 'new progressive property theory'.[72] In this vein, Gerhart advances a theory of property that builds upon the 'communitarian' property theories of Alexander and Peñalver but '. . .unifies communitarian theory with theories of corrective and distributive justice.'[73] At the core of Gerhart's approach is an attempt to find unity between the values of the rights of owners and non-owners in both private and public law contexts. He identifies social recognition as the source of property rights, and as shaping the limits of such rights and of state power over property rights. Most significantly for the purposes of this book, Gerhart contends that state powers over private property are constrained by the need to respect the normative core of property in the public law context, namely: '. . .that owners are promised an appropriate assignment of the burdens and benefits of decisions about resources when the state, representing the community, adjusts the burdens and benefits of ownership.'[74] The requirement is for burdens to be distributed '. . .through processes that are fairly geared to determine the terms of equal treatment.'[75] Due process principles also guide this determination, with Gerhart characterising many judicial determinations that uncompensated regulatory restrictions are unlawful on property rights grounds as better understood as concerned with arbitrary legislation. As will be seen in subsequent chapters, these observations are reflected in Irish constitutional property law, which shows on the one hand, the core area of contention that persists around the impact of constitutional property rights on judicial supervision of the distribution of the burdens of collective life, and on the other hand, the relatively marginal role of constitutional property rights in the overall scheme of rights-protection.[76]

71 See, e.g., Peñalver (n 52), 888, Alexander, *Property and Human Flourishing* (n 1), p. 320.
72 Bray, 'The New Progressive Property' (n 24), 1124.
73 Gerhart, *Property Law and Social Morality* (n 1), p. 38.
74 Ibid., p. 60.
75 Ibid., p. 256.
76 On the marginality of property rights, see Van der Walt, 'The Modest Systemic Status of Property' (n 35).

2.2.5 *Progressive Property Themes*

Mulvaney advances a road-map for the redesign and reinterpretation of property rules based on three progressive themes that offer a useful basis for assessing progressive property in action in the chapters that follow.[77] Echoing Singer, he characterises property as '. . .an open, deliberative, human-created, evolving institution that reflects communal understandings of value and promotes societal interests.'[78] He advocates:

> a system of property in which lawmakers acknowledge that (1) all property rules reflect substantive values (transparency); (2) those values and the body of knowledge on which they are based change over time (humility); and (3) some property interests may enjoy more protection than others due to the plight of those persons implicated by a given declaration of a property right (identity).[79]

In respect of the theme of transparency, he calls for '. . .forthright acknowledgement that property rules are never value-neutral.'[80] Humility signals the need for lawmakers to accept that property rules and arrangements may need to change in light of evolving knowledge and social values.[81] Finally, identity requires that individuals' socio-economic status and needs should impact on the approach that is taken to property disputes.[82] As a consequence of this principle of identity, Mulvaney accepts that legal rules may apply differently depending on the circumstances of the affected individuals in particular cases.[83]

2.3 Progressive Property's Plural Values

2.3.1 *Efficiency and Expectations*

As noted above, progressive property theory positioned itself as a response to the apparent dominance of law and economics in property

[77] Mulvaney, 'Progressive Property Moving Forward' (n 22), 350.
[78] Ibid., 366.
[79] Ibid., 369.
[80] Ibid., 358.
[81] In this regard, Mulvaney broadens the idea of humility as articulated by Peñalver, 'Land Virtues' (n 52).
[82] Mulvaney, 'Progressive Property Moving Forward' (n 22), 368. He identifies a connection between this theme of identity and the work of J. H. Ely, *Democracy and Distrust: A Theory of Judicial Review* (Cambridge, MA: Harvard University Press, 1980). On this theme, see also van der Walt, *Property in the Margins* (n 34).
[83] See also Mulvaney, 'Legislative Exactions' (n 42).

law scholarship. It aimed to encourage a pluralistic understanding of the values secured by protecting property rights as an alternative to the monism that it ascribed to law and economics approaches. However, the tendency towards rhetorical opposition between progressive property theory and information theory co-exists with the recognition by various progressive property scholars of efficiency as a value that is properly secured through the legal protection of property rights, although not to the exclusion of all other values or considerations.[84] As such, the relationship between these schools of thought is more complex than their binary presentation would suggest.

Baron distinguishes progressive property from so-called 'information' theories of property primarily on the basis of their relative acceptance of complexity, with information theorists favouring simple legal signals concerning property rights, for example stemming from the right to exclude.[85] Merrill and Smith characterise such simple signals in terms of 'exclusion rules', which they contend should be the core means of property law.[86] According to Merrill and Smith, '[e]xclusion identifies a person or entity as the manager of a resource (the owner), and then delegates to this manager the discretion to select from among an open-ended set of potential uses.'[87] Exclusion rules are preferred because they send simple on-off signals concerning an owner's rights to the world at large, thereby reducing information costs.[88] 'Governance' rules appropriately replace 'exclusion' rules where control of the use of property is

[84] See, e.g., Peñalver, 'Land Virtues' (n 52), Freyfogle, 'Private Ownership and Human Flourishing', (n 48) 437–38, Singer, 'Democratic Estates', (n 60), 1298.
[85] Baron, 'Contested Commitments', (n 17), 950–51.
[86] T. W. Merrill and H. E. Smith, 'The Property/Contract Interface' (2001) 101 *Columbia Law Review* 773. See also H. E. Smith, 'Exclusion versus Governance: Two Strategies for Delineating Property Rights' (2002) 31 *Journal of Legal Studies* S453; H. E. Smith, 'Mind the Gap: The Indirect Relation Between Ends and Means in American Property Law' (2009) 94 *Cornell Law Review* 959; H. E. Smith 'Property as the Law of Things' (2012) 125 *Harvard Law Review* 1691; H. E. Smith and T. W. Merrill, 'The Morality of Property' (2007) 48 *William & Mary Law Review* 1849 and T. W. Merrill, 'Property and the Right to Exclude' (1998) 77 *Nebraska Law Review* 730.
[87] Merrill and Smith, 'The Property/Contract Interface' (n 86), 791.
[88] Merrill and Smith, 'The Property/Contract Interface' (n 86), 794–95, 802. See also, Smith and Merrill, 'The Morality of Property' (n 86), 1890. Wyman points out that Merrill and Smith also identify positive incentive effects for owners and reduced transaction costs as benefits of their approach: K. M. Wyman, 'The New Essentialism in Property' (2017) 9 *Journal of Legal Analysis* 183, 211.

complex and requires more precise delineation of use-rights.[89] Such rules consist of 'a set of norms picking out important uses of the asset', which allow for more fine-grained control of use.[90] This approach has caused Merrill and Smith to be labelled as 'new essentialists',[91] a label that is also applied to other scholars who identify different 'core' features of property.[92]

While Merrill characterises the right to exclude as the 'sine qua non' of property,[93] Smith emphasises property's focus on rights in respect of things,[94] characterising the right to exclude as a means to property's ends.[95] The difference between progressive and information property theory in respect of complexity is a matter of degree. Although information property theory prefers simplicity, it accepts the need for some fine-grained, contextual decision-making.[96] Equally, progressive property does not disavow all rule-based decision-making on property issues, but rather contends that rules should be open to being reconsidered.[97]

89 This distinction is alternatively framed as the distinction between rules of access and rules of use. See Smith, 'Exclusion versus Governance' (n 86), S454. See also Merrill and Smith, 'The Property/Contract Interface' (n 65), 789–91, 797.

90 See, e.g., Smith, ibid., S470, and Merrill and Smith, ibid., 797–98.

91 Wyman, 'New Essentialism' (n 88).

92 See, e.g., J. E. Penner, *The Idea of Property in Law* (Oxford: Oxford University Press, 2000); L. Katz, 'Exclusion and Exclusivity in Property Law' (2008) 58 *University of Toronto Law Journal* 275; A. Mossoff, 'What Is Property? Putting the Pieces Back Together' (2003) 34 *Arizona Law Review* 371 and C. M. Newman, 'Using Things, Defining Property' in J. E. Penner and M. Otsuka (eds.), *Property Theory* (Cambridge: Cambridge University Press, 2018).

93 Merrill, 'Property and the Right to Exclude' (n 86).

94 Smith, 'Property as the Law of Things' (n 86).

95 Smith, 'Mind the Gap' (n 86), in particular at 964. In their recent work on this issue, Merrill and Smith emphasise property's 'architecture', which allows it to manage significant complexity. T. W. Merrill and H. E. Smith, 'The Architecture of Property' in H. Dagan and B. Zipursky (eds.), *Research Handbook on Private Law Theory* (Cheltenham: Edward Elgar, 2020), pp. 134. They describe its core principles as: a concern with things; the allocation of the right to exclude others from things; hybrids of exclusion and governance rules; modularity; differential formalism; standardization and the *numerus clausus;* a preference for protection via property rules rather than liability rules. See also H. E. Smith, 'Restating the Architecture of Property' in B. McFarlane and S. Agnew (eds.), *Modern Studies in Property Law* (Vol. 10) (Oxford: Bloomsbury, 2019) p. 19, 'The Persistence of System in Property Law' (2015) 163 *U Pa L Rev* 2055, A. S. Gold and 'Sizing Up Private Law' (August 9, 2016), available at https://papers.ssrn.com/sol3/papers.cfm?abstract_id=2821354.

96 Smith, 'Mind the Gap' (n 86), 'Exclusion versus Governance' (n 86).

97 See Singer, 'Property as the Law of Democracy' (n 70), 1307–8 and 'Justifying Regulatory Takings' (2015) 41 *Ohio Northern University Law Review* 601, 618.

Connections between property rights, owners' expectations, and efficient use of resources did not originate with 'information theory', or with law and economics approaches to property law more generally. Bentham argued that property rights must protect expectations *created by law* to encourage productive activity.[98] For Bentham, the anticipation of legal protection enables individuals to plan and work for their futures. The right to property is exhausted by the protection for expectations afforded by law – as Bentham famously put it, '[p]roperty and law are born together, and die together.'[99] While progressive property identifies 'control over wealth' as one of property's plural values, it consistently and robustly rejects the idea that property rights are immutable.[100] Much effort and time has been expended by progressive property theorists in establishing that change is permitted notwithstanding legal protection for property rights,[101] and going further, in arguing that susceptibility to change is an inherent feature of property rights.[102] For the progressive property school of thought, the law should protect some, but not all, expectations that it creates for owners, and should be guided by the common good in making such judgments. That basic approach – qualified protection for legally created expectations – is identifiable in the doctrine and outcomes in Irish constitutional property law that will be analysed in subsequent chapters.

2.3.2 Personality and Personhood

Another important strand of property theory that influences the progressive property school of thought connects private possession of external things to the development of individual personality and personhood. Progressive property theory has generally been sympathetic to the personhood perspective on property.[103]

[98] All references are to Bentham's *Principles of the Civil Code*, taken from his *The Theory of Legislation*. The page references are to the reprint of this edition of Bentham's theory in C. B. MacPherson (ed.), *Property: Mainstream and Critical Positions* (Oxford: Blackwell, 1978) (beginning, p. 41). p. 50 (emphasis in original.)

[99] Ibid., p. 52.

[100] See, e.g., Singer, *Entitlement* (n 23), Freyfogle, 'Property and Liberty' (n 15), Alexander, 'Social-Obligation Norm' (n 49).

[101] On the question of 'how much' stability is appropriate see, e.g., Freyfogle, 'Private Ownership and Human Flourishing' (n 48), 443–46.

[102] See notably the work of Laura Underkuffler on this point: *The Idea of Property in Law* (n 23), 'Property and Change – The Constitutional Conundrum' (2015) 91 *Texas Law Review* 2015. See also Singer, *Entitlement* (n 23).

[103] See, e.g., H. Dagan, *Property: Values and Institutions* (Oxford: Oxford University Press, 2011), pp. 146–47, E. M. Penalver and S. K. Katyal, *Property Outlaws* (New Haven: Yale

In his work, Hegel identifies private property as an important tool in a process of individual development that ultimately culminates in recognising the superiority and primacy of collective interests. Patten identifies two key tenets of Hegel's theory of property: its claims about self-perception and self-development.[104] Property for Hegel allows individuals to personify themselves concretely in the world.[105] By perceiving his independence through seeing the effects of his actions on the world, an individual develops his personality.[106] In this regard, property is 'formative of the self.'[107] Because a person's will becomes embodied in property, it follows for Hegel that such property is privately held; a second possessor in time cannot impose his will on a thing already affected by someone else's will. In order to facilitate self-development, all that is required is that an individual possess *some* property privately.[108] However, according to Patten, Hegel's theory of property provides that '. . .having at least a minimal amount of private property is essential to the development and maintenance of the capacities and self-understandings that make up free personality.'[109] Waldron goes further and contends that Hegel's theory logically requires that all individuals must own significant property capable of meeting their economic needs in order to develop a stable will.[110]

Characterising Hegel's theory as a 'suggestive text',[111] Radin develops a theory of property that connects private ownership and personal

University Press, 2010), pp. 26–27, Alexander, 'Pluralism and Property' (n 17) pp. 1017–19, 1032–35, Singer, 'Democratic Estates' (n 60), pp. 1045–46.

104 A. Patten, *Hegel's Idea of Freedom* (Oxford: Oxford University Press, 1999), p. 147.

105 See D. Knowles, *Hegel and the Philosophy of Right* (London: Routledge, 2002), p. 116, D. Knowles, 'Hegel on Property and Personality' (1983) 33 *The Philosophical Quarterly* 45, 57.

106 Patten, *Hegel's Idea of Freedom* (n 104), p. 149.

107 P. Thomas, 'Property's Properties: From Hegel to Locke' (2003) 84 *Representations* 30, 38. As Patten notes, '[t]he central claim of Hegel's account of property is that it is only in social worlds containing the institution of private property that an agent can become a person; it is only in such a world that he can 'become an actual will'.' ibid., p. 146.

108 Richard Teichgraeber contends it is the attempt to possess property that is crucial to self-development: R. Teichgraeber, 'Hegel on Property and Poverty' (1977) 38 *Journal of the History of Ideas* 47, 54–6.

109 Patten, *Hegel's Idea of Freedom* (n 104), p. 140.

110 Waldron, *The Right to Private Property* (n 142), p. 385. For a sceptical view of Waldron's interpretation, see L. C. Becker, 'Too Much Property' (1992) 21 *Philosophy and Public Affairs* 196.

111 Radin, *Reinterpreting Property* (n 63), pp. 81–2. She acknowledged in hindsight that she should in her earlier work perhaps have made more reference to Kant, and less to Hegel. Ibid., pp. 7–8. See also C. E. Baker, 'Property and Its Relation to Constitutionally

development to assist in *delineating* property rights. Her approach centres on a 'personhood perspective', which she describes as meaning, '. . .to achieve proper self-development – to be a *person* – an individual needs some control over resources in the external environment.'[112] Radin understands personhood as having three overlapping facets: freedom, identity, and contextuality.[113] She argues, '. . .certain categories of property can bridge the gap, or blur the boundary, between the self and the world, between what is inside and what is outside, between what is subject and what is object.'[114] Personal property is the category of property that performs this bridging function.

Radin notes that most people own certain things that they feel are bound up with their personalities, such as houses, wedding rings, and heirlooms.[115] This kind of property can be contrasted with 'fungible property' that is held '. . .purely for instrumental reasons', such as money, commercial property, and generally property that is held in order to perform some service.[116] While in her early work on this topic, Radin referred to the need to identify 'objective criteria' in 'moral consensus' to draw such distinctions, she ultimately rooted such criteria in society's cultural commitments.[117] Radin uses her 'personhood perspective' to set

Protected Liberty' (1986) 134 *University Pennsylvania Law Review* 741, 746–47. Radin's approach differs from Hegel's in important ways. For example, Hegel treats possession of property as one of a number of aspects of the process whereby an individual develops from a state of abstract autonomy to becoming a fully developed individual within the family and the State. In contrast, Radin conceives of the individual as already developed. In addition, while Radin emphasises the importance of secure possession of personal property for individual personhood, Hegel focused on the effects of the *process* of controlling property.

112 Radin, *Reinterpreting Property* (n 63), p. 35.

113 M. J. Radin, 'Market-Inalienability' (1986–87) 100 *Harvard Law Review* 1849, 1904. Radin argues '[f]or appropriate self-constitution, both strong attachment to context and strong possibilities for detachment from context are needed.' M. J. Radin, 'The Colin Ruagh Thomas O'Fallon Memorial Lecture on Reconsidering Personhood' (1995) 74 *Oregon Law Review* 423, 429–30.

114 Radin, 'The Colin Ruagh Thomas O'Fallon Memorial Lecture' (n 113), 426.

115 Radin, *Reinterpreting Property* (n 63), pp. 36–37.

116 Ibid.

117 Radin, 'The Colin Ruagh Thomas O'Fallon Memorial Lecture' (n 113), 427. She acknowledged her change in view in *Reinterpreting Property*, referring in particular to the idea of identifying justifiable connections with property by reference to '. . .shared understandings that are, for now, too entrenched to be revisable by individuals, and are experienced by individuals as coming from outside themselves.' Radin, *Reinterpreting Property* (n 63), p. 5. Stephen Schnalby suggests that Radin's 'personhood perspective' is premised on social consensus that is not immune from legal influence. S. J. Schnably,

up a spectrum of property entitlements ranging from less protected fungible property rights at one end to strongly protected personal property rights at the other end. This 'personhood dichotomy'[118] focuses on subjective relationships between holders and objects, meaning the same piece of property can merit different levels of protection when held by different individuals. In addition, property can become personal over time without changing hands.

Radin's 'personhood' perspective has been widely cited,[119] and evidence of a differentiated approach to judicial review of interferences with property rights based on the type of property involved will be seen in the legal doctrine considered in this book.[120] However, it is important to bear in mind that the personhood perspective has also been challenged, on both normative and empirical grounds. For example, Sharfstein argues, '...personhood has a dark side, as people justify morally unacceptable conduct by investing themselves in their land.'[121] Other critics of the personhood approach query whether the empirical evidence supports claims of particularly strong connections between individuals and 'personal property'.[122] Critics have also argued that there is a 'self-

'Property and Pragmatism' (1993) 45 *Stanford Law Review* 347. See her rejoinder, M. J. Radin, 'Lacking a Transformative Social Theory: A Response' (1993) 45 *Stanford Law Review* 409. On this debate, see J. Williams, 'The Rhetoric of Property' (1998) 88 *Iowa Law Review* 277.

118 Radin, *Reinterpreting Property* (n 63), p. 53.

119 See J. D. Jones, 'Property and Personhood Revisited' (2011) 1 *Wake Forest Journal of Law & Policy* 93, 94 identifying at least 700 citations of Radin's core law review article on the topic. See also F. R. Shapiro, 'The Most-Cited Law Review Articles Revisited' (1996) 71 *Chicago-Kent Law Review* 751, 773.

120 See in particular Chapter 7 on security of possession.

121 D. J. Sharfstein, 'Atrocity, Entitlement, and Personhood in Property' (2012) 98 *Virginia Law Review* 635, 690. Relatedly Schnalby stresses that the home can also be the locus of destructive oppression and violence, inequality and exclusion, and economic domination, as well as a bastion of personhood. Schnalby, 'Property and Pragmatism' (n 117), 366–68. See also Williams, 'The Rhetoric of Property' (n 117), 341.

122 See, e.g., S. M. Stern, 'Residential Protectionism and the Legal Mythology of Home' (2009) 107 *Michigan Law Review* 1093, 1112–13, discussing the psychological literature and arguing that it shows residential real estate to have a primarily self-expressive function rather than a constitutive function. See also S. M. Stern, 'The Inviolate Home: Housing Exceptionalism in the Fourth Amendment' (2009) 95 *Cornell Law Review* 101. Benjamin Barros argues that there is empirical support for Radin's approach, but suggests that aspects of the personhood connection, e.g. to personal property within the home constitutive of identity, are transferable. Barros contends that the non-transferable aspects of the personhood connection primarily relate to community networks rather than real property: B. Barros, 'Legal Questions for the Psychology of Home' (2009) 83 *Tulane Law Review* 645. See also J. A. Blumenthal, '"To Be Human":

perpetuating'[123] tendency in the personhood argument, since the fact of particularly strong legal protection for 'personal' property entrenches a sense that such property is especially important.[124] Distinctive legal protections for 'personal' property are further resisted by some scholars as insufficiently dynamic,[125] including on the basis that they wrongly prioritise stability and stasis as means of realising human flourishing.[126]

2.3.3 *Autonomy*

As noted above, among the property values identified in the Statement were control over one's life, wealth, happiness, and physical security. These broadly stated values capture various dimensions of autonomy that are regarded as secured or enhanced through legal protection for property rights. Blackstone famously described the right of property as '. . .that sole and despotic dominion which one man claims and exercises over the external things of the world, in total exclusion of the right of any other individual in the universe.'[127] However, progressive property consistently argues against such ideas of 'despotic dominion'.[128] Protection for property as a means of securing liberty is regarded as appropriately qualified.[129] For example, Purdy has described human freedom (itself understood as a plural value) as a master-value that is helpful in explaining much legal thinking about property as an institution.[130] On this

A Psychological Perspective on Property' (2009) 83 *Tulane Law Review* 609 and Jones, 'Property and Personhood Revisited' (n 119).

123 Stern, 'Residential Protectionism' (n 122), 1096.

124 As Schnably puts it: '[t]he moment we attempt to identify a value as consensual, we engage in a practice that makes it all too easy for exercises of power to remain hidden. Moreover, since the law itself often shapes consensus, purporting to rely on consensus to shape the law is a dangerous exercise in circularity. In attempting merely to apply a given consensus, we necessarily strengthen it as well.' Schnalby, 'Property and Pragmatism' (n 117), 374.

125 See, e.g., Jones, 'Property and Personhood Revisited' (n 119), 120, arguing '... the spectrum of mental states that interact to constitute an object's value is socially complex and dynamic', not a 'linear continuum' between personal and fungible property.

126 See, e.g., Stern, 'Residential Protectionism' (n 122), 1114–17.

127 William Blackstone, Commentaries on the Laws of England *2 (1765–69).

128 See, e.g., Alexander, 'Social Obligation Norm' (n 49), Singer, 'Democratic Estates' (n 60), Underkuffler, *The Idea of Property* (n 23), Mulvaney, 'Progressive Property Moving Forward' (n 22).

129 Freyfogle, 'Property and Liberty' (n 15), 117.

130 J. Purdy, *The Meaning of Property: Freedom, Community, and the Legal Imagination* (New Haven, CT: Yale University Press, 2010), p. 18. See also J. Purdy, 'People as Resources: Recruitment and Reciprocity in the Freedom-Promoting Approach to

approach, property is understood as involving various distinct values that can be framed as aspects of human freedom, which facilitates human flourishing. Dagan frames property as 'an umbrella of institutions bearing a family resemblance', with a common denominator of rights of exclusion across all institutions deriving from property's function in securing autonomy.[131,132]

A related strand of property theory emphasises the role of property rights in securing privacy. For example, Underkuffler argues, '[p]roperty as an assertion of self and control of one's environment provides human beings with a place of deep psychological refuge.'[133] Barros says that private spheres '...promote the ability of individuals to make basic life choices for themselves by creating physical spaces where they can engage in behaviour frowned on by the rest of the community and where they can withdraw if they want to be alone or to interact only with people of their choice.'[134] Macleod connects property's function in securing a domain of 'dominion' with practical reasonableness, arguing that private property gives individuals '...the freedom to become reasonable by choosing to act for reasons, to shape one's plans and commitments by choosing some possible reasons over others, and to realize one's plans and commitments by pursuing them with commitment and integrity.'[135]

2.3.4 *Natural Rights and Labour*

Progressive property theory challenges the intuitive and rhetorical influence of natural rights thinking in property law.[136] However,

Property' (2007) 56 *Duke Law Journal* 1047 and Purdy, 'A Freedom-Promoting Approach to Property' (n 56).

131 'Autonomy and Property' in H. Dagan and B. Zipursky (eds.), *Research Handbook on Private Law Theory* (Cheltenham: Edward Elgar, 2020), p. 185. Dagan, *Property: Values and Institutions* (n 103), p. xvii, H. Dagan, A Liberal Theory of Property (Cambridge: Cambridge University Press, forthcoming, 2021).

132 He argues that property provides '...some temporally extended control over tangible and intangible resources', enabling individuals to carry out projects and plans. The reference for footnote for the added sentence is Dagan, A Liberal Theory of Property, ibid, p. 2 (available at https://papers.ssrn.com/sol3/papers.cfm?abstract_id=3728796).

133 Underkuffler, *The Idea of Property* (n 23), p. 1. See also M. L. Roark, 'Under-Propertied Persons' (2017) 27 *Cornell Journal of Law and Public Policy* 1.

134 D. B. Barros, 'Property and Freedom' (2009) 4 *New York University Journal of Law & Liberty* 36, 47. See also Waldron (n 142), pp. 295–96.

135 A. J. Macleod, *Property and Practical Reason* (Cambridge: Cambridge University Press, 2015), p. 33.

136 See, e.g., Freyfogle, 'Property and Liberty' (n 15).

notwithstanding the Irish Constitution's progressive framing of its protection for individual property rights, natural law thinking about private ownership emerges as a significant doctrinal influence. As Harris notes, '. . .social conventions commonly incorporate, and are shaped by reference to, the assumption that meritorious work should receive a reward in the form of property.'[137] Locke, in his *Two Treatises on Government*, famously articulated an understanding of the right to private property as a natural right justified by the exertion of labour on external things. Locke began from the premise that the Earth was intended by God to provide sustenance for all men through their cultivation and use of its resources.[138] In light of this purpose, he argued that men must be able to appropriate things in order to make use of them.[139] Locke justified *private* ownership through his 'Labour theory of appropriation', according to which labouring on something gives an individual a claim over that thing, distinguished from the claims of all other people.[140] This theory rested on the idea of self-ownership: an individual owns his own person, which in turn entails ownership of his actions, including labour.[141] The next step in Locke's theory was the notion of 'mixing labour' with objects or resources. By labouring on material resources, an individual transfers his (owned) labour into the resources or things. Locke argued that most of the value in property comes from labour, meaning that appropriation by the first labourer is unobjectionable since his labour made the object worth owning.[142] A related interpretation of Locke's theory is that he justified the appropriation of property as the 'just desert' of a labourer.[143] However, Locke did not regard the boundaries of permissible acquisition and use of property as entirely open-ended, but rather identified limits based on ensuring access to essential

[137] J. W. Harris, *Property and Justice* (Oxford: Oxford University Press, 2002), p. 229.

[138] All references to Locke are to the paragraph numbers in P. Laslett (ed.), *John Locke, Two Treatises of Government* (Cambridge: Cambridge University Press, 1988). See paras. II 26 and II 34.

[139] Ibid., para. II 26.

[140] Ibid., para. II 28.

[141] Ibid., para. II 27. This aspect of the theory has been subject to extensive criticism: see, e.g., R. Nozick, *Anarchy, State and Utopia* (Oxford: Blackwell, 1974), pp. 174–75 and K. Olivecrona, 'Locke's Theory of Appropriation' (1974) 24 *Philosophical Quarterly* 220, 226–27.

[142] On these limits, see his 'spoilation' proviso (Laslett, *Locke* (n 137), para. II 40), and his 'enough and as good in common' requirement (Laslett, *Locke* (n 137), para. II 27).

[143] See J. Waldron, *The Right to Private Property* (Oxford: Oxford University Press, 1990), p. 201.

resources for all (his so-called 'enough and as good' limit[144]) and ensuring acquired property is used (his so-called 'spoilation' proviso[145]).

2.4 Conclusions

Progressive property theory is pluralistic, creating challenges for those charged with deciding between competing incommensurable moral values, for example judges undertaking constitutional property rights adjudication.[146] This chapter provided an overview of some of the most influential property values. Dagan explains property law's plurality as a reflection of 'the heterogeneity of property's real-life manifestations'.[147] The doctrinal analysis that follows in subsequent chapters bears out this assessment, showing that property values variously conflict and overlap, exercising implicit, and sometimes unconscious, influence on judicial decision-making.[148] They often point in different doctrinal directions, resulting in partial implementation as they are weighed against each other.[149] The analysis in this book will show that constitutional property law reflects judicial intuitions of fairness concerning the appropriate mediation of property rights and social justice. Constitutional property law instantiates property theories where they coincide with those judicial intuitions, which in turn are influenced by judges' instincts concerning the merits of private ownership. Accordingly, as manifested in doctrine, constitutional property law's pluralism does not reflect the comprehensive adoption of one, or indeed more than one, of the theories considered in this chapter, but rather intuitive judicial understandings of the value of

144 Laslett, *Locke* (n 137), para. II 27. The traditional interpretation of Locke's theory on this point is that the 'enough and as good' limit was intended as a necessary condition of justified appropriation; see, e.g., A. Ryan, *Property and Political Theory* (Blackwell, 1984), p. 36. However, Waldron argues that it was in fact regarded by Locke simply as a factual consequence of appropriation in circumstances of plenty: J. Waldron, 'Enough and as Good Left for Others' (1979) 29 *The Philosophical Quarterly* 319, 321–22.

145 Laslett, *Locke* (n 137), para. II 31.

146 On this difficulty with pluralistic theories of property, see G. S. Alexander and E. M. Peñalver, *An Introduction to Property Theory* (Cambridge: Cambridge University Press, 2012), pp. 97–101. Alexander argues for 'complementarity analysis', involving '. . .evaluating differences of importance between the goods', rather than balancing as a means of addressing that difficulty: *Property and Human Flourishing* (n 1), p. 205.

147 Dagan, *Property: Values and Institutions* (n 103), p. xii.

148 On these plural values see, e.g., Singer, 'Democratic Estates' (n 60), 1054.

149 For example, securing individual personality and self-development at times signals doctrinal developments that conflict with the dictates of the labour theory of property.

private ownership, which are influenced (often unconsciously, partially, and inconsistently) by those theories.

Waldron distinguishes rights-based and utilitarian general arguments for protecting property rights.[150] However, the analysis in this chapter has shown that property values that might be intuitively classified as right-based (e.g. liberty and privacy, personhood) also can be understood as having important social dimensions (e.g. as a means of securing a proper functioning democratic system). While it is clear that some property values are *primarily* individual or social in nature, the realisation of individual and social values through the protection of private ownership cannot be sharply distinguished.[151] The case-law that is analysed in subsequent chapters shows that both individual property values and property's 'social aspect' are influential and motivate judges to curtail the consistency with which theories on the 'opposite side' of the porous individual/social divide are applied. In that sense, the individual and social values of property that are influential are mutually limiting.

[150] Radin, *Reinterpreting Property* (n 111), pp. 286–87.
[151] Alexander, 'Property's Ends' (n 3), 1296.

3

Property as Ideology, Individual Right, and Institution

3.1 Introduction

Property scholars continue to debate the purpose of constitutional property clauses,[1] as well as the variety of forms that they can take.[2] The shape of such clauses is influenced by the historical circumstances of constitution-making.[3] Their implementation through legal doctrine is affected not just by the relevant constitutional text, but also by the prevailing property values and ideologies in different jurisdictions.[4]

This chapter offers a historically informed explanation of the purpose and form of the property clauses in the Irish Constitution. In doing so, it opens up the impact of the property values considered in the previous chapter in Irish constitutional property law. The argument is not for an originalist reading of the constitutional property clauses strictly in line with the original public meaning of the text.[5] Rather, the contention of this chapter is that the treatment of private property in multiple articles

[1] See, e.g., F. I. Michelman, 'The Property Clause Question' (2012) 19 *Constellations* 152; L. S. Underkuffler, 'What Does the Constitutional Protection of Property Mean?' (2016) 5 *Brigham-Kanner Property Rights Conference Journal* 109; J. Waldron, *The Right to Private Property* (Oxford: Oxford University Press, 1988).

[2] See the analysis of varying types of constitutional property clauses in A. J. van der Walt and R. Walsh, 'Comparative Constitutional Conceptions of Property', in M. Graziadei and L. Smith (eds.), *Comparative Property Law: A Research Handbook* (Cheltenham: Edward Elgar Publishing, 2017), p. 193.

[3] R. Walsh and L. Fox-O'Mahony, 'Land Law, Property Ideologies and the British–Irish Relationship' (2018) 47 *Common Law World Law Review* 7, 16–24.

[4] Van der Walt and Walsh, 'Comparative Constitutional Conceptions of Property' (n 2), p. 215.

[5] On originalism see, e.g., A. Scalia, *A Matter of Interpretation: Federal Courts and the Law* (Princeton: Princeton University Press, 1997); J. O. McGinnis and M. B. Rappaport, *Originalism and the Good Constitution* (Cambridge, MA: Harvard University Press, 2013); L. B. Solum, 'Originalism and the Unwritten Constitution' (2013) 2013 *University Illinois Law Review* 1935. For recent critical analysis of originalism, see T. B. Colby, 'Originalism and Structural Argument' (2019) 113 *Northwestern University Law Review* 1297.

of the Irish Constitution, which has been criticised as confusing,[6] can be illuminated through attending to the historical background to those clauses. As Coffey explains, the Constitution emerged 'in a period of intense historical significance', such that its background 'is relevant to understanding why certain articles are structured in the way that they are'.[7] This historically informed analysis identifies a duality in Irish constitutional property law between qualified protection of *individual* property rights and protection of private ownership as an *institution*, which can usefully inform progressive property theory. It establishes the foundations for a core theme of the book: that positive and negative constitutional property guarantees do not necessarily impede the implementation of social and economic reforms through democratic processes.

As the previous chapters indicated, much ink has been spilled by philosophers and legal theorists concerning the justifications for private ownership.[8] Similarly, the limitation of property rights has been the subject of detailed theoretical and doctrinal analysis.[9] However, relatively little attention has been paid to the consequences of giving private ownership as an institution constitutional status.[10] This is partially

[6] For example, the Constitution Review Group recommended amending the constitution to deal with property rights in one self-contained article, noting criticism of the provisions as confusing: *Report of the Constitution Review Group* (Dublin: Government of Ireland, 1996), pp. 357–67.

[7] D. K. Coffey, *Drafting the 1937 Irish Constitution: Transnational Influences in Interwar Europe* (London: Palgrave Macmillan, 2018), pp. xi–xiii. On the benefits of a historical lens for analysing property law, see also Walsh and Fox-O'Mahony, 'Land Law, Property Ideologies and the British–Irish Relationship' (n 3).

[8] See, e.g., Waldron, *The Right to Private Property* (n 1); J. Tully, *A Discourse on Property* (Cambridge: Cambridge University Press, 1980); S. Munzer, *A Theory of Property* (New York: Cambridge University Press, 1990); A. Ryan, *Property and Political Theory* (Oxford: Basil Blackwell, 1984); J. E. Penner, *The Idea of Property in Law* (Oxford: Oxford University Press, 1997); M. J. Radin, *Reinterpreting Property* (Chicago: University of Chicago Press, 1993).

[9] See, e.g., J. W. Harris, *Property and Justice* (Oxford: Oxford University Press, 1996); F. I. Michelman, 'Property, Utility, and Fairness: Comments on the Ethical Foundations of "Just Compensation" Law' (1967) 80 *Harvard Law Review* 1165; R. Epstein, *Supreme Neglect* (New York: Oxford University Press, 2008).

[10] Some notable exceptions to this neglect include G. S. Alexander, 'Property as a Fundamental Right? – The German Example' (2003) 88 *Cornell Law Review* 733; G. S. Alexander, *The Global Debate Over Constitutional Property: Lessons for American Takings Law* (Chicago: University of Chicago Press, 2006); M. Nakamura, 'Freedom of Economic Activities and the Right to Property' (1990) 53 *Law and Contemporary Problems* 1 (discussing the Japanese 1947 Constitution, which includes in Article 29 a protection of property including an institutional guarantee and limited protection for

explicable by the fact that the jurisdiction with the most active body of constitutional property scholars, the US, does not have a positive guarantee of private ownership. However, positive and negative protections for private ownership are necessarily interlinked. An institutional guarantee of some sort necessarily operates in the background to support *negative* constitutional protection of property rights (protection against State interference for property rights acquired by individuals).[11] As Penner points out, by virtue of having particular interests in respect of items of property that we own, we all also have 'an interest in the practice of property itself', which he argues is best captured by a general right to participate in that practice.[12] As such, a better understanding of the implications of institutional guarantees for private ownership is important for all jurisdictions that afford negative constitutional protection to property rights. As Dorfman rightly emphasises, there is a 'distinction between the very idea of ownership and its substance – its breadth and scope'.[13] The Irish Constitution addresses both these issues in its property clauses. Its institutional guarantee secures general formal access to private ownership as a social and legal institution without rendering any existing distribution of property immutable.

This chapter sets the scene for the analysis of Irish constitutional property doctrine in subsequent chapters by focusing on three foundational dimensions of Irish constitutional property law: the property ideologies that influenced the drafting of the constitutional property clauses and that animate judicial interpretation of those clauses; the individual property rights that the Constitution protects; and its protection of private ownership as an institution. Section 3.2 explains the historical background to the drafting of the property rights provisions in the Irish Constitution provisions and the ideological influences in respect of property that shaped those clauses.[14] Section 3.3 analyses the

individual property rights) and A. J. van der Walt, *Constitutional Property Law*, 3rd ed. (Cape Town: Juta Law, 2011), pp. 34–40, p. 415.

11 See, e.g., David Abraham noting the logical historical addition of a right for all to acquire property to rights *of* property in American law: D. Abraham, 'Liberty without Equality: The Property-Rights Connection in a "Negative Citizenship" Regime' (1996) 21 *Law and Social Inquiry* 1, 4. See similarly Alexander, 'Property as a Fundamental Right?' (n 10), p. 773.

12 Penner, *The Idea of Property* (n 8), pp. 50–51.

13 A. Dorfman, 'Private Ownership' (2010) 16 *Legal Theory* 1, 31.

14 For fuller exploration of some of the historical analysis explored in this chapter, see R. Walsh, 'Private Property Rights in the Drafting of the Irish Constitution: A Communitarian Compromise' (2011) 33 *Dublin University Law Journal* 86; Walsh

doctrine developed by the Irish courts on the relationship between the constitutional property clauses, identifying qualified protection for both individual property rights and private ownership as a legal institution. Section 3.4 concludes.

3.2 Irish Property Ideology in Historical Perspective

3.2.1 Possession/Redistribution Dualism in Pre-Independence Ireland

Attempting to trace the origins of the Irish approach to private property is contentious, with various possible starting points or 'property moments'.[15] Important developments include the Norman Conquest of Ireland in 1171–72, which was followed by the progressive imposition of English common law instead of native Irish (*Brehon*) law,[16] the 'settlement' of Ireland through British plantations in the sixteenth and seventeenth centuries,[17] and the 'Penal Laws' that debarred Irish Catholics from owning Irish land in the eighteenth century.[18] Clark notes, '[b]y the 1840's *over half* of the agricultural holdings in Ireland were too small to provide their occupiers with more than a subsistence livelihood, and *over half* of the adult male agricultural labor force consisted of laborers.'[19] Against this backdrop, the 'Great Hunger' or Famine in Ireland in 1845–47 sparked a dramatic decline in the Irish population, from almost 8.2 million people in 1841 to 4.3 million in 1911.[20]

and Fox-O'Mahony, 'Land Law, Property Ideologies and the British–Irish Relationship' (n 3).

15 N. M. Davidson and R. Dyal-Chand, 'Property in Crisis' (2010) 78 *Fordham Law Review* 1607.

16 G. MacNiocaill, 'The Contact of Irish and Common Law' (1972) 23 *Northern Ireland Law Quarterly* 16.

17 V. T. H. Delaney, 'Irish and Scottish Land Resettlement Legislation' (1959) 8 *International and Comparative Law Quarterly* 299.

18 These were enacted after the consolidation of Protestant control in Ireland from 1690 onwards, and restricted the terms and conditions of lettings to Catholics, as well as outlawing the purchase of interests in land: S. Clark, *Social Origins of the Irish Land War* (Princeton: Princeton University Press, 1979), p. 24. For full discussion, see M. Wall, *The Penal Laws 1691–1760* (Dublin: Dublin Historical Association, 1961).

19 Clark, *Social Origins of the Irish Land War*, p. 53.

20 Although Guinnane attributes less than half of this decline to the Famine itself: T. Guinnane, *The Vanishing Irish: Households, Migration, and the Rural Economy in Ireland* (Princeton: Princeton University Press, 1997), p. 4. For analysis of the Great Famine see, e.g., M. Daly, *The Famine in Ireland* (Dundalk: Dundalgan Press, 1986); C. Portier (ed.), *The Great Irish Famine* (Dublin: Mercier Press, 1995); C. Kinealy,

The Irish experience of material insecurity before and after the Famine generated a strong desire for property rights.[21] Secure possession of land was viewed as both instrumentally and personally important. Lee describes the Irish attitude to property rights as follows:

> Land was equated with security. The idea of property rights in employment, no less than in land, the individual's right to fixity of occupational tenure, was also firmly rooted in public consciousness before the Famine. The concern with property rights was wholly natural in the light of the alternatives facing the holders of land or jobs.[22]

Lee argued that this 'possessor principle', which '… owed its power not to the whims of individuals, but to attitudes deeply rooted in social structure and historical experience',[23] was highly influential in Irish culture until at least the second half of the twentieth century.[24] Demand for security of possession, as well as the need to ensure greater economic sustainability in agriculture, underpinned widespread popular support for land reform and redistribution in the late nineteenth and early twentieth centuries.[25] This movement was intertwined politically with Irish nationalism, with separatists linking expropriation of landlords with independence.[26]

In response to agitation and campaigns of agrarian crime, a series of land reform measures were introduced. Gladstone's Act of 1870 attempted to improve the conditions of tenants through enhanced security of tenure and recognition of the native Irish concept of 'tenant

A Death-Dealing Famine: The Great Hunger in Ireland (London and Chicago: Pluto Press, 1997).

21 Bull notes that the Famine 'created a potent sense of insecurity on the land, which was bound to ensure that any sign of economic reversal would provoke a fierce response'. P. Bull, *Land, Politics and Nationalism: A Study of the Irish Land Question* (Dublin: Gill & Macmillan, 1996), p. 80.

22 J. J. Lee, *Ireland 1912–1985* (Cambridge: Cambridge University Press, 1989), pp. 390–91. See also Michelle Norris, noting '[g]aining access to land was the only route to a living and also to social status for the bulk of the population'. M. Norris, *Property, Family and the Irish Welfare State* (London: Palgrave Macmillan, 2016), p. 95.

23 Lee, *Ireland 1912–1985* (n 22), p. 390.

24 Ibid., p. 392.

25 On the marginalisation of small farmers and agricultural labourers in rural Ireland at the turn of century, see L. M. Cullen, *An Economic History of Ireland since 1660* (London: Batsford, 1987), pp. 134–71.

26 See T. A. M. Dooley, *The Land for the People* (Dublin: University College Dublin Press, 2004), pp. 32–39; Bull, *Land, Politics and Nationalism* (n 21), p. 4; Norris, *Property, Family and the Irish Welfare State* (n 22), pp. 53–54, on this interlinking.

right' in a diluted form,[27] as well as making some provision for tenants to purchase freeholds from landlords.[28] Further acts were introduced in 1881 and in 1885 to enhance the conditions of tenants and to make tenant-purchase more attractive through loans from the British Treasury that were administered by the Land Commission (a public body established through the 1881 Act).[29] The Land Acts of 1903, 1909, 1923, 1933, 1936 and 1939 gave the Commission greater powers to compulsorily acquire land for redistribution to tenant farmers and to owners of uneconomically small farms. Transferees received acquisition loans from the Land Commission, and compensation was paid to dispossessed owners on progressively more attractive terms to encourage their cooperation with the Land Commission's work. These Acts also, as Bull notes, '. . . succeeded in addressing what was symbolically at the heart of the long dispute over land tenure, namely the question of who were the rightful possessors of the soil', given the history of conquest and settlement of Irish land.[30]

The motivations of the politicians who introduced land reform measures were primarily conservative and concerned with consolidating or enhancing power.[31] However, as Lee highlights, property rights were

[27] Dunning describes tenant right as follows: 'a tenant, upon leaving his holding for whatever cause, claimed the privilege of exacting from his successor a sum of money running up to ten or fifteen years' rent'. W. A. Dunning, 'Irish Land Legislation since 1845 I' (1892) 7 *Political Science Quarterly* 57, 59. Bull describes the impact of the 1870 Act as follows: '[w]hile it did very little indeed to satisfy the Irish tenant's claim for recognition of his right of occupancy, by making so substantial an incursion into the normal principles of the English law of contract and property on his behalf it went some way towards vindicating that claim and thus encouraging its further pursuit.' Bull, *Land, Politics and Nationalism* (n 21), p. 53. Bull contends that it was the failure of the 1870 Act to give effect to a principle of fair rent that condemned it to ineffectiveness (p. 78).

[28] For detailed discussion of the process of acquisition and transfer through the Land Commission, and of the evolution in functions over the course of the various Land Acts, see Dooley, *The Land for the People* (n 26), pp. 66–71; B. Edgeworth, 'Rural Radicalism Restrained: The Irish Land Commission and the Courts (1933–1939)' (2007) 42 *Irish Jurist* 1.

[29] Bull characterises this source of funding as significant for nationalists as symbolising that 'the conquest was being undone'. *Land, Politics and Nationalism* (n 21), p. 187.

[30] Ibid., pp. 159–60.

[31] For example, Aalen explains the English approach to Irish land reform as follows: '[r]eforms in Ireland were intended to make a relatively underdeveloped country more capable of laissez-faire; to present an attractive alternative to socialistic solutions and ultimately to strengthen individual enterprise and responsibility and the interests of property and the empire.' F. Aalen, 'Constructive Unionism and the Shaping of Rural Ireland, c 1880–1921' (1993) 4(2) *Rural History* 137, 138.

valued by right-holders not in the abstract, but rather for the economic security that they would bring to precarious occupiers. State intervention in the property system was regarded as a legitimate means of ensuring wider distribution of land.[32] Reflecting on this dimension of Irish land reform, Brian Walsh argued:

> The full popular and social acceptance of compulsory acquisition of lands in accordance with the provisions of the Land Acts, together with other similar statutory provisions, has made our People much less property-oriented than the rest of the English speaking world. The land struggle was regarded as a struggle for social justice.[33]

This assessment misses some of the complexity of the Irish experience. While land reform was undoubtedly understood as serving a social justice function and was advocated on that basis,[34] prior to independence it focused on changing proprietorship by converting tenants into proprietors of their *existing* holdings, not on land redistribution.[35] Through this process, it created a growing population of 'highly conservative small owner-occupier farmers'[36] who in turn embraced the 'possessor principle'.[37] As Aalen puts it, '[c]onservative forces . . . effectively contained the socialistic tendencies in land reform movements'.[38] The new owners exerted significant political power in post-independence Ireland.[39]

[32] See similarly Abraham, 'Liberty without Equality' (n 11), 13 for discussion of the ideological and material force of the idea of universalising property as a means of satisfying the linkage between positive liberty and property in the US context in the late nineteenth century.

[33] B. Walsh, 'Foreword', in J. O'Reilly and M. Redmond, *Cases and Materials on the Irish Constitution* (Dublin: Incorporated Law Society of Ireland, 1980), p. x.

[34] See D. Ferriter, *The Transformation of Ireland, 1900–2000* (London: Profile Books, 2004), p. 210 noting '[a] decree of the Dáil that every Irish man was entitled to a living on his own land was typical of the era'.

[35] Aalen, 'Constructive Unionism' (n 31), 141.

[36] B. Chubb, *The Government and Politics of Ireland*, 2nd ed. (London: Longman, 1970), p. 15. Chubb notes that reforms completed in the first decade of independence created 'a class of owner-occupiers of small farms who came to dominate Irish politics', p. 4.

[37] The tension between the initial demand in Irish society for land redistribution and reform, and the subsequent desire for secure property rights, is highlighted by J. M. Kelly, *Fundamental Rights in the Irish Law and Constitution* (Dublin: Allen Figgis & Co Ltd, 1967), pp. 172–73.

[38] Aalen, 'Constructive Unionism' (n 31), 142.

[39] T. Garvin, 'The Anatomy of a Nationalist Revolution: Ireland, 1858–1928' (1986) 28 *Comparative Studies in Society and History* 468, 469. See also T. Garvin, *The Evolution of Irish Nationalist Politics* (Dublin: Gill & Macmillan, 1981). Private ownership was further

Pre-independence land reform extended the reach of private ownership while also embedding public and political support for the norm of expropriation of land for public purposes, including through private-to-private transfers.[40] This laid the foundations for a complex Irish attitude to private ownership embracing both private ownership as a means of ensuring individual material security and State intervention to secure social justice. Indeed, Norris identifies land reform as an important influence on the future trajectory of the Irish welfare system, arguing:

> ... by conceding the principle of significant government involvement in the redistribution of landownership from landlords to tenant farmers, the Land Acts opened a floodgate of knock-on demands firstly for the provision of higher and higher public subsidies for peasant proprietorship and subsequently for subsidisation of the redistribution of other types of property, principally dwellings, with the result that property redistribution became a major focus of government activity for most of the twentieth century.[41]

Openness to State intervention in the distribution of property rights is accordingly an embedded feature of Irish legal, political, and broader cultural attitudes towards private ownership. At the same time, a desire for individual security in respect of property as a means of ensuring independence is also an entrenched feature of Irish property ideology.

3.2.2 *The 1922 Constitution and the Priority of Social Justice*

Following the Irish War of Independence (1919–21), the UK and Ireland negotiated and signed the Anglo-Irish Treaty. This was adopted in the UK through the Irish Free State (Agreement) Act 1922, approved by Dáil Éireann on 7 January 1922, and ratified through the Constitution of the Irish Free State (Saorstát Éireann) Act 1922. The Irish Free State was born, with the status of Dominion of the British Empire; Northern Ireland was created and remained part of the UK. The process of drafting

extended through the concurrent introduction of subsidies for rural housing from the early 1880s onwards. On this development, see M. Norris, 'Varieties of Home Ownership: Ireland's Transition from a Socialised to a Marketised Policy Regime' (2016) 31 *Housing Studies* 81, 86.

[40] The work of the Commission had other significant implications for the development of Irish land law on the ground, as – through the redistribution process – it carried out the costly, complex work of clarifying boundaries, title, and third party rights in respect of transferred land; Dooley, *The Land for the People* (n 26), p. 9.

[41] Norris, *Property, Family and the Irish Welfare State* (n 22), p. 5.

a Constitution, subject to the terms of the Treaty, was undertaken against the backdrop of a civil war between 1922 and 1923.[42] It also occurred against the backdrop of ongoing land reform. Aalen notes that two thirds of tenants had acquired their holdings by the time independence was achieved, such that 'Ireland, unlike Britain, became essentially a nation of farm proprietors'.[43] However, O'Donnell points out that most of the land was not owned by those who fought in and supported the War of Independence, meaning that land redistribution was a priority in the newly independent state.[44] Attention turned in the post-independence period to redistribution as opposed to tenant-proprietorship, as large farms were broken up to increase the size of smallholdings.

The only provision of the 1922 Constitution of the Irish Free State to ultimately address property was Article 11, which set out the State's rights over natural resources within the national territory.[45] However, the nature and status of private property rights received extensive consideration during the drafting process. The Committee appointed by the Provisional Government of the Free State to draft a Constitution – given one month in which to complete its work[46] – proposed three complete draft constitutions (drafts A, B, and C), signed by different members of

[42] As Kohn notes, through this process, '[t]he conflict between English formalism and Irish dogmatism was transferred to the technical sphere of constitutional detail, but it lost none of its intensity'; L. Kohn, *The Constitution of the Irish Free State* (London: George Allen & Unwin Ltd, 1932), p. 7.

[43] Aalen, 'Constructive Unionism' (n 31), 141.

[44] D. O'Donnell, 'Property Rights in the Irish Constitution: Rights for Rich People, or a Pillar of Free Society?' in E. Carolan and O. Doyle (eds.), *The Irish Constitution – Governance and Values* (Dublin: Round Hall, 2008), p. 417.

[45] Article 11: 'All the lands and waters, mines and minerals, within the territory of the Irish Free State (Saorstát Eireann) hitherto vested in the State, or any department thereof, or held for the public use or benefit, and also all the natural resources of the same territory . . . shall . . . belong to the Irish Free State (Saorstát Eireann), subject to any trusts, grants, leases or concessions then existing in respect thereof, or any valid private interest therein . . . [and] shall not, nor shall any part thereof, be alienated, but may in the public interest be from time to time granted by way of lease or licence to be worked or enjoyed under the authority and subject to the control of the Oireachtas . . .' This represented '. . . only a very incomplete realisation of the socialistic postulates of the "Democratic Programme" of 1919, although it could have potentially facilitated a progressive nationalisation of natural resources.' Kohn, *The Constitution of the Irish Free State* (n 42), pp. 172–74.

[46] L. Cahillane, 'An Insight into the Irish Free State Constitution' (2014) 54 *American Journal of Legal History* 1, 8.

the Committee, on 7 March 1922.[47] All three drafts defined the nature of private property and its relationship with the common good under the new Irish Free State: Drafts A and B addressed these questions in very similar terms; Draft C took a different approach. While Draft C was not adopted, its terms appear to have informed the 1937 Constitution (considered further below).[48] Archival analysis of this process reveals a political consensus, evident in all three drafts, that a socially oriented approach should be taken to property issues.

Article 1 of Draft B, under a section headed 'Fundamental Rights', was clearly inspired by the socialist movement (Draft A contained an almost identical version of Article 1):

> The Nation's sovereignty extends not only to all the men and women of the nation, but to all the material possessions of the nation, the nation's soil and all its resources and all the wealth and wealth-producing processes within the nation; and all right to private property is subordinated to the public right and welfare of the nation. It is the duty of every man and woman to give allegiance and service to the commonwealth, and it is the duty of the nation to ensure that every citizen shall have opportunity to spend his or her strength and faculties in the service of the people. In return for willing service it is the right of every citizen to receive an adequate share of the produce of the nation's labour.[49]

This reflected the social and economic views that developed in the context of the Irish independence campaign. The 1916 Proclamation of the Irish Republic, which was delivered in the context of the 'Easter Rising' (a pivotal moment in the Irish independence movement), declared the 'right of the people of Ireland to the ownership of Ireland'.[50] The socialist-inspired Democratic Programme that was subsequently issued by the first (pre-independence) Dáil in 1919 reaffirmed that statement, declaring 'all right to private property must be subordinated to the public right and welfare'.[51] The Committee also appears to

[47] National Archives of Ireland, Department of an Taoiseach File S/8953 and National Archive Boxes on the Constitution Committee 1922.

[48] On the influence of Draft C's key author, Alfred O'Rahilly, in the drafting of the 1937 Constitution, see B. Kissane, *New Beginnings: Constitutionalism and Democracy in Modern Ireland* (Dublin: University College Dublin Press, 2011), p. 65.

[49] National Archives of Ireland Department of an Taoiseach File S/8953.

[50] The full text of the proclamation is available at www.gov.ie/en/publication/bfa965-proclamation-of-independence/.

[51] See www.oireachtas.ie/en/debates/debate/dail/1919-01-21/15/. See also Richard English, noting the socialist-republican argument: '. . . that the struggle between the oppressed nation (Ireland) and the oppressor nation (England) is necessarily interwoven with the

have been influenced by the property clause of the USSR Constitution,[52] which was included in a book compiled by the Committee entitled *Select Constitutions of the World*.[53] While Article 1 of Draft B did not follow the Soviet model by *abolishing* private ownership, it gave private property no weight over claims of the common good and imposed duties of co-operation and contribution in return for a right to share the common wealth.

The treatment of property in Article 1 of Draft B was criticised by Professor George O'Brien in a memorandum dated 27 March 1922. O'Brien, an economist, argued '... it ought to be made quite clear that no expropriation can take place except for pressing necessity, after full inquiry and with full compensation.'[54] The Constitution Committee rejected this position in a response dated 13 April 1922. It argued that mandating compensation in all cases of expropriation would impose too onerous a limitation on legislative freedom.[55] The 1922 Committee's position on this issue is especially striking because many of the foreign

struggle within Ireland between those classes oppressed by capitalism and those which benefit from it.' R. English, 'Socialist Republicanism in Independent Ireland 1922–49', in M. Cronin and J. M. Regna (eds.), *Ireland: The Politics of Independence, 1922–49* (London: Palgrave Macmillan, 2000), p. 84. English goes on to note that the ambitions of those advancing this argument were never fully realised, although they did significantly influence Irish political life (p. 86).

52 It provided: '[i]n order to establish the socialisation of land, private ownership of land is abolished; all land is declared national property, and is handed over to the workers, without compensation, on the basis of an equitable division, carrying with it the right to use only.'

53 *Select Constitutions of the World* was a collection of constitutions that the Acting-Chairman of the Constitution Committee of 1922 prepared for the information of the Dáil in its capacity as constituent assembly. The collection was updated and republished in 1934 in B. Shiva Rao, *Select Constitutions of the World* (Madras: Madras Law Journal Press, 1934), p. 254. As Kissane notes, given the backgrounds of the drafters in British administration and law: '... the broad frame of reference was noteworthy'; Kissane, *New Beginnings* (n 48), p. 31.

54 National Archives of Ireland Department of a Taoiseach File S/8953. J. J. Lee refers to O'Brien as 'the gifted young professor at University College Dublin who would grace many Free State committees of economic enquiry,' going so far as to call him 'a consultant on the constitution.' Lee, *Ireland 1912-1985* (n 22), p. 129. Lee also notes that O'Brien was a barrister by training, as well as an economist – p. 571.

55 It noted that Article 1 in Drafts A and B was taken '...practically as it stands, from Pádraig Pearce's essay, "The Sovereign People".' Thomas Mohr suggests, '[b]y including this clause, the drafters had hoped to provide the Constitution of the Irish Free State with a link to the events of Easter 1916 and also to Dáil Éireann's "democratic programme" of 1919 which had also used these words.' T. Mohr, 'British Involvement in the Creation of the First Irish Constitution' (2008) 30 *Dublin University Law Journal* 166, 172.

constitutions that it considered took the approach advocated by O'Brien.[56] Furthermore, O'Donnell highlights that closer to home, both the Home Rule Bill 1893 and s. 5 of the Government of Ireland Act 1920 prohibited uncompensated takings.[57]

Unlike Drafts A and B, Draft C recognised and protected private property rights, although in significantly qualified terms: for example, Article 62.1 provided: '[t]he right to hold private property, like other rights, implies a correlative duty, and it must not be exercised to the detriment of the community'. Property rights were dealt with under Part IX, entitled 'Economic Life', which contained principles of social policy, individual rights, and duties over property and State powers over private property and natural resources. Further property issues, including land policy, were covered in Articles 63 (which limited rights of private property over natural resources in the public interest and asserted a claim of State ownership over all unappropriated natural resources) and 64(1) (which provided: '[o]wnership, inheritance, distribution and use of land are superintended by the State, so as to ensure to every citizen a healthy residence, and to secure an efficient exploitation of the soil and in the interests of the community'). Article 64 also provided that landholders had a duty to use land efficiently and that all increases in land value not attributable to the labour or expenditure of the landholder would accrue to the community rather than the holder.

Following consideration of the drafts, the Provisional Government selected Draft B,[58] and chief negotiator Michael Collins took it to London for approval.[59] The British Government rejected the proposed

[56] The records of the work of the Committee contain copies of the constitutions of Greece, Denmark, and the Netherlands, which each provided that expropriation of private property could only take place pursuant to law, in fulfilment of the demands of public utility and with the payment of compensation or indemnity. National Archives Boxes on the Constitution Committee 1922 (National Archives of Ireland) at M1, T1, and S2.

[57] O'Donnell, 'Property Rights in the Irish Constitution' (n 44), p. 416. As will be seen in Chapter 8, Irish resistance to absolute compensation entitlements has persisted over time, with judicial recognition of a *presumptive* constitutional entitlement to full compensation for expropriation, but one that is capable of being displaced or modified by social justice and other common good considerations.

[58] National Archives of Ireland Department of an Taoiseach File S/8953.

[59] J. M. Curran, *The Birth of the Irish Free State 1921–1923*, (Tuscaloosa, AL: University of Alabama Press, 1980), p. 201. Leo Kohn notes, '[t]he Irish Government, as was expressly admitted by the British Colonial Secretary in the House of Commons, was under no obligation to consult the British Cabinet. Inasmuch, however, as the Constitution represented an implementation of the Treaty and would, therefore, require to be confirmed by the British Parliament, it was obviously expedient prior to the publication of the Draft to

Constitution, expressing particular concern with Article 1 in light of its assertion of sovereignty and the socialist overtones of its property clauses.[60] The Irish leadership drew up a revised Constitution,[61] with an express statement of the Free State's co-equal status within the Commonwealth and without draft Article 1's treatment of property.[62] In this way, to secure British agreement and to bolster the Free State's political independence, the Constitution of the Irish Free State (Saorstát Éireann) Act 1922 was silent on private ownership.[63] As such, an important political event caused English property ideology to shape the constitutional treatment of property in post-independence Ireland.[64]

3.2.3 *Bunreacht na hÉireann 1937: A Rights-Based Framing of Ownership*

By the mid-1930s, political energy in Ireland was focused on breaking free of residual post-Independence British control. During the Anglo-Irish Trade War 1932–38, the Irish government withheld the payment of land annuities (debt owed to the British Treasury linked to financing of Irish leasehold enfranchisement) and the British government retaliated through trade quotas and tariffs. The dispute was eventually resolved through a once-off payment to the British government of £10 million.[65] This political clash prompted a (largely failed) emphasis on

secure an assurance from the British Government that it was regarded by Great Britain as conforming to the terms of the Treaty.' Kohn, *The Constitution of the Irish Free State* (n 42), p. 78.

60 Mohr notes, '[a]side from the sustained emphasis on Irish sovereignty, the British were shocked by what Austen Chamberlain, then Lord Privy Seal, called the "Soviet character" of these articles.' Mohr, 'British Involvement' (n 55), 172.

61 Curran, *The Birth of the Irish Free State* (n 59), p. 213. See also the discussion of this point by Kissane, *New Beginnings* (n 48), p. 37.

62 Mohr, 'British Involvement' (n 55), 172; see also Cahillane, 'An Insight into the Irish Free State Constitution' (n 46), 21, noting that Hugh Kennedy wrote to Michael Collins suggesting that he would propose omitting parts of Articles 1 and 2 that were suggested as having a 'communistic tendency'. For details, see Hugh Kennedy Papers, UCD Archives, P4/362 and 363.

63 It addressed property already vested in the State and natural resources in Article 11.

64 The role of English property ideologies and historical events in shaping the Irish approach to property is further developed in Walsh and Fox O'Mahony, 'Land Law, Property Ideologies and the British–Irish Relationship' (n 3).

65 The annuity stood at around £5 million per annum prior to independence. See P. Neary and C. O'Grada, 'Economic War and Structural Change: The 1930s in Ireland' (1991) *Irish Historical Studies* 27 (10) 250 and C. Ó Gráda, *A Rocky Road: The Irish Economy Since the 1920s* (Manchester: Manchester University Press, 1997), pp. 5–6.

self-sufficiency in Irish economic policy. As Kissane notes, '[b]y 1937 the Irish state was diplomatically isolated, dependent on protectionist economic policies, and culturally defensive.'[66] Ongoing land reform, by this stage centred on the break-up of large farms, was consistent with this isolationist outlook.[67] To move Ireland out of the shadow of English political power, the President of the Executive Council (the title of the leader of the government at that time), Eamon de Valera, decided that constitutional reform was required. Kissane characterises de Valera's approach to constitutional reform as an Irish version of the 'Whig' tradition, which had been exported from Britain and Europe to North America: his vision was of a virtuous citizenry amenable to restraints on individual rights to secure the common good.[68] In 1934, de Valera gave a committee of civil servants the task of reviewing the 1922 Constitution to identify the provisions contained in that document that should be protected as fundamental.[69] This process eventually evolved into a plan to draft a new Constitution.[70]

Given the complex Irish cultural attitude towards private property, the drafters faced a difficult task. They had to balance the demand of owners for security of possession with the need for the State to retain power to redistribute land to enable the ongoing work of the Land Commission. Any constitutional treatment of private property had to avoid unravelling or calling into question the extensive land redistributions that had occurred up to 1937.[71] Dooley suggests that the impact of the Land Commission on Irish society was surpassed only by that of the Catholic

66 Kissane, *New Beginnings* (n 48), p. 57.

67 Ferriter, *The Transformation of Ireland* (n 34), p. 313.

68 Kissane, *New Beginnings* (n 48), p. 58.

69 The Committee consisted of four senior civil servants, Stephen Roche, Michael McDunphy, John Hearne, and Philip O'Donoghue, and met 10 times between 28 May and 3 July 1934 before reporting to de Valera. G. Hogan, 'The Constitution Review Committee of 1934', in F. Ó Muircheartaigh (ed.), *Ireland in the Coming Times – Essays to celebrate T. K. Whitaker's 80 Years*, (Dublin: Institute of Public Administration, 1997), pp. 342, 347. See also D. Keogh and A. McCarthy, *The Making of the Irish Constitution 1937* (Cork: Mercier Press, 2008), pp. 65–9.

70 For full treatment of the drafting process, see G. Hogan, *Origins of the Irish Constitution 1928–1941* (Dublin: Royal Irish Academy, 2012) and Coffey, *Drafting the 1937 Irish Constitution* (n 7).

71 R. Keane, 'Property in the Constitution and in the Courts' in B. Farrell (ed.) *Dev's Constitution and Ours* (Dublin: Gill and Macmillan, 1988), pp. 137, 138.

Church.[72] In this context, political discourse shifted away from the socialist ideals that influenced Drafts A and B of the 1922 Constitution towards the approach adopted in Draft C of protecting private ownership and individual property rights in the context of a detailed social and economic framework for State intervention.[73]

3.2.4 *Property Rights, Social Justice, and Social Policy in the Drafting Process*

In line with this shift, the right to own property and rights over owned property were included in the new draft Constitution from an early stage.[74] Archival records of the drafting process from early 1937 onwards reveal that the inclination of those preparing the new Constitution was for a single constitutional provision that would both protect individual property rights and specify the principles of social policy that should delimit such rights.[75] The *opportunity to own property* was to be recognised in the Constitution as a natural right, but the *exercise* of property rights was to be considered in light of the effects that such exercise could have on society as a whole, and particularly on vulnerable members of the community.[76] On this approach, private ownership and social justice would be balanced by giving the State a clear constitutional mandate to restrict the exercise of property rights and concrete constitutional guidance on the meaning of social justice as a delimiting principle.

To this end, as late as March 1937, the draft Constitution grouped the property rights guarantees alongside delimiting principles of social

72 Dooley, *The Land for the People* (n 26), p. 28. Similarly, Kissane suggests that by 1937, '[the three most important institutions south of the border were the Catholic Church, the State, and the Land Commission.' Kissane, *New Beginnings* (n 48), p. 84.

73 While draft C was not adopted by the Provisional Government in 1922, its echoes are evident in the 1937 Constitution, particularly in relation to the separation of social principles from judicially enforceable rights; B. Farrell, 'The Drafting of the Irish Free State Constitution: III' (1971) 6 *Irish Jurist* 110, 111–12.

74 See the documentation of early drafts at UCDAD/P150/2371, analysed in Walsh, 'Private Property Rights in the Drafting of the Irish Constitution' (n 14), 89–90.

75 See the documentation at UCDAD/P150/2385 and UCDAD/P150/2387, analysed in Walsh, 'Private Property Rights in the Drafting of the Irish Constitution', (n 14), 91–3.

76 See, e.g., G. S. Alexander, E. M. Peñalver, J. W. Singer and L. S. Underkuffler, 'A Statement of Progressive Property' (2009) 94 *Cornell Law Review* 743; J. W. Singer, *No Freedom Without Regulation: The Hidden Lesson of the Subprime Crisis* (New Haven: Yale University Press, 2015) and J. W. Singer, *Entitlement: The Paradoxes of Property* (New Haven: Yale University Press, 2000).

policy.[77] Those principles articulated the need to promote the welfare of all, with justice and charity as guiding principles, and the associated need for material resources be distributed to secure the common good. They enshrined de Valera's Whig-inspired vision for a strong agrarian economy with as many families settled on the land as was practicable; they also established controls on credit, competition, and wages, and articulated a special commitment to protecting the needs of vulnerable people.

3.2.5 *The Influence of Catholic Thinking on Private Ownership*

Catholic social teaching was a very significant influence on the drafting process, with for example Moyn citing the Irish Constitution as an important early instance of 'religious constitutionalism'.[78] There are extensive references in the archival material on the drafting of the property rights provisions to *Rerum Novarum* and *Quadragesimo Anno*, Papal Encyclicals issued by Pope Leo XIII and Pope Pius XI respectively.[79] Dr John Charles McQuaid, Archbishop of Dublin and a key religious advisor on the drafting of the 1937 Constitution, submitted numerous draft articles to de Valera that drew heavily on *Rerum Novarum* and *Quadragesimo Anno*.[80] Rev. Edward Cahill (a Jesuit priest who was involved in the drafting process from 1936 onwards in conjunction with a Committee of leading Jesuits) drew upon the Papal Encyclicals as well as other Catholic constitutions in Europe in his submissions.[81]

[77] National Archives of Ireland Department of an Taoiseach File S/9715 A. The same draft appears to be contained in de Valera's papers, at UCDAD/P150/2401.

[78] S. Moyn, 'The Secret History of Constitutional Dignity' (2014) 17 *Yale Human Rights and Development Journal* 39, 41. See D. Keogh and A. McCarthy, 'The Catholic Church and the Writing of the 1937 Constitution' (2005) 13 *History Ireland* 36.

[79] *Rerum Novarum* was issued on 15 May 1891 by Pope Leo XIII (http://w2.vatican.va/content/leo-xiii/en/encyclicals/documents/hf_l-xiii_enc_15051891_rerum-novarum.html). *Quadragesimo Anno* was issued on 15 May 1931 by Pope Pius XI (http://w2.vatican.va/content/pius-xi/en/encyclicals/documents/hf_p-xi_enc_19310515_quadragesimo-anno.html). See Keogh and McCarthy, *The Making of the Irish Constitution 1937* (n 69), pp. 117–20, for a helpful comparison of these encyclicals and the first printed draft of the Constitution.

[80] These are set out in archival documentation, University College Dublin Archives: UCDAD/P150/2395. See also the discussion of McQuaid's input in Keogh and McCarthy, *The Making of the Irish Constitution* (n 69), pp. 117–21.

[81] This contribution is set out in documentation contained at UCDAD/P150/2393. S. Faughnan, 'The Jesuits and the Drafting of the Irish Constitution of 1937' (1988) 26

The Encyclicals can be understood as advocating right-based protection of private ownership subject to State-imposed limitations designed to secure social justice.[82] For Leo XIII, the propagation and protection of private ownership was the favoured means of ensuring the sustenance of all men, peaceful relations between the classes, and the efficient use of natural resources; natural rights to private ownership required that the State could limit, but not abolish, private property. Leo XIII argued that an individual's effort in labouring on property *itself* created a natural entitlement to that property. As such, Leo XIII's view of labour as property's basis was 'surprisingly but obviously in the liberal and Lockean tradition.'[83] He also characterised labour as a means by which an individual could impose his personality on external things, reflecting a Hegelian understanding of the role of property rights in personal development. The archival evidence suggests that drafters of the 1937 Constitution were influenced by the limited adoption of the Lockean and Hegelian property theories identifiable in the Encyclicals rather than by significant direct engagement with those theories.

In *Quadragesimo Anno*, Pope Pius XI also stressed the social aspect of private ownership, arguing:

> . . .twin rocks of shipwreck must be carefully avoided. For, as one is wrecked upon, or comes close to, what is known as 'individualism' by denying or minimising the social and public character of the right of property, so by rejecting or minimising the private and individual character of this same right, one inevitably runs into 'collectivism' or at least closely approaches its tenets.[84]

In light of this concern, in finalising the treatment of individual property rights in the new Constitution, the drafters sought to establish a framework for balanced protection of property rights and social justice.

Irish Historical Studies 79, highlights the extent to which Cahill acted as spokesman for a wider Jesuit committee; see also Keogh and McCarthy, *The Making of the Irish Constitution* (n 69), p. 104. Article 99 of the Polish Constitution was influential at an early stage in the drafting of the property rights provisions, although its influence was attenuated in later versions: Coffey, *Drafting the 1937 Irish Constitution* (n 7) p. 237. However, see in contrast Kissane's view that the Polish Constitution's statement of a State aim of wide distribution of private productive property did influence the Constitution as adopted: Kissane, *New Beginnings* (n 48), p. 66.

82 Moyn notes the significance of the timing of the anti-communist Papal Encyclical, *Divini Redemptoris*, in the context of the Irish drafting process. The encyclical was issued on 19 March 1937: Moyn, 'The Secret History' (n 78), 48–9.

83 J. M. Kelly, *A Short History of Western Legal Theory* (Oxford: Clarendon Press, 1992), p. 338.

84 *Quadragesimo Anno*, [46].

3.2.6 *Decoupling Property Rights and Social Justice*

At a late stage in the drafting process, the property rights guarantees were separated from the delimiting principles of social policy and the decision was taken to make the principles of social policy non-cognisable by the courts.[85] These changes were prompted by political concerns about the possibility that the draft social policy principles would be relied upon by individuals to establish *positive* rights through judicial review, for example, through actions to compel the redistribution of land by the State.[86] They were not motivated by any desire to weaken the power of the State to restrict the exercise of individual property rights. A full draft Constitution was published and circulated generally on 1 May 1937 protecting private property rights in the terms now contained in Articles 40.3.2° and 43 of the 1937 Constitution.[87] The principles of social policy were set out in Article 45, which was stated to be for the sole cognisance of the legislature. The Constitution was approved by the Oireachtas on 14 June and adopted by the people on 1 July, coming into operation on 29 December 1937.[88]

Commenting on Article 43, Cahill foresaw some of the problems that courts have subsequently encountered in interpreting that provision, saying:

> The term social justice (Article 43.2.1) which is so often used in the Encyclicals of Pius XI, and has for the student of Catholic Social Science a clear and definite meaning, is probably quite unknown in our current jurisprudence, or, if known, has a meaning different from its meaning in the Papal Encyclicals.[89]

He argued that most Irish judges and lawyers were trained in the liberal English common law legal tradition, with the result that the Constitution's commitment to securing social justice could be frustrated. As will be seen throughout this book, the interplay between that legal tradition and the Constitution's distinctive, progressively framed approach to protecting individual property rights continues to shape Irish constitutional property law, with 'social justice' receiving relatively little doctrinal attention.[90]

85 See the draft clause circulated on 2 April 1937 at UCDAD/P150/2416.
86 See Walsh, 'Private Property Rights in the Drafting of the Irish Constitution' (n 14), 93–7.
87 UCDAD/P150/2429.
88 Keogh and McCarthy, *The Making of the Irish Constitution* (n 69), p. 124.
89 UCDAD/P150/2393.
90 Although see the judicial analysis of the relationship between 'the principles of social justice' and 'the exigencies of the common good', discussed below at (n 104)–(n 114).

The late-stage decoupling of the property rights guarantees and the principles of social policy made the reference in Article 43.2 to 'the principles of social justice' appear vague rather than a short-hand reference to an express constitutional statement of principles of social policy as had been intended in the early drafts. The separation of the principles of social policy from Article 43 and the rendering of those principles non-justiciable resulted in a protection of private property rights that left the definition of property's 'social aspect'[91] largely up to the elected branches of government. However, the intention was clearly not to entrench an absolutist protection for private property rights. Rather, the drafters sought to crystallise within the text of the Constitution a creative tension between the cultural attraction to the security afforded by property rights on the one hand, and resistance to absolutist conceptions of ownership as impediments to social justice on the other hand. This cultural attitude was shaped by local, national, and international factors, including the legacy of the Famine and the Penal Laws, the economic significance of land reform and its connections with the independence movement, the influence of the Catholic church on leading law-makers, and the tensions surrounding private ownership in the wider European political context. Against this multi-faceted backdrop, the Constitution's property clauses sought to strike a compromise between competing property ideologies – individual possession and socially oriented redistribution – that both had strong cultural salience and deep historical roots.

3.3 Understanding the Functions of the Constitutional Property Clauses

The historical evidence discussed in the previous part suggests that Article 40.3.2° is properly regarded as the source of constitutional protection for individual rights over property actually owned (i.e. rights *of* ownership), while Article 43.1 guarantees the individual right to private ownership of property (i.e. an *institutional* guarantee of private ownership). The current judicial consensus is that individual rights over owned property are protected by Article 40.3.2°, but that the concept of 'unjust attack' in Article 40.3.2° must be read considering 'the principles of social justice' and 'the exigencies of the common good' referenced in Article

[91] A. M. Honoré, 'Ownership', in A. G. Guest (ed.) *Oxford Essays in Jurisprudence* (Oxford: Oxford University Press, 1961), pp. 144–45.

43.2. This part analyses the doctrinal pathway to this settlement of the relationship between Articles 40.3.2° and 43 and the significance of this delineation of the Constitution's two property rights guarantees.

3.3.1 Evolving Judicial Interpretations of the Relationship between Articles 40.3.2° and 43

Over time, three distinct judicial approaches to the relationship between Articles 40.3.2° and 43 have been adopted. First, in 1950, the Supreme Court rejected the contention that Article 43.1 was an institutional guarantee of private property, in particular emphasising its natural law language.[92] The Court characterised Article 43.1 as recognising natural individual rights to private property, albeit subject to the State's regulatory power as set out in Article 43.2.[93] Second, in 1960, Article 43.1 was interpreted as an institutional guarantee by Davitt P in the High Court in *Attorney General* v. *Southern Industrial Trust.*[94] He identified three distinct facets of the Irish constitutional protection of private property rights: first, a guarantee of general access to the institution of private ownership; second, security of possession of owned property; third, freedom of use of owned property. Davitt P characterised Article 40.3.2°, rather than Article 43, as the source of the second and third types of rights.[95] Third, in the Supreme Court in *Southern Industrial Trust*, on appeal from Davitt P's decision, Lavery J held that the property rights protected under Article 40.3.2° were the same as those defined and declared by Article 43, namely the general rights to own, transfer, bequeath, and inherit property. He said that statutes and regulations

[92] *Buckley* v. *AG* [1950] IR 67.

[93] *Buckley* was followed in *Foley* v. *The Irish Land Commission.* In the High Court, Dixon J did not refer to Article 40.3.2°, but rather analysed the property rights question in the case by reference to Article 43, noting that the protection given to individual property rights by Article 43.1 was limited by Article 43.2. In the Supreme Court, O'Byrne J referred to Article 40.3.2°, and said it dealt with personal rights including the right to private property, which right was specifically dealt with in Article 43. The Court concluded that the impugned restriction on property rights did not constitute an abolition of the right of private ownership under Article 43.1.2°, and moreover was a restriction on property rights that was permitted by Article 43.2.2°, as it was designed to reconcile the exercise of the appellant's rights with the exigencies of the common good and the principles of social justice. [1952] IR 118 at 152–54.

[94] (1960) 94 ILTR 161.

[95] However, he held that he was bound by *Buckley* to find that Article 43 protected individual rights over property actually owned. Ibid. at 172.

allowing for the expropriation without compensation of private property did not abolish the private ownership of external goods, or the other general rights protected by Article 43.1. Rather, such measures delimited the exercise of those rights in accordance with Article 43.2 provided they were in the interests of the common good and social justice.[96] According to Lavery J, the Constitution *only* protected general rights in relation to private ownership, not individual rights over owned property.

In *Blake* v. *The Attorney General*, the Supreme Court approved Davitt P's approach in *Southern Industrial Trust* and interpreted Articles 40.3.2° and 43 as having distinct functions in protecting property rights.[97] O'Higgins CJ characterised Article 43 as a statement concerning the attitude of the Irish State towards private ownership, involving an institutional guarantee (including the right for all to participate in that institution), coupled with a statement of the circumstances in which the exercise of rights flowing from that institutional guarantee (property rights) could be restricted. Individual property rights were dealt with alongside other personal rights in Article 40.3.2°. Based on this interpretation of Articles 40.3.2° and 43, O'Higgins CJ described the Constitution as providing 'a double protection for the property rights of a citizen'.[98] Since the impugned legislation in *Blake* (a rent control law) affected individual property rights rather than the right *to own*, O'Higgins CJ held that its constitutionality fell to be assessed under Article 40.3.2°. He did not specify whether the delimiting principles set out in Article 43.2 were relevant to this assessment or whether they were only engaged when considering restrictions imposed on the *institutional* guarantee in Article 43.1.

3.3.2 A Harmonious Interpretation of Article 40.3.2° and Article 43 and the Meaning of Social Justice

Subsequent decisions have mediated between these competing judicial approaches by drawing on both Articles 40.3.2° and 43 to achieve a

96 Ibid. at 175–77.
97 [1982] IR 117.
98 Ibid. at 135. A. J. van der Walt discusses various types of 'double property clauses' in A. J. van der Walt, 'Double Property Guarantees: A Structural and Comparative Analysis' (1998) 14 *South African Journal of Human Rights* 560, 561 noting, '...the "property clause" can and often does consist of a complex of different provisions that are more or less closely related to the constitutional property guarantee in the narrow sense of the term'.

harmonious interpretation of the two property rights clauses.[99] For example, in *Re Article 26 and Part V of the Planning and Development Bill 1999*,[100] the Supreme Court characterised the approach adopted in *Blake* whereby the impugned restriction was analysed solely by reference to Article 40.3.2° as drawing an unduly rigid line between the two provisions. It noted that in most cases where legislation was challenged based on its impact on property rights, debate would arise over the consistency of the legislation with 'the exigencies of the common good' and 'the principles of social justice'.[101] The Court did not explicitly state its view on the function of Article 43.1 as an institutional and/or an individual rights guarantee, but it clearly advocated a holistic reading of the two private property provisions.[102]

This is a plausible and practicable interpretation of the relative functions of Articles 40.3.2° and 43. The regulatory power set out in Article 43.2.2° is stated to be over the 'exercise' of the rights set out in Article 43.1. The *prima facie* right to own private property is exercised through individual property rights, meaning that the institution of private ownership and the individual rights that flow from participation in that institution are not hermetically sealed from one another. The right *to own* is intimately related to rights *of ownership*, with for example Penner describing the right to own as 'a general contingent right to participate in the practice [of property] by acquiring special rights to specific forms of property according to the well-recognized modes of the practice, principally gift and contractual transfer.'[103] As such, control of the institution will necessarily impact on rights of ownership, making it logical for

[99] See, e.g., *PMPS* v. *Attorney General* [1983] IR 355; *Cafolla* v. *O'Malley* [1985] IR 486; *Madigan* v. *Attorney General* [1986] ILRM 136; *Lawlor* v. *Minister for Agriculture* [1990] 1 IR 356; *An Blascaod Mór Teoranta* v. *Commissioners of Public Works* [1998] IEHC 38 and *Re Article 26 and the Employment Equality Bill 1996* [1997] 2 IR 321 at 366–67.

[100] *Re Article 26 and the Employment Equality Bill 1996* (n 99).

[101] Ibid. at 348.

[102] See also *Dreher* v. *Irish Land Commission*, where Walsh J stated, 'I think it clear that any State action that is authorised by Article 43 of the Constitution and conforms to that Article cannot by definition be unjust for the purpose of Article 40.3.2': [1984] ILRM 94 at 96. Interestingly, both Henchy J and Griffin J agreed with Walsh J's judgment, but referred simply to the failure of the applicant to show any inconsistency between the impugned compensation provision and Article 40.3 of the Constitution. Ibid. at 98–9. This statement was approved the Supreme Court in *O'Callaghan* v. *Commissioners for Public Works* [1985] ILRM 364 at 368 and *ESB* v. *Gormley* [1985] 1 IR 129 at 150. See similarly *Carrigaline Community Television Broadcasting Co Ltd* v. *Minister for Transport* [1997] 1 ILRM 241 at 288.

[103] Penner, *The Idea of Property* (n 8), p. 51.

courts to have regard to the same principles in considering restrictions imposed on the institution of private property and on individual rights generated by the operation of that institution.

The judicial preference for a harmonious interpretation of Articles 40.3.2° and 43 begs the question of the distinct meaning of the delimiting principles in Article 43.2, if any. In a number of early cases, judges disclaimed any role in considering whether restrictions on the exercise of property rights were required by 'the exigencies of the common good' and 'the principles of social justice', regarding such decisions as lying exclusively within the purview of the legislature. The most striking example of this approach was *Pigs Marketing Board* v. *Donnelly,* where Hanna J held that the concept of 'social justice' in Article 43 was non-justiciable, and that the Oireachtas alone should decide the appropriate limits that could be placed on property rights.[104] He commented in relation to the phrase 'social justice':

> I cannot define that phrase as a matter of law. It cannot be the old standard of the greatest good of the greatest number, for, at the present day, it may be considered proper that the claim of a minority be made paramount on some topic...I cannot conceive social justice as being a constant quality, either with individuals or in different states. What is social justice in one State may be the negation of what is considered social justice in another State. In a Court of law it seems to me to be a nebulous phrase, involving no questions of law for the Court, but questions of ethics, morals, economics, and sociology which are, in my opinion, beyond the determination of a Court of law, but which may be, in their various aspects, within the consideration of the Oireachtas, as representing the people, when framing the law.[105]

Hanna J contended that the Oireachtas should judge the legitimacy of restrictions on property rights and that any argument that a delimitation of the exercise of property rights was contrary to the common good

[104] [1939] IR 413. Hanna J characterised 'social justice' as '...a vague phrase, a kind of political shibboleth', the meaning of which would be determined by 'the individual view of each particular Judge, or body of Judges, on the theory of government and their knowledge of political science.' Hanna J made these comments in reference to Article 12 of the Irish Free State Constitution of 1922 (which referred to 'peace, order, and good government of the State'), and then said that the same critique could be applied to Article 43 of the 1937 Constitution – at 418.

[105] Ibid. Hanna J clearly regarded 'the principles of social justice' as having a meaning distinct from a utilitarian conception of the common good, consistent with the origins of Article 43 in Catholic teaching on property and social justice.

would need to be clearly proven.[106] A similar approach was adopted by Lavery J in *Attorney General* v. *Southern Industrial Trust*, where he held that the legislature 'has the primary function in securing that the laws enacted by it have regard to "the requirements of the common good" and are regulated by the principles of "social justice".'[107]

However, the Supreme Court exercised jurisdiction under Article 43.2 in *Buckley* v. *The Attorney General*, holding that if the intention had been to deny judges the power to apply that provision, it would have been made expressly non-cognisable by the courts, as was done with the Directive Principles of Social Policy in Article 45.[108] Building on the assertion of jurisdiction in *Buckley*, the Supreme Court has since held that the structure of Article 43 means that the State can only legitimately delimit the exercise of property rights in accordance with 'the principles of social justice'.[109] The decisions of the Supreme Court in *Re Article 26 and the Health (Amendment) (No 2) Bill, 2004*,[110] and Peart J in the High Court in *Shirley* v. *AO Gorman*,[111] give some indication of the judicial understanding of the meaning of 'the principles of social justice' as compared with 'the exigencies of the common good'. In the former case, the Court held that the reference in Article 43.2 to 'the principles of social justice' meant that greater protection should be afforded to the property rights of 'persons of modest means'.[112] The Court further held that it would stretch the meaning of the reference to social justice '. . .to extend it to an expropriation of property solely in the financial interests of the State', barring evidence of a serious risk of economic crisis.[113] Peart J in *Shirley* considered extensive expert evidence on the meaning of 'social justice' in Article 43.2 and concluded, '[i]t seems to me that social justice in the context of property rights means that there ought to be at

106 Ibid. at 422–23. Hanna J rejected the argument that the Pigs and Bacon Acts of 1935 and 1937 were unconstitutional as being contrary to good government and social justice, because he felt there was no standard that could be applied by the Court to determine that issue.

107 *Southern Industrial Trust* (n 94) at 176.

108 [1950] IR 67 at 83.

109 *Re Article 26 and the Employment Equality Bill, 1996* (n 99) at 366–67. See also on this point D. Barrington, 'Private Property under the Irish Constitution' (1973) 8 *Irish Jurist* 1, 3; J. M. Kelly, G. W. Hogan and G. Whyte, *The Irish Constitution (Supplement to the Second Edition)* (Dublin: Jurist Publishing, 1987), p. 190.

110 [2005] 1 IR 105.

111 [2006] IEHC 27.

112 *Re Article 26 and the Health (Amendment) (No 2) Bill, 2004* (n 110) at 202.

113 Ibid. at 205–06.

least a fair, as opposed to equal, distribution of property amongst all members of the society, so that justice is achieved.'[114]

3.3.3 *Understanding the 'Double Protection' of Property Rights*

Doyle argues '. . .the intellectual lineage of Article 43 unquestionably lies in the natural law tradition'.[115] The previous part of this chapter demonstrated the complexity of that lineage, with natural law thinking about private ownership filtered into the Irish Constitution through Catholic teaching that also recognised an important social dimension to the protection of property rights. Accordingly, constitutional recognition of the right to private ownership as a natural right never entailed property absolutism.

However, that begs the question of what the natural right to private ownership in Article 43.1 *does* entail. The Irish courts have not addressed this foundational question, notwithstanding the clarification of the relationship between Articles 40.3.2° and 43 considered in the previous section. Waldron argues persuasively that while the reference in Article 43.1.1° of the Irish Constitution to the 'natural right' to private ownership of external goods might superficially seem like a guarantee of *individual* property rights, in fact it can also be interpreted as simply meaning '. . .there is something about human nature (the nature we all share) which makes it wrong to exclude any (or all) of us from the class of potential proprietors'.[116] On this understanding, all individuals have the right '. . .not to be ruled out of the class of people who *may* own property'.[117] Read in light of this interpretation of Article 43.1.1°, Wheare's criticism of Article 43 as 'a classic example of giving a right

[114] *Shirley* (n 111). Peart J envisaged the 'principles of social justice' as determining the *reasons* that the State could advance to justify restricting the exercise of property rights, while the 'exigencies of the common good' delimited the permissible *means* that could be adopted to achieve socially just public objectives.

[115] O. Doyle, *The Constitution of Ireland: A Contextual Analysis* (Oxford: Hart, 2018), p. 94.

[116] Waldron, *The Right to Private Property* (n 1), p. 21. He notes that while it seems that Article 43.1 guarantees a certain level of immunity against expropriation for existing property rights, expropriation of the property rights of some individuals is not inconsistent with the preservation of private property in general, and everyone's potential right to own private property – p. 22. A. J. van der Walt adopts a similar reading of the nature of the Irish Constitution's protection for private property. A. J. van der Walt, *Constitutional Property Clauses: A Comparative Analysis* (Cape Town: Juta, 1999), p. 234.

[117] Waldron, *The Right to Private Property* (n 1), p. 20–21. See also Penner, *The Idea of Property* (n 8), p. 51.

with one hand and taking it back with the other' fundamentally misunderstands the nature of Article 43.[118] The right to participate in a private ownership system is 'given' (in fact 'acknowledged') by Article 43.1, and is not 'taken away' by Article 43.2. Rather, individual rights obtained through participation in that system are subjected to the possibility of regulatory control.[119] The State is prohibited from setting down exclusionary rules about who can and cannot own property or avail of the major incidents of ownership, such as the right to transfer and bequeath property. Everyone has the right *to own*, which arises without the need for any action on their part, or any other contingent occurrence. While the introduction of legal rules preventing certain individuals or groups from acquiring property is unlikely now,[120] in 1937 the influence of communism meant that such fear existed and shaped the Catholic teaching on property that was relied on by the Constitution's drafters.[121] Furthermore, Ireland had experienced exclusionary property laws through the Penal Laws and its history of settlement, including the imposition of the feudal system of landholding. Article 43 guards against such exclusionary laws without rendering any distribution of property rights immutable. As Brian Walsh argues, '[t]he natural right to the private ownership of property is very different from a right to retain all

[118] K. C. Wheare, *Modern Constitutions* (Oxford: Oxford University Press, 1966), p. 43.

[119] Kenny J in *Central Dublin Development Association* v. *The Attorney General* argued that the Irish text of Article 43.1.1° recognised 'a natural right to his own private share of worldly wealth', which appeared consistent with a guarantee of an individual right over owned property rather than an institutional guarantee of private ownership: (1975) 109 ILTR 69 at 83. See also O'Donnell, 'Property Rights in the Irish Constitution' (n 44), p. 428 for this translation of the Irish text. However, the literal translation of the Irish text provided by Micheál Ó Cearúil is consistent with an institutional reading of Article 43.1.1°. He says it means, '[t]he State acknowledges, because man has the gift of reason, that he has a natural right to have worldly assets of his own privately, a right which is more ancient than human statute.' M. Ó Cearúil, *Bunreacht na hEireann – A Study of the Irish Text* (Dublin: Stationary Office, 1999), p. 619.

[120] Although it is worth noting in this context that in recent years several common-law jurisdictions have introduced new restrictions over who may access their residential property sectors: see, e.g., Overseas Investment Amendment Act 2018 (NZ) 2018/25; Foreign Acquisitions and Takeovers Act 1975 (Cth), 1975/92 as amended; Land Transfer Tax Act, RSO 1990, c L.6, s 2.1. For analysis, see S. Hamill, 'Restricting Access to Property: Citizens, Owners, Residents, and Claims to Property' (unpublished manuscript, on file with author).

[121] See, e.g., Keane, 'Property in the Constitution and in the Courts' (n 71), p. 139, noting '[c]ommunism, rather than fascism, was seen in Catholic terms – at least in Irish Catholic Terms – as the most dangerous of political systems, and this is reflected in the first section of article 43.'

the property one has legally acquired.'[122] In this way, the Irish example demonstrates that a Constitution can recognise a natural right of private ownership without thereby entrenching the status quo in terms of property distribution.[123]

Article 43.1.2° prohibits the State from abolishing the general right to transfer, bequeath, or inherit property. Davitt P in *Southern Industrial Trust* appeared to interpret this as meaning that once an individual acquired property, he or she could not be deprived of the core incidents of ownership in respect of that property. In this interpretation, Article 43.1's institutional guarantee prescribes the core content of the individual rights flowing from the protected private ownership system.[124] However, this interpretation neglects the reference to 'general right' in the constitutional text. In *O'B* v. *S*, which concerned statutory limitations on the right to inherit, the Supreme Court emphasised the general nature of the guarantees of transfer, bequest, and inheritance in Article 43.2, holding that legislation could prevent succession to property by individuals in some circumstances.[125] Consequently, Article 43.2 does not guarantee a protected core of rights of transfer and bequest for all owners in all circumstances – rather, it prohibits the *general abolition* of these aspects of the institution of private ownership. It suggests that if the sale of property was prohibited in all circumstances, or if wills in general were rendered wholly ineffective through a change in the law, the Constitution might be infringed. What is unclear is how significant and wide-reaching an interference with one of these aspects of ownership would need to be to constitute an unlawful interference with the general right. As Kleyn puts it in discussing the German institutional guarantee, 'the guarantee of the institution is a direction to the legislature neither to abolish the institution *nor to water it down to such an extent that it cannot be*

[122] B. Walsh, 'The Judicial Power, Justice and the Constitution of Ireland' in D. Curtin and T. F. O'Keeffe (eds.), *Constitutional Adjudication in European Community and National Law – Essays of the Hon. Mr. Justice T. F. O'Higgins* (Dublin: Butterworths, 1992), pp. 145, 148. See also Dorfman, distinguishing between the idea of private ownership (which he defines as 'an authority to fix in some measure the normative standing of others in relation to an object') and its breadth and scope: 'Private Ownership' (n 13), 28.

[123] See Alexander, 'Property as a Fundamental Right?' (n 10), 772, making a similar argument concerning the German constitutional protection of property.

[124] Dorfman argues '. . .the power of alienation is the surface manifestation of the very idea of private ownership', with outright elimination of that right going to the very core of the idea of private ownership. Dorfman, 'Private Ownership' (n 13), 34.

[125] [1984] 1 IR 316.

characterised as property any longer'.[126] It remains to be seen how far-reaching an alteration of transfer, bequest, or inheritance would need to be to infringe Article 43.1.2° of the Irish Constitution.[127] *O'B* indicates that generally applicable *restrictions* on freedom of testation are constitutionally permissible.

However, the institutional guarantee means that private ownership is made a permanent aspect of the Irish social and political structure. While the proposed Article 1 of the 1922 Constitution would have embraced a socialist economic and legal system, Article 43.1 means that the State is absolutely precluded from abolishing private ownership in general.[128] Nonetheless, Article 45, which includes principles concerning access to property and State control of ownership, indicates that a mixed economy, including legislatively mandated redistribution, is constitutionally permissible. This is reinforced by the regulatory power expressly conferred by Article 43.2. Protecting private ownership as an institution in this way complicates the application by judges of any 'balancing' framework purporting to juxtapose public policy/the public interest against the protection of individual property rights in reviewing restrictions on such rights.[129] Changes to the protection of individual property rights affect the institution of private ownership. Equally, changes to the institution affect the rights flowing from that institution. In limiting individual property rights to pursue one policy goal, Article 43.1 suggests that the State must also factor in the impact that the change has on the *institutional* protection of private

126 D. Kleyn, 'The Constitutional Protection of Property: A comparison between the German and the South African approach' (1996) 11 *SA Publiekreg/Public Law* 402, 414–15 (emphasis added). Article 14 of the German Basic Law provides: '(i) Property and the right of inheritance shall be guaranteed. (ii) Their substance and limits shall be determined by law.' Lubens identifies a judicial commitment to protecting a 'core field' of property rights (*Kernbereich*): R. Lubens, 'The Social Obligation of Property Ownership: A Comparison of German and US Law' (2007) 24 *Arizona Journal of International and Comparative Law* 389, 414. In the context of the US Takings Clause of the Fifth Amendment, the Supreme Court in *Hodel v. Irving* 481 U.S. 704 (1987) invalidated a law (s. 207 of the Indian Land Consolidation Act 1983) on the basis that it effectively abolished (for those adversely affected by the law, which concerned Indian lands) the descent and devise of a particular class of property.

127 In the German context, a major alteration in the incidents of ownership that would significantly curtail the freedom entailed by ownership could be inconsistent with the institutional protection of property in Article 14 of the Basic Law. See *Hamburg Flood Control Case* (1968) 24 BverfGE 36 and *Groundwater case* (1981) 58 BverfGE 300.

128 Waldron, *The Right to Private Property* (n 1), p. 21.

129 See L. S. Underkuffler, *The Idea of Property in Law – Its Meaning and Power* (Oxford: Oxford University Press, 2003) for analysis of the consequences of the same interests or values being implicated on both sides of the property 'balancing scales', e.g. pp. 74–6 and 128.

ownership. That is not to suggest that the institutional guarantee prevents the restriction of individual property rights – any such suggestion should be strongly resisted as inconsistent with the division of labour contemplated by the two types of property guarantees in the Irish Constitution. It is simply to emphasise that property rights protection exists in the Irish constitutional order as both an individual right and a social institution and that restrictions must be assessed bearing in mind that duality. Equally, the social nature of property, which is reflected in its institutional protection and in the strong statement of the State's regulatory power in Article 43.2, supports the limitation of property rights to ensure that they contribute to realising the common good.

Finally, the constitutional recognition of both a general right *to own* and individual rights *of ownership* impacts on the arguments for legal protection of property rights that are relevant in the Irish constitutional context. Waldron distinguishes between 'special rights', which accrue to an individual because of some contingent occurrence, and 'general rights', which everyone has and which are not so contingent.[130] This distinction helps to explain the distinction in types of property rights identifiable in the Irish Constitution. Article 40.3.2° secures special rights, namely the rights that accrue to individuals in respect of property that they come to acquire over the course of their lives. Article 43.1 secures general rights: the right of all individuals in Ireland to live in a private ownership system that recognises rights of transfer, bequest, and inheritance, and the right of all individuals to be permitted (although not enabled) to own property. Article 43.2 subjects special rights in respect of property to restriction to secure the common good and social justice.

Waldron argues that different arguments for private property are pertinent depending on the type of property right that is in issue:

> An argument for private property is *SR-based* if and only if it is right-based and *either* (i) the interest which it takes to be important arises out of some contingent event or transaction *or* (ii) the particular importance of the interest in question arose out of some contingent event or transaction.[131]

[130] Waldron, *The Right to Private Property* (n 1), p. 112. This distinction is also drawn by H. L. A. Hart, 'Are There Any Natural Rights?' in J. Waldron (ed.), *Theories of Rights* (Oxford: Oxford University Press, 1984), p. 77, with general rights understood as those rights that we have by virtue of our status as human beings. See also Penner, *The Idea of Property* (n 8), pp. 20–23.

[131] Waldron, *The Right to Private Property* (n 1), p. 117.

In contrast, general-right-based arguments are not rooted in a particular contingent event or transaction, but contend that an interest is important because of its quality.[132] For example, while Lockean labour arguments for private ownership are necessarily *SR-based*, since they depend on the contingent event of labouring on a resource, Hegelian personality arguments are *GR-based*, flowing as they do from the nature of individuals as persons. *SR-based* arguments concerning the justification and functions of private ownership tend to dominate modern discourse, particularly given the rise of law and economics analysis of property, although a resurgence in interest in *GR-based* arguments may be emerging, for example in the human flourishing approaches considered in the previous chapter.[133] Institutional property guarantees expand the range of the debate over the justification of private ownership by bringing both *GR-based* and *SR-based* arguments to bear on constitutional interpretation.

This chapter has shown that the Irish constitutional scheme for the protection of property rights couples an absolute guarantee that no person will be excluded from the institution of private ownership with a qualified protection for individual rights arising out of a contingent event or transaction, i.e., the acquisition of external goods. This structure makes it highly unlikely that any single, overarching justification for the protection of private ownership, and for the protection of individual rights flowing from participation in that institution, will fit the complex combination of rights in relation to property protected by the Irish Constitution. Following Waldron, the form of the Irish Constitution's property rights guarantees means that constitutional property law is appropriately influenced by both '*GR-based*' and '*SR-based*' arguments for private ownership. This assessment is supported by the doctrinal analysis that follows in subsequent chapters, which shows that judicial decision-making in this context is immanently and incompletely influenced by a wide range of property values and ideologies, both special-right-based and general-right-based.

[132] Ibid., p. 116.

[133] See G. S. Alexander and E. M. Peñalver, 'Properties of Community' (2009) 10 *Theoretical Inquiries in Law* 127; *An Introduction to Property Theory* (Cambridge: Cambridge University Press, 2012); E. M. Peñalver, 'Land Virtues' (2009) 94 *Cornell Law Review* 821 and G. S. Alexander, 'The Social Obligation Norm in American Property Law' (2009) 94 *Cornell Law Review* 745.

3.4 Conclusions

MacDonagh describes Article 43 of the Irish Constitution as 'a convergence of traditions', citing as key influences:

> ...the insistence of Locke and various successors on the connection between private property and freedom, the nineteenth-century struggle of the dispossessed Irish for property rights, particularly in land, and the developing Catholic emphasis on the right to private property in the face of socialist and communist manifestoes.[134]

What emerges from the historically informed analysis of the property rights clauses in this chapter is a distinctive constitutional scheme for the protection of property rights shaped by Ireland's history of identifying land as an essential means to material security. That experience generated a cultural desire for legal protection for property rights that was tempered by an acute awareness of the potential exclusionary impacts of such rights. Both attitudes towards property rights were reflected in the 1937 Constitution, through institutional protection for private ownership, qualified legal protections for individual property rights, and express recognition of the State's power to regulate the exercise of such rights to secure the common good and social justice. The 'double protection' for both the institution of private ownership and individual property rights, which has been criticised as confusing[135], in fact reflects the prevailing duality in Irish property ideology at the time the Constitution was drafted. That duality was also shaped by global turns of event, including notably an entrenchment of the 'possessor principle' in Catholic teaching in response to contemporary political developments. These key 'property moments'[136] influenced the emergence of a hybrid property ideology driven by a liberal, common law understanding of ownership layered with an openness to State intervention for socially just public purposes. The approach adopted in the Constitution in

[134] E. McDonagh, 'Philosophical-Theological Reflections on the Constitution' in F. Litton (ed.), *The Constitution of Ireland 1937–1987* (Dublin: Institute of Public Administration, 1988), pp. 192, 199.

[135] For example, the Constitution Review Group recommended amending the constitution to deal with property rights in one self-contained article, noting criticism of the provisions as confusing: see Report of the Constitution Review Group (Dublin: Government of Ireland, 1996), at 357–67. See also G. Hogan, 'The Constitution, Property Rights and Proportionality' (1997) 32 *Irish Jurist* 373, 386, characterising as fruitless '...the search for what might be termed the exegetical solution to the Article 40.3.2/Article 43 conundrum'.

[136] Davidson and Dyal-Chand (n 15).

1937 marked a significant shift away from the 1922 Constitution, which had not guaranteed individual property rights or a private ownership system. However, the protection given to property rights was socially oriented, reflecting what might be termed a 'qualified progressive' approach to constitutional protection for property rights. The tension between the 'individual' and 'social' aspects of private ownership was reproduced in the Constitution, with political representatives and judges both given roles in mediating that tension.

As subsequent chapters will demonstrate, Irish judges have generally embraced the socially oriented, qualified nature of the protection for property rights that was enshrined in the Constitution in 1937. Their interpretation of those protections has not imposed significant or wide-ranging constraints on legislative freedom. Nonetheless, a myth of property absolutism exists in Irish culture, rooted in part in the lived experience with land analysed in this chapter.[137] Bull argues that following the resolution of the Irish land question, Irish political culture was unable '. . .to free itself of the habits of mind and action created by the land issue', a tendency that persists, whether wilfully or unconsciously, particularly in Irish political life.[138] The felt-need for secure individual possession of property remains strong, with for example Ireland classified as a 'home ownership society' with amongst the highest rates of home ownership in the world for most of the twentieth century.[139] That cultural attitude co-exists with an openness to property redistribution rooted in the Irish history of land reform and reflected in the welfare system.[140] These competing attitudes and priorities reflect the core tensions concerning the mediation of property rights and social justice that are tackled in progressive property theory and are identifiable influences in Irish constitutional property doctrine and in political approaches to property issues, which are explored in detail in the rest of this book.

[137] Examples of this myth explored in subsequent chapters include the provision of compensation for planning controls in the first Irish planning statute, and ongoing arguments about rent freezes, which Irish politicians have repeatedly resisted as unconstitutional.

[138] Bull, *Land, Politics and Nationalism* (n 21), p. 176.

[139] Norris, 'Varieties of Home Ownership' (n 39), 86.

[140] Norris, *Property, Family and the Irish Welfare State* (n 22), p. 5.

4

Engaging Constitutional Property Rights

4.1 Introduction

To develop a clear understanding of the effect of any constitutional protection for property rights, it is necessary to identify the reach of that protection – when are constitutional property rights engaged? This threshold question is surprisingly underexplored in constitutional property law, and its judicial treatment to date has been highly *ad hoc*.[1] The sphere of protection of constitutional property rights guarantees is undefined and an argument must be had in at least some cases about whether a particular valuable interest is or is not protected.[2] Generally, courts in jurisdictions with constitutional property rights guarantees take an inclusive approach by recognising a wide range of interests as protected.[3] That does not necessarily lead to widespread invalidation of public law restrictions of such rights, which depends in large part on the standards of review applied by judges and on the stringency with which those standards are applied (issues that are considered in Chapters 5 and 6). In a jurisdiction like Ireland that has both private law and constitutional protection for property rights, those sources of legal protection necessarily interact, with conceptions and techniques formulated in the private law context influencing (often implicitly)

1 See, e.g., T. W. Merrill, 'The Landscape of Constitutional Property' (2000) 86 *Virginia Law Review* 885, 891 noting the limited attention paid to this threshold question in US property law and theory.

2 See, e.g., Laura Underkuffler, arguing '[p]roperty is not a preordained or acontextual concept – it is a socially constructed concept, with all of the flux and change which that involves': L. S. Underkuffler, *The Idea of Property* (Oxford: Oxford University Press, 2003), p. 134. Elsewhere, she refers to 'the notorious problem of defining property for constitutional purposes' – L. S. Underkuffler, 'Property as a Constitutional Myth' (2007) 92 *Cornell Law Review* 1239, 1245.

3 For discussion of this point, see A. J. van der Walt and R. Walsh, 'Comparative Constitutional Conceptions of Property' in M. Graziadei and L. Smith (eds.), *Comparative Property Law* (Cheltenham: Elgar Publishing, 2017), p. 193, pp. 195–200.

judicial approaches to ownership and property rights in the constitutional context.

This chapter analyses the threshold question of engagement through the prism of Irish constitutional property law. Section 4.2 analyses the conception of ownership that applies in Irish constitutional property law. Section 4.3 addresses the circumstances in which constitutional property rights protection has been held to be engaged. Private law rights and other established categories of legal rights, such as intellectual property rights, are at the centre of the constitutional property guarantees' sphere of protection. The degree of judicial policing of engagement increases as one moves away from this centre and the level of constitutional protection decreases, resulting in an implicit hierarchy of constitutional property rights. Different, and at times conflicting, rhetorics and metaphors concerning property rights and ownership combine and interact to establish a dynamic, non-determinative 'definition' of property rights for constitutional purposes. Section 4.4 assesses the implications of a broadly applicable constitutional property rights guarantee, responding to the progressive concern that constitutional protection for property rights can entrench the distributive status quo. It argues that while a broad approach to the engagement of constitutional property rights is not outcome-determinative, a wide-reaching constitutional property rights guarantee is rhetorically significant. Furthermore, it may have a chilling effect on legislative reform. Consequently, there are risks from a progressive property perspective with a broad interpretation of the reach of constitutional property rights protection even if the strict legal effect of that interpretation is minimised through deferential application of standards of review.

4.2 Understanding 'Ownership' in the Irish Constitutional Context

4.2.1 The 'Bundle of Rights' Metaphor

In *Central Dublin Development Association* v. *The Attorney General*, Kenny J stated in respect of Article 43: '[t]he word "ownership" in the English text is, I think, misleading because there is no known legal right of ownership. There is a bundle of rights which, for brevity, is called ownership'.[4] This description of ownership as a 'bundle of rights' has

[4] (1975) 109 ILTR 69, hereafter *Central Dublin Development Association*. Ronan LJ. termed ownership a 'bundle of rights' in *Guinness & Co* v. *Commissioners of Inland Revenue* [1923] 2 IR 186, 208.

been much analysed in property law and theory.[5] In the constitutional context, it can most basically be understood as characterising ownership as a variety of relations between persons, often (but on this view not necessarily) pertaining to things, which form a package but are separable and capable of being 're-bundled' in various ways.[6] It is usually associated with legal realism[7] and with the work of Hohfeld, in particular his fine-grained analysis of jural relations as involving opposites and correlatives (such as privilege/duty and privilege/no-right) and his distinction between paucital rights (availing against one or a small group of persons) and multitital rights (availing against a very large and indefinite class of people).[8]

The 'bundle of rights' understanding of ownership reflects what has been variously termed a 'legalistic', 'sophisticated', or 'scientific' conception of property, as opposed to a lay person's understanding of property as things.[9] As Grey put it, '[m]ost people, including most specialists in their unprofessional moments, conceive of property as *things* that are *owned* by *persons*.'[10] The usefulness of the bundle metaphor has been

5 See, e.g., J. B. Baron, 'Rescuing the Bundle-of-Rights Metaphor in Property Law' (2013) 82 *University of Cincinnati Law Review* 57 and S. Glackin, 'Back to Bundles: Deflating Property Rights, Again' (2014) 20 *Legal Theory* 1, for analysis supporting the 'bundle' model.

6 As Glackin puts it, '[t]he bundle theory regards these individual and separable rights, or 'sticks', as having no substantive, essential connection to each other.' Glackin, 'Back to Bundles' (n 5), 5.

7 See H. E. Smith, 'The Persistence of System in Property Law' (2015) 163 *University of Pennsylvania Law Review* 2055, particularly 2059–64. For a critical perspective on this development see, e.g., T. C. Grey, 'The Disintegration of Property', in J. R. Pennock and J. W. Chapman (eds.), *Property: Nomos XXII* (New York: New York University Press, 1980), p. 69.

8 See W. N. Hohfeld, 'Some Fundamental Legal Conceptions as Applied in Judicial Reasoning' (1913) 23 *Yale Law Journal* 16, and W. N. Hohfeld, 'Fundamental Legal Conceptions as Applied in Judicial Reasoning' (1917) 26 *Yale Law Journal* 710. For analysis see, e.g., A. Kocourek, 'The Hohfeld System of Fundamental Legal Concepts' (1920) 15 *Illionois Law Review* 24; J. W. Singer, 'The Legal Rights Debate in Analytical Jurisprudence' (1982) 6 *Wisconsin Law Review* 975. For a contemporary Hohfeldian approach to property, see S. Douglas and B. MacFarlane, 'Defining Property Rights' in J. E. Penner and H. E. Smith (eds.), *Philosophical Foundations of Property Law* (Oxford: Oxford University Press, 2013), p. 219.

9 On this see, e.g., J. Williams, 'The Rhetoric of Property' (1997) 83 *Iowa Law Review* 277; B. A. Ackerman, *Private Property and the Constitution* (New Haven: Yale University Press), pp. 113–67; S. R. Munzer, *A Theory of Property* (New York: Cambridge University Press, 1990), p. 16 and K. Gray, 'Equitable Property' (1994) 47 *Current Legal Problems* 157.

10 Grey, 'Disintegration of Property' (n 7), 68.

hotly contested in property theory in recent times, including through arguments that property is properly understood as concerned with relations to things, or with relations *concerning* things.[11] The bundle metaphor has been criticised as entailing unwieldy and unpredictable contextual analysis and as failing to give due weight to lay intuitions concerning property, thereby heightening information costs and undermining the efficiency of property.[12] It has been further challenged for failing to adequately distinguish between the purposes of property law and the legal means used to achieve those purposes.[13] As alternatives, the right to exclude and the right to control the use of property have been variously defended as property's readily understood, intuitive 'core' or essence.[14] Mediating between these positions, some scholars emphasise exclusion as the means through which property law achieves its goals, including protecting an owner's right of use.[15] The bundle of rights

[11] For a useful summary of the concerns with the 'bundle of rights' model see, e.g., H. E. Smith, 'Property is Not Just a Bundle of Rights' (2011) 8 *Econ Journal Watch* 279, and Smith, 'The Persistence of System' (n 7). See further E. R. Claeys, 'Property 101: Is Property a Thing or a Bundle?' (2009) 32 *Seattle University Law Review* 617; L. Katz, 'Exclusion and Exclusivity in Property Law' (2008) 58 *University of Toronto Law Journal* 275. T. W. Merrill, 'Property and the Right to Exclude' (1998) 77 *Nebraska Law Review* 730; T. W. Merrill and H. E. Smith, 'Optimal Standardization in the Law of Property: The Numerus Clausus Principle' (2000) 110 *Yale Law Journal* 1; A. Mossoff, 'What Is Property? Putting the Pieces Back Together' (2003) 45 *Arizona Law Review* 371, and J. E. Penner, 'The "Bundle of Rights" Picture of Property' (1996) 43 *UCLA Law Review* 711.

[12] On this point see, e.g., Smith, 'The Persistence of System' (n 7) and T. W. Merrill and H. E. Smith, 'The Morality of Property' (2007) 48 *William & Mary Law Review* 1849.

[13] See, e.g., H. E Smith, 'Property as the Law of Things' (2012) 125 *Harvard Law Review* 1691, 1693: '[r]ealism tends to assume a one-to-one and relatively direct relationship between the features of property and the purposes they serve'.

[14] On exclusion as property's core see, e.g., Merrill, 'Property and the Right to Exclude' (n 11), 730: '[t]he right to exclude others is more than just 'one of the most essential' constituents of property – it is the *sine qua non.*' On the right to use see, e.g., C. M. Newman, 'Using Things, Defining Property' in J. E. Penner and M. Otsuka (eds.), *Property Theory: Legal and Political Perspectives* (Cambridge: Cambridge University Press, 2018), p. 69, L. Katz, 'Exclusion and Exclusivity in Property Law' (n 11).

[15] See, e.g., J. E. Penner, *The Idea of Property in Law* (Oxford: Oxford University Press, 1997), 71 arguing '[t]he right to property is a right to exclude others from things which is grounded by the interest we have in the use of things'. Penner argues that 'use serves a justificatory role for the right, while exclusion is seen as the formal essence of the right'. See similarly Smith, 'Property is Not Just a Bundle of Rights' (n 11), 281. Avihay Dorfman points out that owners are often protected in excluding others even where such exclusion is not related to their use of the property: 'The Normativity of the Private Ownership Form' (2012) 75 *Modern Law Review* 981. Dorfman emphasises the normative standing that ownership gives an owner relative to others, for example contending: '[p]rivate

metaphor is often considered in conjunction with the account of the incidents of ownership contained in any protected 'bundle' given by Honoré.[16] His liberal conception of ownership includes: the right to possess; the right to use; the right to manage; the right to the income; the right to the capital; the right to security; the incident of transmissibility; the incident of absence of term; the prohibition on harmful use; and the liability to execution.[17]

The Irish courts have repeatedly used the 'bundle of rights' metaphor in their decisions.[18] However, they tend to use it as a description of the scope of the powers entailed by ownership rather than as a constitutive theory of property.[19] After expressly recognising the right to own, transfer, and bequeath property in Article 43.1, the Irish constitutional text appears to assume an established understanding of 'full ownership' along the lines suggested by Honoré, with the State simply empowered in Article 43.2 to 'delimit the exercise' of such rights. This suggests that the State's role is in limiting, not defining, property rights. There has been no definitive or exhaustive doctrinal enumeration of the 'sticks' in the bundle. However, in the High Court, Shanley J in *Fitzpatrick* v. *The*

ownership presupposes a status authority that owners purport to possess over anyone else, demanding that the latter take the former as reason-providing for them:' 'Private Ownership and the Standing to Say So' (2014) 64 *University of Toronto Law Journal* 402, 441.

16 See, e.g., Penner, 'Bundle of Rights' (n 11), 712, noting, '[i]n its conventional formulation, the bundle of rights thesis is a combination of Wesley Hohfeld's analysis of rights and A. M. Honoré's description of the incidents of ownership'. Penner is critical of this elision, arguing that the two theories are conceptually distinct: Penner, 'Bundle of Rights' (n 11), 738–39. See also M. A. Heller, 'The Tragedy of the Anticommons: Property in the Transition from Marx to Markets' (1998) 111 *Harvard Law Review* 621, 663: 'Honoré's list is now commonly accepted by property theorists as a starting point for describing the core bundle of private property rights . . . although some theorists challenge the inclusion of one incident or another.'

17 A. M. Honoré, 'Ownership', in A. G. Guest (ed.) *Oxford Essays in Jurisprudence* (Oxford: Oxford University Press, 1961), pp. 107–23. Frank Snare identifies six key aspects of the core concept of ownership: rights of use, exclusion, and transfer; punishment for interference with the use of private property by others without consent; damages for harm caused to private property by others, and liability rules for damage to property. F. Snare, 'The Concept of Property' (1972) 9 *American Philosophical Quarterly* 200, 201–5.

18 For example, it was applied in *PMPS* (n 18) at 349 and *Cafolla* v. *O'Malley* [1985] IR 486 at 493. More recently, the 'bundle of rights' metaphor was referred to by O'Neill J in *M & F Quirke & Sons* v. *An Bord Pleanála* [2010] 2 ILRM 91 at 110.

19 See Penner, 'Bundle of Rights' (n 11), 741, arguing, 'the bundle of rights perspective on property is entirely innocuous if regarded merely as an elaboration of the scope of action that ownership provides'. See similarly Smith, 'Property as the Law of Things' (n 13), 1694 describing the bundle of rights as 'more of a description than a theory'.

Criminal Assets Bureau discussed the nature of some of the incidents of ownership and how they fit together:

> In Austin's *Jurisprudence*, Austin defined 'ownership' as the right to indefinite user, the right to unrestricted disposition and the right of enjoyment unlimited in duration. It is generally accepted that that definition of what constitutes the bundle of rights known as 'ownership' has not stood the test of time and that in modern society the ownership of chattels personal, such as motor cars, is restricted by law both as to user and disposition. A definition which is seen as more appropriate temporally is that of Sir Frederick Pollock who defined ownership as 'the entirety of the powers of use and disposal allowed by law'.
>
> The power of use embraces the right of exclusive enjoyment and the right of maintaining and recovering possession from all other persons. The power of disposal includes the right of destruction of the goods, the right to alter the goods, and the right to alienate or transfer ownership in the goods: all these rights are regarded as comprising the 'bundle of rights' which together merge into one general right of ownership in goods.[20]

Shanley J's analysis can be understood as advancing a conception of ownership as what Harris terms 'full-blooded ownership of things', which Harris contends:

> . . .entails a relationship between a person (or persons) and a thing such that he (or they) have, *prima facie*, unlimited privileges of use or abuse over the thing, and, *prima facie*, unlimited powers of control and transmission, so far as such use or exercise of power does not infringe some property-independent prohibition.[21]

Shanley J's analysis further suggests that ownership in the Irish context is understood as both disaggregated and unitary – it comprises several distinct rights and yet is understood as a coherent whole, with each right taken together to form an overall right of ownership rather than subsisting individually. Nonetheless, those rights can clearly be split up and vested in different individuals in respect of the same resource, even at the same time.

Shanley J emphasised the powers of use and disposal, rather than exclusion, as key. However, exclusion is clearly *a* stick in the recognised

[20] [2000] 1 IR 217 at 234 (citations omitted). The case did not raise or decide a constitutional point as regards private property, but sheds useful light on the Irish judicial understanding of the meaning of ownership. Austin's definition was referred to approvingly by Ronan LJ in *Guinness* (n 4) at 208, where Ronan LJ stressed the rights of possession, enjoyment, and disposition as the important rights of ownership.

[21] J. W. Harris, *Property and Justice* (Oxford: Oxford University Press, 1996), p. 30.

bundle of ownership rights in the Irish constitutional context. For example, in *Reid* v. *Industrial Development Agency*, the Supreme Court referred to '. . .an entitlement to undisturbed enjoyment of one's property and if necessary, the right to rebuff all unwelcome interferences with it' as being intrinsic to the right to own.[22] Furthermore, rights of exclusion in respect of dwellings are strongly protected by Article 40.5 of the Constitution, which guarantees the inviolability of the dwelling.[23] The case-law interpreting Article 40.5 showcases the core image of property rights held by the courts as legal rights over physical property, with home-ownership emerging as the paradigm of private property.[24]

4.2.2 Doctrinal Unpredictability and the Relationship between Property as 'Things' and Property as 'Rights'

Dagan argues that the bundle approach demonstrates the fact that property law is '. . .a human creation that can be, and has been, modified in accordance with human needs and values', which does not involve a fixed, *a priori*, list of incidents or apply only to a prescribed range of resources.[25] Rather, Dagan suggests, reference to 'property' triggers a normative inquiry, requiring frank and open analysis by judges.[26] The foundational (and contextual) question of fair balance arises where

[22] *Reid* v. *IDA* [2015] IESC 82 at 42. See also *Ashbourne Holdings* v. *An Bord Pleanála* [2003] 2 IR 114 at 128, where Hardiman J described the right to exclude the public from private property as an incident of the ownership of land, and *O'Sullivan* v. *Department of the Environment* [2010] IEHC 376 at 49, where McKechnie J described the rights of ownership as 'normally' including '. . .the right to stop, restrict or condition entry as well as removing or ejecting those unlawfully present'.

[23] For full discussion of Article 40.5, see G. W. Hogan, G. F. Whyte, D. Kenny, R. Walsh, *Kelly: The Irish Constitution*, 5th ed. (Dublin: Bloomsbury Professional, 2018), pp. 2019–61. For analysis of the relationship between the constitutional property clauses and Article 40.5, see R. Walsh, 'Reviewing Expropriations: Looking Beyond Constitutional Property Clauses' in H. Mostert and L. Verstappen (eds.), *Rethinking Public Interest in Expropriation Law* (The Hague: Eleven International Publishing, 2015) p. 125.

[24] As Joseph Singer notes, '[i]n imagining the meaning of property, people call on a particular set of core conceptions, images, examples, and pictures of the social world. Property is about ownership, and the core image of ownership is ownership of a home.' J. W. Singer, *Entitlement: The Paradoxes of Property* (New Haven: Yale University Press, 2000), p. 29.

[25] H. Dagan, 'The Craft of Property' (2003) 91 *California Law Review* 1517, 1532.

[26] Ibid., 1533.

judges are called upon to determine an owner's 'normal' or 'presumptive' 'bundle of rights'.[27]

Accordingly, Baron contends that the 'bundle' approach encourages frank judicial engagement with the relational nature of property.[28] However, this chapter will show that the Irish courts have at once employed the bundle metaphor and adopted an intuitive, under-reasoned approach to defining the 'terms of engagement' of the Constitution's property rights guarantees. The idea of constitutional property as protecting rights in respect of things continues to shape judicial interpretations of the constitutional property rights guarantees, as well as influencing how the legislature responds to those guarantees. As the doctrinal analysis in the next part of this chapter will demonstrate, ideas of property as rights and property as things interact and assert mutual influence, with the understanding that is applied in Irish constitutional property law perhaps best captured by Munzer's definition of property as '. . . a constellation of Hohfeldian elements, correlatives, and opposites; a specification of standard incidents of ownership and other related but less powerful interests; and a catalogue of "things" (tangible and intangible) that are the subject of those incidents'.[29] Another helpful definition is offered by Lametti, who usefully emphasises the interplay of rights between individuals and rights concerning 'things' and the definitional impact of the public interest, saying, '[p]rivate property is a social institution that comprises a variety of contextual relationships among individuals through objects of social wealth and is meant to serve a variety of individual and collective purposes.'[30]

[27] See G. S. Alexander, 'The Social-Obligation Norm in American Property Law' (2009) 94 *Cornell Law Review* 745, 801, arguing for abandonment of the bundle of rights model in the context of US Takings Law in favour of a direct focus on the nature and content of an owner's social obligations, on the basis that bundle analysis is question begging in the Takings context.

[28] Baron, 'Rescuing the Bundle-of-Rights Metaphor' (n 5), 94. From a law and psychology perspective, experiments have suggested that a 'bundle' framing enhances the acceptability of limitations and restrictions: see, e.g., J. R. Nash, 'Packaging Property: The Effect of Paradigmatic Framing of Property Rights' (2009) 83 *Tulane Law Review* 691, and J. R. Nash and S. M. Stern, 'Property Frames' (2010) 87 *Washington University Law Review* 449.

[29] Munzer, *A Theory of Property* (n 9), p. 23.

[30] D. Lametti, 'The Concept of Property: Relations through Objects of Social Wealth' (2003) 53 *University of Toronto Law Journal* 325, 326.

4.2.3 *Property Baselines and 'Unbundling' Ownership*

Conceiving of ownership as a 'bundle of rights' does not provide a baseline for constitutional property rights analysis; it does not allow courts to deductively reach conclusions about permissible or impermissible delimitations of such rights.[31] The 'bundle' approach further raises the risk of what Radin famously termed 'conceptual severance', whereby the various incidents of ownership are 'unbundled' and treated as distinctly protected. Radin explains that where a 'conceptual severance' approach is adopted, '[e]very curtailment of any of the liberal indicia of property, every regulation of any portion of an owner's "bundle of sticks", is a taking of the whole of that particular portion considered separately.'[32] Merrill rightly points out that such an approach increases the likelihood that government regulation will seem draconian, thereby triggering constitutional protection for property rights.[33] Such a risk is potentially problematic from a progressive property perspective, as it could impede the enactment and implementation of regulatory measures in the public interest.[34]

However, 'conceptual severance' is not an inevitable consequence of adopting the 'bundle of rights' metaphor as a description of the powers attendant upon ownership; the Irish courts have largely avoided this pitfall.[35] As will be seen in more detail in Chapter 8, the Irish courts generally assess the need for compensation by reference to the impact of a measure on an owner's total 'bundle of rights', rather than on discrete incidents of ownership.[36]

31 On this point, see Baron, 'Rescuing the Bundle of Rights Metaphor' (n 5), 69–70.

32 M. J. Radin, *Reinterpreting Property* (Chicago: University of Chicago Press, 1993), p. 129. She explains that conceptual severance '. . .hypothetically or conceptually "severs" from the whole bundle of rights just those strands that are interfered with by the regulation, and then hypothetically or conceptually construes those strands in the aggregate as a separate whole thing.' p. 129. She argues that this is usually avoided on the basis of 'crystallised expectations or ordinary language and culture', which treat property as defined by its previous real-life usage, not by its conceptual possibilities, ibid.

33 Merrill, 'The Landscape of Constitutional Property' (n 1), 899.

34 See Alexander, 'The Social-Obligation Norm' (n 27), arguing against using a bundle of rights model in the context of the Takings Clause of the Fifth Amendment of the US Constitution on this basis.

35 See Kenny J in *Central Dublin Development Association* (n 4). Rather than every interference with an individual incident of ownership giving rise to a claim for compensation, Kenny J held that an interference with some of the 'sticks' in the 'bundle of rights', falling short of outright appropriation of all of the 'sticks', could require compensation only where that interference would otherwise be 'unjust'.

36 Ibid., at 84.

4.3 The Reach of Constitutional Property Rights

4.3.1 Synthesising the Reach of the Constitution's Property Rights

Overall, the Irish courts have interpreted the constitutional property rights guarantees as having wide-ranging application, with for example Hardiman J stating in *Dellway* v. *National Asset Management Agency*:

> [t]he property rights of the citizen are not limited to land or 'real property' to which one holds the title nor to the right to money or monies worth to which one is entitled. It has been recognised for a long time as being more extensive, and extending to established contractual rights, to the right to earn a living, to the rights to one's entitlements under an appointment to an office or under a contract of employment, and to rights to pensions, gratuities or other emoluments for which one has contracted, or has earned.[37]

The Irish courts intuitively identify as constitutionally protected a range of 'core' rights resting largely on private law rights or closely related rights, without offering detailed supporting analysis.[38] As Alexander puts it, '[t]he private law meaning of property is a rhetorical trope that runs throughout the entire legal discourse of property.'[39] The gravitational pull of private law rights reflects the existing common law culture onto which the Constitution was superimposed and with which it interacts.[40] Where cases raise the possibility of constitutional protection that are further away from this implicit 'core', judges undertake more detailed analysis of engagement. In this 'periphery', Lockean ideas of private property as a reward for individual effort have influenced judicial interpretations of the reach of the property rights guarantees, albeit inconsistently and partially.

[37] *Dellway* v. *National Asset Management Agency* [2011] IESC 13, [2011] 4 IR 1 at 287.

[38] To borrow from Frank Michelman, writing in the different context of South African eviction law: '... it seems that the property-right claims based in the common law are perceived to be in some sense worthier or solider – in some sense more *real* – than claims based in political legislation.' F. I. Michelman, 'Expropriation, Eviction and the Gravity of the Common Law' (2013) 24 *Stellenbosch Law Review* 245, 253. This tendency was explicitly endorsed by the High Court in *Dellway*, which held that an interest must be a legal right, or very similar to, or connected to, a legal right, in order to be recognised as a property right for constitutional purposes. [2010] IEHC 364 at [7.32].

[39] G. S. Alexander, *The Global Debate over Constitutional Property* (Chicago: University of Chicago Press, 2006), p. 18.

[40] As Alexander notes, '[p]re-existing legal and political traditions and culture continue strongly to influence the stability and security of property rights even where those traditions and culture seemingly conflict with or are in tension with constitutional expressions.' Ibid., p. 245.

4.3.2 *Constitutional Property's 'Core'*

Most straightforwardly, the right to control the use of land, rights over personal property, and rights in respect of money have been accepted as constitutionally protected.[41] In this way, an understanding of property as rights in respect of things is reflected in an intuitively recognised core of protected rights delineated by private law. Relatedly, in *Dellway* v. *National Asset Management Agency*, Finnegan J and Hardiman J characterised the equity of redemption as a valuable interest in property that engaged the constitutional protection for property.[42] Fennelly J referred to the rights of a mortgagor in respect of mortgaged property, including the right to an income stream from such property, other contractual relations associated with such property, and a mortgagor's reputation as a borrower, as 'aspects of, or closely related to' property rights.[43]

Contractual rights are also protected by the Irish Constitution's guarantee of property rights, again reflecting the 'private law trope' identified by Alexander.[44] However, the scope of constitutional protection for contractual rights is primarily determined by the terms of the relevant contract and the law of contract. For example, in *J & J Haire & Company*

[41] See, e.g., in respect of land *Central Dublin Development Association* (n 4) and *O'Callaghan* v. *Commissioners for Public Works* [1983] ILRM 391. In *Whelan* v. *Cork Corporation*, Murphy J said '[i]t is clear that a right, even a negative right, over the property of another person may be a valuable intangible right of property': [1991] ILRM 19 at 26. However, the case was not decided on a constitutional basis. In respect of personal property and money, see *Fitzpatrick* (n 20); *Attorney General* v. *Southern Industrial Trust* (1960) 94 ILTR 161; *Buckley* v. *Attorney General* [1950] IR 67 and *In re Eylewood Ltd* [2010] IEHC 57. In *Tuffy* v. *O'Neill* [2013] IEHC 231, rights under guarantees, and rights of indemnity, were recognised as constitutionally protected.

[42] On this point, see also *National Asset Loan Management Ltd v. McMahon*; *National Asset Loan Management* v. *Downes* [2014] IEHC 71 at 47, where Charleton J referred to the equity of redemption in mortgage contracts '. . .as among the most important of property rights', but went on to stress that such rights were not afforded absolute or unlimited protection by the Constitution.

[43] *Dellway* (n 38) at 51.

[44] As Gerard McCormack notes, '[p]roperty rights as distinct from physical goods are protected by Article 43, and there is no obvious reason for distinguishing legal rights over property from legal rights under contracts'. G. McCormack, 'Contractual Entitlements and the Constitution' (1982) 17 *Irish Jurist* 340, 341. For examples of recognition of contractual rights as property rights see, e.g., *East Donegal Co-Operative Society* v. *The Attorney General* [1970] 1 IR 317 at 332, *Foley* v. *The Irish Land Commission* [1952] IR 118 at 131, *Dunne* v. *Hamilton* [1982] ILRM 290, and *PMPS* (n 18). McWilliam J in *Condon* v. *Minister for Labour* distinguished the right to enter into and enforce a contract from rights under a contract, characterising the former right as a personal right, and the latter as property rights: 11 June 1980 (HC) at 9–10.

Ltd v. *Minister for Health*,[45] the plaintiff pharmacists argued that regulations enacted pursuant to s. 9 of the Financial Emergency Measures in the Public Interest Act 2009, which reduced the rates payable to them by the State for the provision of public services, were an unconstitutional interference with their contractual rights.[46] In the High Court, McMahon J rejected the plaintiffs' argument on the basis that they had no contractual right to a specific level of fees in the future. Consequently, they had no property rights capable of being unjustly interfered with by the impugned reductions. McMahon J held that the principles of contract law were the primary source of protection for contractual entitlements, but he did indicate that in the event of the failure or inadequacy of those principles, resort could be had to the constitutional guarantee of private property to fill any gaps in protection.

Other intangible rights protected by the Constitution include shares and intellectual property rights. For example, Carroll J stated in *PMPS* v. *Attorney General*, '[o]wnership of shares is one of the bundle of rights which constitute ownership of private property.'[47] In *Re Sugar Distributors Ltd*, Keane J characterised a share as in itself a bundle of proprietary rights.[48] However, property rights in shares do not extend to the value of those shares at any particular level.[49] Furthermore, as Collins J noted in *Permanent Holdings TSB plc* v. *Skoczylas*, '. . .these rights are not abstractions and cannot be meaningfully delineated without reference to the articles of association'.[50] In *Phonographic Performance (Ireland) Ltd* v. *Cody*, Keane J held that intellectual property rights are constitutionally protected, and that such rights, although susceptible to regulation in the interests of the common good, cannot be abolished.[51] In

45 [2009] IEHC 562.

46 The regulations in question were the Health Professionals (Reduction of Payments to Community Pharmacy Contractors) Regulations 2009 (SI No 246 of 2009).

47 *PMPS* (n 18) at 349. See also *Attorney General* v. *Paperlink* [1984] ILRM 373 at 383.

48 [1995] 2 IR 194 at 207. In *In re Eylewood* [2011] 1 ILRM 5 at 22, Finlay Geoghegan J characterised the ownership of shares as conferring 'a right of participation', which was protected even in circumstances where the shares themselves were economically valueless as a result of the insolvency of the relevant company. See also the Court of Appeal in *Dowling v Minister for Finance* [2018] IECA 300 at [102], characterising shareholders as acquiring 'a bundle of intangible legal rights' protected by the Constitution.

49 *Dowling* v. *Minister for Finance* [2012] IEHC 436 at [173].

50 *Permanent TSB Group Holdings Plc* v. *Skoczylas* [2020] IECA 1, at [85].

51 [1998] 4 IR 504 at 511. On appeal, the Supreme Court did not address the constitutional status of intellectual property rights – [1998] 4 IR 504 at 518. However, Keane CJ in *Maher* v. *Minister for Agriculture* clearly indicated that he regarded intellectual property rights as constitutionally protected. [2001] 2 IR 139 at 186–87.

reaching this conclusion, Keane J emphasised the creative input into the value of those rights. Nonetheless, statute remains the primary source of protection for intellectual property rights.[52] Relatedly, commercial goodwill has been recognised by the courts as coming within the reach of the Constitution's property rights clauses.[53] In *DPP (Long)* v. *McDonald*, the Supreme Court recognised franchises, in this case concerning the holding of a market, as constitutionally protected.[54] Central to that decision was the fact that the right in question was recognised in private law as an intangible right gained through long usage.[55]

4.3.3 *Constitutional Property's 'Periphery'*

Outside the intuitively identified 'core' of constitutional property, the Irish courts have adopted a more cautious, less intuitive attitude, giving more explicit attention in their reasoning to the threshold question of engagement. The degree of individual contribution to the value of an interest that is claimed to engage constitutional protection is a highly influential factor, demonstrating the partial and implicit influence of Lockean thinking about property rights. Absent private law recognition, labour serves as an intuitive marker of property rights for the Irish courts.

Pensions straddle the 'core' and the 'periphery' of the Constitution's property rights guarantees, as many pensions are based on contract and as such are readily recognised as protected. Much of the litigation that has come before the Irish courts has concerned pensions paid to public-sector employees regulated by statutory schemes. Even in these cases, the connection of the statutory pension entitlements to contractual rights prompted the courts to recognise them as constitutionally protected

52 For example, Charleton J in *EMI Records (Ireland) Ltd* v. *UPC Communications Ireland Ltd* held that courts must defer '...to the manner in which the Oireachtas circumscribes and regulates the enforcement of those rights.' [2007] IEHC 377 at 85–6. See similarly *Sony Music Entertainment (Ireland) Ltd* v. *UP Communications Ireland Ltd (No 1)* [2015] IEHC 317, [2016] IECA 231.

53 *Cork Institute of Technology* v. *Minister for Transport* [2017] IEHC 762. See also *Falcon Travel Ltd* v. *Owners Abroad Group plc* [1999] 1 IR 175, and *Dellway* (n 37), recognising commercial goodwill as a property right without reference to the Constitution.

54 [1983] ILRM 223.

55 Ibid. at 226. However, in *Simmonds* v. *Ennis Town Council* [2012] IEHC 281, Clarke J stressed that insofar as an established right to trade at a franchise market was recognised as a species of property rights, such rights were not absolutely protected and were subject to limitation in the public interest.

property rights deserving of strong judicial protection. For example, in *Cox* v. *Ireland*, Finlay CJ held, '. . .the unilateral variation and suspension of contractual rights, including rights which may involve the entitlement to a pension to which contribution over a period has been made, constitutes a major invasion of those particular property rights.'[56] The Irish courts have recognised pensions as deferred payment for employment such that the holder of a contributory pension has a vested right to its economic value.[57] This again suggests that judges are likely to recognise an interest as constitutionally protected where the holder of the interest contributed to its value through independent effort. However, outside the contractual context, the case for constitutional protection is regarded as much weaker. For example, in *PC* v. *Minister for Social Protection*,[58] the Supreme Court suggested *obiter* that the susceptibility of the regime for state pensions to legislative change meant that entitlements accruing to individuals through its operation could not be regarded as constitutionally protected.

The Irish courts have variously characterised statutory licences as privileges not protected by the Constitution and as constitutionally protected property rights that are heavily circumscribed by the interests of the common good.[59] In framing such entitlements as unprotected privileges,[60] the courts apply an assumed and unarticulated image of private property rights as concerned with the control of physical property, as well as a preference for characterising long-established private law interests, rather than public law entitlements, as constitutionally protected. In decisions where licences are classified as constitutionally protected, they are seen by the courts as held subject to the public interest.[61] While a licence holder is entitled to fair procedures prior to

[56] *Cox* v. *Ireland* [1992] 2 IR 503 at 522. He referred to a suite of property rights protected by the Constitution: '. . .the right to a pension, gratuity or other emoluments already earned, or the right to the advantages of a subsisting contract of employment'. See also *Lovett* v. *The Minister for Education* [1997] 1 ILRM 89, and *Re Article 26 and the Employment Equality Bill, 1996* [1997] 2 IR 321 at 342.

[57] *District Judge McMenamin* v. *Ireland* [1996] 3 IR 100 at 134 and 139.

[58] [2017] IESC 63.

[59] On the various distinguishing moves open to judges in this context, see C. A. Reich, 'The New Property' (1964) 73 *Yale Law Journal* 733, 740.

[60] See, e.g., *The State (Pheasantry)* v. *District Judge Donnelly* [1982] ILRM 512; *Sherry* v. *Brennan* [1979] ILRM 113 at 116–17; *Macklin* v. *Greacen & Co Ltd* [1983] IR 61 at 66; *PMPS* (n 18) and *Hand* v. *Dublin Corporation* [1989] IR 26.

[61] For example, in *Cafolla* v. *O'Malley*, Finlay CJ held that since the legislature was entitled to prohibit the operation of fruit machines in gaming halls altogether, where it chose to

the revocation of such a licence,[62] he or she is held to lack a substantive claim to the licence itself, or to retain it on particular terms, where such retention is inconsistent with the interests of the common good. Furthermore, the value of a licence is not guaranteed through compensation.[63] For example, in *Hempenstall* v. *Minister for the Environment*, in rejecting a constitutional challenge to deregulation in the taxi industry, Costello J stated:

> Property rights arising in licences created by law (enacted or delegated) are subject to the conditions created by law and to an implied condition that the law may change those conditions. Changes brought about by law may enhance the value of those property rights…or they may diminish them…But an amendment of the law which by changing the conditions under which a licence is held reduces the commercial value of the licence cannot be regarded as an attack on the property right in the licence – it is the consequence of the implied condition which is an inherent part of the property right in the licence.[64]

Accordingly, constitutional protection for licences is very limited, since the terms upon which such licences are held are regarded as changeable at the will of the legislature.[65]

In the same vein, the Irish courts have characterised production quotas as the by-product of a justified restriction of an owner's right to make productive use of his or her land, and accordingly as privileges that can be conferred, withheld, or conditioned by the legislature so as best to

allow it, it could subject such operation to onerous conditions going so far as to make it unprofitable. *Cafolla* (n 18) at 500.

[62] See on this point *Hygeia Chemicals Ltd* v. *Irish Medicines Board* [2005] IEHC 226, recognising an entitlement to fair procedures prior to the deprivation of a licence.

[63] McKechnie J in the High Court in *Neurendale Ltd* v. *Dublin City Council* stated in respect of waste collection licences, '…interests generated by State regulation will not generally give rise to a compensable right.' [2009] IEHC 588 at 191. He referred to *Hempenstall* (n 64), and *Maher* (n 51) in support of this conclusion.

[64] *Hempenstall* v. *Minister for the Environment* [1994] 2 IR 20 at 28. See also *Gorman* v. *Minister for the Environment* [2001] 2 IR 414 and in *J & J Haire & Company Ltd* (n 45).

[65] *Hempenstall* was recently invoked by McMahon J in *J & J Haire & Company Ltd* (n 45) at [45] as authority for the view that it was always open to the Oireachtas to 'fundamentally alter' the statutory regime set out in the Health Acts, even if such adjustments had a profound effect on pharmacists. Similarly, *Hempenstall* was approved on this point by the High Court in *Dellway* (n 37)at [7.14]–[7.15]. It may be significant that many of the cases on this issue have concerned occupational licences – permissions to carry on certain restricted activities as a means of earning one's livelihood. As will be discussed in the next section of this chapter, the right to earn a livelihood is constitutionally protected, but is susceptible to extensive restriction in the public interest. See also *Muldoon* v. *Minister for the Environment* [2015] IEHC 649, and *Gorman* (n 64).

fulfil the public policy grounding the restriction itself.[66] In *Maher* v. *Minister for Agriculture*, the Supreme Court held that production quotas for milk created through (as it then was) European Community regulatory control were not protected under Articles 40.3.2˚ and 43.[67] Three key justifications for this conclusion emerge from the various judgments in *Maher*: first, individual labour and effort is emphasised as a prerequisite for the recognition of a valuable interest as constitutional property – the simple fact of economic value is insufficient; second, the public-interest function and origin of a regulatory system is regarded as delimiting the scope and status of the interests it produces; third, participation in a regulated market is said to entail acceptance of both the benefits and burdens of regulatory changes.

The Irish courts have yet to definitively clarify whether they regard grants of planning permission as 'new' property rights that are protected by Articles 40.3.2˚ and 43 or whether planning control is understood as a legitimate constraint on the exercise of property rights that impacts on land values through the granting and refusing of applications for development consent.[68] The dominant judicial characterisation of planning permission has shifted over time towards treating a grant of planning permission as enhancing the value of land, with planning control framed as a legitimate and proportionate restriction of property rights.[69] Most recently, the Supreme Court rejected the suggestion that there could be a constitutional right to build a house on foot of an invalid planning permission.[70] Development of land no longer appears to be a constitutionally protected 'incident of ownership'. This change reflects an evolving social acceptance of the permissibility of land-use control, involving

[66] See *Lawlor* v. *Minister for Agriculture* [1990] 1 IR 356 and *Maher* (n 51).

[67] *Maher* (n 51).

[68] For examples of the 'restriction conception' see, e.g., *Frescati Estates* v. *Walker* [1975] IR 177 at 187, *In re Viscount Securities Ltd* (1978) 112 ILTR 17 at 20, *Grange Developments Ltd* v. *Dublin County Council* [1986] 1 IR 246 at 256, *Waterford County Council* v. *John A Wood* [1999] 1 IR 556 at 561, *McDonagh & Sons Ltd* v. *Galway Corporation* [1995] 1 IR 191 at 202 and *Butler* v. *Dublin Corporation* [1999] 1 IR 565. On the enhancement conception, see most significantly the decision of the Supreme Court in *Pine Valley Developments* v. *Minister for the Environment* [1987] IR 23. For a more recent example, see Peart J's analysis in *Muldoon* (n 65) at 178: 'If one views a planning permission as a licence permitting the owner of the land to build on certain land, the land may gain an increased value as a result. But that licence itself does not have value separate from the enhanced value of the land in respect of which it is granted.'

[69] See, e.g., on this point the *obiter* comments of Clarke J in *Sister Mary Christian v Dublin City Council* [2012] IEHC 163 at [12.11].

[70] *Treacey* v. *An Bord Pleanála* [2019] IESC 70, at [27].

what Michelman terms '. . .a jurisprudence of adaptive and evolving principles including expansive principles of public trust and social responsibility,' according to which the entitlements of owners are not fixed, but rather are shaped by social, cultural, and economic developments.[71]

4.3.4 *Dual Protection – Personal and Property Rights*

Rights of action and the right to earn a livelihood have been recognised by the Irish courts as protected by *both* the property rights and personal rights guarantees in the Constitution.[72] For example, the right to a livelihood or the right to work has been variously classified by the courts as a personal right,[73] a property right,[74] or

[71] F. I. Michelman, 'Property, Federalism and Jurisprudence: A Comment on *Lucas* and Judicial Conservatism' (1993) 35 *William & Mary Law Review* 301, 317. He notes as an example of this approach the view that '[o]ur law makes allowance for the fact that what appears to one age to be innocent use of one's own property may sometimes justifiably come to appear to a successor age to be an unreasonable encroachment on the property-based interests of others or of the public at large.' Ibid., 316. On the idea of change as a facet of property, see also Underkuffler, *The Idea of Property* (n 2) and Harris, *Property and Justice* (n 21), p. 77.

[72] On rights of action see, e.g., *O'Brien* v. *Keogh* [1972] IR 144; *O'Brien* v. *Manufacturing Engineering Company Ltd* [1973] IR 334; *Moynihan* v. *Greensmyth* [1977] 1 IR 55; *Brady* v. *Donegal County Council* [1989] ILRM 282, and *Re Article 26 and the Health Amendment (No. 2) Bill 2004* [2005] 1 IR 105. On livelihood see, e.g., *Brendan Dunne Ltd* v. *Fitzpatrick* [1958] 1 IR 29; *Murphy* v. *Stewart* [1973] 1 IR 97; *Cafolla* (n 18); *Re Article 26 and the Employment Equality Bill 1996* (n 56), *O'Brien* v. *The Personal Injuries Assessment Board* [2005] IEHC 100, [2008] IESC 71 and *Cork Institute of Technology* (n 53).

[73] *Murphy* (n 72) at 117. Kenny J in the earlier case of *Murtagh Properties Ltd* v. *Cleary* [1972] 1 IR 330 at 336, had identified an equal right for all citizens to the right to earn a livelihood, by drawing on Article 45 in interpreting Article 40.3.1°. *Murphy* v. *Stewart* was approved by Finlay P in *Rodgers* v. *Irish Transport and General Workers' Union* [1978] ILRM 51 at 61, and by Costello J in *Paperlink* (n 47) at 384–85. See *White* v. *Bar Council of Ireland* [2016] IECA 363 at 50, where a right to livelihood is referred to solely in context of Article 40.3.1° but it is stressed that this does not extend to a right to earn a livelihood by any particular means or through the exercise of any particular occupation. See, e.g., *Casey* v. *Minister for the Environment* [2004] 1 IR 402 at 419. The Court held that the right could not guarantee an individual access to property owned by a third party for business purposes. Ibid. at 420. *Casey* was applied by de Valera J in *Lough Swilly Shellfish Growers Co-Operative Society Ltd* v. *Bradley* (29 June, 2010) (HC), and by McKechnie J in *O'Sullivan* (n 22) at 61. In the latter case, McKechnie J stated that the right to earn a livelihood was protected by Article 40.3.1°. Ibid. at 60. In *NVH* v. *Minister for Justice and Equality* [2017] IESC 35, the Supreme Court treated the right to work as a personal freedom.

[74] See, e.g., *Re Article 26 and the Employment Equality Bill 1996* (n 56); *Dellway* (n 37); *White* v. *Bar Council* [2016] IEHC 406 and *O'Connell* v. *BATU* [2016] IECA 86 (where Peart J noted that the right to earn a livelihood was also sometimes described as a personal right), *Cork Institute of Technology* (n 53).

both.[75] Rights flowing from specific employment are often characterised as property rights due to the constitutional status of contractual rights. However, beyond the contractual context, any constitutional protection for the right to a livelihood is negative in nature.[76]

Judges have generally equated the effect of the Constitution's protection of both property rights and personal rights. The Supreme Court attempted to explain this equation in the context of rights of action in *Re Article 26 and the Health (Amendment) (No 2) Bill*.[77] The case concerned a bill that would have retrospectively validated the imposition of charges for the provision of nursing home care in cases where the care ought legally to have been provided free of charge. The bill provided that except in cases where recovery proceedings had already been commenced, the charges were to be deemed to have always been lawful.[78] The Supreme Court held that rights of action to recover such wrongfully paid charges were 'a species of personal property known as a *chose in action*'.[79] This right of action was assignable and formed part of the estate of a deceased person.[80] The Court also acknowledged that the right to litigate such a claim was a personal right and it suggested that the distinction between personal and property rights might not be material in this context.[81] It noted the argument to this effect in earlier decisions[82] and said:

> Implicit in the statement that there would be no material difference in the constitutional protection provided is the assumption that the Oireachtas may have been involved in deciding whether the principles of social

[75] See, e.g., *O'Neill* v. *Minister for Agriculture* [1998] 1 IR 539, where the judges in the Supreme Court referred to both property rights and the right to work in considering regulations that restricted the granting of licences for artificial insemination of animals. They did not clarify the constitutional source of these rights.

[76] For example, in *Neurendale Ltd* v. *Dublin City Council*, McKechnie J held that the right to earn a livelihood was not a right to earn a livelihood through any particular means, but rather a right not to be prevented from earning a livelihood by the State. *Neurendale* (n 63) at 193. See similarly O'Donnell J in *NVH* v. *Minister for Justice* describing the right to work as '. . .freedom to seek work which however implies a negative obligation not to prevent the person from seeking or obtaining employment, at least without substantial justification.' (n 73) at 12.

[77] *Re Article 26 and the Health Amendment (No. 2) Bill 2004* (n 72).

[78] Section 1 amended s. 53 of the Health Act 1970 s (1)(b) by inserting sub-s. 5: '[s]ubject to subsection (6), it is hereby declared that the imposition and payment of a relevant charge is, and always has been, lawful.'

[79] *Re Article 26 and the Health Amendment (No. 2) Bill 2004* (n 72) at 178.

[80] Ibid. at 202.

[81] Ibid. at 182.

[82] *Tuohy* v. *Courtney* [1994] 3 IR 1 and *White* v. *Dublin City Council* [2004] 1 IR 545.

> justice required the regulation of the exercise of the property rights in question and whether their delimitation was therefore justified by the exigencies of the common good.[83]

In this view, the protection afforded to rights of action by recognition as either property rights or personal rights could be regarded as the same if the legislature had taken the delimiting principles set out in Article 43.2 into account in drawing up the legislation. This raises the as-yet unanswered question of whether such legislative consideration should be presumed (which would be consistent with the presumption of constitutionality that applies to all legislation and all administrative action in the Irish context[84]), or whether courts could review the legislative process to identify whether consideration was given to the delimiting principles in Article 43.2. In general, Irish courts tend not to review the processes involved in preparing and passing legislation.

The tendency to collapse the distinction between personal rights and property rights marginalises the significance of Article 43.2, which as was discussed in Chapter 3 specifies the justifications for the exercise of the State's regulatory power. The harmonious reading of Articles 40.3.2° and 43 advocated by the Irish courts, which was analysed in the previous chapter as a plausible and constructive interpretation of the relationship between the Constitution's two property rights guarantees, means that if a right is a *property right* as opposed to another kind of personal right, the delimiting principles set out in Article 43 should inform judicial interpretation of the 'unjust attack' standard in Article 40.3.2˚. Therefore, whether a right is treated as a property right or a personal right or both may in fact influence judicial analysis and outcomes.

4.4 The Impact of Wide-Reaching Constitutional Property Clauses

An oft-cited progressive concern about constitutional property clauses is that they entrench the status quo and impede social and economic reform.[85] This concern is raised even in respect of progressively framed constitutional guarantees. For example Alexander argues:

83 *Re Article 26 and the Health Amendment (No. 2) Bill 2004* (n 72) at 200.

84 On the presumption of constitutionality, see Hogan, Whyte, Kenny and Walsh, *Kelly: The Irish Constitution* (n 23), pp. 982–1009.

85 See, e.g., J. Nedelsky, 'Should Property Be Constitutionalized? A Relational and Comparative Approach' in G. E. van Maanen and A. J. van der Walt (eds.), *Property Law on the Threshold of the Twenty-first Century* (Antwerp: Maklu, 1996), pp. 417, 425,

> [i]n a society with a strong legal tradition of protecting the extant holdings of property, a property clause that was designed to have politically progressive, or even transformative, results, may be effectively neutered by a community of judicial interpreters who were all acculturated in the old regime and whose own legal consciousness has not been transformed.[86]

Judicial interpretation of constitutional property clauses as including a wide range of interests may heighten these concerns by expanding the reach of such clauses, thereby creating further impediments to progressive change. This part considers this risk in light of the Irish courts' inclusive interpretation of the reach of the Irish Constitution's property rights guarantees. The doctrinal analysis in the previous part demonstrated that the constitutional conception of property is expansive, taking in intangible as well as tangible interests. Such a doctrinal position is consistent with the nature of the State's power in respect of property rights under Article 43, which is focused at the right-limiting, rather than right-defining, stage.[87] However, it may impact on cultural attitudes towards private ownership and on ideas of the constraining impact of constitutional property rights on legislative freedom.[88]

The decision to identify an interest as coming within the sphere of the Constitution's property rights guarantees has an important impact insofar as it triggers judicial analysis of the legitimacy of any impugned restriction on that interest. Furthermore, such a decision draws upon, and in turn shapes, cultural understandings of private property. As Penner puts it: '[i]t is incontrovertible that calling something "property" ramifies in all sorts of ways, legal, political, social, and cultural.'[89] Framing a claim in terms of property rights has long been recognised

Private Property and the Limits of American Constitutionalism: The Madisoninan Framework and its Legacy (Chicago: University of Chicago Press, 1990); Underkuffler, 'Property as a Constitutional Myth' (n 2); A. J. van der Walt, 'The Constitutional Property Clause: Striking a Balance between Guarantee and Limitation' in J. MacLean (ed.), *Property and the Constitution* (Oxford: Hart Publishing, 1999), p. 109 and C. M. Rose, 'Property as the Keystone Right?' (1996) 71 *Notre Dame Law Review* 329.

86 Alexander (n 39), p. 18.

87 On this point, see van der Walt and Walsh, 'Comparative Constitutional Conceptions of Property' (n 3), p. 196.

88 Underkuffler describes a 'mythology of property. . .as a free-standing entity, defined from the individual perspective alone, and nearly absolute in nature', and argues that popular belief in that mythology will itself restrain legislative freedom. Underkuffler, 'Property as Constitutional Myth' (n 2), 1247–48.

89 Penner, 'Bundle of Rights' (n 11), 799.

as a powerful rhetorical tool.[90] Insofar as judges focus on the limitation stage rather than the definition stage in interpreting the constitutional property guarantees, they invite litigants and advocates outside the courts to argue themselves into the sphere of protection of those guarantees in a wide range of contexts.[91] From a legal perspective, concerns have been raised that a wide constitutional conception of property risks making property at once all-encompassing and meaningless.[92]

The inclusive interpretation adopted by the Irish courts raises the *possibility* of constitutional challenge on property rights grounds in a wide range of circumstances. In this regard, van der Walt rightly stresses the importance of '. . .the space between the doctrinal detail of property rules and practices on the one hand and the abstract, rhetorical and affective value of paradigmatic rights talk on the other'.[93] As will be seen in the doctrinal analysis in the chapters that follow, the Irish constitutional property clauses have not generally been interpreted by judges as significantly constraining legislative freedom. In most cases, legislative and administrative restrictions on the exercise of property rights are upheld against constitutional challenge, with outlier cases of invalidation generally involving distinctive or unusual features, such as absurdity or irrationality or procedural unfairness. Overall, the Irish constitutional protection for property rights is in Michelman's terms 'soft', involving balancing analysis rather than rule-based protection for property rights and generating outcomes that usually favour the public interest.[94]

Nonetheless, political conservativism concerning property rights linked to the Constitution is a persistent feature of Irish political life.[95]

90 As Carol Rose points out, as a metaphor, the idea of exclusive possession of property '. . .is a particularly potent metaphor for dignity and personal efficacy', which as such is attractive to ordinary persons and can be harnessed by those advancing rights-claims. C. M. Rose, 'Canons of Property Talk, or, Blackstone's Anxiety' (1998) 108 *Yale Law Journal* 601, 630. See also Gray, 'Equitable Property' (n 9), 46 referring to '. . .the insidiously powerful leverage of the primal claim, "it's mine"' and 'the enormous symbolic and emotional impact of the property attribution'.

91 For discussion of expanded property concepts as a form of political property rhetoric, see Harris, *Property and Justice* (n 21), pp. 154–61.

92 See K. J. Vandevelde, 'The New Property of the Nineteenth Century: The Development of the Modern Concept of Property' (1980) 29 *Buffalo Law Review* 325, 329.

93 A. J. van der Walt, *Property in the Margins* (Oxford: Hart Publishing, 2009), p. 37.

94 F. I. Michelman, 'Constitutional Protection for Property Rights and the Reasons Why: Distrust Revisited' (2012) 1 *Brigham Kanner Property Rights Journal* 217, 235.

95 Jennifer Nedelsky notes a similar disconnect in the US context, stating 'judicial practice does not yet seem to have shaken the popular force of the idea of property as a limit to the legitimate power of government': J. Nedelsky, 'American Constitutionalism and the

For example, four bills have been referred to the Supreme Court by the President for pre-enactment constitutional review in respect of constitutional property rights issues out of a total of 15 referrals over the lifetime of the Constitution.[96] Successive governments have adopted a cautious attitude towards initiating legislative reforms that restrict the exercise of property rights, apparently influenced by the legal advice provided to government by the Attorney General (AG). The AG advises the government on matters of law and legal opinion and is provided for in Article 30 of the Constitution. The AG is usually an eminent barrister nominated by government and sits in Cabinet meetings. The AG's advice is not usually published as a matter of convention, but successive governments have cited the advice of the AG concerning constitutional property rights as a reason for not initiating legislative reforms.[97] Recent examples include reform of upward-only rent review clauses, measures to deter land hoarding, tenant protection measures, mortgage interest rate caps, and regulation of vulture funds.[98] The constitutional protection for property rights was also repeatedly cited by government ministers as a reason for opposing private members bills designed to rectify post-economic crisis problems on issues such as housing,

Paradox of Private Property' in J. Elster and R. Slagstad (eds.), *Constitutionalism and Democracy* (Cambridge: Cambridge University Press, 1988), pp. 241, 263.

[96] On patterns in respect of Article 26 references, including the particularly high attrition rate of Article 26 references, see in further detail G. W. Hogan, D. Kenny and R. Walsh, 'An Anthology of Declarations of Unconstitutionality' (2015) 54 *Irish Jurist* 1.

[97] For analysis of this phenomenon, see D. Kenny and C. Casey, 'Shadow Constitutional Review: The Dark Side of Pre-Enactment Political Review in Ireland and Japan' (2019) 18 *International Journal of Constitutional Law* 51.

[98] Legislation was introduced with the purpose of nullifying existing upward-only rent review clauses, but was abandoned on the basis that the AG had advised that such legislation would be unconstitutional. See the statement of Minister for State Michael Ring, www.justice.ie/en/JELR/Pages/SP13000346 (last visited 11 September 2020). The Constitution was also cited as the reason for not pursuing other measures in response to the Irish housing crisis: see P. Melia and C. Treacy, 'Constitution blocked me in bid to supply homes – Kelly'. Irish Independent, 1 April 2016: www.independent.ie/business/personal-finance/property-mortgages/consttitution-blocked-me-in-bid-to-supply-homes-kelly-34589603.html (last visited 11 September 2020), quoting former Environment Minister Alan Kelly as saying, 'I was repeatedly blocked from making provision for what I believed was the common good by the strength by which property rights are protected under Article 43 of the Constitution'. For a helpful overview, see Finn Keyes, Oireachtas Library and Research Centre Briefing Paper, 'Property Rights and Housing Legislation' (19 June 2019) and Hilary Hogan and Finn Keyes, 'The Housing Crisis and the Constitution' (November 16, 2020), available at https://ssrn.com/abstract=3731506.

mortgages, and pensions.[99] It was used to justify rejecting proposed amendments to government bills brought forward in these contexts during the course of the economic crisis,[100] and as a response to calls for measures such as depriving bankers involved in the economic crisis of accrued bonuses and pensions.[101]

The 2020 general election cast a spotlight on this issue as parties debated the constitutionality of a rent freeze, with the outgoing government and major opposition party both citing legal advice that such a freeze would be unconstitutional.[102] Most controversially, the advice of the previous and current Attorneys General was that a temporary freeze on rent increases and evictions introduced as a response to the

[99] See, e.g., Minister for Housing, Planning and Local Government Eoghan Murphy's comments in Dáil Éireann responding to the Residential Tenancies (Prevention of Family Homelessness) Bill 2018 (28 March 2019), characterising that Bill as unconstitutional '. . . because it is an unjust attack on a sub-group of people for a societal problem that is far more complex than simply someone selling property'. The bill would have prevented the sale of a property for rent with tenants in situ, which the Minister stated on the advice of the Attorney General, was unconstitutional. See https://www.oireachtas.ie/en/debates/debate/dail/2019-03-28/67/. A review of the Dáil debates shows that there are many similar examples where Government ministers have cited the constitutional protection of property rights as preventing the enactment of proposed bills, e.g., in response to the Housing Emergency Measures in the Public Interest Bill 2018, the Urban Regeneration and Housing (Amendment) Bill 2018, the Residential Tenancies (Greater Security of Tenure and Rent Certainty) Bill 2018, the Mortgage Arrears Resolution (Family Home) Bill 2017, Media Ownership Bill 2017, Pensions (Amendment) (No. 2) Bill 2017, Anti-Evictions Bill 2016, Central Bank (Variable Rate Mortgages) 2016.

[100] See, e.g., the comments of Minister of State for Justice and Equality, David Stanton, in Dáil Éireann on 13 December 2016 rejecting a proposed amendment to the Courts Bill 2016 to protect tenants where dwellings are repossessed or a receiver is appointed, on the basis that the measure as drafted extended to tenants of commercial premises, which he argued was inconsistent with the social justice requirement of Article 43. See https://www.oireachtas.ie/en/debates/debate/dail/2016-12-13/28/.

[101] See, e.g., J. Clarke, 'Taoiseach Welcomes Cut to Ex-AIB Chief's Pension', *Journal*, i.e., 7 November 2012, available at www.thejournal.ie/ex-aib-boss-agrees-to-pension-cut-664702-Nov2012/ (last visited 14 September 2020), reporting the Taoiseach's statement that bankers' pensions could not be changed by government on the basis of their status as constitutionally protected property, R. Riegel, 'Gormley Pledges to Force €1m Fingleton Payback', *Irish Independent*, 24 April 2010, available at www.independent.ie/irish-news/gormley-pledges-to-force-1m-fingleton-payback-26652663.html (last visited 14 September 2020), reporting the Environment Minister's view that recouping bankers' bonuses was difficult due to the constitutional protection of property rights.

[102] For analysis, see R. Walsh, 'Housing Crisis: There Is No Constitutional Block to Rent Freezes in Ireland' *Irish Times*, 3 February 2020, available at www.irishtimes.com/opinion/housing-crisis-there-is-no-constitutional-block-to-rent-freezes-in-ireland-1.4159367 (last visited 14 September 2020).

COVID-19 crisis could not be extended once the phased reopening of the economy had been largely completed without raising a significant risk of legal challenge.[103] This advice influenced the nature of the temporary protections for tenants introduced in the Residential Tenancies and Valuation Act 2020 to respond to the economic hardship caused by COVID-19. In response to this culture of political conservativism grounded in the Constitution, non-governmental organisations and other housing bodies have characterised the constitutional protection for property rights as a significant impediment to effective legislative responses to the current Irish housing crisis.[104] There have been repeated calls, both by NGO's and by opposition politicians, for a referendum to amend the Constitution to include an express right to housing and/or to alter the existing constitutional property clauses to make it easier to introduce measures that impact adversely on private property rights.[105] That call was apparently heard by the current coalition government, which committed to holding a referendum on a right to housing in its Programme for Government in 2020, although no date has yet been set for any such a referendum.[106]

[103] On these developments, see R. Walsh, 'COVID-19's Silver Lining – Housing, the Constitution, and the Scope for Post-Crisis Reform' COVID-19 Law and Human Rights Blog (19 June 2020) http://tcdlaw.blogspot.com/2020/06/covid-19s-silver-lining-housing.html.

[104] See, e.g., the Home for Good group and the Raise the Roof campaigns the comments of Barnardos chairman Fergus Finlay, characterising the Constitution as containing '. . .the strongest set of property rights anywhere in the world and one of the major stumbling blocks and obstacles to addressing the housing crisis'. See J. H. Jones, 'Right to a Secure Home Must Be Added to Constitution, Say Advocates' *Irish Times*, 28 February 2019, www.irishtimes.com/news/social-affairs/right-to-a-secure-home-must-be-added-to-constitution-say-advocates-1.3808858 (last visited 11 September 2020), E. Dalton, 'Right to Property Adding to Housing Crisis, Says Council Chief', *Irish Times*, 17 September 2018, www.irishtimes.com/news/social-affairs/right-to-property-adding-to-housing-crisis-says-council-chief-1.3631244?mode=sample&auth-failed=1&pw-origin=https%3A%2F%2Fwww.irishtimes.com%2Fnews%2Fsocial-affairs%2Fright-to-property-adding-to-housing-crisis-says-council-chief-1.3631244 (last visited 11 September 2020), reporting that the chief executive of Waterford City and County Council cited the constitutional right to property as the key impediment to local authorities easing the housing crisis.

[105] See, e.g., the Thirty-fifth Amendment of the Constitution (Right to a Home) Bill 2016, a private members bill seeking to insert a right to housing into the Constitution that was defeated by vote on 31 May 2016. See also D. Linnane, 'Labour Party Want Right to Home Put Into the Constitution', *Evening Echo*, 6 November 2018, reporting that the Labour Party had passed a motion unanimously calling for the right to a home to be inserted into the Constitution.

[106] See https://static.rasset.ie/documents/news/2020/06/draft-programme-for-govt.pdf.

How should we understand this divergence between the political interpretation of the effect of the Constitution's property rights guarantees and the overall doctrinal position – between Irish property 'mythology' and property 'actuality'?[107] Any such explanation is necessarily speculative, and this question will be returned to in Chapter 9. The following are suggested as some relevant factors tending to explain the divergence between judicial and political interpretations of the effect of the constitutional property rights provisions, to be borne in mind in assessing Irish constitutional property law through the prism of its doctrine and outcomes in subsequent chapters.

The culture of political conservativism in respect of property rights arguably reflects the complex Irish historical relationship with property rights detailed in the previous chapter, which embedded a cultural commitment to both individual possession and social justice-oriented redistribution. It may also reflect the influence of the institutional protection of private ownership in Article 43, which entrenches private ownership as a feature of Ireland's social, economic, and legal landscape. In addition, politicians and their legal advisers may have over-learnt lessons from some rare, but high profile, defeats in the courts on constitutional property rights, for example in respect of rent control, which are explored further in Chapter 6.[108] The office of the Attorney General, although independent of government, is a political appointment and the Attorney General works very closely with government.[109] The legal advice given to governments on constitutional issues has been referred

[107] This contrast is borrowed from Underkuffler, 'Property as a Constitutional Myth' (n 2), 1249.

[108] For example, former Taoiseach Garret Fitzgerald cited '…concern about possible restrictive interpretation of the Articles on private property' as a 'major impediment' to necessary legislative reforms in respect of taxation and revenue, land use and planning controls, environmental protection, consumer protection, and archaeological and historical preservation. G. Fitzgerald, 'Time to Exorcise the Ghosts of Past British Concerns', *Irish Times*, 27 July 1996. He expressed public concern about the inhibiting effect of the constitutional protection for property rights while Taoiseach: see D. Grogan, 'Property Rights Too Strong – Taoiseach', *Irish Times*, 5 September 1985. The invalidation of rent control by the Supreme Court in *Blake* v. *Attorney General* [1982] 1 IR 117, and of the proposed replacement scheme in *Re Article 26 and the Housing (Private Rented Dwellings) Bill* [1983] IR 181 (considered further in Chapter 5) seem to have made a strong impression on Irish politicians in the 1980s.

[109] See, e.g., McCarthy J in *Attorney General v Hamilton* [1993] 2 IR 250, 282, noting that since the AG is appointed by the government and subject to termination by the government, the AG 'must be presumed to be acting with at least the tacit consent of the Government'.

to as 'court-mimicking' and highly qualified, focused on the prospects of legislation being invalidated.[110] Accordingly, one or a small number of invalidations in a particular context are likely to exert disproportionate influence on the advice given by an Attorney General. This in turn stymies the initiation of new measures that might be challenged, thereby allowing the courts to clarify contentious issues in constitutional property law.[111]

Against this backdrop, political actors may genuinely misunderstand or be unaware of the *overall* tenor of Irish constitutional property law as developed by judges, and as a result may misconceive the constitutional property clauses as significant barriers to social and economic reforms. Their interpretation of the constraining effect of the Constitution's protection for individual property rights may reflect a sincere attempt to understand the text in light of legal advice, with such advice treated as binding by government.[112] On the other hand, the Constitution's property rights guarantees may serve as a convenient means for politicians to excuse legislative inaction on social and economic issues where they perceive constituent constraints or other political challenges. In this respect, it is significant that governments have initiated and passed various restrictions on the exercise of property rights, suggesting that where the political will exists, perceived constitutional barriers can be overcome.[113]

Whatever the explanation for the political interpretation of the constitutional property clauses as imposing strong constraints on legislative freedom, the broad *prima facie* reach of the Irish constitutional property rights guarantees means that the Constitution may at least be plausibly raised in a wide array of contexts as an impediment to the initiation of reforming legislation. Such invocation of the Constitution in turn influences wider perceptions about the strength of protection for property

[110] D. Kenny and C. Casey, 'A One Person Supreme Court? The Attorney General, Constitutional Advice to Government, and the Case for Transparency' (2019) 42 (1) *DULJ* 89, p. 95.

[111] Ibid.

[112] Kenny and Casey stress that the government is not in fact bound by AG's advice. Ibid.

[113] For example, the National Asset Management Agency Act 2009 was enacted despite far-reaching impacts on property rights, which were noted by the Supreme Court in *Dellway* (n 37). Similarly, austerity measures were introduced in the context of the economic crisis, and rights-restrictive measures such as rent pressure zones and vacant site levies were introduced in response to the ongoing housing crisis. Most recently, far-reaching restraints on the exercise of property rights were introduced in response to the COVID-19 crisis, for example requiring the closure of businesses.

rights and its constraining effect on legislative freedom.[114] This result is potentially in tension with the progressive framing of Article 43 and with its clear empowerment of the State in respect of social justice and the common good. Furthermore, this book will show through doctrinal analysis that it does not reflect the predominant judicial interpretation of the constraining effects of the Constitution's property rights guarantees, which largely favours the public interest.

4.5 Conclusions

At its core, the doctrine on the engagement of Articles 40.3.2° and 43 analysed in this chapter reflects the interplay between judges' evolving intuitive understandings of the justification for, and scope of, private ownership (derived in large part from the common law) and the overtly distributive inquiry presupposed by the delimiting principles in Article 43.2.[115] Distinctions between protected and unprotected valuable interests have not been coherently or consistently justified by the courts, demonstrating Harris' contention that once an extended property concept is adopted, '. . .stopping-points tend to be *ad hoc* and unexplained.'[116] The threshold question of engagement receives very limited judicial attention for cases falling within the intuitive 'core' of constitutional property clauses. That core is centred on an understanding of property rights as rights earned through individual effort and/or protected by law, reflecting Lockean and positivist influences. More focus is placed on the threshold question in circumstances falling outside this core. This suggests that the information costs critique of the 'bundle of rights' metaphor may be most significant in respect of interests that are not protected in private law.[117]

[114] See, e.g., Kenny and Casey, 'A One Person Supreme Court' (n 110), p. 109, arguing that negative political invocation of the Constitution on foot of undisclosed AG's advice '. . .fosters no image of the Constitution as an empowering document and store of public values which affirmatively empowers politicians and the people to grapple with social and economic problems.'

[115] As Cribbet puts it: '. . . the judiciary calls property that which they protect, and that which they protect is forever in transition' J. E. Cribbet, 'Concepts in Transition: The Search for a New Definition of Property' (1986) *University of Illinois Law Review* 1, 41.

[116] Harris, *Property and Justice* (n 21), p. 146.

[117] See, e.g., Smith, 'Property is Not Just a Bundle of Rights' (n 11), in particular 283–84, arguing for an architectural or modular theory of property that responds to such costs.

The Irish experience further demonstrates that a progressively framed constitutional property clause, even when coupled with the 'bundle of rights' metaphor, does not prevent the idea of 'property as things' from having impact. Understandings of 'property as things', 'property as relations between persons', or a merged 'property as relations between persons concerning things' that are presented in contrasting terms in property theory in fact interact doctrinally, particularly where common law protection for property rights is overlaid with constitutional property rights guarantees. Each of these understandings of property are applied, incompletely, and often implicitly or indeed unconsciously, by judges. As Williams puts it: '. . .judges, commentators, and the general public often mix intuitive imagery with imagery that conflicts with it, or combine two rhetorics to form new mixtures, or, occasionally, new compounds that achieve a stable presence in the rhetoric of property' in a way that is '. . .pragmatic, and often unreflective'.[118] Where such an unreflective approach is adopted, judgments as to the appropriate balance between public and private interests may be concealed within a court's determination that an interest does or does not engage the Constitution's protection for property rights. As Radin notes, '. . .our very recognition of the existence of property rights is intertwined with our perceptions of their justice.'[119] This intertwining is heightened where constitutional property clauses explicitly address distributive issues like social justice.

A less intuitive judicial approach to the question of engagement, involving greater transparency concerning the reasons why constitutional property rights protection is or is not triggered in respect of various valuable individual interests, would facilitate more reasoned analysis and critique of the dominant political interpretation of the property clauses as strongly protecting property rights. A key lesson from the Irish experience is that *political* and *non-judicial legal* interpretations of constitutional property clauses may in fact be just as significant as judicial interpretations in acting as potential barriers to progressive reforms. However, these spheres of interpretation are interlinked – ambiguity in legal doctrine about the reasons for judicial decisions facilitates

[118] Williams, 'The Rhetoric of Property' (n 9), 280. See also Harris, criticising the contrast between property as a relationship to a thing and as a relationship between persons, arguing '[c]onclusions that certain relations obtain between persons follow, for laymen and lawyers alike, from conceptions of ownership interests in things.' Harris, *Property and Justice* (n 21), p. 119.

[119] Radin, *Reinterpreting Property* (n 32), p. 168.

the type of constitutionally rooted political conservativism identifiable in the Irish context. Progressive approaches to property need to be alive to this fact, and to the rhetorical impact of interpretations of the reach of constitutional property rights provisions. They should not neglect the risk that an inclusive interpretation of constitutional property rights provisions can create, bolster, or serve to justify political conservativism, even where legal doctrine predominantly favours the public interest.[120]

[120] On this concern see, e.g., Underkuffler, *Property as Constitutional Myth*, (n 2), for example noting '[t]he popular belief in the separateness and sanctity of property of property will restrain government action even if it does not do so in the way the belief itself demands': 1248.

5

Standards of Review and the Form of Constitutional Property Rights

5.1 Introduction

Many jurisdictions with constitutional property rights guarantees apply some standard of review capturing a principle of fairness to structure judicial review of public law restrictions on individual property rights.[1] The choices judges make *between* standards of review and in *applying* the selected standard(s) impact upon the constraining effect of constitutional property rights on legislative freedom. This chapter analyses the standards of review that are applied in Irish constitutional property law and their relationship to the form of the Constitution's property rights provisions. The standards of review provide the framework through which the delimiting principles in Articles 40.3.2° ('unjust attack') and 43.2 ('the exigencies of the common good' and 'the principles of social justice') are given concrete effect. In this way, standards of review provide the legal techniques through which the aspects of the Irish constitutional property clauses that are particularly consistent with progressive property ideas are interpreted and applied.

The Irish experience has been that general standards of review have proven more influential in constitutional property rights adjudication than the specific form of the Constitution's property rights provisions. The courts variously apply the proportionality principle, the rationality test, and a text-based approach advanced by the Supreme Court in *Re Article 26 and the Health (Amendment) (No 2) Bill, 2004,*[2] with differing degrees of stringency. Each of these approaches is analysed in this chapter, as well as the relationship between them. Overall, the picture that emerges is of a high level of doctrinal uncertainty concerning the identification of the appropriate standard of review and a high level of

[1] For discussion of the general trend in comparative constitutional property law, see A. J. van der Walt and R. Walsh, 'Comparative Constitutional Property Law' in M. Graziadei and L. Smith (eds.), *Comparative Property Law – Global Perspectives* (Cheltenham: Edward Elgar Publishing, 2017), p. 193, in particular pp. 202–4.

[2] [2005] 1 IR 105.

deference to the legislature in the application of standards of review. The specific wording of the Constitution's property rights provisions has had limited doctrinal impact. In light of the Irish experience, this chapter argues that direct judicial engagement with the question of fair balance that is posed by constitutional property clauses (particularly clauses like Articles 40.3.2° and 43 that have an explicitly progressive orientation) is preferable. It contends that the *Health Bill case* marks a welcome, if as yet tentative, move in that direction. Insofar as general standards of review are applied in the constitutional property context, Irish constitutional property law indicates that a clear statement of judicial reasons for particular applications of those standards is generally not forthcoming.

Section 5.2 analyses the standards of review that are applied in Irish constitutional property law. Section 5.3 highlights the overlap between those standards. Section 5.4 considers their application, in particular the predominantly deferential approach adopted by the Irish courts to the judgments of elected branches of government concerning the appropriate mediation of property rights and social justice. Section 5.5 concludes.

5.2 Overlapping Standards of Review

5.2.1 Proportionality

As in many other jurisdictions that constitutionalise property rights, the dominant standard of review in Irish constitutional property law is the proportionality principle.[3] The principle sets out a series of questions for judges to answer in assessing the constitutionality of a restriction on the exercise of property rights.[4] However, it can be applied with varying degrees of stringency depending on the posture adopted by the reviewing

[3] For discussion of this trend in constitutional property law see, e.g., G. S. Alexander, *The Global Debate over Constitutional Property* (Chicago: University of Chicago Press, 2006), in particular pp. 199–215.

[4] In the Irish context, specifically focused on constitutional property rights adjudication, see G. W. Hogan, 'The Constitution, Property Rights and Proportionality' (1997) 32 *Irish Jurist* 373, and R. Walsh, 'The Constitution, Property Rights and Proportionality: A Reappraisal' (2009) 31 *Dublin University Law Journal* 1. There is an enormous scholarly literature on the proportionality principle more broadly: see, e.g., A. Barak, *Proportionality: Constitutional Rights and the Limitations* (Cambridge: Cambridge University Press, 2012); M. Cohen-Eliya and I. Porat, *Proportionality and Constitutional Culture* (Cambridge: Cambridge University Press, 2013); J. Rivers, 'Proportionality and Variable Intensity of Review' (2006) 65 *Cambridge Law Journal* 174 and V. Jackson, 'Constitutional Law in an Age of Proportionality' (2015) 125 *Yale Law Journal* 3095.

judge *vis-á-vis* the legislature. In and of itself, the proportionality principle is not a guarantor of objectivity, nor is it outcome-determinative.[5] Rather, as Alexander puts it, proportionality analysis '. . .is a form of contextualized practical judgment.'[6]

The statement of the proportionality principle that is applied by the Irish courts was articulated by Costello J in *Heaney* v. *Ireland*, albeit not in the context of property rights.[7] Costello J approved the Supreme Court of Canada's well-known formulation of the proportionality principle as set out in *Chaulk* v. *R*:

> The objective of the impugned provision must be of sufficient importance to warrant overriding a constitutionally protected right. It must relate to concerns pressing and substantial in a free and democratic society. The means chosen must pass a proportionality test. They must:
>
> (a) be rationally connected to the objective and not be arbitrary, unfair or based on irrational considerations;
> (b) impair the right as little as possible, and
> (c) be such that their effects on rights are proportional to the objective.[8]

The Supreme Court in *Re Article 26 and Part V of the Planning and Development Bill, 1999* expressly approved the proportionality principle set out in *Heaney* as the appropriate approach to assessing the constitutionality of a restriction on the exercise of property rights.[9]

5 On this point, see the statement of O'Donnell J in the Supreme Court in *Nottinghamshire County Council* v. *B*: '[p]roportionality in itself is not an entirely transparent concept. It can be applied strictly to strike down legislation or generously to sustain it. It is important to remember that proportionality is a tool for analysis, rather than an end in itself. The mere statement that something is *proportionate* is almost as Delphic as the statement that it is reasonable. The analysis of whether any particular restriction or limitation is consistent to the Constitution may be assisted by the structure proportionality analysis provides, but only if it is explained *why* any particular provision is permitted by the Constitution, and is proportionate.' [2013] 4 IR 622 at [87]. See also Hogan, 'The Constitution, Property Rights and Proportionality' (n 4) 393, and A. O'Neill, 'Property Rights and the Power of Eminent Domain', in E. Carolan and O. Doyle (eds.), *The Irish Constitution: Governance and Values* (Dublin: Thomson Round Hall, 2008), p. 438.

6 Alexander, *The Global Debate over Constitutional Property* (n 3), p. 203.

7 [1994] 3 IR 593, hereafter *Heaney*. The case concerned a challenge to a restriction imposed on the right to silence in s. 52 of the Offences Against the State Act, 1939.

8 [1990] 3 SCR 1303 at 1335–36, adopted by Costello P in *Heaney* (n 7) at 607.

9 [2000] 2 IR 321 at 349–50. The proportionality test has been repeatedly approved in recent constitutional property rights decisions of the High Court, for example: *Daly* v. *Revenue Commissioners* [1995] 3 IR 1; *Gilligan* v. *The Criminal Assets Bureau* [1998] 3 IR 185; *Gorman* v. *The Minister for the Environment* [2001] 2 IR 414; *Shirley* v. *AO*

However, as will be seen, other approaches have continued to be adopted by judges, alongside or instead of the proportionality principle.

5.2.2 *Rationality*

Notwithstanding the primacy of the proportionality principle, if the Irish courts characterise a legislative restriction as designed to reconcile competing constitutional rights or duties, they sometimes apply rationality review in assessing its constitutionality.[10] The Irish doctrine suggests that the difficult distributional assessments involved in constitutional property rights adjudication may prompt judges to gravitate towards the facially deferential rationality standard or to overlay the proportionality standard with rationality review.[11]

Finlay CJ articulated the rationality standard in *Tuohy* v. *Courtney*, which concerned the constitutionality of a limitation statute that he characterised as balancing competing individual rights. He stated:

> The Court is satisfied that in a challenge to the constitutional validity of any statute in the enactment of which the Oireachtas has been engaged in such a balancing function, the role of the courts is not to impose their view of the correct or desirable balance in substitution for the view of the legislature as displayed in their legislation but rather to determine from an objective stance whether the balance contained in the impugned legislation is so contrary to reason and fairness as to constitute an unjust attack on some individual's constitutional rights.[12]

Notwithstanding the emphasis in this passage on 'balance of rights' as the trigger for rationality review, rationality review has been applied in some cases where the most obvious understanding of the legislation was as a restriction on property rights in the public interest, making it an

Gorman [2006] IEHC 27; *BUPA Ireland Ltd* v. *The Health Insurance Authority* [2006] IEHC 431; *J & J Haire Company Ltd* v. *Minister for Health* [2009] IEHC 562; *Dellway Investment Ltd* v. *National Asset Management Agency* [2010] IEHC 364; *Island Ferries Teoranta* v. *Galway County Council* [2013] IEHC 587; *Aer Lingus Ltd* v. *Minister for Finance* [2018] IEHC 198, *Rafferty v. Minister for Agriculture* [2014] IESC 61.

10 *Tuohy* v. *Courtney* [1994] 3 IR 1.

11 See, e.g., *Shirley* (n 9); *BUPA Ireland Ltd* (n 9).

12 *Tuohy* (n 10) at 47. The language of the test is reminiscent of the unreasonableness test applied in judicial review of administrative action and set out in *The State (Keegan)* v. *The Stardust Victims Compensation Tribunal*, whereby an administrative decision may be quashed if it '. . .plainly and unambiguously flies in the face of fundamental reason and common sense.' [1986] 1 IR 642 at 658.

apparent candidate for proportionality analysis.[13] The rationality standard was cited with approval by the Supreme Court in *Re Article 26 and the Employment Equality Bill 1996*, although the stringency of the Court's application of the standard varied greatly throughout the judgment.[14] *Tuohy* rationality is also identifiable in the Supreme Court's decision in *Re Article 26 and Part V of the Planning and Development Bill 1990*.[15] The Court in that case expressly approved and applied the proportionality principle as the framework for its review of the constitutionality of the Bill. However, it drew on the rationality standard to justify the deferential stance it adopted in considering the proportionality of the Bill, thereby overlaying the proportionality principle with rationality. In support of this approach, the Court said it was '. . .peculiarly the province of the Oireachtas to seek to reconcile in this area the conflicting rights of different sections of society'.[16] This example illustrates the blurred line that has been drawn between rationality and proportionality review, with the resulting potential for unpredictability concerning the standard of review that will be applied where a restriction on the exercise of property rights is challenged.

5.2.3 *The Health Bill Case Approach*

Neither the proportionality principle nor rationality review is tailored to, or informed by, the specific language of the constitutional property rights guarantees, in particular the delimiting principles in Article 43.2. Rather, they are generally applicable standards of review for considering claims that legislative measures (or in some cases administrative decisions) violate individual rights protected by the Irish Constitution. However,

13 See, e.g., *Landers* v. *AG* (1975) 109 ILTR 1; *Hanrahan Farms Ltd* v. *The Environmental Protection Agency* [2006] 1 ILRM 275.

14 [1997] 2 IR 321.

15 *Re Article 26 and Part V of the Planning and Development Bill 1990* (n 9).

16 Ibid. at 357–58. There is a strong presumption in Irish law of the compatibility of laws passed by the legislature with the Constitution, for example stated by the Supreme Court in *Re Article 26 and the Offences Against the State (Amendment) Bill 1940* [1940] IR 470 at 478: 'Where any particular law is not expressly prohibited and it is sought to establish that it is repugnant to the Constitution by reason of some implied prohibition or repugnancy, we are of opinion, as a matter of construction, that such repugnancy must be clearly established.' For analysis, see B. Foley, *Deference and the Presumption of Constitutionality* (Dublin: Institute of Public Administration, 2008), and G. W. Hogan, G. F. Whyte, D. Kenny and R. Walsh, *Kelly: The Irish Constitution*, 5th ed. (Dublin: Bloomsbury Professional, 2018), pp. 982–84 and 994–1015.

the Supreme Court has also articulated a distinctive text-based approach to reviewing restrictions on the exercise of property rights focused on the delimiting principles contained in Articles 40.3.2° and 43: 'unjust attack'; 'the exigencies of the common good'; and 'the principles of social justice'.

Rather than applying either the proportionality principle or the rationality test, the Supreme Court in *Re Article 26 and the Health (Amendment) (No. 2) Bill 2004*[17] drew directly on the wording of Articles 40.3.2° and 43 in articulating the standard of review to be applied to the bill:

> [T]he Court is satisfied that the correct approach is: firstly, to examine the nature of the property rights at issue; secondly, to consider whether the Bill consists of a regulation of those rights in accordance with principles of social justice and whether the Bill is required so as to delimit those rights in accordance with the exigencies of the common good; thirdly, in the light of its conclusions on these issues, to consider whether the Bill constitutes an unjust attack on those property rights.[18]

These steps emphasise the nature of the property rights at issue in any given case, and the extent of the impact of a restriction on those rights. This is consistent with the analysis in the previous chapter, which indicated that different interests recognised as constitutional property rights may be subject to varying levels of protection, e.g., benefits derived from regulatory schemes as compared to real property. This factor is not an explicit consideration in proportionality or rationality analysis. In contrast, the *Health Bill case* expressly acknowledges the relevance of such differentiation. In this way, it fills a gap left open by the proportionality principle, which does not provide judges with a framework for analysing the important questions identified in the previous chapter, namely whether the constitutional property clauses are engaged in respect of particular individual interests, and to what degree. The *Health Bill case* approach also reflects the harmonious interpretation of the relationship between Articles 40.3.2° and 43 now favoured by the Irish courts, which was analysed in Chapter 3. It does so by explicitly linking the 'unjust attack' standard in Article 40.3.2° with Article 43.1's guidance on the nature of the property rights protected by the Constitution and with the delimiting principles in Article 43.2.

[17] *Re Article 26 and the Health (Amendment) (No. 2) Bill 2004* (n 2).

[18] Ibid. at 201.

5.3 Disentangling Overlapping Standards of Review

The Irish courts have failed to explain the co-existence and inter-relationship of these overlapping standards of review. In their decisions, judges have not clearly distinguished the three standards, nor have they justified their choice of test in any given case. For example, in *Bupa Ireland Ltd* v. *The Health Insurance Authority*, McKechnie J accepted an approach argued for by counsel that was almost identical to the *Health Bill case*.[19] Nonetheless, he upheld the constitutionality of the impugned regulations by applying the proportionality principle.[20] To further add to the confusion, he also referred to the rationality standard set out in *Tuohy*, and said it was '...of general application in dealing with a constitutional challenge.'[21]

The circumstances in which proportionality review or rationality review is appropriate are blurred. The basic premise of the rationality standard is that it is for the legislature to decide how to reconcile conflicting constitutional rights and duties, thereby clearly instructing the courts to refrain from reviewing the means adopted in such cases. In this way, the rationality standard indicates deferential review of legislative means in a way that the proportionality principle, on its face, does not.[22] In some instances, the courts regard the State's performance of its constitutional duty to legislate in the public interest as sufficient to bring the rationality standard into play.[23] In others, they break what would traditionally be regarded as a 'public interest' down into the individual rights that the public interest in question protects. They characterise the restriction as a collective enforcement of those rights, thereby constructing a 'clash of rights and duties' sufficient to bring the case within the ambit of the rationality principle.[24]

19 *BUPA Ireland Ltd.* (n 9). Counsel suggested that the approach that the court should adopt was ' . . . to examine the nature of the property rights in question, to consider whether the impugned provisions constitute a regulation of those rights in accordance with the principles of social justice, to see whether those provisions are required so as to delimit the exercise of those rights in accordance with the exigencies of the common good and having come to a conclusion on these issues to determine whether the legislative provisions constitute an unjust attack on the applicant's property rights.' at 237–38.

20 McKechnie J asserted that the scheme was 'fair, reasonable and proportionate'. Ibid. at 290.

21 Ibid. at 238.

22 See, e.g., *Landers* (n 13) at 6, and *Re Article 26 the Employment Equality Bill 1996* (n 14).

23 See, e.g., *Landers* (n 13) at 293–94, discussed below. For a theoretical argument in favour of such a breakdown, see L. S. Underkuffler, *The Idea of Property in Law: Its Meaning and Power* (Oxford: Oxford University Press, 2003).

24 See, e.g., *Tuohy* (n 10). See also *Hanrahan* v. *The Environmental Protection Agency* [2006] 1 ILRM 275, at 298.

Further overlap and ambiguity emerges when the *Health Bill case* approach is considered. The test set out by the Supreme Court in the *Health Bill case* has not in fact replaced proportionality review. In some decisions, the courts purportedly applied both approaches.[25] In still other cases, the courts applied the proportionality principle without referring to the *Health Bill case* or distinguishing that decision.[26] The courts have not articulated any principles explaining when either approach should be adopted, suggesting that the *Health Bill case* approach may be best understood as a gloss on the general standards of review (proportionality and rationality) that is applicable only in constitutional property rights adjudication. However, the substantive impact (if any) of that gloss is as yet unclear, as the *Health Bill case* approach has not been consistently applied since its articulation by the Supreme Court in 2005.

Accordingly, there is doctrinal ambiguity and inconsistency concerning appropriate standard of review to be applied in considering a challenge to the constitutionality of a restriction on the exercise of property rights. This creates scope for judges to choose the standard that they wish to apply based on the extent to which they feel the legislature's judgment is owed respect, without justifying such deference.

5.4 Deference and the Application of Standards of Review

The level of deference that judges show to the legislature when applying standards of review has a substantial impact on whether a restriction on the exercise of property rights is upheld.[27] Overall, the Irish courts tend to privilege the public interest over private property rights when

[25] See, e.g., *NALM* v. *McMahon* [2014] IEHC 71, where the High Court purported to apply the Health Bill case approach, but also referred to proportionality, and *McGrath* v. *Limestone* [2014] IEHC 382.

[26] See, e.g., *Rafferty* v. *Minister for Agriculture* [2008] IEHC 344; *Unite the Union* v. *Minister for Finance* [2010] IEHC 354; *Sister Mary Christian* v. *Dublin City Council (No 1)* [2012] 2 IR 506; *NALM* v. *Breslin* [2017] IECA 283 and *Dowling* v. *Minister for Finance* [2018] IECA 300 (although notably in that case the Court of Appeal emphasised Article 40.3.2°'s reference to 'as far as practicable' as qualifying the duty of the State to safeguard property rights).

[27] See similarly T. Allen, *Property and the Human Rights Act 1998* (Oxford: Hart, 2005), p. 125, arguing '[i]n many property cases, the most important issue is the level of scrutiny: how much leeway does the court allow other decision-makers in setting general policy and resolving specific cases?' Aileen Kavanagh offers a useful definition of deference as '. . .a matter of assigning weight to the judgment of another, either where it is at variance with one's one assessment, or where one is uncertain of what the correct assessment should be.' A. Kavanagh, 'Deference or Defiance? The Limits of the Judicial Role in

reviewing legislative restrictions on the exercise of property rights.[28] This reflects general patterns of judicial resistance to intervening through judicial review on issues with distributive implications.[29] At the same time, the reference in Article 43.2 to 'the exigencies of the common good' and 'the principles of social justice' expressly engages judges in the consideration of matters with distributive implications.[30] The next sections outline the Irish judicial approach to reviewing the objectives, means, and impact of interferences with the exercise of property rights under the three standards of review that are variously applied in Irish constitutional property law.

5.4.1 *Objectives and Means Analysis*

In general, although they do not adopt an entirely hands-off approach, the Irish courts defer substantially to the legislature in assessing the legitimacy of the objective of a legislative or administrative interference with property rights before then going on to give it predominant weight in their analysis.[31] Limited supporting analysis is provided – as Kenny puts it, '. . .objectives are merely stated to be important.'[32] Moreover,

Constitutional Adjudication' in G. Huscroft (ed.), *Expounding the Constitution – Essays in Constitutional Theory* (Cambridge: Cambridge University Press, 2008), pp. 184–215, 185. On deference and proportionality more generally see, e.g., A. Kavanagh, *Constitutional Review under the UK Human Rights Act* (Cambridge: Cambridge University Press, 2009); A. Brady, *Proportionality and Deference under the UK Human Rights Act: An Institutionally Sensitive Approach* (Cambridge: Cambridge University Press, 2012) and T. R. S. Allan, 'Human Rights and Judicial Review: A Critique of Due Deference' (2006) 65 *Cambridge Law Journal* 671.

28 For full analysis, see R. Walsh, 'The Constitution, Property Rights and Proportionality' (n 4).

29 See, e.g., *O'Reilly* v. *Limerick Corporation* [1989] 1 ILRM 181, and *TD* v. *Minister for Education* [2001] 4 IR 259.

30 Frank Michelman accurately captures the nature of the distributional decision involved in his discussion of US takings law saying, '[a] court assigned to differentiate among impacts which are and are not "takings" is essentially engaged in deciding when government may execute public programs while leaving associated costs disproportionately concentrated upon one or a few persons.' F. I. Michelman, 'Property, Utility, and Fairness: Comments on the Ethical Foundations of "Just Compensation" Law' (1967) 80 *Harvard Law Review* 1165, 1165.

31 See, e.g., *Re Article 26 and the Employment Equality Bill 1996* (n 14), and *Re Article 26 and Part V of the Planning and Development Bill 1999* (n 916). See also Walsh, 'Property Rights and Proportionality' (n 4), 10–20.

32 D. Kenny, 'Proportionality and the Inevitability of the Local: A Comparative Localist Analysis of Canada and Ireland' (2018) 66 *American Journal of Comparative Law* 537, 543.

judges tend to define the legislature's objective with an eye to upholding or striking down the restriction; construction of the objective is influenced by the apparent fairness of the restriction. The public interest dominates judicial analysis, generally favouring collective concerns over individual property rights.

Each of the standards of review applied by the courts requires judges to assess the means adopted by the legislature to achieve its stated goal. However, the characterisation of the legislature's objective by a court and its determination of what means are rational or proportionate to achieve that end are closely interlinked.[33] Where the courts adopt a relatively specific purpose, the range of means that the legislature can adopt is narrowed, whereas if a broad objective is adopted, a very wide range of means could conceivably be adopted for its attainment. Accordingly, judges do much of the work in constitutional property rights adjudication when they attribute a hypothetical purpose to a measure. The dominant judicial trend in Irish constitutional property law has been to defer to the legislature's selection of means once the motivating objective has been held to be legitimate. Hypothetical justification suffices; anything done in pursuance of such an aim is constitutionally permissible if it could conceivably contribute to the aim's attainment.[34] Given that the courts require only hypothetical or conceivable justification and relevance, a very wide range of measures can conceivably be regarded as relevant to reconciling the exercise of competing constitutional rights or duties. For instance, if the aim of a measure is construed as the reconciliation of the competing property rights of plaintiffs and defendants, a huge range of means could be reasonably adopted in pursuance of that aim.

In *Rafferty* v. *Minister for Agriculture*, the Supreme Court appeared to distinguish object analysis and proportionality analysis, regarding the latter as focused on *means* rather than *ends*. Delivering the majority judgment, Denham CJ suggested that legislative exceptions to the default constitutional requirement for full compensation for the deprivation of property '...would be subject to strict scrutiny by the court as to the legitimacy of the grounds limiting full compensation for loss actually sustained, and subject also to the principle of proportionality.'[35] This appears to neglect the significance of objective analysis *as an aspect of*

[33] O. Doyle, *Constitutional Equality Law* (Dublin: Thomson Round Hall, 2004), p. 118.
[34] See, e.g., *Re Article 26 and Part V of the Planning and Development Bill* (n 9), and *Shirley* (n 9).
[35] *Rafferty v. Minister for Agriculture* [2014] IESC 61, [23].

proportionality analysis. It could alternatively be construed as advocating searching objective analysis within proportionality review in the compensation context in a move away from the predominantly deferential approach to the question of purpose in Irish constitutional property law, which is considered further in Chapter 7.

5.4.2 *Impact Analysis*

Of the standards of review considered in this chapter, only the proportionality principle expressly requires judges to consider the impact of a restriction on individual property rights. It states that restrictions should 'impair the right as little as possible' and 'be such that their effects on rights are proportional to the objective.'[36] The rationality standard and the *Health Bill case* approach may do so, but this depends on how 'fairness' and 'unjust attack' are construed and applied by the courts.[37]

In applying the proportionality principle, the Irish courts generally pay scant attention to the limbs of the test requiring 'minimal impairment' *and* overall proportionality between objective and impact.[38] By and large, Irish judges seem to presume that in deciding that an objective warrants the enactment of legislation that restricts property rights, the legislature considers the balance between the public interest and the affected individual right. Accordingly, they treat the legitimacy of the objective pursued by the legislation as largely determinative of its proportionality.[39] As such, Allen's assessment of proportionality review in the property jurisprudence of the European Court of Human Rights is equally applicable in the Irish context: '…reasons for judgments are cast in an almost impressionistic way, where the courts seem to do little more than say that a particular interference imposed an excessive impact on the victim or not'.[40]

[36] *Chaulk* (n 8) at 1335–36.

[37] *Tuohy* (n 10) requires judges to limit themselves to considering whether the balance struck in legislation '…is so contrary to reason and fairness as to constitute an unjust attack on some individual's constitutional rights'. The *Health Bill case* similarly asks whether a restriction is an unjust attack on property rights. *Re Article 26 and the Health (Amendment) (No. 2) Bill 2004* (n 2) at 201.

[38] For detailed elaboration of this point, see Walsh, 'The Constitution, Property Rights and Proportionality' (n 4), 23–7.

[39] See, e.g., *Re Article 26 and Part V of the Planning and Development Bill 1990* (n 9), and *BUPA Ireland Ltd* (n 9).

[40] Allen, *Property and the Human Rights Act* (n 27), p. 165. See similarly, Kenny, 'Proportionality and the Inevitability of the Local' (n 32), 555, arguing '[t]he typical

The Supreme Court's decision in *Re Article 26 and Part V of the Planning and Development Bill 1999*[41] is a good example of this tendency, although consideration of the impact of the impugned restriction on the exercise of property rights in that case may have been hampered by the fact that it was an Article 26 reference and so involved no actual plaintiffs.[42] The referred Bill provided for the contribution for social and affordable housing purposes of up to 20 per cent of a development in the form of sites, serviced sites, built units, or cash equivalent by developers of residential or mixed residential and commercial developments over four hectares. Developers were to receive compensation for that contribution reflecting the value of the land *prior to* the grant of planning permission (its so-called existing use value). In reviewing the constitutionality of the Bill, the Court deferred to the legislature's judgment on the validity of its objectives, concluding that they were socially just and advanced the common good. It said that the key question was whether the means employed constituted an unjust attack on property rights, or whether they impaired the affected property rights no more than was required by the aims of the Bill. The Court stated that a grant of planning permission led to an enhancement of land values, part of which could be clawed-back to help attain the public interest in social and affordable housing provision. On that basis, it asserted that the requirements of the proportionality test were satisfied:

> Applying the tests proposed by Costello J in *Heaney* v. *Ireland* and subsequently endorsed by this court, the court in the case of the present Bill is satisfied that the scheme passes those tests. They are rationally connected to an objective of sufficient importance to warrant interference with a constitutionally protected right and, given the serious social problems which they are designed to meet, they undoubtedly relate to concerns which, in a free and democratic society, should be regarded as pressing and substantial. At the same time, the court is satisfied that they impair those rights as little as possible and their effects on those rights are proportionate to the objectives sought to be attained.[43]

balancing analysis of an Irish court is to simply state, without analysis, that a measure is acceptable. This is often, but not always, said in the same breath as the declaration that the law has passed minimum impairment.'

41 See also *Blehein* v. *Minister for Health* [2009] 1 IR 275.

42 *Re Article 26 and Part V of the Planning and Development Bill 1990* (n 9). On the Article 26 reference procedure in the Irish Constitution, which allows the President to refer a Bill passed by the Houses of the Oireachtas to the Supreme Court for review before signing it into law, see Hogan, Whyte, Kenny and Walsh, *Kelly* (n 16), pp. 477–93.

43 *Re Article 26 and Part V of the Planning and Development Bill, 1999* (n 9) at 354.

In this way, the Court simply restated the proportionality principle as a justification for its conclusion that the Bill was constitutional rather than applying the principle to assess the balance struck between individual rights and the public interest.[44]

Kenny suggests two plausible explanations for the general lack of rigour in the impact analysis of the Irish courts: '[p]erhaps very little balancing at all is done in Ireland, or perhaps whatever balancing is done in the background always favours the state.'[45] Other potential explanations include: that the Irish courts may be slow to identify the distinct nature of the various questions posed by the proportionality principle; that they may be predisposed to defer to the legislature, or (most likely); that some combination of these factors operates in different cases to generate different degrees of stringency of review. The nature of the right to private property makes impact analysis particularly difficult, since as the previous chapter highlighted, the denominator by reference to which impact is to be analysed is unclear.[46] This ambiguity surrounding the applicable baseline in constitutional property rights adjudication means that impact analysis necessarily reproduces questions about the nature and content of the protected right as well as questions about the balance between the public interest and the protection of the right. This problem is not unique to constitutional property law, but arises acutely in that context.

Deferential application of the proportionality principle in constitutional property rights adjudication is not inevitable; the degree to which the public interest is allowed to obscure the impact of a restriction on individual rights depends on the attitude of the reviewing judge. It clearly is possible to carry out impact analysis if a judge is so minded, and there are rare instances of robust minimal impairment and/or impact review in Irish constitutional property doctrine.[47] A notable recent example is the

[44] As O'Neill notes, '[t]his passage, with its formulaic repetition of the *Heaney* test, seems rather disengaged. This passage appears at the end of a lengthy judgment in which the issues are discussed and while it detracts nothing from what precedes it, perhaps the more pertinent question is what does it add?' O'Neill, 'Property Rights and the Power of Eminent Domain' (n 5), p. 438.

[45] Kenny, 'Proportionality and the Inevitability of the Local' (n 32), 557.

[46] See similarly Lorna Fox O'Mahony, arguing proportionality analysis cannot be conducted without 'a coherent concept of the interest at stake in any given claim'. L. Fox-O'Mahony, *Conceptualising Home: Theories, Laws and Policies* (Oxford: Hart Publishing, 2007), p. 456.

[47] See, e.g., *Gilligan* (n 9). Budd J in *The Dunraven Limerick Estates Company* v. *The Commissioners for Public Works* [1974] 1 IR 113 engaged robustly with the impact of a

decision of the Court of Appeal in *Dowling* v. *Minister for Finance*, one of a number of decisions analysing the constitutionality of legislative responses to the economic crisis that adversely impacted upon property rights.[48] *Dowling* involved a constitutional challenge to a Ministerial direction order issued as part of a broader project of bank recapitalisation. Its effect was to compulsorily acquire shares in Irish Life and Permanent (an Irish financial services institution) in a manner that shareholders argued did not satisfy the 'minimal impairment' limb of the proportionality test. The shareholders objected to the recapitalisation on a number of grounds, notably: the failure to provide for a pre-emptive offer by shareholders; the failure to provide for an option whereby shares could be bought back if the bank proved to be over-capitalised following re-capitalisation; and the price paid for the shares, which they argued was artificially low due to Government announcements related to the recapitalisation and a 10 per cent discount on share value applied at the time of acquisition.

Hogan J held that the recapitalisation legislation clearly pursued a rational objective. He suggested that 'minimal impairment' could not be taken literally, arguing, '. . .some flexibility must necessarily be allowed to decision makers, not least in cases of this kind where the decision in question had large scale macro-economic implications and where it was required to be taken urgently and against the background of an acute emergency.'[49] He stressed that Article 40.3.2° required property rights to be defended against unjust attack 'as far as practicable', and rejected the alternatives raised by the shareholders as unrealistic in the circumstances prevailing at the time of the recapitalisation. Accordingly, the impugned direction order was upheld as imposing a proportionate limit on the exercise of property rights.

5.4.3 *The Role of the Delimiting Principles in Article 43.2 in Impact Analysis*

All of this raises the question of the effect, if any, of the language of the delimiting principles in Article 43.2 on the approach of judges to impact

restriction on affected property rights. Another good example is *Daly* (n 9). See also the victim focus displayed in the *Re Article 26 and the Health (Amendment) (No. 2) Bill 2004* (n 2), and *Re Article 26 and the Employment Equality Bill 1996* (n 14).

48 *Dowling* (n 26).

49 Ibid. at [145].

analysis; what is the doctrinal significance of the form of the Constitution's property rights provisions, in particular the progressive framing of the State's regulatory power?

In one interpretation, Article 43.2's reference to 'the exigencies of the common good' could be satisfied by an objective falling substantially short of being necessary in the interests of the common good. Judges hypothesise as to what could reasonably be regarded as being in the public interest in deciding if a restriction is justified.[50] Coupled with the presumption of constitutionality, this approach means that where there is any plausible public interest justification for a restriction, it must be upheld. An alternative interpretation takes the word 'exigencies' literally and requires that a particular restriction on the exercise of property rights be shown to be necessary to achieve the common good, taking in a consideration of means as well as objective. While the potential for hypothetical justification still exists under this interpretation, the justifications must meet the higher threshold of being conceivably *necessary* in the interests of the common good. A further distinction can be drawn between the standard by reference to which 'exigencies' are assessed – necessity, or something less – and the manner in which the chosen standard is applied to particular cases – looking for hypothetical or actual justification on the basis of the standard adopted. Regardless of the interpretation of 'exigencies' adopted, a judge must decide whether to require a restriction to be factually or actually justified in the particular case in the interests of the common good, or whether to accept a hypothetical justification. These two considerations overlap and are rarely distinguished in judicial analysis.[51]

In most cases, a hypothetical justification meeting the chosen standard of 'exigencies' has been held to suffice.[52] However, in rare instances, a

[50] Doyle notes, '[t]here is a crucial difference between questioning whether something is justified or whether it could reasonably be justified. The latter question imports some deference to the judgment of someone else, in the case of constitutional adjudication that of the Oireachtas.' *Constitutional Equality Law* (n 33), p. 113.

[51] See, e.g., *Central Dublin Development Association* v. *Attorney General* (1975) 109 ILTR 69 at 84, where Kenny J argued that courts should consider, '... whether the legislation has been passed with a view to reconciling the exercise of property rights with the exigencies of the common good, whether the Oireachtas may reasonably hold that view and whether the restriction would be unjust without the payment of compensation'. In *Shirley* (n 9), Peart J favoured actual justification, but adopted a deferential understanding of the meaning of 'the exigencies of the common good'.

[52] See, e.g., *Condon* v. *Minister for Labour*, (11 June 1980) (HC); *J & J Haire Company Ltd* (n 9), and *Madigan* v. *AG* [1986] ILRM 136. For analysis, see Kenny, arguing in

more searching approach has been adopted by the courts.[53] For example, the Supreme Court in the *Health Bill case* sought actual as opposed to hypothetical justification for the retrospective abrogation of the rights of action of elderly people to recover illegal nursing home charges levied upon them by the State. The Attorney General argued that the Bill was justified by the need to protect the public finances against the cost of repaying the illegal charges, which it suggested would amount to €500 million. The Court held that although this unexpected financial burden was substantial, it was not '. . .anything like catastrophic', and could be dealt with by the State through ordinary budgetary management.[54] Consequently, it determined that the asserted legislative objective did not actually justify the restriction imposed on property rights by the Bill.[55] The stringency of the Court's review was clearly influenced by the profile of the victims of the proposed restriction, who were characterised as vulnerable, and by the retrospective nature of the interference with individual rights. In addition, the State had knowingly imposed charges without legal authority over a long period of time, which the Court held weakened its claim to avoid making repayments.

5.5 Conclusions

Proportionality analysis forms a central part of constitutional property rights adjudication in many jurisdictions with constitutional property clauses, and progressive property scholars have argued for its transplantation to jurisdictions where it is not currently applied.[56] For example, Alexander points to the experience of Canada, Australia, Germany, and South Africa and suggests that the application of a general proportionality principle in US Takings law would mean '. . .the courts would more frankly disclose what considerations were the driving force in their decisions and

'Proportionality and the Inevitability of the Local' (n 32), 544: '[t]hey have never been willing to look to subjective motivation, and, without much sustained analysis in the constitutional context, have chosen to hypothesize the motivations for laws.'

53 See, e.g., *Blake* v. *The Attorney General* [1982] 1 IR 117, and *An Blascaod Mór Teoranta* v. *Commissioners for Public Works* [1998] IEHC 38.

54 *Re Article 26 and the Health (Amendment) (No. 2) Bill 2004* (n 2) at 205.

55 Ibid. at 206.

56 On the international trend see, e.g., van der Walt and Walsh, 'Comparative Constitutional Property Law' (n 1), pp. 201–3, describing proportionate effect on property owners as a validity requirement for regulatory public interest limitations on the use of private property. See also A. J. van der Walt, *Constitutional Property Law*, 3rd ed. (Cape Town: Juta Publishing, 2011), pp. 241–42.

they would more directly acknowledge competing considerations and the reasons why those considerations did not carry the day.'[57]

The Irish experience of the proportionality principle in constitutional property rights adjudication presents a less optimistic picture. It suggests that application of the proportionality principle will not in and of itself prompt a judicial turn to what Mulvaney terms 'transparency' concerning the mediation of property rights and social justice.[58] Generally applicable standards of review such as proportionality and rationality have in fact obscured the reasons for decisions in Irish constitutional property law, thereby reducing clarity and predictability concerning the scope of protection for property rights. Rather than acknowledging the choices that they are required to make in constitutional property rights cases and articulating and defending them through reasoned argument, the Irish courts attempt to cast their decisions as the products of the application of outcome-determinative standards of review. They treat the proportionality and rationality principles as rules that can be recited to justify a conclusion, when in fact they provide analytical frameworks for judgment, or as Michelman puts it, 'a protocol for use in constitutional discourses'.[59] The proportionality and rationality principles do not *answer* the core questions concerning fairness that arise in constitutional property rights adjudication, and in fact do not even reach some of them, notably the question of the range of interests protected by a constitutional property rights guarantee that was considered in the previous chapter.

However, judicial obfuscation concerning the reasons for outcomes in constitutional property rights adjudication is not a necessary or inevitable consequence of proportionality or rationality review. These standards of review can be applied with much more rigour.[60] To do so, judges must squarely address the value choices that are necessarily involved in constitutional property rights adjudication. As Alexander puts it, '[a] legal culture that is still preoccupied with denying that judges make

[57] Alexander, *The Global Debate over Constitutional Property* (n 3), pp. 204–5.

[58] T. M. Mulvaney, 'Progressive Property Moving Forward' (2014) 5 *Calif L Rev Circ* 349, 358–61.

[59] F. I. Michelman, 'Proportionality Outside the Courts (With Special Reference to Popular and Political Constitutionalism)', in V. Jackson and M. Tushnet (eds.), *Proportionality: New Frontiers, New Challenges* (Cambridge: Cambridge University Press, 2020) p. 30.

[60] See e.g. T. Hickman, 'The Substance and Structure of Proportionality' (2008) *Public Law* 694, arguing for the need for a more considered and principled approach to proportionality analysis in the UK context. See also Kavanagh, *Constitutional Review under the UK Human Rights Act* (n 27); Brady, *Proportionality and Deference under the UK Human Rights Act* (n 27).

controversial value choices is one in which a general, Canadian-style proportionality balancing may not play well.'[61] Article 43.2 gives important distinctive guidance about the nature and purpose of the State's regulatory power, which ought to be attended to in constitutional property rights adjudication. As O'Donnell J argued in the Supreme Court in *Nottinghamshire County Council* v. *B*: '. . .it is an error to approach the constitutional issue by simply asking, almost in the abstract, whether any particular provision is proportionate as an almost self-standing test of constitutionality and detached from careful consideration of the text and the values necessarily implied by it.'[62] The *Health Bill case* approach marks a welcome refocusing on the distinctive treatment of property rights in Article 43, but it has not been consistently applied and its relationship to the general standards of review has not been explained by the courts.

If general standards such as proportionality and rationality are to be retained in the constitutional property context, greater frankness is required from judges concerning the reasons for their decisions, as well as an acknowledgment of the fundamental question of fairness that lies behind the general standards. Such clarity would allow patterns and principles to emerge within the framework of the contextual adjudication presupposed by those standards.[63] The task given to judges by Articles 40.3.2° and 43.2 is at once simple and intuitive, and highly complex and opaque. As will be seen further in the next chapter's analysis of the multi-factorial judicial enquiry required by Article 40.3.2°, clearly articulating outcomes based on a standard such as 'unjust attack' is challenging for judges. As Michelman puts it, '[f]airness. . .is a subtle compound, whose presence in any given situation we can often sense. . .but only through a mental chemistry hard to reconstruct except through impressionistic, almost conclusory discourse.'[64] However, a sustained and considered attempt on the part of judges to offer reasons to support their applications of standards of review in the constitutional property context would help to clarify the relative scope of individual freedoms and State powers in respect of property.

[61] Alexander, *The Global Debate Over Constitutional Property* (n 3), p. 214.

[62] *Nottinghamshire County Council* (n 5) at [87].

[63] J. W. Singer, 'The Rule of Reason in Property Law' (2013) 46 *UC Davis Law Review* 1369, 1389.

[64] Michelman, 'Property, Utility, and Fairness' (n 30), p. 1249.

6

Adjudicating Fairness

The 'Unjust Attack' Assessment

6.1 Introduction

As we have seen, the Irish courts review public law interferences with individual property rights to determine whether they unjustly attack such rights. They carry out such review cognisant of the Constitution's requirement that the exercise of property rights should be 'regulated by the principles of social justice', which informs the State's constitutional power to delimit the exercise of property rights to secure the 'exigencies of the common good'. In this chapter, the scope of that regulatory power is analysed by identifying and assessing the factors that the Irish courts consider in adjudicating fairness through the prism of Article 40.3.2°'s 'unjust attack' standard. As such, it analyses the meaning that courts give through case-law to a broadly stated constitutional test of fairness.[1] The focus is primarily on delimitations that fall short of outright deprivation, with Chapters 7 and 8 considering expropriation and compensation issues.

In *J & J Haire & Company Ltd* v. *Minister for Health*, McMahon J in the High Court gave a good synopsis of the doctrine that will be explored, saying that 'unjust' in Article 40.3.2° '. . .refers to matters such as retrospectivity, lack of fair procedures, unreasonableness and irrationality, discrimination, lack of proportionality and, in some cases, lack of compensation.'[2] Compensation will be considered in Chapter 8, while proportionality was addressed in Chapter 5. The nature of the other factors identified by McMahon J and the role that they play in judicial determinations of fairness in constitutional property rights adjudication will be assessed in this chapter. That assessment shows that judges are often reluctant to squarely address the distributional issues raised by a broadly

[1] On this approach to clarifying the meaning of 'fairness' standards, see J. W. Singer, 'Justifying Regulatory Takings' (2015) 41 *Ohio Northern University Law Review* 601.

[2] [2009] IEHC 562, approved by Kearns P in *Unite the Union* v. *Minister for Finance* [2010] IEHC 354.

stated constitutional test of fairness, opting instead to employ other factors as loose proxies for fairness. That strategy allows identifiable patterns to emerge from judicial decisions over time notwithstanding the absence of upfront 'transparency' concerning the core question of fairness.[3] However, most of the factors employed deflect direct analysis of the tension between property rights and social justice through a non-property focus. Thus even where judges are expressly mandated by progressively framed constitutional property clauses to mediate that tension, they prove reluctant to do so directly.

Section 6.2 considers the relevance of retrospectivity and related Rule of Law considerations. Section 6.3 considers fair procedures. Section 6.4 analyses the significance of unreasonableness and irrationality in legislative interferences with property rights. Section 6.5 turns to discrimination and distributional fairness. Section 6.6 concludes.

6.2 'Retrospectivity'

6.2.1 Introduction

Retrospectivity weighs against the constitutionality of a restriction on the exercise of property rights because it interferes with an owner's security of expectation and is inconsistent with general rule of law principles prioritised in Irish constitutional law.[4] In most cases, the Irish courts avoid finding retrospective effect through the application of interpretative presumptions such as the presumption against interferences with vested rights and the presumption of constitutionality.[5] These are

[3] T. M. Mulvaney, 'Progressive Property Moving Forward' (2014) 5 *Calif L Rev Circ* 349, 358–61.

[4] Jeremy Waldron describes the Rule of Law in formal and procedural terms as follows: 'Laws should be clear, public, and prospective, they should take the form of stable and learnable rules, they should be administered fairly and impartially, they should operate as limits on state action, and they should apply equally to each and every person, no matter how rich and powerful they are.' J. Waldron, *The Rule of Law and the Measure of Property (Hamlyn Lectures)* (Cambridge: Cambridge University Press, 2012), p. 45. See also, pp. 6–7. On the Rule of Law generally see also, e.g., A. V. Dicey, *Introduction to the Study of the Law of the Constitution*, 8th ed., (Indianapolis, IN: Liberty Classics, 1982); F. Hayek *The Constitution of Liberty* (Chicago: University of Chicago Press, 1960); J. Raz, 'The Rule of Law and its Virtue' in *The Authority of Law* (Oxford: Clarendon Press, 1979), p. 224 and L. Fuller, *The Morality of Law* (New Haven, CT: Yale University Press, 1964).

[5] For a full analysis of the presumption of constitutionality in Irish constitutional law, see G. W. Hogan, G. F. Whyte, D. Kenny and R. Walsh, *Kelly: The Irish Constitution*, 5th ed., (Dublin: Bloomsbury Professional, 2018), pp. 982–1009.

generally applicable legal principles that are not rooted in the property rights clauses of the Constitution.[6] However, in some cases the Irish courts have directly addressed the relevance of retrospectivity to the constitutionality of interferences with individual property rights. In such cases, retrospectivity does not always result in a finding of 'unjust attack', but it heightens the attention that judges pay to the protection of the adversely affected rights.

6.2.2 *The Presumption against Interference with Vested Rights*

The presumption against interference with vested rights requires legislation to be interpreted insofar as is possible to avoid retrospectively interfering with property rights, thereby guaranteeing owners' security of expectations concerning their property. It is a specific application of the more general presumption against retrospective application.

A good example of the presumption against retrospectivity in Irish constitutional property law is *Hamilton* v. *Hamilton*, which concerned the scope of application of the Family Home Protection Act, 1976.[7] Section 6.3 provided that where a spouse purported to convey an interest in the family home without the written consent of the other spouse, the purported conveyance would be null and void. The plaintiff obtained an order for specific performance of a contract for the sale of the disputed property in 1975, but before the sale closed, the vendor's wife applied to court for a declaration that the conveyance was void under the terms of s. 3, as she had not consented in writing. In the High Court, Gannon J granted this request and stayed all further proceedings in the specific performance action. The plaintiff appealed this decision to the Supreme Court. The Court held that if s. 3 applied to pre-Act contracts for sale, it would deprive the purchaser of his rights and interests in respect of the property without any compensation.[8] O'Higgins CJ rejected the

[6] For example, the Supreme Court in *Albatros Feeds Ltd* v. *Minister for Agriculture* held that the issuance of 'seizure and detention notices' by the Minister in relation to feeding products could result in the deprivation of private property and its potential destruction, meaning that such powers had to be clearly authorised by law. Given the '...drastic intrusion into individual property rights' involved, the Court invalidated such notices where no legal authority existed for them. [2007] 1 IR 221 at 235. See also *In re Linen Supply of Ireland Ltd* [2010] IEHC 28 at [21].

[7] [1982] IR 466. Other important examples include *Vone Securities* v. *Cooke* [1979] IR 59; *In re Deansrath Investments* [1974] IR 228; *Limerick Corporation* v. *Sheridan* (1956) 90 ILTR 50 and *Neurendale Ltd* v. *Dublin City Council* [2009] IEHC 588.

[8] *Hamilton* (n 7) at 476.

suggestion that the Act could have been intended to upset contractual rights that pre-dated its enactment, because such interference would constitute an unjust attack on property rights contrary to Article 40.3.2° of the Constitution.[9] Property rights were on both sides of the scales in *Hamilton*; on the one hand, the plaintiff's interest in the security of his investment and on the other hand, the defendant's interest in the secure possession of her home. Since, as the majority saw it, prior to the Act the law had explicitly fostered the former expectation but had not fostered the latter expectation, the presumption against retrospective effect gave the plaintiff's expectation primacy.[10] In this way, the presumption against retrospectivity functions somewhat like the 'first in time' presumption in private law, prioritising property rights in the order of their vesting.[11]

Grealy v. *Dublin County Council* demonstrates that this temporal dimension influences not only competition between competing property rights, as in *Hamilton*, but also the degree of susceptibility of property rights to uncompensated public law control.[12] *Grealy* concerned the interpretation of s. 25 of the Local Government (Planning and Development) Act 1976, which provided that where development was carried out pursuant to a permission that contained an explicit or implicit condition requiring the developer to provide or maintain open space, the planning authority could serve notice on the owner requiring him/her to provide, level, plant, or otherwise adapt or maintain the open space in a specified manner. Absent compliance with such a condition, the planning authority could put in motion compulsory acquisition proceedings. The defendants in 1984 became the owners of a plot of undeveloped land in a housing estate that was built pursuant to a

[9] Ibid. at 477. Similarly, Henchy J held that since the 1976 Act was not clearly retrospective in effect, the spouse's veto could only apply to agreements for sale entered into after the coming into operation of the Act. Unlike O'Higgins CJ, Henchy J did not consider whether the Act would have been unconstitutional if it expressly intended to interfere with pre-Act contracts, simply commenting that the State's primary responsibilities in respect of property rights arose under Article 40.3, but that the State's duty to respect those rights would have to be balanced with its other constitutional duties, such as the protection of marriage and the family. Ibid. at 487. Griffin and Hederman JJ agreed with both Henchy J and O'Higgins CJ.

[10] Contractual rights were protected through similar reasoning in *Re Ranks (Ireland) Ltd* [1989] 1 IR 1 at 7.

[11] On property and time in the private law context, see usefully C. R. Beitz, 'Property and Time' (2018) 27 *Journal of Political Philosophy* 419.

[12] [1990] 1 IR 77. *See also Child* v. *Wicklow County Council* [1995] 2 IR 447 at 451.

permission granted in 1957, and the council sought to apply s. 25 to their land. Blayney J held that to allow such application would be to impair the defendant's ownership of the plot by making it liable to be taken away in circumstances created for the first time by s. 25 and by imposing a new maintenance obligation.[13]

6.2.3 *Retrospectivity as 'Unjust Attack'*

Where an interference with property rights is found to be retrospective, the courts identify procedural protections for adversely affected owners as relevant factors in preventing an 'unjust attack' on property rights.[14] However, the decision of the Supreme Court in *Re Article 26 and the Health (Amendment) (No 2) Bill, 2004* demonstrates how the retrospective nature of an interference with property rights can trigger a finding of 'unjust attack'.[15] The legislature proposed to enact legislation to retrospectively declare lawful the imposition and payment of nursing home charges that were levied by successive Governments without any legal basis and with knowledge of the lack of legal basis.[16] The aim of the Bill was to avoid the costs of meeting claims for the *recovery* of the charges that had been paid, not to retrospectively penalise non-payment of such charges. Its practical effect was to expropriate a chose in action, namely the right to sue to recover the monies paid to the State. As was seen in Chapter 4, the Supreme Court recognised such a right as protected by the Constitution's property rights guarantees, as well as a personal right. The Supreme Court held that those who had received care were legally entitled to receive it free of charge, and accordingly that the charges

13 Ibid. at 81.

14 See, e.g., *Chestvale Properties* v. *Glackin* [1993] 3 IR 35, where Murphy J stated *obiter* that the statutory requirement that a Minister be satisfied that the public interest demand the appointment of an inspector to a particular company meant that the legislation in question appropriately balanced the common good and social justice.

15 [2005] 1 IR 105.

16 In *Maud McInerney, in re* [1976–67] ILRM 229, the Supreme Court had held that the imposition of charges on medical cardholders in receipt of medical care in the relevant institutions was unauthorised. In addition, the Court in the *Health Bill case* noted that before the commencement of the Health (Miscellaneous Provisions) Act 2001, the entitlement to free care only extended to medical card holders, whereas after 1 July 2001, it was extended to all persons over 70. The Court noted, '[t]hus from the entry into force of that provision, all persons aged 70 or more were automatically and by that fact alone deemed to be fully eligible. Thereafter, any charge imposed on such a person was indisputably imposed in direct contravention of s. 53 (2) of the Act of 1970', [2005] 1 IR 105, at 175–76.

imposed on them were unlawful. As such, any recovery of those charges by individuals who paid them could not be characterised as a windfall.[17] It did not matter that recipients had not necessarily expected their care to be free. The Bill was designed to alter the legal effect of completed transactions in circumstances where that legal effect had been created by statute.[18] Consequently, the Court concluded that the retrospective provisions of the Bill were an unjust attack on property rights.[19] This decision reflects the view that individuals are entitled to rely on the law as it exists at the time that they perform various actions affecting their property rights, echoing in this respect Bentham's characterisation of property rights as guaranteeing the preservation of the legal status quo once relied upon. The courts will guarantee security in the legal conditions upon which expectations are legitimately based, at least absent some relatively compelling countervailing public interest. The decision in *Health Amendment Bill* requires no evidence of actual reliance – even where no expectations have *in fact* built up around a law, retrospective abrogation of legally acquired property rights will not usually be permissible.[20]

The application of a rule against retrospective effect in the context of property rights has the potential to impose high costs on the exchequer, as in the *Health Bill case*.[21] A further complicating factor is the fact that even *prospective* interferences with property rights often adversely impact upon established expectations and investments in respect of the future use and value of land and other property.[22] To the extent that retrospective interference with vested property rights is involved, rule of law concerns are engaged, triggering a strict judicial approach. However, where prospective interferences upset settled expectations in respect of the future use, possession, or value of property, judges return to the

[17] Ibid. at 195.

[18] Ibid. at 204.

[19] The absence of retrospective interference with vested rights was stressed by McMahon J in *J & J Haire & Company Ltd* (n 2) as a factor tending to show that the impugned restriction was not an unjust attack on property rights.

[20] For discussion of reliance ideas as a justification for government forbearance in respect of property rights, see L. S. Underkuffler, 'Property, Sovereignty, and the Public Trust' (2017) 18 *Theoretical Inquiries in Law* 329, 334–41. See also J. W. Singer, 'The Reliance Interest in Property Revisited' (2011) 7 *Harvard Journal of the Legal Left* 79.

[21] In the *Health Bill case*, the State argued that the figure to be repaid for recovery claims within the Statute of Limitations could be in the order of 500 million euros.

[22] On this point, see Christopher Serkin, 'Existing Uses and the Limits of Land Use Regulations' (2009) 84 *New York University Law Review* 1222, 1264.

foundational question of fairness. As Underkuffler puts it, a finding that government forbearance should extend to *prospective* interferences with established expectations '. . .is rooted in the quasi-moral, common, and intuitively powerful idea that government should forbear because the individual *deserves to be protected* against changes in the rules of the property-entitlement game.'[23] The test of 'unjust attack' in Article 40.3.2° poses precisely this quasi-moral question for judges.[24]

6.3 'Lack of Fair Procedures'

6.3.1 Introduction

Administrative processes established by legislation can impact on property rights in diverse contexts, for example planning control, social welfare, land registration, and environmental protection. This raises complex questions of administrative law, since it connects the protection of property rights to '. . .the accountable and legitimate application of such regulatory processes.'[25] The presence of structures for guaranteeing fair procedures, and their proper application, impacts on the constitutionality of individual administrative decisions and the legislative schemes that generate such decisions. If burdens are imposed transparently through fair processes, there is arguably less scope for arbitrary or unfair singling-out of individuals to bear disproportionate burdens in the public interest.[26] In addition, participation rights allow an owner to argue *ex ante* that his or her property rights should not be restricted in the

[23] Underkuffler, 'Property, Sovereignty, and the Public Trust' (n 23), 334. See also L. S. Underkuffler, *The Idea of Property* (Oxford: Oxford University Press, 2003), pp. 28–30, discussing property's 'temporal dimension'.

[24] To quote Waldron, '[w]e can't have the Rule of Law endorsing a fanatic stabilization which underwrites every expectation of profit that people happen to have conceived in a particular legal context.' Waldron, *The Rule of Law* (n 4), p. 71. He suggests that the principle prohibiting retroactive legislation should not apply to statutes that affect the use of land purchased before enactment, at least where no specific action inconsistent with the statute was taken prior to enactment (e.g., the commencement of construction prior to a building restriction being imposed) – pp. 83–4.

[25] E. Scotford and R. Walsh, 'The Symbiosis of Property and English Environmental Law – Property Rights in a Public Law Context' (2013) 76 *Modern Law Review* 1010, 1040.

[26] See R. Walsh, 'Belfast Corporation v. O.D. Cars [1959]: Setting Parameters for Restricting Use' in S. Douglas, R. Hickey and E. Waring eds., *Landmark Cases in Property Law* (Oxford: Hart, 2015) p. 227, pp. 247–51, arguing that good participation can help to establish reciprocity of advantage, whereby burdened owners are shown to be benefited by regulatory restrictions imposed on their rights.

public interest, thereby providing a means of vindicating owners' interests in secure possession and control of use.[27]

A restriction on the exercise of property rights or a deprivation of property is more likely to be found to be an 'unjust attack' where there is no provision for owner-participation. In such circumstances, courts will generally 'read-in' procedural rights by interpreting the provision in accordance with the presumption of constitutionality. Three key overlapping procedural safeguards emerge from the Irish doctrine: a right to be heard, a right to notice, and a right to challenge an adverse decision.[28] Characteristic of these safeguards is their importance in securing an effective voice for owners in administrative processes that have the potential to adversely affect their property rights, as distinct from a right to veto such decisions or a right to compensation for losses flowing from such decisions.

6.3.2 *The Right to Be Heard*

The right to be heard has been consistently emphasised by the Irish courts as legitimising restrictions imposed on property rights through planning control. This has shaped judicial interpretation of such restrictions and the outcomes of constitutional challenges.

For example, on the interpretation point, in *Finn* v. *Bray UDC*,[29] Butler J held that one of the purposes of a development plan was to control and regulate the use and development of property by setting out the kinds of development that would be permitted within the relevant area.[30] Since a plan could adversely affect property values, he interpreted the Local Government (Planning and Development) Act, 1963 as guaranteeing owners notice of proposed plans and an opportunity to be heard prior to their adoption.[31] In the context of a constitutional challenge to planning control in *Central Dublin Development Association* v. *Attorney General*, Kenny J invoked the procedural rights afforded to owners under

[27] For full discussion of this argument, see R. Walsh, 'The Evolving Relationship between Property and Participation in English Planning Law' in N. Hopkins (ed.) *Modern Studies in Property Law: Volume 7* (Oxford: Hart Publishing, 2013), p. 263, especially pp. 281–82.

[28] Various derivative and related procedural rights have also been recognised. These include for example the right to clear procedures, the right to reasons, and the right to access materials required to make effective representations.

[29] [1969] IR 169.

[30] Ibid. at 174.

[31] Ibid. at 178.

various provisions of the Local Government (Planning and Development) Act 1963 Act in support of his decision to uphold the restrictions imposed by the Act on property rights.[32] Similarly, in *Byrne* v. *Fingal County Council*, which involved a challenge to a decision on the location of a halting site, McKechnie J reiterated the importance of participation rights to the constitutionality of the planning code, emphasising the significance of allowing all individuals to be informed about proposals and to have their views heard and taken into account.[33] McKechnie J concluded that where proper procedure is followed, those adversely affected by planning decisions '. . .must suffer the pain, undergo the loss and concede to the public good.'[34]

The constitutional significance of the right to be heard in the administration of restrictions on property rights has also been emphasised by the Irish courts beyond the planning context. As a general principle, they have held that administrators are required to engage effectively with owners and to give real meaning to their right to be heard in matters that affect their property rights.[35] This emerged most notably in *Dellway Investments* v. *National Asset Management Agency*.[36] There, it was contended that fair procedures were constitutionally required to be afforded to an individual or company before the National Asset Management Agency (NAMA) decided to acquire its loan agreements with banks. NAMA was created by the National Asset Management Agency Act 2009, the purpose of which was stated in its long-title to be '. . .to address a serious threat to the economy and to the systemic stability of credit institutions in the State.' Its function was to acquire 'eligible assets' (defined in s. 2 of the Act) and manage them to maximise the return to the State.[37] The basic aim was to restructure bank debt by transferring loans of systemic significance

[32] (1975) 109 ILTR 69 at 89. Kenny J held that planning authorities were bound under the Act to consider objections in relation to the boundaries of obsolete areas (which were designated areas that could be compulsorily acquired for redevelopment) and determined, '. . .any objector is entitled to require that he should be given an opportunity to state his case before a person appointed by the planning authority.'

[33] [2001] 4 IR 565.

[34] Ibid. at 580. As Finlay Geoghehan J noted in *North Wall Quay Property Holding Company Ltd* v. *Dublin Docklands Authority*, owners can take comfort in the fact that any development permitted in the area controlled by a plan will be required to conform to such a plan: [2008] IEHC 305 at [68].

[35] *The Dunraven Limerick Estates Company* v. *The Commissioners of Public Works* [1974] 1 IR 113 at 133 and 139.

[36] [2011] IESC 14, [2011] 4 IR 1.

[37] The power to prescribe classes of bank assets susceptible to acquisition is conferred on the Minister for Finance by section 69 of the 2009 Act, which was done through the National Asset Management Agency (Designation of Eligible Bank Assets) Regulations 2009.

(generally associated with development land) to a state body that would work out those loans in an orderly fashion, thereby removing uncertainty surrounding development loans and restoring confidence in the Irish banking sector. Two key property rights points arose in *Dellway* in relation to this legislative scheme. First, the appellants argued that they had an entitlement to be heard in advance of the acquisition of their loans based on the significant impact that acquisition would have on their property rights. Second, the appellants argued that the Act was an 'unjust attack' on their property rights insofar as the breadth of its definition of eligible assets and the vagueness of the criteria for the exercise of the Agency's power of acquisition impeded challenges to acquisition decisions.

The Supreme Court decided that that the potential adverse impact of the acquisition of the appellants' bank loans by NAMA required that they be afforded fair procedures, including a right to be heard, in advance of any acquisition. The Court identified a real risk of adverse effects flowing from such acquisition, including the loss of the right to deal freely with a property portfolio and the loss of the equity of redemption *qua* mortgagor. Accordingly, the Court held that the appellant had a right to be heard notwithstanding the urgent nature of the economic crisis that the 2009 Act was designed to address.[38] Murray CJ subsequently delivered the Court's separate judgment on the constitutionality of the Act, concluding that it was a proportionate interference with property rights.[39] He held that the procedural protections for owners identified as a result of the Supreme Court's decision on the impugned acquisition decision mitigated in part the possibility of any 'unjust attack'.

6.3.3 *The Right to Notice*

Effective participation rights demand a right to notice of a decision that may adversely affect property rights, for example to enable an owner to exercise the right to be heard.[40] The right to notice is often secured by the Irish courts through their application of the presumption of constitutionality. For

NAMA in turn is given the power to acquire an eligible bank asset of a participating institution under section 84(1) of the 2009 Act.

38 As Fennelly J put it, '[i]f a decision made concerning me or my property is liable to affect my interests in a material way, it is fair and reasonable that I should be allowed to put forward reasons why it should not be made or that it should take a particular form. It would be unjust to exclude me from being heard.' *Dellway* (n 36) at [99].

39 [2011] IESC 13.

40 *The Dunraven Limerick Estates Company* (n 35) at 134.

example, in *O'Callaghan* v. *Commissioners for Public Works*, the plaintiff argued that the making of a preservation order in respect of his land was an 'unjust attack' on his property rights, because s. 8 of the National Monuments Act 1930 (as amended) did not require notice to be given prior to the making of such an order or provide for an opportunity for review or appeal of an order. The Supreme Court presumed that the Commissioners would exercise their powers constitutionally by giving notice of their intention to make a preservation order where practicable.[41]

However, a right to notice is not always guaranteed – the public interest may justify a lack of notice. For example, *National Asset Loan Management Ltd* v. *McMahon* involved a constitutional challenge to two key provisions of the National Asset Management Agency Act 2009: section 84, which sets out the circumstances in which NAMA may acquire loans, and section 147, providing for the appointment of a statutory receiver by NAMA without notice in prescribed circumstances. Charleton J in the High Court stressed that the Act addressed a serious threat to the economy. He further emphasised that a borrower adversely affected by the Act could avail of a wider array of substantive and procedural rights than those arising in a wholly private context.[42] In respect of the criteria for acquisition, he held that in light of the Irish experience over the course of the economic crisis, it was unsurprising that banks were given no say in determining the assets to be transferred to NAMA, as that would have undermined the scheme of the Act.[43] He upheld the constitutionality of section 147 on the basis that circumstances could arise wherein the appointment of a receiver without notice might be justifiable on a prudential basis, e.g., to avoid a real risk of destruction or disposal of assets or where a borrower failed to reply to requests for submissions.[44]

6.3.4 The Right to Challenge an Adverse Decision

The right to challenge an administrative decision adversely affecting one's property rights has been recognised by the Irish courts.[45] The

[41] [1985] ILRM 364 at 368–69. See also *Eircell Ltd* v. *Leitrim County Council* [2000] 1 IR 479; *MacPharthalain* v. *The Commissioners of Public Works* [1992] 1 IR 111 (HC), [1994] 3 IR 353 (SC); *ESB* v. *Cork County Council* 28 June 2000 (HC, Finnegan J).

[42] *O'Callaghan* (n 41) at [46], [47].

[43] Ibid.

[44] Ibid. at [45].

[45] See, e.g., *Cassels* v. *Dublin Corporation* [1963] 1 IR 193 on the right to challenge a demolition order.

Supreme Court has held that procedures for challenging an adverse administrative decision must be clear and accessible to satisfy the requirements of natural and constitutional justice.[46] The existence of an internal appeals mechanism weighs in favour of the constitutionality of a legislative scheme that restricts property rights.[47] The extent to which an owner is entitled to an *independent* appeal remains unsettled in Irish law. In *O'Brien* v. *Bord na Móna,* the Supreme Court held that the absence of a right of appeal or external confirmation of a compulsory acquisition order did not violate constitutional rights.[48] However, in *Reid* v. *Industrial Development Agency (Ireland),* the Supreme Court suggested *obiter* that an opportunity for independent appeal or review should form a part of all compulsory acquisition procedures.[49]

6.3.5 *Participation Rules as a Tool for Mediating Property Rights and Social Justice*

The increasing judicial focus on administrative procedures as spaces where property rights can be balanced with competing rights and/or the public interest reflects the expanded scope of the regulatory state and its intensifying impact on property rights. While property rights were traditionally understood to be protected by either 'property rules', granting owners a veto power, or 'liability rules', entitling owners to compensation for loss of rights, 'participation rules' are an increasingly important additional source of protection for owners.[50] However, they are sometimes included in statutory schemes to secure wider stakeholder involvement rather than to protect property rights. As such, they are an important legal tool for mediating individual and wider social interests in property. The participation rules considered in this section reflect what

[46] *Hygeia Chemicals Ltd* v. *Irish Medicines Board* [2010] IESC 4.

[47] See, e.g., *Deighan* v. *Hearne* [1986] 1 IR 603 (HC), [1990] 1 IR 499 (SC).

[48] [1983] 1 IR 255.

[49] [2015] IESC 83 at paras [83]–[84].

[50] The distinction between 'property rules' and 'liability rules' has its origins in G. Calabresi and A. D. Melamed, 'Property Rules, Liability Rules, and Inalienability Rules: One View of the Cathedral' (1972) 85 *Harvard Law Review* 1089, in particular at 1092. It has been developed by other scholars; see, e.g., H. E. Smith, 'Exclusion and Property Rules in the Law of Property' (2004) 90 *Virginia Law Review* 965, 980; A. Bell and G. Parchomovsky, 'Pliability Rules' (2002) 101 *Michigan Law Review* 1, 7; C. Rodgers, 'Nature's Place? Property Rights, Property Rules and Environmental Stewardship' (2009) 68 *Cambridge Law Journal* 550, 565.

Rose refers to as 'mud doctrine' rather than 'crystal rules'.[51] Whereas 'crystalline' property rules and liability rules presume a fixed fungible entitlement on the part of an owner, participation rules treat the scope of an owner's freedom of possession and use of private property as context-dependent. They treat the scope of an owner's rights in respect of the use and/or possession of property as, at least in the public sphere, dynamic and contextually determined.

In this way, the prioritisation of inclusive administrative procedures reflects Singer's 'democratic model' of property, according to which property is collectively constructed through an ongoing, value-focused public/private dialectic.[52] Following this approach, the scope of private ownership is determined bearing in mind that the protection afforded to property rights *through* democratic decisions in turn impacts *on* democracy.[53] The increasing priority given to process and participation rights can also be understood as practical illustrations of the emphasis placed by Peñalver on the right of entrance as a core facet of private ownership.[54] Peñalver argues that property rights allow owners to engage with, and develop, local communities.[55] Using participation rules to protect property rights in public law contexts gives effect to this vision of property as performing a binding function, since property rights can only be asserted and defined through participation in regulatory processes designed to capture collective interests in respect of the use and/or possession of property. However, participation rules may not always be effective as a means of protecting property rights[56] and may in fact have *exclusionary* effects in some contexts.[57] Accordingly, for the presence of such rules to

[51] C. M. Rose, 'Crystals and Mud in Property Law' (1988) 40 *Stanford Law Review* 577.

[52] J. W. Singer, 'Democratic Estates: Property Law in a Free and Democratic Society' (2009) 94 *Cornell Law Review* 1009.

[53] Walsh, 'The Evolving Relationship' (n 27).

[54] E. M. Peñalver, 'Property as Entrance' (2005) 91 *Virginia Law Review* 1889.

[55] Ibid. at 1894.

[56] As Arnstein notes: 'There is a critical difference between going through the empty ritual of participation and having the real power needed to affect the outcome of the process.' S. R. Arnstein, 'A Ladder of Citizen Participation' (1969) 35 *Journal of American Planners* 216.

[57] For full discussion of the potential for participatory procedures to have exclusionary effects see, e.g., Walsh, 'The Evolving Relationship' (n 27); C. Allen, *Housing Market Renewal and Social Class* (London: Routledge, 2008); G. Macleod and C. Johnstone, 'Stretching Urban Renaissance: Privatizing Space, Civilizing Place, Summoning "Community"' (2012) 36 *International Journal of Urban and Regional Research* 1; B. Nevin, 'Housing Market Renewal in Liverpool: Locating the Gentrification Debate in History, Context and Evidence' (2010) 25 *Housing Studies* 715.

appropriately weigh against a judicial finding of 'unjust attack', either in respect of an individual decision or a legislative scheme, judges should be satisfied that such rules secure meaningful owner participation in administrative decision-making processes.[58]

6.4 'Unreasonableness and Irrationality'

Blake v. *The Attorney General* provides a good example of judicial invalidation of an outdated and irrational legislative scheme as an 'unjust attack' on property rights.[59] The plaintiff landlords argued that Parts II and IV of the Rent Restrictions Act, 1960, as amended by the Rent Restrictions (Amendment) Act, 1967, and the Landlord and Tenant (Amendment) Act, 1971 unconstitutionally interfered with their constitutional property rights. The Act applied only to properties of a specified rateable value and fixed the rents payable by tenants at 1966 levels.[60] However, many of the affected properties had been subject to earlier temporary rent restriction schemes. The depressed rents applicable under those schemes were carried forward in 1966 so that most of the affected properties received rents fixed at 1946 levels, although some were fixed at 1914 levels. Landlords remained liable for repairs and were heavily restricted in their ability to recover possession.

In the Supreme Court, O'Higgins CJ first held that the Act interfered with the exercise of property rights. He noted that the evidence showed that the rents obtainable on the open market were between 9 and 19 times more than could be recovered by the plaintiffs and that this was not an abnormal consequence of the application of the Act.[61] The legislation was mandatory in effect, unlimited in duration, and operated to override contractual arrangements. Second, O'Higgins CJ considered whether that interference amounted to an 'unjust attack'. He held that the Act restricted rents in certain cases without any rational basis for the selection of controlled properties:

58 For further elaboration of this argument, see Walsh, 'The Evolving Relationship' (n 27), Walsh, '*Belfast Corporation v OD Cars*' (n 26).

59 [1982] IR 117.

60 Under the terms of the Act, properties outside the valuation limits, and all properties built after 1941, were exempt from rent control. Local authorities were exempted from the application of the Act in cases where they were landlords.

61 He further noted that the obligation to repair the controlled premises was burdensome, particularly in respect of old properties requiring heavy maintenance but yielding only low rents. The evidence in relation to one of the plaintiffs' properties was that a loss of £35 would be sustained by the landlord on the property if repairs were carried out.

> Neither the means of the tenant nor the lack of means of, or possible hardship to, the landlord may be considered in determining the permitted rent. Therefore, it is apparent that in this legislation rent control is applied only to some houses and dwellings and not to others; that the basis for the selection is not related to the needs of the tenants, to the financial or economic resources of the landlords, or to any established social necessity; and that, since the legislation is now not limited in duration, it is not associated with any particular temporary or emergency situation.[62]

In addition, the lack of provision for review was a 'circumstance of inherent injustice'.[63] There was no provision for compensation or for modifying the application of the Act. Consequently, O'Higgins CJ concluded that it was arbitrary and unfair and unjustly attacked landlords' property rights.

Arbitrariness was also central to the Supreme Court's decision in *Brennan* v. *The Attorney General.*[64] *Brennan* concerned the valuation of land by reference to the Griffith Valuation, which was carried out over a period of 14 years between 1852 and 1866. No revision was ever carried out, and there was no provision for individual landowners to appeal their valuations. The Supreme Court struck down s. 11 of the Local Government Act 1946 insofar as it authorised the collection of county rates (a form of local taxation) on the basis of those valuations. It held: '. . .the valuation used is many years out of date, has never been revised, is inconsistent even within the same county, has failed to reflect fundamental changes in agricultural methods and soil evaluation and for all of these reasons lacks fairness and uniformity.'[65]

Overall, *Blake* and *Brennan* indicate that out-dated, anachronistic, or irrational legislation will be struck down as an unjust attack on property rights. The impugned legislation in both cases was blatantly ineffective and anomalous, and as such, unfair. However, in more borderline cases, the courts have been slower to intervene.[66] Perfect rationality is not

[62] *Blake* (n 59) at 138.

[63] Ibid.

[64] [1983] ILRM 449; [1984] ILRM 355.

[65] [1984] ILRM 355 at 362–63.

[66] See, e.g., *Madigan* v. *Attorney General* [1986] 1 ILRM 136, upholding the constitutionality of a residential property tax imposed by Part VI of the Finance Act 1983 in the face of an arbitrariness challenge, and *Browne* v. *Attorney General* [1991] 2 IR 58, upholding the rationality of s. 4 of the Finance Act 1982, providing for taxation of the use of a company car for private purposes. In both decisions, the courts held that interferences with property rights could impact on individuals to different degrees without that fact alone causing an 'unjust attack'. It is significant in this respect that *Madigan* and *Browne*

required, and restrictions can have particularly oppressive, or even anomalous, impacts on some owners without necessarily constituting an 'unjust attack'.[67] However, the Irish courts have failed to clearly distinguish permissible and impermissible irrationality – where a given case falls on the line between arbitrariness and legitimacy appears to be driven by the judges' intuitive understanding of the fairness of the impugned restrictions.

6.5 'Discrimination'

6.5.1 Introduction

The Irish courts have drawn on principles of equality and non-discrimination in delineating the State's power to restrict the exercise of property rights through their application of the 'unjust attack' test. Their decisions reflect a concern with distributional fairness, as well as narrower non-discrimination concerns. However, they have been inconsistent in their response to legislative measures that burden particular groups of owners with the costs of securing collective goods. This raises in a doctrinal context a recurring tension in progressive property between on the one hand, facilitating a strong regulatory power through emphasising the non-absolute nature of property rights, including through ideas of owner obligations, and on the other hand, protecting owners against unfair exploitation in the public interest.[68] Progressive property is criticised for being ambiguous on this point.[69] The case-law considered in this section demonstrates that the question of what Gerhart terms 'appropriate burdening'[70] does not readily lend itself to a clear answer that is capable of coherent justification and consistent application by judges. The quest for what Singer terms 'adequate justification' of the circumstances in which owners can legitimately be disproportionately

concerned taxation measures, and in both instances the courts stressed the need to defer to the legislature in relation to such statutes.

67 See, e.g., *Shirley* v. *AO Gorman* [2006] IEHC 27 and *Greene* v. *Minister for Agriculture* [1990] 2 IR 1 at 24.

68 See, e.g., G. S. Alexander and E. M. Peñalver, 'Properties of Community' (2009) 10 *Theoretical Inquiries in Law* 127, 144, G. S. Alexander, 'The Social Obligation Norm in American Property Law' (2009) 94 *Cornell L Rev* 745, 772–73.

69 See, e.g., H. Dagan, 'Reimagining Takings' in G. S. Alexander and E. M. Peñalver, *Property and Community* (Oxford: University Press, 2010) p. 39, at p. 44.

70 P. M. Gerhart, *Property Law and Social Morality* (Cambridge: Cambridge University Press, 2014) p. 60.

burdened in the public interest is not simple.[71] Rather, it represents a core contested aspect of constitutional property law.

6.5.2 *Fairness in the Distribution of Collective Burdens*

In some cases where the Irish courts invalidated restrictions on property rights as unjust, they emphasised that there was unfairness in the distribution of the costs of attaining social goods.[72] This reasoning reflects the view that social goods should be paid for out of general taxation so that the costs are spread evenly across society rather than being concentrated on a discrete category of individuals. It echoes Gerhart's argument, considered in Chapter 2, that a right to 'appropriate burdening' forms the 'normative core' of property.[73] Gerhart argues that '...owners are promised an appropriate assignment of the burdens and benefits of decisions about resources when the state, representing the community, adjusts the burdens and benefits of ownership.'[74] The question of 'appropriate burdening' has been at the core of some of the most high profile legal and political debates about constitutional property rights in Ireland, for example featuring heavily in current political disagreements about permissible legislative responses to Ireland's on-going housing crisis.[75] The Irish courts have found some (but not all) legislation that secures

[71] Singer, 'Justifying Regulatory Takings' (n 1).

[72] Frank Michelman identified a similar trend in US takings jurisprudence, saying '[a] court assigned to differentiate among impacts which are and are not 'takings' is essentially engaged in deciding when government may execute public programs while leaving associated costs disproportionately concentrated upon one or a few persons.' F. I. Michelman 'Property, Utility, and Fairness: Comments on the Ethical Foundations of "Just Compensation" Law' (1967) 80 *Harvard Law Review* 1165, 1165. See also R. Keane, 'Property in the Constitution and in the Courts', in B. Farrell (ed.), *De Valera's Constitution and Ours* (London: Gill & MacMillan, 1988), p. 137, pp. 143–44.

[73] Gerhart, *Property Law and Social Morality* (n 70), p. 60.

[74] Ibid.

[75] On these debates, see R. Walsh, 'Housing Crisis: There is no constitutional block to rent freezes in Ireland' (*Irish Times*, 3 February 2020), available at www.irishtimes.com/opinion/housing-crisis-there-is-no-constitutional-block-to-rent-freezes-in-ireland-1.4159367?mode=sample&auth-failed=1&pw-origin=https%3A%2F%2Fwww.irishtimes.com%2Fopinion%2Fhousing-crisis-there-is-no-constitutional-block-to-rent-freezes-in-ireland-1.4159367 (last visited 11 August 2020), and 'What Would the 'Referendum on Housing' Be About and Do We Really Need One? (*Irish Times*, 22 July 2020), available at www.irishtimes.com/opinion/what-would-the-referendum-on-housing-be-about-and-do-we-really-need-one-1.4285592?mode=sample&auth-failed=1&pw-origin=https%3A%2F%2Fwww.irishtimes.com%2Fopinion%2Fwhat-would-the-referendum-on-housing-be-about-and-do-we-really-need-one-1.4285592 (last visited 11 August 2020).

public benefits by targeting discrete groups to be unconstitutional. The explicit empowerment of the State in Article 43.2 to realise social justice and the common good seems inconsistent with a strict anti-redistribution principle. This is reflected in the case law, which as the next two sections show, oscillates between striking down and upholding targeted burdening without any cogent, consistently applicable justification being offered for shifts in approach. The intuitive sense of fairness held by the deciding judges appears to determine outcomes, rather than any clear and consistently applied legal principle.

6.5.3 *'Inappropriate Burdens'*

In *Blake*, the Supreme Court ruled that it was not permissible for the legislature to secure social benefits by shifting the cost of those benefits onto particular groups of owners, at least where that was done in an irrational manner and on a permanent basis.[76] As already noted, *Blake* concerned the Rent Restrictions Act 1960, which froze rents for selected properties and limited the ability of landlords to recover possession. The Supreme Court was influenced by the Act's distribution of burdens:

> In the opinion of the Court, the provisions of Part II of the Act of 1960 (as amended) restrict the property rights of one group of citizens for the benefit of another group. This is done, without compensation and without regard to the financial capacity or the financial needs of either group, in legislation which provides no limitation on the period of restriction, gives no opportunity for review and allows no modification of the operation of the restriction.[77]

Accordingly, the lack of attention in the legislative scheme to the relative means of the benefited and burdened groups was highly significant, as was its open-ended nature.

[76] [1982] 1 IR 117.

[77] Ibid. at 139–40. The Court emphasised these conclusions further in analysing the restrictions on recovery of possession imposed by the Act as: '. . .an integral part of the arbitrary and unfair statutory scheme whereby tenants of controlled dwellings are singled out for specially favourable treatment, both as to rent and as to the right to retain possession, regardless of whether they have any social or financial need for such preferential treatment and regardless of whether the landlords have the ability to bear the burden of providing such preferential treatment.' Ibid. at 140. McCormack is critical of the Court's rejection of the legitimacy of the distinctions drawn by the Rent Restrictions Act: G. McCormack, '*Blake-Madigan* and its Aftermath' (1983) 5 *Dublin University Law Journal* 205, 214–15.

Following *Blake*, the legislature introduced a new Bill designed to remedy the problems created by the invalidation of the 1960 Act. It provided that in the context of controlled dwellings, rent should be either agreed or fixed by the District Court on essentially a market value basis.[78] Under s. 9, tenants whose rents were increased would pay their old rent plus 40 per cent of the increase in 1982, rising to 55 per cent of the increase in 1984, 70 per cent in 1985, reaching the full amount in 1986. The Bill also improved the ability of the landlord to recover possession of a controlled property.[79] Nonetheless, the Supreme Court held that it was unconstitutional because it deferred payment of the 'just rent' and as such involved '. . .different but no less unjust deprivations' than the Act struck down in *Blake*.[80]

As the analysis in the previous part of this chapter demonstrated, the anachronistic nature of the impugned rent control scheme was central to the Supreme Court's decision in *Blake*.[81] The 1981 Bill was introduced to respond to the problems created by the decision in *Blake*, so it covered the same controlled properties, arguably carrying over some of the irrationality of the previously invalidated legislation. Indeed the Supreme Court noted the coverage of the 1981 Bill and the criticism of the selection criteria in *Blake* as not grounded in any clearly established social need, but it accepted that the basis for selection in the 1981 Bill was determined by *Blake*. However, the Court focused on the phased introduction of market rents in determining that the Bill involved an 'unjust attack' on property rights.[82] As it saw it, there was no justification for postponing the right to receive market rent. This presupposes that landlords have an absolute right to market-value returns on their properties. In subsequent decisions, the Irish courts have been much more

[78] Section 6 of the Bill provided that the rent fixed by the court would be that which in the opinion of the court a willing lessee who was not in occupation would give and a willing lessor would take for the dwelling on the basis of vacant possession being given to the tenant and having regard to the other terms of the tenancy and the letting values of dwellings of a similar character and location.

[79] For example, the Bill removed the entitlement of a tenant to assign the controlled tenancy and limited the rights of the family of such a tenant to take over the tenancy.

[80] *Re Article 26 and the Housing (Private Rented Dwellings) Bill, 1981* [1983] IR 181 at 191.

[81] On this point, see also J. Casey, *Constitutional Law in Ireland*, 3rd ed., (Dublin: Round Hall, 2000), p. 671 and H. Kelly, *Private Property Rights Under the Irish Constitution* (PhD thesis, University College Dublin, 2010), p. 115.

[82] R. Keane, 'Land Use, Compensation and the Community' (1983) 18 *Irish Jurist* 23, 30 notes, '. . .even when a conspicuous attempt was made to substitute legislation which did not appear invidious and discriminatory, it perished on the rock of no compensation.'

accepting of restrictions on the profitable use of private property.[83] The decision might be explained by the fact that the Bill carried forward the underpinning selection criteria for controlled properties that had been invalidated in *Blake*, thereby tainting the 1981 Bill with the same irrationality. The Court did acknowledge that an immediate demand for fair rents could cause some tenants hardship, but it regarded such hardship as appropriately remedied by the State rather than private landlords.[84] As such, it did not treat the risk of hardship to tenants as a 'constitutionally permitted justification' for phased introduction of market rents.

A more clear-cut anti-redistribution position was adopted by the Supreme Court in *Re Article 26 and the Employment Equality Bill, 1996*.[85] The referred Bill precluded discrimination in employment on a variety of grounds, including disability. Section 16 required employers to take all reasonable steps to accommodate the needs of disabled persons, including making provision where necessary for special treatment or facilities that would enable a disabled person to perform the duties and tasks associated with a job. Section 35 created an exemption from this obligation where, having regard to all the relevant circumstances, it would cause undue hardship to an employer. The exemption was to be applied by the administrative bodies empowered under the Bill to deal with disputes concerning employment equality.[86] The Supreme Court held that despite the public interest advanced by the Bill, it was unjust to require employers to pay for adaptations to workplaces, reasoning: '. . .the difficulty with the section now under discussion is that it attempts to transfer the cost of solving one of society's problems on to a particular group.'[87] This conclusion was reached despite the exemption provision,

[83] See, e.g., *Hempenstall* v. *Minister for Environment* [1994] 2 IR 20, *Gorman* v. *Minister for Environment* [2001] 2 IR 414, *Re Article 26 and Part V of the Planning and Development Bill 1999* [2000] 1 IR 321. McCormack characterises the rent-control decisions as '. . . a beatification of the market economy through the Constitution': '*Blake-Madigan* and its Aftermath' (n 77), 214.

[84] *Re Article 26 and the Housing (Private Rented Dwellings) Bill, 1981* (n 80) at 191–92.

[85] [1997] 2 IR 321.

[86] The applicability of the exemption was to be determined with regard to the nature of the facilities and/or treatments required by the disabled person, the cost of same, the financial circumstances of the employer, the disruption that would be caused by the provision of the facilities and/or treatments, and the nature of any benefit or detriment which would accrue to any persons likely to be affected by the provision of the treatment or facilities.

[87] *Re Article 26 and the Employment Equality Bill, 1996* (n 85) at 367–68. Although the judgment was not referred to by the Supreme Court, this clearly echoes Justice Black's

which allowed the financial circumstances of an individual employer to be taken into account.[88] Consequently, the decision in the *Employment Equality Bill* case imposed a strong substantive limit on the State's regulatory power by foreclosing the transfer of the costs of social benefits to discrete groups. The stance adopted by the Supreme Court is particularly striking given the extreme reluctance of the Irish courts to address matters of distributive justice outside the property rights context.[89] It suggests that while the courts will not involve themselves with the appropriate allocation of *common resources*, they will analyse the justice of the allocation of *common burdens*.

The Supreme Court attempted to limit the scope of its holding in the *Employment Equality Bill case* by giving examples of permissible targeted burdens. It cited health and safety legislation, pollution remediation, and the facilitation of disabled access to public buildings and private buildings intended to be open to the public, arguing that these costs could legitimately be regarded as part of restricted owners' operating costs.[90] Hogan and Whyte characterised these examples as embracing:

> …two distinct qualifications to the general principle – first, a person responsible for the creation of a social problem may be required to pay for its resolution and, second, the State may, as a condition of granting permission to an individual to pursue a course of action that would

statement in *Armstrong* v. *United States*, 364 US 40, 49 (US 1960) concerning the Takings Clause in the US Constitution: 'The Fifth Amendment's guarantee that private property shall not be taken for a public use without just compensation was designed to bar Government from forcing some people alone to bear public burdens which, in all fairness and justice, should be borne by the public as a whole.'

88 In line with the general presumption of constitutionality in Irish law, the Court was required to presume that the exemption provision would be applied in accordance with the Constitution. However, the Court stressed that the Bill did not exempt small firms and held that it defined 'disability' in such broad terms that an employer could not assess his liabilities in advance. Furthermore, the Court emphasised that the Bill required an employer to reveal confidential financial information if it wished to be considered for an exemption from the accommodation requirement. *Re Article 26 and the Employment Equality Bill, 1996* (n 85) at 368.

89 The seminal decision is *O'Reilly* v. *Limerick Corporation* [1989] ILRM 181 at 194, where Costello J distinguished between distributive and commutative justice and characterised distributive matters as appropriately pursued through political, not legal, channels. Costello J's distinction between distributive and commutative justice was approved in the Supreme Court by Hardiman J in *Sinnott* v. *Minister for Education* [2001] 2 IR 545 at 699–702, and by Denham and Hardiman JJ in *TD* v. *Minister for Education* [2001] 4 IR 259 at 305 and at 359 and 363 respectively.

90 Ibid. at 367.

> otherwise not be permitted, require that person to comply with a social policy designed for the benefit of a specific section of the community.[91]

This synthesis of the Court's examples is insufficiently precise. The examples are not limited to cases where legislative permission of some kind is required to engage in an activity. The examples offered by the Court do all reflect the view that where individuals or discrete groups in society profit from an activity carried on in the public sphere, they can be required to accept limits on the scope for profit in the public interest – a polluter must pay for pollution-remediation, an industrialist must run a safe workplace, and an operator who wishes to have the benefit of public access to its premises must ensure that the premises are accessible for all individuals. However, the profit-making rationale cannot explain the Court's decision on the Employment Equality Bill itself. The employers affected by the Bill were making profits in the public sphere through operating workplaces, and as such, following the Court's line of reasoning, could have been required to make such profits in an accessible environment. Therefore, while the profit-making context loosely explains the Court's examples, that rationale should arguably have prompted the Court to uphold the Bill.

The other rationale for the exceptions identified by Hogan and Whyte is the harm/benefit distinction. Following this approach, where individuals engage in activity that has harmful effects (such as, for example, causing pollution), it may be permissible for the legislature to transfer the costs of remediation to them. The application of this distinction depends on an assumed prior understanding of the 'ordinary' rights of an owner that can be asserted without any question of harm-creation arising.[92] Such a benchmark is not articulated in the *Employment Equality Bill case*. It may be possible to identify a cultural consensus of some kind on the meaning of 'harm' and 'benefit' at the extreme ends of the spectrum. Alexander argues that an ordinary person has no difficulty distinguishing

[91] G. Hogan and G. Whyte, *Kelly: The Irish Constitution*, 4th ed., (Dublin: LexisNexis Butterworths, 2003), p. 2003.

[92] As Singer points out, '. . .our conceptualization of property rights powerfully affects our understanding of when an externality is present and when an action should be viewed as legitimately self-regarding. And those conceptions are powerfully influenced by both conscious and unconscious norms.' J. W. Singer, 'How Property Norms Construct the Externalities of Ownership' in G. S. Alexander and E. M. Peñalver (eds.), *Property and Community* (Oxford: Oxford University Press, 2010), p. 57, 70.

between harmful and beneficial uses of private property.[93] However, once one strays beyond relatively 'easy' cases such as pollution and other forms of environmental degradation, reasonable judgments will vary as to the appropriate classification of any given burden imposed on an owner. Taking *Blake* as an example, it was clearly open to the Court, particularly in light of Article 43.2's express invocation of social justice, to characterise charging people high rents as an injurious use of private property. On the other hand, it was also plausible, based on a robust understanding of an owner's right to control the use of property, to characterise rent restriction as transferring a benefit from landlords to tenants or as requiring the private realisation of a public benefit. Therefore, the harm/benefit distinction often re-poses the question of fairness that it is invoked to answer.

The anti-redistribution strain in the courts' 'unjust attack' doctrine, which worked against progressive goals in the *Employment Equality Bill case*, was deployed in *defence of* such goals by the Supreme Court in the *Health Bill case.*[94] As has already been discussed, the Bill at issue retrospectively validated the imposition of charges on elderly people receiving medical care in public institutions to cover their shelter and maintenance even though they were entitled to receive this service for free under s. 53 of the Health Act 1970.[95] In assessing the constitutionality of the Bill, the Court stated:

> The right to the ownership of property has a moral quality which is intimately related to the humanity of each individual. It is also one of the pillars of the free and democratic society established under the Constitution. Owners of property must, however, in exercising their rights respect the rights of other members of society. Article 43.2.1, therefore, declares that these rights, 'ought, in civil society, to be regulated by the principles of social justice.' The property of persons of modest means must necessarily, in accordance with those principles, be deserving of particular protection, since any abridgement of the rights of such persons will normally be proportionately more severe in its effects.[96]

The Court thus invoked Article 43.2.1°'s reference to the 'principles of social justice' to support a presumptive two-tier scheme of property

[93] G. S. Alexander, 'The Social-Obligation Norm in American Property Law' (2009) 94 *Cornell Law Review* 745, at 798. See also Singer (n 92), p. 65.

[94] *Re Article 26 and the Health (Amendment) (No 2) Bill, 2004* (n 15).

[95] The Bill also required the Minister for Health to introduce regulations providing for the imposition of such charges in the future.

[96] *Re Article 26 and the Health (Amendment) (No 2) Bill, 2004* (n 15) at 201–2.

rights protection under which the property rights of individuals of limited means were to be treated as most deserving of protection.[97] The Court stressed that the Bill targeted the property rights of the most vulnerable members of society. It was particularly concerned that most old people would have been relatively powerless to protest at the charges levied upon them, if indeed they even knew they were unlawful. Drawing on this analysis, Doyle and Whyte identify a concern with unfair burdening as central to the Court's decision.[98]

The *Health Bill case* presents a more nuanced judicial approach to unfair burdening than the *Employment Equality Bill case*, as it is focused on opposing redistributive measures targeted at those of limited means rather than rejecting redistributive measures *per se*. Furthermore, the *Health Bill case* demonstrates judicial awareness of the connections between democracy, socio-economic status, political empowerment, and property rights that were discussed in Chapter 2 and is more consistent with the progressive tenor of the delimiting principles set out in Article 43.2, in particular the express focus on social justice.

6.5.4 'Appropriate Burdening'

Despite the decisions in *Blake*, the *Employment Equality Bill case*, and the *Health Bill case*, the courts have often rejected challenges to legislation based on alleged unfairness in the distribution of the costs of securing public goods. The focus in such decisions is on the public interest served by the restriction. The courts have invoked a variety of factors to distinguish these decisions, only some of which are consistent with the anti-redistribution decisions. The outcomes provide guidance on the meaning of 'appropriate burdening' in Irish constitutional property law.

One explanation for the examples of appropriate burdens offered in the *Employment Equality Bill case* was that owners could legitimately be

[97] Eoin O'Dell and Gerry Whyte correctly suggest that this may require 'heightened judicial scrutiny of legislation that primarily affects vulnerable persons of modest means'. They also suggest that hardship exceptions in fiscal legislation may be required. E. O'Dell and G. Whyte, 'Is This a Country for Old Men and Women? – *In re Article 26 and the Health (Amendment) (No. 2) Bill 2004*' (2005) 27 *Dublin University Law Journal* 368, 390. The same point is made in O. Doyle and G. Whyte, 'The Separation of Powers and Constitutional Egalitarianism after the *Health (Amendment) (No. 2) Bill Reference*', in E. O'Dell (ed.), *Older People in Modern Ireland – Essays on Law and Policy* (Dublin: First Law, 2006), p. 391, 406.

[98] Doyle and Whyte, ibid., p. 415.

required to give up profits earned in the public sphere in the public interest. This reasoning was applied by the Supreme Court to *uphold* the constitutionality of a targeted burden in *Re Article 26 and Part V of the Planning and Development Bill, 1999.*[99] The Bill in issue empowered local authorities to require developers to cede up to 20 per cent of their land, serviced sites, or built units for social and affordable housing as a condition of a grant of planning permission.[100] Compensation was payable reflecting the existing use value of the land, which assumed that no development other than exempted development would be allowed on the land at the time it was transferred.[101]

The arguments made by counsel opposing the Bill's constitutionality drew heavily on the earlier anti-redistribution decisions, contending that the Bill entailed an impermissible imposition of social costs on a discrete group of owners.[102] Nonetheless, the Supreme Court held that the Bill did not constitute an unjust attack on property rights. It reasoned that since the effect of Part V was simply to claw back part of the value contributed to the land by a grant of planning permission, less than market value compensation was permissible.[103] The Court also rejected the argument that Part V unfairly discriminated between those who were burdened under its terms and those who benefited from it. The Court acknowledged that insofar as the scheme benefited individuals in need of housing support at the expense of landowners, it did provide for unequal

[99] *Re Article 26 and Part V of the Planning and Development Bill, 1999* [2000] 2 IR 321.

[100] Developments consisting of four or fewer houses or of housing on 0.2 hectares or less were exempt from these obligations: S. 97. This exemption was probably a response to the criticism of the absence of an exemption for small businesses in the Employment Equality Bill, 1996 by the Supreme Court in *Re Article 26 and the Employment Equality Bill, 1996* (n 87) at 368.

[101] Where houses and/or sites were transferred, the compensation paid to the developer would include the building and attributable development costs as agreed between the parties, including profit on that cost. In addition, in certain circumstances the compensation payable under s. 96 could be greater than the existing use value of the land. If the developer bought the land before 25 August, 1999, he could claim the price actually paid for the land plus interest if that sum was greater than the existing use value of the land on the date of transfer. However, where land was acquired as a gift or through inheritance before that date, the owner could only claim a sum equal to the market value of the land on the valuation date estimated in accordance with s. 15 of the Capital Acquisitions Tax Act, 1976, or the existing use value, whichever was greater. The valuation date was the date of the gift or the date of the death of the person from whom the land was inherited.

[102] *See Re Article 26 and Part V of the Planning and Development Bill, 1999* (n 99) at 339–41.

[103] Ibid. at 354–56.

treatment. However, the Court held that this was constitutionally permissible, particularly considering the need to afford substantial leeway to the legislature to deal with controversial social and economic matters and to reconcile the conflicting claims of different sections of society. The Court also emphasised that while the obligations in relation to social and affordable housing only applied to a discrete category of individuals, they formed part of a wider code of planning control to which all land was subject, and which consequently limited the expectations that all owners could legitimately form in relation to land-use. Accordingly, the decision in the *Planning and Development Bill case* fits the exceptions set out in the *Employment Equality Bill case* – where a profit is earned by an operator in the public sphere, that profit can be limited in the interests of the common good where there is some connection between the reason for the limitation and the profitable activity in question, at least where investments have not already been made on foot of the prior regulatory regime.[104] It also reflects the distinction drawn by Hogan and Whyte between cases involving regulatory permissions and other interferences with property rights; the 'added value' of regulatory permits can be clawed back in the public interest. Finally, the formally equal application of the measure to all owners weighed against a finding of unfair targeting.

The Irish courts have also relied upon the harm/benefit distinction to support decisions upholding restrictions on the exercise of property rights, but have rejected attempts by owners to use it to strike down restrictions. The central idea is that an owner has no right to begin or continue a nuisance-like use of property, meaning that restricting or prohibiting such a use does not require compensation.[105] Such an

[104] For similar 'profit claw-back' reasoning, see *Carrigaline Community Television Broadcasting Co Ltd* v. *Minister for Transport* [1997] 1 ILRM 241 at 290; *BUPA Ireland Ltd* v. *Health Insurance Authority* [2006] IEHC 431 and *Island Ferries Teoranta* v. *Galway County Council* [2013] IEHC 587.

[105] See J. L. Sax, 'Takings and the Police Power', (1964) 74 *Yale Law Journal* 36, 37, for a classic analysis of this concept. This 'noxious use' doctrine, originally articulated in the context of judicial and academic analysis of the Takings Clause of the Fifth Amendment of the US Constitution, has fallen into disfavour with the US Supreme Court on the basis that the harm/benefit distinction upon which it turns is indeterminate. For instance in *Lucas* v. *South Carolina Coastal Commission*, which involved a prohibition on development of coastal lands, Justice Scalia for the majority characterised the 'noxious use' doctrine as a simplistic device used before the case-law developed a broad acceptance that the State could restrict property rights in the interests of the common good, and argued that the difference between 'harm' and 'benefit' was in the eye of the beholder. (1992) 505 US 1003 at 1022–26. For a strong scholarly rejection of the doctrine, see G. S.

approach was adopted in *M & F Quirke* v. *An Bord Pleanála*, where O'Neill J noted:

> Apart from statutory provision, the law of nuisance has long recognised that activity carried out on land may be restrained where that activity causes deleterious effects to escape which cause damage to adjoining property. It could never be said that there was an unrestricted right to use property for any activity, including quarrying, regardless of the effects that activity had on the enjoyment of other persons of their lives, health and properties.[106]

O'Neill J clearly regarded nuisance law as an important guide to the limits of an owner's control of use, thereby reflecting the view that harmful uses do not form part of an owner's protected 'bundle of rights', at least where they would be liable to result in an award of damages or to be otherwise restricted through private law. However, the consequence of a particular use being found to be unreasonable in nuisance law could be an injunctive remedy, but it might instead be remedied through an award of damages.[107] In contrast, the public law measures in issue in *M&F Quirke* ruled out any unpermitted use of the properties in question for quarrying – an owner lacked the possibility of avoiding the restriction on use through payment of damages. Furthermore, O'Neill J did not delineate a category of uses falling short of common law nuisances but sufficiently 'nuisance-like' or 'noxious' to warrant restriction without compensation.[108] The deeper root of this indeterminacy is the lack of clarity in Irish constitutional property doctrine surrounding the 'bundle

Lunney, 'Responsibility, Causation and the Harm-Benefit Line in Takings Jurisprudence' (1995) 6 *Fordham Environmental Law Journal* 433.

106 [2010] 1 ILRM 93 at 111. However, the tort of nuisance also protects property rights. As the Supreme Court stated in *Hanrahan* v. *Merck, Sharpe and Dohme*, the tort of nuisance is '...an implementation of the State's duties under the [Constitution's] provisions as to the personal rights and property rights of the plaintiffs as citizens.' [1988] ILRM 629 at 635. See also *Smyth* v. *Railway Procurement Agency* (5 March 2010) (HC) at [32.3] and *Grant* v. *Roche Products (Ireland) Ltd* [2008] 4 IR 679 at 700–01.

107 On the relationship between property rights and environmental regulation as mediated through nuisance law, see Scotford and Walsh (n 25) 1030–33. See also H. E. Smith, 'Exclusion and Property Rules in the Law of Nuisance' (2004) 90 Va L Rev 965.

108 Although in *M&F Quirke Ltd*, which concerned statutory provisions that required quarry owners to re-apply for planning permission for their operations in certain circumstances, O'Neill J left open the possibility that if permission for the continuation of a quarry was not granted on foot of such an application or was granted subject to conditions requiring cessation, compensation might be payable: [2010] 2 ILRM 91 at 112.

of rights' that an owner is presumed to have, which was analysed in Chapter 4.

The Irish courts have also on occasion invoked the related idea of 'reciprocity of advantage' to support their decisions upholding public law restrictions on property rights: where a constraint is imposed on the exercise of property rights that is linked to benefits accruing to the adversely affected owner, uncompensated restrictions are permissible.[109] From this perspective, burdens imposed by a regulatory system do not suffer from distributional unfairness where they are offset by benefits that accrue to an individual within such a system.[110] However, reciprocity analysis suffers from similar indeterminacy to that identified in relation to the harm/benefit distinction. Absent a clear understanding of the 'incidents of ownership' ordinarily accruing to an owner, judges are free to construe the meaning of 'benefit' broadly or narrowly. Judges could, and likely do, consciously or unconsciously draw on their sense of community practice and 'normal behaviour',[111] as well as on their intuitive understanding of the baseline entitlements of owners,[112] in undertaking such an evaluative exercise. Distinguishing harms and benefits in this way requires that judges

[109] See, e.g., *the Planning and Development Bill case* (n 99), where the Supreme Court held that the increased land value flowing from a grant of compensation justified a claw-back from that increase in the public interest. See also *Hanrahan* v. *The Environmental Protection Agency* [2005] IEHC 5867, [2006] 1 ILRM 275, *Hempenstall* (n 83), *Gorman* (n 83).

[110] In contrast, something like spot zoning, whereby the use of small pockets of land is restricted, but the surrounding land is not subject to the same restrictions, appears to unfairly single out an owner for the benefit of his neighbours. In such a case, the targeted owner is required to limit his use of his property, without any reciprocity of advantage. For discussion of zoning as an example of reciprocity of advantag see, e.g., A. Bettman, 'Constitutionality of Zoning' (1923–1924) 37 *Harvard Law Review* 834; R. Coletta, 'Reciprocity of Advantage and Regulatory Takings: Toward a New Theory of Takings Jurisprudence' (1990–1991) 40 *American University Law Review* 297 and L. S. Oswald, 'The Role of "Harm/Benefit" and "Average Reciprocity of Advantage" Rules in a Comprehensive Takings Analysis' (1997) 50 *Vanderbilt Law Review* 1447.

[111] Various defences of the harm/benefit distinction have been mounted, focusing on the ability to discern shared social assumptions about what exercises of property rights constitute harms. See, e.g., J. E. Fee, 'The Takings Clause As A Comparative Right' (2002–2003) *Southern California Law Review* 1003, 1046–49; W. A. Fischel, *Regulatory Takings: Law, Economics and Politics* (Cambridge, MA: Harvard University Press, 1995), p. 354; A. L. Peterson, 'The Takings Clause: In Search of Underlying Principles: Part II – Takings as Intentional Deprivations of Property Without Moral Justification' (1990) 78 *California Law Review* 55, 91 and Oswald, 'The Role of "Harm/Benefit" and "Average Reciprocity of Advantage" Rules' (n 110).

[112] Singer, 'How Property Norms Construct the Externalities of Ownership' (n 92), Lunney, 'Responsibility, Causation, and the Harm-Benefit Line' (n 105), 464–65.

'. . .perform a quintessential legislative task, namely to balance public need against private harm in a redistributive context.'[113]

Both broad and narrow interpretations of the meaning of reciprocity of advantage have been advanced.[114] For example, adopting a narrow approach, Epstein characterises parallel benefits generating reciprocity of advantage as 'implicit in-kind compensation' that justify otherwise unconstitutional takings of private property rights.[115] Epstein requires direct returns for an owner adversely affected by a land-use regulation from the imposition of the same regulation on other owners. More general societal benefits do not establish reciprocity of advantage on this view. This strict interpretation of reciprocity of advantage has been persuasively criticised on the basis that even where 'direct' reciprocity is identifiable, it will not make all individuals 'whole', due to differences in subjective preferences.[116] Perhaps most fundamentally from the perspective of Irish constitutional property law, the reasoning behind a strict reciprocity standard does not sit comfortably with the progressively framed emphasis on the common good and social justice in Article 43.2.[117]

Responding to some of these concerns, Dagan argues that a *long-term* view of reciprocity of advantage is appropriate for identifying justifiable uncompensated regulations of property rights. He contends that public authorities should be absolved from paying compensation if:

> . . .[T]he disproportionate burden of the public action in question is not overly extreme and is offset, or is likely in all probability to be offset, by benefits of similar magnitude to the landowner's current injury that she

[113] W. M. Treanor, 'The Original Understanding of the Takings Clause and the Political Process' (1995) 95 *Columbia Law Review* 782, 877–78.

[114] H. Dagan, *Property: Values and Institutions* (New York: Oxford University Press, 2011), pp. 102–3.

[115] R. Epstein, *Supreme Neglect* (New York: Oxford University Press, 2008), p. 49.

[116] B. A. Lee, 'Average Reciprocity of Advantage', in J. E. Penner and H. E. Smith (eds.), *Philosophical Foundations of Property Law* (Oxford: Oxford University Press, 2013), p. 99. He argues that true reciprocity of advantage will only arise where a coordination problem is solved. For similar criticism, see D. Lewinsohn-Zamir, 'Compensation for Injuries to Land Caused by Planning Authorities: Towards a Comprehensive Theory' (1996) 46 *University of Toronto Law Journal* 47, 105–6. For an alternative approach, focused on the probability of reciprocal advantages, see L. A. Fennell 'Taking Eminent Domain Apart' (2004) *Michigan State Law Review* 957.

[117] As Alexander argues, '. . .if we limit recognition of our contributory obligations strictly to circumstances where an individual eventually receives a benefit as valuable as the burden the individual has sustained, then we weaken our conception of community and hinder it from fostering human flourishing.' 'The Social-Obligation Norm in American Property Law' (n 93), 772.

> gains from other – past, present, or future – public actions (which harm neighbouring properties).[118]

Accordingly, Dagan is concerned with the likelihood of burdens and benefits equalling out in a relatively rough way over time. However, he requires a more clearly defined benefit to the burdened individual than simply participation in the public interest. He characterises this principle of reciprocity as a means of ensuring that owners act in a socially responsible manner in using their land while at the same time protecting them against effacement in the public interest.

This approach suffers from some of the same problems as the narrow understanding of reciprocity of advantage. It does not make owners 'whole' through ensuring compensation in all circumstances. Perhaps more significantly, it requires judges not only to adjudicate upon the fairness of the distribution of the burdens created by an impugned interference with property rights, but to go further and hypothesise about the likely direction of regulatory policy, as well as assessing the impact of *past* public law measures. Such an assessment takes judges into the realm of speculation, as well as requiring a complex evaluation of the history of regulatory control of property rights. It is questionable whether this is a task that courts could, practically speaking, undertake. In the context of the prevailing Irish adjudication culture, it is certainly a responsibility that they would be reluctant to assume.

If reciprocity of advantage is to be employed as a proxy for fairness in constitutional property rights adjudication, it is probably best understood in a looser sense as tending to establish overall reasonableness in the distribution of the burdens of securing public goods.[119] Lee suggests a touchstone of ensuring 'equality of civic status' through compensation provision that shows respect to a burdened owner and the community at large.[120] He characterises reciprocity of advantage as an important proxy

118 Dagan, *Property* (n 114), p. 103. For a long-term view of reciprocity, see also Michelman, 'Property, Utility and Fairness' (n 72), 1225.

119 As Lee points out, accounts of reciprocity of advantage are usually vague on the details concerning the exact distribution of benefits and burdens required, relying instead on a more intuitive requirement that they even out over time: Lee, 'Average Reciprocity of Advantage' (n 116). See for example Oswald, 'The Role of "Harm-Benefit" and "Average Reciprocity of Advantage" Rules' (n 110), 1520–21, arguing, '. . .average reciprocity of advantage does not require a one-to-one equivalency between the burden imposed by the regulation and the resulting benefit to the property owner – a rough approximation will suffice.'

120 Lee, 'Average Reciprocity of Advantage' (n 116), p. 126.

for identifying the risk of unfair exploitation and disrespect.[121] Following this approach, if judges cannot identify a rough offsetting of burdens with related benefits, that can flag the risk of an 'unjust attack' on property rights warranting careful judicial consideration.

In this vein, in *O'Callaghan* v. *Commissioners for Public Works*, the Irish Supreme Court framed its decision that the costs of the preservation of national monuments could be imposed on the private owners of such monuments in terms of the common civic duty of owners to contribute to preserving national heritage.[122] The case concerned a constitutional challenge to a preservation order issued in respect of an historic promontory fort pursuant to s. 8 of the National Monuments Act 1930 as amended, which prohibited the owner from, among other things, excavating, digging, ploughing, or otherwise disturbing the ground within, around, or in proximity to the fort without consent from the Commissioners for Public Works. The Supreme Court held that the impugned provision of the National Monument Act was not an unconstitutional interference with property rights. O'Higgins CJ stressed that the legislation did not deprive the plaintiff of his ownership of the property, or the right to use the property in any way not inconsistent with its preservation. It simply prohibited the plaintiff from destroying the monument.[123] Furthermore, the legislation was not arbitrary or selective, as it applied to all national monuments regardless of who owned them.[124] O'Higgins CJ countered the concern raised about the distribution of the costs generated by the legislation by characterising the burden imposed on the affected landowners as '. . .a requirement of what should be regarded as the common duty of all citizens – to preserve such a monument.'[125] He held that this duty meant that the restriction involved in a preservation order constituted a reconciliation of the use of land with the exigencies of the common good, as set out in the Preamble and Article 1 of the Constitution. O'Higgins CJ did not indicate the legal origin or scope of the 'common duty' to protect heritage

[121] Ibid., p. 125.

[122] *O'Callaghan* (n 41). In the earlier decision of *Tormey* v. *Commissioners for Public Works* (21 December 1972) (SC), the Supreme Court clearly indicated that compensation was required where land was compulsorily acquired for preservation purposes.

[123] *O'Callaghan* (n 41) at 367.

[124] Ibid.

[125] Ibid.

property that he identified.[126] However, drawing on Lee's approach, O'Higgins CJ's focus on citizens' common duty in respect of preservation can be understood as shorthand for a conclusion that the common interest in the benefits of historical preservation meant that it was not a mark of disrespect or a neglect of an individual's equal civic status to require an uncompensated contribution to securing that collective good.

Finally, the Irish courts have drawn on prevailing adverse economic conditions to justify restrictions that on their face could have fallen foul of the strict anti-redistribution position adopted in the *Employment Equality Bill* case. *Condon* v. *The Minister for Labour* provides an interesting early example. *Condon* concerned the constitutionality of the Regulation of Banks (Remuneration and Conditions of Employment) (Temporary Provisions) Act 1975, which empowered the Minister for Labour to prohibit increases in wages that were inconsistent with agreements that had been negotiated at the instance of government between unions and employer representatives to stabilise wages. The Minister exercised this power to prohibit the bringing into effect of a pay agreement between the Irish Bank Officials Association and the Bank Staff Relations Committee.[127] McWilliam J in the High Court rejected the argument that the prohibition unfairly singled out one group of workers for special punitive treatment.[128] He concluded that the difficult economic circumstances in which the Act was introduced meant that the selection of bank officials for restrictions was not arbitrary and that it was reasonable for the government to think the Act would promote the common good.[129]

126 A clearer distinction offered by the Court was the fact that the landowner in *O'Callaghan* was on notice of the preservation order before he purchased the property, meaning his expectations in relation to the use of the property could be regarded as shaped by the order.

127 In *Condon* v. *The Minister for Labour* [1981] IR 62, the Supreme Court held that the introduction of an Expiration Order by the Minister in 1976 – causing the 1975 Act, and orders made under it, to expire – did not mean that the challenge to the constitutionality of the Act and the order was moot.

128 11 June 1980 (HC) at 9.

129 Ibid. at 12. McWilliam J devoted considerable attention to the economic context within which the Act was introduced, noting that at the relevant time inflation was at over 20 per cent, the balance of payments deficit was too high and the government was advised that urgent measures were needed to regulate the economy. He also stressed that the Acts were temporary in application and had not operated so as to permanently deprive anyone of any pecuniary advantage – at 5.

More recently, economic conditions fell to be considered in several cases that arose in the context of austerity measures introduced during Ireland's economic crisis between 2008 and 2011. In *J & J Haire & Company Ltd* v. *Minister for Health*, McMahon J in the High Court interpreted the decision of the Supreme Court in the *Health Bill case* to mean that where an 'extreme financial crisis or a fundamental disequilibrium in public finances' exists, the abrogation of property rights in the interests of the public finances could be justified.[130] He reasoned:

> . . .the State is facing an unprecedented economic crisis, whereby the State is forced to introduce drastic economies and cuts across the board. These economic realities must inform the interpretation of the constitutional phrases in assessing what the State can do and what distributive measures it must take to ensure not only the stability of the economy, but the stability of the State itself.[131]

Accordingly, any notion of fairness in the distribution of collective burdens contained in the courts' understanding of 'unjust attack' must accommodate the economic challenges facing the State in times of crisis.

Haire concerned the constitutionality of changes made to the fees for the provision of public services paid to pharmacists that were introduced in regulations enacted pursuant to s. 9 of the Financial Emergency Measures in the Public Interest Act 2009. McMahon J held that the plaintiffs did not have a contractual right to continued fees at a particular level, and consequently he determined that the legislation was not an 'unjust attack' on property rights. However, he also concluded *obiter* that even if the plaintiffs did have such a property right, it would not have been unjustly attacked by the impugned reductions, which involved proportionate restriction of property rights.[132] Significantly, McMahon J did not indicate when, between the decision of the Supreme Court in the *Health Bill case* (at which time the Supreme Court considered that the potential risk to the exchequer posed by the referred provision was not

[130] *J & J Haire & Company Ltd* (n 2).

[131] Ibid., reference omitted, approved in *Unite the Union* (n 2). See similarly *MacDonncha* v. *Minister for Education* [2013] IEHC 226, where Hogan J stated that the wisdom of the overall fiscal consolidation policy was not a matter for the courts, and that judges should be sensitive to economic realities but could not on that basis turn a blind eye to *ultra vires* executive and administrative action.

[132] He noted the provision for consultation, the specification of matters required to be taken into consideration by the relevant Minister, the provision for annulment and review by the Oireachtas, and the facility for pharmacists to withdraw from providing services upon service of 30 days' notice, in reaching this conclusion.

sufficiently extreme or serious to justify the restriction involved in that case) and his decision in *Haire*, economic circumstances in Ireland shifted into crisis-mode.[133] In reality, economic conditions are *always* likely to be a relevant factor in an 'unjust attack' determination, with that relevance heightened in adverse economic circumstances. Such sensitivity to prevailing economic circumstances seems consistent with the clear requirement in Article 43.2 that the exercise of property rights should be regulated by the principles of social justice.

In *Unite the Union* v. *The Minister for Finance*, Kearns P. in the High Court upheld the constitutionality of s. 2 of the Financial Emergency Measures in the Public Interest Act 2009, which provided for the imposition of a pension levy in respect of public sector pensions.[134] Drawing on *Haire*, he stressed that the legislation responded to a serious economic crisis. He concluded that even if the deductions involved in the pension levy could be said to interfere with property rights, they were not disproportionate given the 'dire financial circumstances' in which the Act was passed and considering the benefit of a public sector pension. As already noted, in *Dellway* v. *National Asset Management Agency*, the Supreme Court upheld the constitutionality of the definition of 'eligible assets' and the grounds for acquisition under the National Asset Management Agency Act 2009.[135] In doing so, it made reference to relevant aspects of the economic climate that led to the introduction of the legislation.[136] It held that a broad definition of eligible assets was necessary to ensure that all bank assets of systemic significance could be dealt with by NAMA, particularly given the importance of perception in restoring confidence in the sector.[137] Most recently, in *Dowling*

[133] As Gerard McCormack presciently noted, commenting on *Condon* (n 128), '[t]he Irish economy (like that of all other countries) is nearly always beset by some difficulty, whether it be high unemployment, budgetary deficits, poor growth, or an adverse balance of payments, which could be characterised as an emergency with as much (or as little) plausibility as inflation.' G. McCormack, 'Contractual Entitlements and the Constitution' (1982) 17 *Irish Jurist* 340, 343.

[134] *Unite the Union* (n 2).

[135] The definition of eligible assets, which governed the acquisition of assets by NAMA, was set out in s. 69 of the Act and amplified through regulations (the National Asset Management Agency (Designation of Eligible Bank Assets) Regulations 2009 (S.I. No. 568 of. 2009).

[136] See similarly the High Court in *National Asset Loan Management* (n 38).

[137] [2011] 4 IR 1 at 192–94. It further noted that banks had to opt into NAMA, and that NAMA had to decide to acquire particular assets for specified purposes set out in s. 2 of the Act.

v. *Minister for Finance,*[138] the Court of Appeal stressed the dire economic circumstances in which the Credit Institutions (Stabilisation) Act 2010 was introduced in upholding the constitutionality of that Act. The Court held that the prevailing adverse economic context meant that the bank in question was within days of being wound-up at the moment of acquisition of shares that was challenged in that case. On this basis, it held that the resulting dilution of the value of the shareholdings could not be regarded as a violation of constitutionally protected property rights, but rather represented legitimate 'burden-sharing' between the State and shareholders.[139]

6.5.5 *Illegitimate Discrimination and Bills of Attainder*

A restriction that discriminates between owners but does not advance a legitimate objective will be struck down as unconstitutional, primarily on equality grounds. Relatedly, measures that affect only one or a small group of owners are particularly susceptible to being struck down as unconstitutional.

This is well illustrated by *An Blascaod Mór Teoranta* v. *Commissioners for Public Works.*[140] The plaintiffs in the case taken together were the largest landowners on the Great Blasket Island, located off Ireland's Atlantic coast. In a comment reflecting the intuitive influence of Lockean thinking about property rights on judicial decision making, Budd J noted that they had all '...expended time, energy and money on trying to preserve the ambience of the island and buildings on the island.'[141] On the basis of s. 4 of the An Blascaod Mór National Historic Park Act, 1989, compulsory purchase orders were issued in respect of their land. However, under the terms of the Act, the Commissioners could not acquire land owned or occupied by someone since the date the island was evacuated (17 November 1953) who was ordinarily resident

[138] *Dowling* v. *Minister for Justice* [2018] IECA 300. See relatedly *Aurelius Capital Master Ltd v Minister for Finance* [2011] IEHC 267, where Cooke J also stressed the circumstances in which the Credit Institutions (Stabilisation) Act 2010 was enacted, arguing for a strict construction and a conservative application of its provisions given the far-reaching impact on contractual and property rights. His decision on this point was approved by the Court of Appeal in *Dowling* at [115].

[139] Ibid. at [160].

[140] [1998] IEHC 38, [2000] 1 IR 6.

[141] [1998] IEHC 38 at [54].

on the island before that date, or land owned or occupied by a relative or lineal descendant of such a person.

In the High Court, Budd J highlighted the Act's unusual features: first, it was not framed in general terms, but rather concerned one island[142]; second, it provided that a small group of owners on the island could have their land expropriated whilst others, who might be unconnected with Ireland, could be exempted.[143] While he accepted that an exemption limited to former inhabitants who remained actively associated with the island might have been less objectionable, he concluded that the discrimination involved in the legislation was unconstitutional.[144] The subjective relationship (or lack thereof) between a category of owners and their property, both in terms of the time spent living in the property, and the level of personal input into the property, influenced his assessment of the fairness of the impugned Act.[145] The plaintiffs in *An Blascaod Mór Teoranta* also argued that the Act was akin to a bill of attainder because it applied in effect only to them. Budd J agreed, concluding that the Act was unconstitutional as it involved, '. . .the targeting in reality of only the Plaintiffs whereby the Plaintiffs' lands are subjected to the power of compulsory acquisition.'[146] On appeal, the Supreme Court upheld Budd J's decision, but it focused on the constitutional guarantee of equality in Article 40.1 rather than on Articles 40.3.2° and 43.[147] In characterising the 1989 Act as akin to a bill of attainder, Budd J construed that concept relatively broadly, since the 1989 Act did not expressly single the plaintiffs out for targeted burdens, but rather contained a wide-ranging *exemption* that excluded most other potentially affected landowners from its terms. The breadth of application required to avoid characterisation as a bill of attainder is not evident from Budd J's decision. In the unusual factual circumstances of *An Blascaod Mór Teoranta*, the affected group was small and was delineated geographically. However, in another case, more debate could arise over the degree of 'singling out' that a measure in fact involves and the extent of 'singling out' required for legislation to constitute a bill of attainder.

142 Ibid. at [39].
143 Ibid. at [41].
144 Ibid. at [185]–[195].
145 There are clear echoes here of the intuitions driving Radin's personhood theory of property: M. J. Radin, *Reinterpreting Property* (Chicago: University of Chicago Press, 1993).
146 Ibid. at [209]–[210].
147 [2001] 1 IR 6 at 18.

This raises the question of whether the *sole* purpose of the constitutional property clauses could be to prevent discrimination in respect of property? As has already been discussed, Gerhart characterises an entitlement to 'appropriate burdening' as property's 'normative core'.[148] Fee goes further, characterising the Takings Clause of the Fifth Amendment of the US Constitution as a comparative right, specifically 'a right to be treated legally the same as other property owners in a community, or to receive compensation when differential treatment is justified'.[149] Fee argues that by ensuring that restrictions on property rights apply generally, courts can prevent the majority from imposing unfair burdens on minority groups, as the majority must either subject itself to the restriction on property rights or compensate the singled-out minority.[150] He suggests that compensation is required where a regulation does not on its face apply to a 'broad community of owners'.[151] Fee acknowledges that there is a group definition problem that must be overcome in order for his approach to be workable. To know whether some person or group has been unfairly burdened by a restriction on property rights, we need to know how big a group of potential targets we should look at.[152] For example, is a law singling out a discrete class of property owners, such as landlords, unfair? Relative to society at large, landlords are a narrow group, but relative to property owners, the group is larger and the singling-out more limited.[153] If a singled-out group must be very small, the equality function of constitutional property rights guarantees would be triggered rarely, whereas if a singled-out group could be relatively large, the implications for legislative freedom would increase. In seeking to overcome this problem, Fee falls back on the harm/benefit distinction. He suggests that the relevant group should be identified by assessing whether the regulation's main *beneficiaries* are those *burdened* by it. However, this approach is dependent on identifying reciprocal advantages, which as discussed above, is difficult unless the level of generality at which the concept of 'benefit' is to be construed is clear. Fee equivocates

[148] Gerhart, *Property Law and Social Morality*, (n 70) p. 60.
[149] Fee, 'The Takings Clause As A Comparative Right' (n 111), 1003.
[150] Ibid., 1053–54.
[151] Ibid., 1050.
[152] Ibid., 1054–55.
[153] Fee suggests rent control laws are not 'takings' because they apply generally to prohibit all individuals from charging higher rents than those designated by legislation. Ibid., 1052.

on this point, suggesting that it will fall to judges to determine what degree of directness of benefit is required to establish reciprocity.

Accordingly, once one moves beyond a narrow focus on irrational discrimination and/or bills of attainder narrowly understood, a comparative or equality-focused approach to the application of a constitutional property rights guarantee collapses back into the broader question of fairness. Furthermore, unlike Gerhart's approach, Fee closes off inquiry into *other* values or goals that may influence constitutional property law. Irish constitutional property law suggests that distributional fairness or discrimination is the most contentious aspect of the protection afforded by constitutional property rights, which most squarely raises the tension between such rights and social justice. Furthermore, it lends support to Gerhart's characterisation of 'appropriate burdening' as property's 'normative core', because the other factors considered in this chapter – retrospectivity, fair procedures, arbitrariness, and irrationality – are concerns of constitutional law *generally*, not distinctive concerns of constitutional property law.[154] However, that fact shows that while appropriate burdening may well be the core area of contention in constitutional property law, it is not its sole focus. This is reinforced by the analysis in the next chapter, which considers the protection for security of possession in Irish constitutional property law. It shows that there are interferences with property rights that courts are likely to resist even if generally applicable, meaning that any notion of 'appropriate burdening' cannot be framed solely in comparative terms.

6.6 Conclusions

The overall picture that emerges from this chapter's analysis of the factors that influence Irish courts when adjudicating upon the question of 'unjust attack' is that the State has broad power to limit the exercise of property rights. The courts invoke a variety of factors to justify their delineation of the State's regulatory power and they systematically seek to portray their decisions as constrained by principle. The courts have failed to directly engage with the contextual assessment of fairness in the distribution of benefits and burdens entailed by the 'unjust attack' standard, tending rather to obfuscate regarding the '…judicial gut-felt

[154] See similarly Singer, 'Justifying Regulatory Takings' (n 1), 663, noting that 'non-constitutional law' does a good job at protecting property rights against illegitimate interference, thereby contributing to the low number of successful regulatory takings challenges.

principles of fundamental fairness' that drive their decisions.[155] In this respect, the Irish experience highlights the doctrinal difficulties that can arise where judges are asked to adjudicate based on a standard like 'unjust attack'.[156]

Notwithstanding these problems, patterns emerge from the case-law analysed in this chapter that help to clarify the scope of the State's power to restrict the exercise of property rights.[157] Overall, that scope is broad and restrictions on the exercise of property rights falling short of deprivations are rarely invalidated by the courts.[158] Three kinds of 'non-property' problems weigh in favour of invalidation: first, retrospective application; second, an absence of provision for fair procedures; and third, the related problems of arbitrariness, unreasonableness, and irrationality. While it overlaps with equality, the 'discrimination' factor most directly raises the appropriate mediation of property rights and social justice and is the most distinctive contribution of the property rights provisions identified in the doctrine explored in this chapter. However, its application is replete with inconsistencies and ambiguities. Judges obscure the question that most of their analysis under the rubric of 'discrimination' is in fact directed towards, namely whether a minority is being unfairly singled out to bear the costs of a benefit in the interests of the majority. Instead of developing and articulating a coherent understanding of 'the principles of social justice' that could assist in answering that question, or of the idea of fairness that drives their application of the 'unjust attack' test, the courts employ indeterminate, overlapping distinctions that presuppose a clear, settled conception of the presumptive content of an owner's 'bundle of rights'. These include the harm/benefit distinction, the related 'noxious use' doctrine, and the reciprocity principle. While the courts clearly regard it as part of their function in

[155] A. G. McFarlane, 'Rebuilding the Public-Private City: Regulatory Taking's Anti-Subordination Insights for Eminent Domain and Redevelopment' (2009) 42 *Indiana Law Review* 97, 137. For similar criticism of US regulatory takings law, see Serkin, 'Existing Uses' (n 22), 1290.

[156] As Singer argues, '. . .while "fairness and justice" are admirable goals and certainly mean *something*, they represent essentially-contested concepts and certainly cannot constrain decision making by themselves without significant elaboration.' 'Justifying Regulatory Takings' (n 1), 632. On the constraining effect of concepts like fairness, see J. W. Singer, 'Normative Methods for Lawyers'(2009) 56 *UCLA Law Review* 899.

[157] See similarly Singer, 'Justifying Regulatory Takings' (n 1), 606, arguing for attention to the results of regulatory takings cases as a means of identifying predictable patterns.

[158] On this tendency, see R. Walsh, 'The Constitution, Property Rights and Proportionality: A Reappraisal' (2009) 31 *DULJ* 1.

constitutional property rights adjudication to ensure what Gerhart terms 'appropriate burdening' of individuals in the public interest, the degree of burdening that is legally permissible is not clear.[159] This doctrinal ambiguity has practical effects; the political conservativism surrounding the restriction of the exercise of property rights discussed in Chapter 4 finds its primary constitutional 'hook' in the small number of 'anti-redistribution' decisions analysed in this chapter.[160]

Overall, while Article 40.3.2° calls on judges to ask the right question in reviewing interferences with property rights from a progressive property perspective – namely to determine whether they are unfair in light of the demands of the common good and social justice – Irish judges have generally not embraced the holistic, contextual assessment that is required to answer that question.[161] They avoid standard-based adjudication or conceal such adjudication behind rule-like distinctions.[162] As such, the Irish experience demonstrates that even where judges are given an express constitutional mandate to adopt a contextual approach focused on ensuring fairness in individual cases, they may resist that role, or may fulfil it in a manner that does not reflect the important progressive property theme of 'transparency'.[163] In this way, it reaffirms that cultures of adjudication, particularly concerning distributive issues, exercise considerable influence on reasoning processes and outcomes in constitutional property law, regardless of the text of a given constitutional property clause.[164]

159 Gerhart, *Property Law and Social Morality* (n 70), p. 60.

160 See Walsh, 'Housing Crisis' (n 75).

161 See J. W. Singer, 'The Ownership Society and Takings of Property: Castles, Investments, and Just Obligations' (2006) 30 *Harvard Environmental Law Review* 309, 336, arguing '[t]he question of justice and fairness does not relieve us of the burden of judgment, and that – perhaps more than any reason – explains why it is the right question.' The 'unjust attack' standard captures the idea of 'adequate justification' advanced by Singer as the core inquiry in regulatory takings law: 'Justifying Regulatory Takings' (n 1).

162 For critical analysis of similar patterns in US Takings Law, see, e.g., F. I. Michelman, 'Possession vs. Distribution in the Constitutional Idea of Property' (1987) 72 *Iowa Law Review* 1319; E. M. Peñalver, 'Is Land Special?' (2004) 31 *Ecology Law Quarterly* 227; Peñalver, 'Property as Entrance' (n 54); J. Paul, 'The Hidden Structure of Takings Law' (1991) 63 *Southern California Law Review* 1393; E. R. Claeys, 'The *Penn Central* test and Tensions in Liberal Property Theory' (2006) 30 *Harvard Environmental Law Review* 339.

163 Mulvaney, 'Progressive Property Moving Forward' (n 3), 358–61.

164 G. S. Alexander, *The Global Debate Over Constitutional Property* (Chicago: University of Chicago Press, 2006), p. 245.

7

Security of Possession in a Progressive Constitutional Context

7.1 Introduction

As the previous chapter illustrated, many of the constraints imposed on the State's power to control the exercise of property rights by the Constitution's property rights guarantees in fact replicate in various ways protections secured by other constitutional rights, such as fair procedures and equality.[1] In this chapter and the next, two distinctive constraints stemming from the constitutional protection of property rights are analysed: first, in this chapter, the constitutional requirement that the State's power to control the exercise of property rights, whether through deprivation or regulation, can only be exercised for purposes consistent with 'the principles of social justice' and 'the exigencies of the common good'; second, in the next chapter, the requirement that the State pay compensation in *some* circumstances to owners adversely affected by the exercise of that power. These constraints provide constitutional protection for owners' interests in security of possession and security of value respectively.

The primary focus of this chapter is on interventions that result in the deprivation of real or personal property – of some 'thing', whether tangible or intangible, that is owned. Where this occurs, whether through the intentional exercise of compulsory acquisition powers or otherwise, many jurisdictions require that the aim must be to benefit the public.[2]

[1] Writing in the US context, Frank Michelman similarly argues that the equal protection and due process clauses are capable of securing '...basic general fairness in the operations of a regulatory state:' F. I. Michelman, 'Good Government, Core Liberties, and Constitutional Property: An Essay for Joe Singer' (2016) 5 *Brigham-Kanner Property Rights Conference Journal* 27, 32.

[2] As Kevin Gray puts it, one of 'the more ancient and majestic themes of global jurisprudence' is that '...private necessity can never demand that the lands of one individual be taken peremptorily and given to another individual exclusively for his or her personal benefit or profit.' K. Gray, 'Human Property Rights: The Politics of Expropriation' (2005) 16 *Stellenbosch Law Review* 398, 398. See also L. Verstappen, 'Rethinking Public Interest in Expropriation Law: Introductory Observations' in B. Hoops, E. Marais, H. Mostert, J. A.

This creates a so-called 'public purpose requirement': a state cannot exercise its power to deprive owners of property except for a public purpose. However, judicial supervision of the legislative purposes is a highly sensitive exercise since it involves reviewing public policy goals that often have distributive implications. As this chapter will illustrate using the example of Irish constitutional property law, judges predominantly defer to the decisions of the elected branches of government concerning the aims and necessity of such measures. The question of 'economic development takings' is a particularly controversial example of such deference in action; Irish courts, like courts in other jurisdictions,[3] have generally accepted the aim of securing economic development as sufficiently 'public' to justify compulsory acquisition of property for transfer to a private developer. However, depending on the owners who are adversely affected, such a deferential judicial approach may be inconsistent with social justice or other progressive property goals.

The decision of the US Supreme Court in *Kelo v City of New London* cast these concerns into sharp relief[4] *Kelo* held that non-pretextual deprivations ('takings' in the terminology of the US Constitution) for public–private partnership economic development projects were constitutional.[5] The decision was largely consistent with earlier Supreme Court authorities on the issue,[6] but there were strong dissenting judgments[7] and reactionary legislation and constitutional amendments at state level.[8]

M. A. Sluysmans, and L. C. A. Verstappen (eds.), *Rethinking Expropriation Law I: Public Interest in Expropriation* (The Hague: Eleven International Publishing, 2015), p. 15, tracing the historic roots of the public purpose requirement to Grotius.

3 A. J. van der Walt and R. Walsh, 'Comparative Constitutional Property Law' in M. Graziadei and L. Smith, *Comparative Property Law* (UK, USA: Edward Elgar, 2017) p. 192, pp. 205–6.

4 545 U.S. 469 (2005). For reflection on *Kelo*'s impact see, e.g., D. Merriam, 'Time to Make Lemonade from the Lemons of the *Kelo* Case' (2016) 48 *Connecticut Law Review* 1569.

5 For discussion of the meaning of 'pretextual' in this context see, e.g., D. Kelly, 'Pretextual Takings: Of Private Developers, Local Governments, and Impermissible Favortism' (2009) 17 *Supreme Court Economic Review* 173 and I. Somin, 'Controlling the Grasping Hand: Economic Development Takings After *Kelo*' (2007) 15 *Supreme Court Economic Review* 183.

6 See, e.g., *Berman* v. *Parker* 348 US 26 (1954); *Hawaii Housing Authority* v. *Midkiff* 467 US 229 (1984) for similarly broad understandings of 'public purpose'.

7 Justice O'Connor dissented, joined by Chief Justice Rehnquist, Justice Thomas and Justice Scalia. Justice Thomas delivered a separated dissent. See *Kelo* (n 4) at 494–523.

8 For discussion, see Somin, 'Controlling the Grasping Hand' (n 5), 244–59; C. Calfee, '*Kelo* v. *City of New London*: The More Things Stay the Same, the More They Change' (2006) 33 *Ecology Law Quarterly* 545.

In the wake of *Kelo*, significant academic energy was devoted to developing methods of tightening the public purpose requirement flowing from the Takings Clause of the Fifth Amendment of the US Constitution. As will be discussed in this chapter, scholars within the progressive property school of thought argued that values such as political participation,[9] dignity[10] and human flourishing[11] should guide judicial review of takings. Other scholars, cognisant of the sensitivity of substantive judicial review of the *aims* of takings, advocated heightened *means-ends* scrutiny to constrain the enactment and exercise of takings powers.[12] Still others argued for a ban on takings for certain purposes, in particular economic development and the renewal of blighted property,[13] or for a focus on due process and compensation as alternative sources of protection for owners.[14]

This chapter considers these complex and controversial issues through the lens of Irish constitutional property law. It illustrates how a 'public purpose' requirement has been inferred and applied in the context of a

[9] L. S. Underkuffler, 'Kelo's Moral Failure' (2006) 15 *William & Mary Bill of Rights Journal* 377.

[10] E. M. Peñalver, 'Property Metaphors and *Kelo* v. *New London*: Two Views of the Castle' (2006) 74 *Fordham Law Review* 2971.

[11] G. S. Alexander, 'The Public Use Requirement and the Character of Consequentialist Reasoning' in B. Hoops, E. Marais, H. Mostert, J. A. M. A. Sluysmans, and L. C. A. Verstappen (eds.), *Rethinking Expropriation Law II: Public Interest in Expropriation* (The Hague: Eleven International Publishing, 2015) p. 113.

[12] See, e.g., J. J. Lazzarotti, 'Public Use or Public Abuse' (2000) 49 *University of Missouri-Kansas City Law Review* 69; L. Mansnerus, 'Public Use, Private Use, and Judicial Review in Eminent Domain' (1983) 58 *New York University Law Review* 409 and N. Stelle-Garnett, 'The Public Use Question as a Takings Problem' (2003) 71 *George Washington Law Review* 934.

[13] See, e.g., Somin, 'Controlling the Grasping Hand' (n 5) and C. E. Cohen, 'Eminent Domain after *Kelo* v. *City of New London*: An Argument for Banning Economic Development Takings' (2006) 29 *Harvard Journal of Law and Public Policy* 491.

[14] See, e.g., J. E. Krier and C. Serkin, 'Public Ruses' (2004) *Michigan State Law Review* 859; A. Bell and G. Parchomovsky, 'Taking Compensation Private' (2007) 59 *Stanford Law Review* 871; E. F. Gallagher, 'Breaking New Ground: Using Eminent Domain for Economic Development' (2005) 73 *Fordham Law Review* 1837 and R. D. Godsil, 'Viewing the Cathedral from Behind the Color Line; Property Rules, Liability Rules, and Environmental Racism' (2004) 53 *Emory Law Journal* 1807. Lee Anne Fennell argues that to protect owners' autonomy, a self-assessment system should be used to identify owner consent to a proposed private-to-private taking for an unclear public purpose involving an opportunity to opt-in to a takings system in exchange for tax benefits: L. A. Fennell, 'Taking Eminent Domain Apart' (2004) *Michigan State Law Review* 957. See also J. D. Mahoney, 'Kelo's Legacy: Eminent Domain and the Future of Property Rights' (2005) *Supreme Court Review* 103, 128–29 for criticism of the potential for procedural reforms and changes to compensation rules to provide adequate protection for property rights.

constitutional text that expressly recognises that property rights are appropriately limited by social justice and common good considerations. It analyses the 'public purpose' doctrine developed by the Irish courts from a progressive property perspective to illuminate the outcomes that can emerge concerning public purpose when progressive property ideas have a constitutional foothold.

After addressing some terminological issues in Section 7.2, this chapter considers in Section 7.3 the relationship between security of possession and the right to exclude. Section 7.4 builds on this analysis in assessing the case-law flowing from the delimiting principles in Article 43.2 to determine if, and to what extent, they constrain the purposes for which the State can interfere with individual property rights. Section 7.5 considers the complexity of progressive property approaches to the 'public purpose' question in light of the analysis of Irish constitutional property law. Section 7.6 concludes.

7.2 Terminology

The core question analysed in this chapter is how, if at all, the Constitution constrains the purposes for which the State's regulatory power can be exercised. The basic constitutional requirement considered in this chapter – that the aim of an interference with property rights be justifiable by reference to 'the principles of social justice' and 'the exigencies of the common good' – applies to *all* State interferences with property rights, including those falling short of outright deprivation.[15] The primary focus of this chapter is on the justification that is required by the Constitution for public law measures or decisions that have the effect of taking away an owner's property rights in some thing (whether real or personal, tangible, or intangible), as opposed to merely restricting or otherwise regulating the exercise of such rights. To the extent that the Constitution as interpreted by the courts imposes strong constraints on purpose, it can be understood to robustly protect owners' security of possession.

The text of the Irish Constitution makes no reference on its face to the State's power to deprive an owner of property, whether through compulsory acquisition or otherwise, nor does it mention compensation. However, the statement in Article 43.2 of the State's power to regulate the exercise of property rights has been consistently interpreted by the

[15] See, e.g., *Buckley* v. *Attorney General* [1950] IR 67 and *Re Article 26 and Part V of the Planning and Development Bill 1999* [2000] 2 IR 321.

Irish courts as including a deprivation power. Most often, this occurs through the compulsory acquisition of land pursuant to statute.[16] However, there are other examples of State actions involving deprivation without any acquisition (what Fennell terms 'confiscatory non-takings'[17]), for example, the compulsory culling of animals to stop the spread of disease[18] and the statutory abrogation of rights of action against the State.[19] These examples indicate that the Constitution's relevance in respect of security of possession is not confined to compulsory acquisition of real property; it may also arise in respect of deprivations of personal property or intangible property rights. Furthermore, there is no requirement of *transfer* to the State, or indeed to some person or entity nominated by the State. Rather, the Constitution also captures public law measures that extinguish or destroy physical or intangible property. Consequently, this chapter will primarily refer to 'deprivations' rather than 'takings', 'expropriations', or 'eminent domain'.

7.3 Security of Possession and the Right to Exclude

Security of possession is intimately connected with the right to exclude others from privately owned property, but it goes further than merely prohibiting trespass to include at least some control over the alienation of property. Where security of possession is protected, as Calabresi and Melamed famously argued, 'property rules' allow owners to veto any proposed transfer, sale, or other loss of their property rights.[20] Accordingly, owners are entitled to *retain* their property rather than

[16] Irish legislative provisions generally refer either to compulsory acquisition or to compulsory purchase, reflecting the common-law tradition. The use of the term 'compulsory acquisition' is identifiable in constitutional property clauses rooted in the common-law tradition: see, e.g., s. 142 of the Constitution of Guyana; s. 18 of the Constitution of Jamaica; s. 13(2) of the Constitution of Malaysia; s. 8 of the Constitution of Mauritius. S. 51(xxxi) of the Australian Commonwealth Constitution refers to 'acquisition of property on just terms'. A notable exception is the Takings Clause of the Fifth Amendment of the US Constitution, which uses the term 'takings'.

[17] Lee Anne Fennell terms these 'confiscatory non-takings' to highlight the fact that compensation is not required for such takings: L. A. Fennell, 'Picturing Takings' (2012) 88 *Notre Dame Law Review* 57. As will be seen in the next chapter, the Irish courts have held that compensation is required for some such deprivations of property.

[18] *Rafferty* v. *Minister for Agriculture* [2014] IESC 61.

[19] *Re Article 26 and the Health (Amendment (No 2) Bill 2004* [2005] 1 IR 105.

[20] They contrast property rules with liability rules, which guarantee compensation but deny an owner a veto, and inalienability rules, which prevent all transfers of entitlement, regardless of an owner's wishes: G. Calabresi and A. D. Melamed, 'Property Rules,

merely being entitled to monetary compensation in the event of loss of property.[21]

Building on this idea, Kochan identifies a category of 'keepings rules', which assist owners in retaining their property.[22] Kochan argues '. . .it is precisely the ability to keep property that motivates its acquisition and that serves as a necessary element in offering any property up in a transaction.'[23] He contends that framing constitutional protection for property rights in terms of a 'right to keep' can trigger closer scrutiny of the legitimacy of deprivations.[24] Michelman suggests that protecting a 'right to keep' may be the distinctive function of constitutional property rights.[25] McFarlane characterises 'the right to keep' as an extension of 'the right to be free from expropriation', which she contends is central to realising property's underlying purpose of securing stability.[26] She argues that the right to keep is '. . .a necessary corollary of all of the other sticks in the bundle', which enables individuals to maintain social relations.[27]

The Irish constitutional protection for property rights includes security of possession, although as this chapter will demonstrate, the 'right to keep' has been emphasised in judicial rhetoric more than in outcomes. In

Liability Rules, and Inalienability: One View of the Cathedral' (1972) 85 *Harvard Law Review* 1089, 1092. Subsequent scholarship has focused on the further development of this typology: see, e.g., A. Bell and G. Parchomovsky, 'Pliability Rules' (2002) 101 *Michigan Law Review* 1; C. Rodgers, 'Nature's Place? Property Rights, Property Rules and Environmental Stewardship' (2009) 68 *Cambridge Law Journal* 550 and R. Walsh, 'The Evolving Relationship between Property and Participation in *English* Planning Law' in N. Hopkins (ed.), *Modern Studies in Property Law Volume 7* (Oxford: Hart Publishing, 2013), p. 263.

21 As G. S. Alexander puts it, '[t]he public-use requirement *represents* a recognition that property's core values are not compensable by monetary damages but can be adequately protected only by preventing the state from acting in the first place'. Alexander, 'The Public Use Requirement' (n 11), p. 123.

22 D. J. Kochan, 'Keepings' (2015) 23 *New York University Environmental Law Journal* 355. See also D. J. Kochan, 'The [Takings] Keepings Clause: An Analysis of Framing Effects from Labelling Constitutional Rights' (2018) 45 *Florida State University Law Review* 1021.

23 Kochan, 'Keepings' (n 22), 356.

24 Kochan, 'The [Takings] Keepings Clause' (n 22), 1081.

25 Michelman, 'Good Government' (n 1), 36.

26 A. G. McFarlane, 'Properties of Instability: Markets, Predation, Racialized Geography, and Property Law' (2011) 5 *Wisconsin Law Review* 855. She argues that stability secured through property law enables investment and protects individual identity. On stability of relations between individuals and assets as the core function of property law, see also A. Bell and G. Parchomovsky, 'A Theory of Property' (2005) 90 *Cornell Law Review* 531.

27 Ibid., 916.

Reid v. Industrial Development Agency,[28] which concerned the compulsory acquisition of residential property to incentivise private industrial development, McKechnie J (delivering the Supreme Court's judgment), described security of possession in these terms:

> The right to own what is one's own is as ancient as the earliest form by which unit groups of society regulated the affairs of those within them. Intrinsic to such a right is an entitlement to undisturbed enjoyment of one's property and if necessary, the right to rebuff all unwelcome interferences with it. This right has always been recognised as a bedrock of the common law, with Blackstone describing it as the 'third absolute right inherent in every Englishman…' (*Commentaries on the Laws of England* (176: Vol. 3: 138)).[29]

A key means by which a 'right to keep' is practically protected is through imposing constraints on the kinds of reasons or purposes for which the State can legitimately deprive an individual of his/her property, regardless of any compensation that might be payable.[30] In *Clinton* v. *An Bord Pleanála*, the Supreme Court held '…compensation as such is no substitute for the property itself.'[31] Geoghegan J stated that an acquiring authority would have to be satisfied that any particular compulsory acquisition was justified by the exigencies of the common good.[32] It is through this requirement of justification by reference to the delimiting principles in Article 43.2 that Irish constitutional law guarantees limited security of possession to owners.

[28] [2015] IESC 82.

[29] Ibid. at [40].

[30] See, e.g., Kochan arguing that a tighter public use requirement moves the Takings Clause in the US Constitution in the direction of a property rule, affording owners a veto on acquisitions regardless of compensation: D. J. Kochan, '"Public Use" and the Independent Judiciary: Condemnation in an Interest-Group Perspective' (1998) 3 *Texas Review of Law and Politics* 49, 90. See also R. A. Epstein, 'A Clear View of the Cathedral: The Dominance of Property Rules' (1997) 106 *Yale Law Journal* 2091 explaining the additional layer of institutional constraints on the exercise of the takings power and A. B. Lopez, 'Weighing and Reweighing Eminent Domain's Political Philosophies Post-Kelo' (2006) 41 *Wake Forest Law Review* 237, framing the relationship between public use and compensation in the Takings Clause in terms of a balance between republicanism and liberalism.

[31] [2007] 4 IR 701 at 723. See similarly G. S. Alexander, *Property and Human Flourishing* (Oxford: Oxford University Press, 2018) noting '[t]he public use requirement represents a recognition that property's core values are not compensable by monetary damages but can be adequately protected only by preventing the state from acting in the first place': p. 219.

[32] *Clinton* (n 31) at 723–24.

7.4 'The Principles of Social Justice' and 'the Exigencies of the Common Good' as Purpose Constraints

7.4.1 *The Recognition of an Ambiguous Purpose Constraint in Article 43.2*

In describing the incidents of ownership, Honoré argued:

> A general power to expropriate any property for any purpose would be inconsistent with the institution of ownership. If, under such a system, compensation were regularly paid, we might say either that ownership was not recognized in that system, or that money alone could be owned, 'money' here meaning a strictly fungible claim on the resources of the community.[33]

From this perspective, a public purpose is required to justify the exercise of compulsory acquisition powers to ensure that the possession of property, rather than merely its exchange value, is protected. Like Honoré, van der Walt characterises this requirement as a feature of a liberal understanding of ownership, saying '[t]he foundation of the requirement is the classic liberal view that state infringements of private property – and particularly expropriation – should be restricted to instances where the relevant action is unavoidable.'[34] Van der Walt identifies a spectrum of stringency in the interpretation of public purpose requirements:

> [t]he public purpose requirement can be interpreted in at least three different ways: very narrowly to restrict expropriations to actual public use; slightly wider to include some public benefits that exceed actual public use; or very widely to include almost any purpose that is vaguely beneficial to the public weal.[35]

Similarly Kochan distinguishes 'strong constraint versions' and 'weak constraint versions' of the 'public use' clause of the Takings Clause of the US Constitution.[36] The stricter the public purpose requirement,

[33] A. M. Honoré, 'Ownership', in A. G. Guest (ed.), *Oxford Essays in Jurisprudence*, (Oxford: Oxford University Press, 1961), pp. 107, 120.

[34] A. J. van der Walt, *Constitutional Property Law* (Cape Town: Juta Publishing, 2005), p. 242.

[35] Ibid., p. 243.

[36] Kochan, 'The [Takings] Keepings Clause' (n 22), 1066. For analysis of the variety in interpretations of the 'public use' requirement of the Takings Clause of the Fifth Amendment of the US Constitution see, e.g., N. A. Sales, 'Classical Republicanism and the Fifth Amendment's "Public Use" Requirement' (2000) 49 *Duke Law Journal* 339 and J. W. Scott, 'Public Use and Private Profit: When Should Heightened Scrutiny be Applied

according to both Honoré and van der Walt, the more liberal the institution of ownership.

As already noted, in interpreting Article 43 the Irish courts have held that it is only where a regulation of the exercise of property rights is adopted in pursuance of the exigencies of the common good and the principles of social justice that it can be held to be justifiable.[37] In *An Blascaod Mór Teoranta* v. *Commissioners for Public Works*, the High Court held that 'exigencies' in Article 43.2.2° required evidence of 'the existence of a pressing social need' for a deprivation.[38] In stark contrast, in *Shirley* v. *AO Gorman*, Peart J held that a meaning falling far short of necessity was appropriate.[39] The Supreme Court indicated in *Re Article 26 and the Health (Amendment) (No 2) Bill, 2004* that an *extreme crisis* would be required for an uncompensated abrogation of property rights for purely financial reasons to be justifiable under Article 43.[40] The next sections in this part analyse controversial purposes for deprivations that have been accepted by the Irish courts. These outcomes demonstrate that the purpose-constraint imposed by Article 43.2 is weak, falling within van der Walt's third category of very wide interpretations of the public purpose requirement.

7.4.2 Land Redistribution

The constitutionality of the compulsory acquisition of private property for redistribution to other private individuals was almost a foregone conclusion in the Irish context, since as was seen in Chapter 3, land redistribution was central to Irish social and economic policy when the Constitution was adopted. Through the Land Purchase Acts, the Land Commission compulsorily acquired land (upon payment of compensation) and sold it to tenant farmers and farmers with unprofitably small

to "Public-Private" Takings?' (2003) 12 *Journal of Affordable Housing and Community Development Law* 466.

37 See *Central Dublin Development Association* v. *Attorney General* (1975) 109 ILTR 86; *In re the Employment Equality Bill 1996* [1997] 2 IR 117 at 367 and *Shirley* v. *AO Gorman* [2006] IEHC 27.

38 [1998] IEHC 38 at 150.

39 *Shirley* (n 37) at 66. He reasoned, '. . .otherwise the legislature would be under such a strict requirement of proof of absolute necessity in every instance where they wish to amend the law in relation to delimiting property rights that the situation would become impossible.'

40 *Re Article 26 and the Health (Amendment (No 2) Bill 2004* (n 19) at 206.

agricultural holdings who could buy from the Land Commission with the assistance of State subsidised loans.[41] Given this historical backdrop, the constitutional legitimacy of the compulsory acquisition powers contained within the Land Acts was unsurprisingly repeatedly affirmed by the Irish courts. For example, in *Fisher* v. *Irish Land Commission*, Maguire CJ noted, '[i]t is not contested that the Legislature has the power to expropriate owners so as to make land available for public purposes.'[42] Similarly, in *Foley* v. *The Irish Land Commission*, O'Byrne J characterised the Land Acts as 'a very important branch of our social legislation',[43] while Walsh J stated in *Dreher* v. *Irish Land Commission* that the acquisition of private property pursuant to the Land Acts was compatible with Article 43 of the Constitution because it advanced peasant proprietorship.[44]

The Irish courts have also endorsed the legitimacy of land redistribution outside the context of the Land Acts, at least where it has been held to be plausibly directed towards achieving social justice. For example, in *Re Article 26 and Part V of the Planning and Development Bill 1999*,[45] the Supreme Court upheld the constitutionality of a social housing contribution requirement for developers, identifying the aims of the Bill as being to enable individuals to purchase housing at a time of very high prices and to ensure the physical integration of social and affordable housing with other types of housing. The Court said: '[i]t can scarcely be disputed that it was within the competence of the Oireachtas to decide that the achievement of these objectives would be socially just and required by the common good.'[46] Addressing the constitutionality of

[41] In *Fisher* v. *Irish Land Commission*, Maguire CJ succinctly explained how land redistribution operated under the Land Acts: '[t]he main task set the Land Commission was to create a peasant proprietorship of a certain standard. This it was to do, first, by expropriating the landlords and by making available advances to tenants to enable them to purchase their holdings, and secondly, by taking untenanted land, and in the case of large holdings by taking these holdings or portions thereof for the purpose of creating economic holdings. To make available land for these purposes wide powers of expropriation were given. Owners of untenanted land in the congested counties lost their land by virtue of the statute. Untenanted land elsewhere became liable to be taken by executive or administrative action. Tenanted land could be taken by the machinery of s. 5 of the Land Law (Ir.) Act, 1881, adapted specially for the purpose.' [1948] IR 3 at 26.

[42] Ibid. at 23.

[43] [1952] IR 118 at 153.

[44] [1984] ILRM 94 at 96.

[45] *Re Article 26 and Part V of the Planning and Development Bill 1999* (n 15).

[46] Ibid. at 349.

a statutory scheme for tenant enfranchisement[47], Peart J in *Shirley* v. *AO Gorman* held:

> In an extreme example, where the vast majority of property in the State was permitted by the laws of the State to remain in the ownership of a small group at the top of the tree so to speak, it could be seen as a justifiable interference with the property rights of those in such a protected and privileged position that they be required to make a share of that wealth available for the many at the middle or bottom of the tree, albeit on the basis of purchase or compensation. The passing of laws to facilitate the ownership of property being thus enjoyed by a greater number of persons in society would constitute the pursuit of a principle of social justice.[48]

Peart J held that this would be the case even if some of the beneficiaries of the policy did not in fact need to so benefit in order to secure social justice. On this view, property rights can be legitimately redistributed even where *particular* private-to-private transfers do not advance social justice, provided that the redistribution scheme aims to secure social justice.[49]

7.4.3 Urban Regeneration

In a series of cases, the Irish courts accepted the constitutionality of compulsory acquisition for urban regeneration. While they reaffirmed the need for compulsory acquisition to be undertaken only in the interests of the common good, and for the exercise of such powers to be subject to strict scrutiny, they accepted non-specific purposes such as 'redevelopment', 'renewal', and 'regeneration' as sufficiently 'public' in nature.[50] Furthermore, they accepted that compulsorily acquired property could be transferred to private developers.

Perhaps least controversially, the compulsory acquisition of derelict sites was upheld as being in the public interest.[51] However, much wider

[47] Under the relevant scheme, compensation was payable to landlords at 1/8th of the market value of the property.

[48] *Shirley* (n 37).

[49] The transfer at issue in Shirley was in fact between two commercial operations, not from a landlord to a residential tenant.

[50] For detailed analysis, see R. Walsh, '"The Principles of Social Justice": The Compulsory Acquisition of Private Property for Redevelopment in the US and Ireland' (2010) 32 *Dublin University Law Journal* 1.

[51] *Egan* v. *An Bord Pleanála* [2011] IEHC 44.

statutory powers of compulsory acquisition for regeneration purposes have also been upheld. In *Central Dublin Development Association* v. *The Attorney General*[52], which involved a challenge to the Local Government (Planning and Development) Act 1963 (the first comprehensive legislative scheme for planning and development control in Irish law), the High Court upheld statutory powers designed to secure the redevelopment of 'obsolete' areas.[53] Section 77 of the Act gave planning authorities the power to compulsorily acquire land in such areas to be let to private developers for redevelopment.[54] The applicant argued that this power was an 'unjust attack' on property rights. Kenny J rejected this contention, saying that private redevelopment might be the most efficient means of regenerating an area and noting that the High Court could review the decisions of planning authorities delineating obsolete areas. He also rejected the claim that dispossessed owners should have a right to *reinstatement* in the premises that they previously owned post-redevelopment, as that would create practical difficulties and undermine the feasibility of regeneration schemes.[55] He upheld s. 75 of the Act, which provided that land acquired by a planning authority for the purposes of the Act could be sold or leased, holding that such a power was necessary to enable private redevelopment.

The holding in *Central Dublin Development Association* is reinforced by the High Court's decision in *Crosbie* v. *Custom House Docks Development Authority*.[56] The plaintiff owned lands in the Docklands area of Dublin City, and the Custom House Dock Development Authority, acting under s. 5 of the Urban Renewal (Amendment) Act, 1987, issued a compulsory acquisition order in respect of those lands. The plaintiff agreed to sell but later challenged the constitutionality of s. 5 of the 1987 Act.[57] He argued that since his land was initially sought for a

[52] (1975) 109 ILTR 69.

[53] An obsolete area was defined under s. 2 of the Act as 'an area consisting of land. . .which, in the opinion of the planning authority, is badly laid out or the development of which has, in their opinion, become obsolete, together with such land contiguous or adjacent to the principal land as, in the opinion of the planning authority, is necessary for the satisfactory development or user of the principal law.'

[54] *Central Dublin Development Association* (n 52) at 87.

[55] For instance, he noted that new buildings might not be suitable for old purposes, and new rents would have to be fixed post-redevelopment. Ibid.

[56] [1996] 2 IR 531.

[57] Section 9 imposed a general duty on the Authority to secure the redevelopment of the Custom House Docks Area. It empowered the Authority 'to acquire, hold, and manage land' in the relevant area, 'for its development, redevelopment, or renewal by either the

national sports stadium that was not ultimately developed, he should be entitled to *reacquire* his property.[58] Costello P determined that the Authority was entitled to choose a broad purpose for the acquisition.[59]

In *Clinton* v. *An Bord Pleanála*, the Irish courts again endorsed the use of compulsory acquisition powers to facilitate private redevelopment for regeneration and economic development purposes.[60] *Clinton* concerned the compulsory acquisition by Dublin City Council of the applicant's property as part of a plan to regenerate Dublin city centre. The order stated that the property was required for 'development purposes'. Clinton sought to have the compulsory purchase order quashed on the basis that the acquiring authority had to specify a *particular* purpose for which it intended to use the acquired property. In the Supreme Court, Geoghegan J held that while some compulsory acquisitions were for clear predefined purposes that might need to be specified, that was not the case with the acquisition of the applicant's land for redevelopment. As Geoghegan J put it:

> . . .the whole process would usually involve private developers in some form at least and plans as yet unknown which they would propose and envisage and which would eventually require planning permission. That is quite different from property required for the purposes of council offices or a public swimming pool, for instance.[61]

Since private regeneration could happen in a variety of ways, the Council simply had to show that acquisition was desirable in the public interest to achieve that broad aim. At the same time, Geoghegan J endorsed heightened scrutiny by judges of individual compulsory acquisition

Authority or by any other person', thereby clearly envisaging private involvement in redevelopment projects.

58 Despite the fact that he had actually sold his land to the authority, Costello P accepted that the applicant had standing to make these arguments before the court, because the contract for sale would not have been entered into if the Authority had not threatened to acquire his property. *Crosbie* (n 56) at 550.

59 Ibid. at 550. Costello P held that since the Oireachtas had imposed a duty on the Authority to secure the redevelopment of the Docklands area and had given it the power to compulsorily acquire the relevant land, the Oireachtas had '. . .in effect concluded that the public good which is to be achieved by urban renewal requires the limitations on the objector's constitutionally protected rights.' Ibid. at 544–45.

60 [2005] IEHC 84, [2007] 4 IR 701. Prior to *Clinton*, Budd J doubted the appropriateness of passing control of compulsorily acquired land to private citizens or entities in *An Blascaod Mór Teoranta* v. *Commissioners for Public Works*. He expressed surprise at the fact that powers in respect of land compulsorily acquired pursuant to the An Blascaod Mór National Historic Park Act, 1989 could be delegated pursuant to statute to a private company limited by guarantee. *Blascaod Mór Teoranta* (n 38) at 255.

61 *Clinton* (n 31) at 717.

decisions.[62] On the facts, he determined that the Council had satisfied itself appropriately that the acquisition of the applicant's property was necessary in the public interest.

The effect of these urban renewal decisions is that the degree of security of possession protected by the Constitution is limited, despite the adoption of a heightened scrutiny approach. An almost unfettered legislative power to select the means for realising broad public objectives through deprivation emerges. Geoghegan J's conclusion in *Clinton* that specificity of purpose is not required where real property is compulsorily acquired for complex projects involving third parties means that where a project's goals are loosely defined, an acquiring authority is understood to have less of an obligation to specify the purpose(s) of the acquisition than in circumstances of acquisition for a defined project, e.g., the construction of a particular road.[63] This makes it attractive for acquiring authorities to employ broad language in describing the aims of particular acquisitions.[64]

However, the context of these regeneration decisions is significant. *Clinton* and *Crosbie* required the courts to weigh the property rights of developers at the height of the economic boom against the public interest in urban renewal. In this context, and bearing in mind the progressive tenor of Article 43.2, it is perhaps unsurprising that security of possession did not win out; flexible compulsory acquisition powers were clearly in the interests of the common good in circumstances where high demand for land and resulting costs might otherwise have impeded the realisation of the public interest.[65]

7.4.4 *Economic Development*

A different, more controversial compulsory acquisition scenario fell to be considered in *Reid* v. *The Industrial Development Agency (Ireland)*, which

[62] He held that the reasonableness of such determinations would not be decided on review by merely considering whether the making of the order was irrational or fundamentally contrary to reason or common sense, because that approach would have insufficient regard to the fact that a compulsory purchase order was an invasion of constitutionally protected property rights.

[63] On this point, see also E. E. Meidinger, 'The "Public Uses" of Eminent Domain: History and Policy' (1981) 11 *Environmental Law Journal* 1, 49.

[64] For discussion of the particular problems of private takings see, e.g., Gray, 'Human Property Rights' (n 2); N. Stelle-Garnett, 'The Neglected Political Economy of Eminent Domain' (2006) 105 *Michigan Law Review* 115 and E. Waring, *Private-to-Private Takings: Rhetoric and Reality* (Oxford: Hart Publishing, forthcoming 2021).

[65] On the importance of expropriation powers in the public interest, see Alexander, 'The Public Use Requirement' (n 11).

arose during the economic crisis and squarely raised the issue of economic development takings.[66]

Reid concerned section 16 of the Industrial Development Act 1986, which empowered a semi-state body, the Industrial Development Authority (now known as IDA Ireland), to compulsorily acquire land to provide or facilitate the provision of sites for the establishment, development, or maintenance of an industrial undertaking, under certain circumstances.[67] The property in issue in *Reid* was the first that the IDA sought to acquire using this power, indicating that previously it had negotiated strategic land acquisitions without resorting to compulsory acquisition.[68] The site in question was situated near a key technology industry site in the Greater Dublin area, but the land was not zoned for industrial use. It was occupied as a residential property that was protected because of its historical significance. The IDA issued notice of intention to acquire the property and held an information-gathering inquiry presided over by a senior barrister at which the applicants made representations and were legally represented. The acquisition order that was made by the IDA following this inquiry was challenged as a disproportionate interference with the adversely affected owner's constitutional property rights.

In the High Court, Hedigan J held that an industrial undertaking did not have to be identified for a site prior to a compulsory acquisition decision. While he acknowledged the significant interference with rights involved in the compulsory acquisition of an historic family home, he prioritised the public interest in economic development and deferred to the expert judgment of the IDA concerning the need for the acquisition.[69] On appeal, the Supreme Court adopted a stricter approach but did not squarely address the constitutionality of compulsory acquisition for economic development. The Court held that the constitutional protection afforded to property rights meant that a statute conferring a compulsory acquisition power had to be interpreted strictly, and furthermore,

66 [2013] IEHC 433 (HC); [2015] IESC 82 (SC).

67 It must be of the opinion that industrial development will or is likely to occur as a result of the acquisition, and that such development will conform to the statutory criteria set out in s. 21, such as providing or maintaining employment.

68 As Bell and Parchomovsky point out, it is usually less costly in both economic and political terms to secure consensual agreement: Bell and Parchomovsky, 'A Theory of Property' (n 26), 605.

69 He recounted in detail the previous successes of the IDA in attracting industry to Ireland, and the value of such development to the broader Irish economy

had to be applied by administrators in a manner consistent with the Constitution. Accordingly, it concluded that a power to compulsorily acquire property for land-banking would have to be expressly stated in legislation, which was not the case in the 1986 Act. Significantly, it did not suggest that an express statutory power to land-bank would be an unconstitutional interference with property rights, nor did it intimate that private redevelopment was an impermissible use of compulsorily acquired property.

However, *Reid* does indicate that constraint may be imposed on *administrative* freedom in two ways: first, through strict construction of statutory provisions conferring compulsory acquisition powers based on the need to protect constitutional property rights; and second, through closer judicial supervision of the exercise of such powers. The Court held that the impact of an acquisition on the right to private property must be justified by the 'exigencies of the common good' informed by 'the principles of social justice', that compensation will almost always form an important part of the overall constitutional protection for property rights, and that the grant and exercise of compulsory acquisition powers must adhere to the principle of minimal impairment of rights.

7.4.5 Assessing Heightened Scrutiny as a Response to Weak Purpose-Constraint

The analysis in the previous sections of this part has shown that Irish constitutional property law does not limit the State to depriving individuals of property for 'public use' – transfers to private parties are permitted. At the same time, the courts have held that interferences with property rights by the State must be in pursuance of social justice and that the exercise of compulsory acquisition powers will be subjected to heightened scrutiny. However, they have interpreted and applied these requirements very deferentially and have generally upheld broad purposes for deprivations, for example urban renewal. In general, provided compensation is paid, the State will be permitted to take privately owned property. Accordingly, on the issue of security of possession, the progressive tenor of the delimiting principles in Article 43.2 influences Irish judges more than any intuitive liberal conception of ownership that would indicate a narrow interpretation of the State's deprivation powers.

Analysing this issue in the context of US Takings law, Merrill argued that deference flows naturally from an ends-focus, since '. . .the question naturally arises: which institution is better suited to determine permissible ends-the courts or the legislature? In a society committed to majoritarian rule, not surprisingly the answer has been the legislature.'[70] This tendency has been attributed by various commentators to judges' concerns about their qualification to review the aims of public projects and policies, and about the democratic legitimacy of such review.[71] Perhaps in light of this judicial disinclination, many academics arguing for tighter judicial control of the exercise of public powers that deprive an owner of property have focused their attention on strict or heightened means-ends scrutiny.[72] For example, Garnett contends that heightened means-ends scrutiny is required whenever 'eminent domain' powers are exercised.[73] Merrill adopts a narrower approach, arguing for heightened

[70] T. W. Merrill, 'The Economics of Public Use' (1986) 72 *Cornell Law Review* 61, 64. See also L. A. Fennell, 'Picturing Takings' (n 17), 85, arguing: '. . .the public use line embodies a means-ends test that is highly deferential to legislative and executive actors, on the grounds that they are best able to determine how to achieve legitimate governmental objectives.'

[71] For example, Paul Boudreaux argues, '[d]emanding more exacting scrutiny of the justifications for eminent domain is likely to lead courts into an inextricable bog of trying to assess and weigh the benefits of public development projects – a fact-finding job that is a legislative, not judicial, function.' P. Boudreaux, 'Eminent Domain, Property Rights, and the Solution of Representation Reinforcement' (2005) 83 *Denver University Law Review* 1, 5. On this point, see also Krier and Serkin, 'Public Ruses' (n 14), 864–65 and G. S. Alexander, 'Eminent Domain and Secondary Rent-Seeking' (2005) 1 *New York University Journal of Law and Liberty* 958, 961. For a contrary view, see Mahoney, arguing that expertise and legitimacy concerns do not mean that judicial oversight of eminent domain is not beneficial, since such oversight provides the important safeguard of multiple veto points for rearrangements of property rights: J. D. Mahoney, 'Kelo's Legacy: Eminent Domain and the Future of Property Rights' (n 14), 130.

[72] See, e.g, J. J. Lazzarotti, 'Public Use or Public Abuse' (n 12), arguing for rationality review of the exercise of eminent domain power. Similarly, Laura Mansnerus advocates an 'actual rationality' test, 'requiring evidence that the condemnor did reasonably consider the taking to serve a public purpose': Mansnerus, 'Public Use, Private Use, and Judicial Review' (n 12). Nader and Hirsh argue that strict scrutiny of eminent domain takings is required where the acquired land is transferred to a private party, and where 'the individual interest of those whose land is taken is particularly strong and monetary compensation cannot significantly compensate for the loss', and the dispossessed owner (s) are relatively politically powerless: R. Nader and A. Hirsh, 'Making Eminent Domain Humane' (2004) 49 *Villanova Law Review* 207, 219–24. Some scholars have objected to such heightened scrutiny approaches on the basis that the courts lack the necessary legitimacy and expertise: see, e.g., L. E. Blais, 'The Public Use Clause and Heightened Rational Basis Review' (2016) 48 *Connecticut Law Review* 1497.

[73] She argues that courts should require '. . .that a given exercise of eminent domain is "reasonably necessary" to advance or, put differently, "related in nature and extent" to the public purpose used to justify it': Stelle-Garnett, 'The Public Use Question as a Takings Problem' (n 12), 964.

scrutiny by judges of 'eminent domain' decisions in three types of situations: first, in circumstances where they impose high uncompensated subjective losses on a dispossessed owner; second, where there is a strong likelihood of secondary rent-seeking by one or a small number of individuals capturing a taking's surplus[74]; and third, where the acquirer has bypassed the opportunity to acquire the relevant property in a 'thick' market, either intentionally or negligently.[75]

Others have confined their call for heightened scrutiny to circumstances involving acquisition/deprivation of particular types of property. Perhaps most famously, Radin sought to increase protection for 'personal property', which she defined as property that is bound up with an individual's identity.[76] She argued that 'personal property' should be immune from compulsory acquisition, or if not so immune, that the government should be required to show a 'compelling state interest' to justify its acquisition, and further that the acquisition was the 'least intrusive alternative'.[77] In the same vein, Barros contended that compulsory acquisitions of homes should be permissible only once it was shown that the property could not be purchased voluntarily, and that there was no reasonable alternative course of action that would achieve the same public goal.[78] Similarly van der Walt argued for heightened scrutiny of deprivation and/or regulation for economic or general redevelopment purposes causing displacement or dispossession of homes.[79]

[74] Merrill argues, '[c]ases involving delegation of eminent domain to one or a few private parties, or involving condemnation followed by retransfer of the property to one or a few private parties, present the primary situations where such secondary rent seeking is likely to occur.' Merrill, 'The Economics of Public Use' (n 70), 87–88. This approach is approved in Alexander, 'Eminent Domain and Secondary Rent-Seeking' (n 71).

[75] Merrill, (n 70), 89. Merrill describes a 'thick market' as '...any situation where market conditions do not allow a seller to extract economic rents from a buyer.' Ibid., 76.

[76] Radin contrasts 'personal property' with property that is held for instrumental reasons, which she terms 'fungible property'. M. J. Radin, 'Property and Personhood' (1982) 34 *Stanford Law Review* 957, 960. Key in drawing this distinction is whether the loss of the object '...causes pain that cannot be relieved by the object's replacement': ibid., 959. For criticism of this aspect of Radin's thesis, arguing for at most legal protection of socio-cultural meanings attached to resources, see J. D. Jones, 'Property and Personhood Revisited' (2011) 1 *Wake Forest Journal of Law & Policy* 93.

[77] Ibid., 1006. A similar approach is endorsed by Stephen Jones in the context of third-party transfers: see S. J. Jones 'Trumping Eminent Domain Law: An Argument for Strict Scrutiny Analysis Under the Public Use Requirement of the Fifth Amendment' (2000) 50 *Syracuse Law Review* 285.

[78] B. Barros, 'Home as a Legal Concept' (2006) 46 *Santa Clara Law Review* 255, 297–98.

[79] A. J. van der Walt, 'Housing Rights in the Intersection between Expropriation and Eviction Law' in L. Fox O'Mahony and J. A. Sweeney (eds.), *The Idea of Home in Law: Displacement and Dispossession* (Farnham: Ashgate, 2011) p. 55, 86, and 99.

Whether these (and other) heightened scrutiny approaches require project-specific justification for compulsory acquisition decisions depends largely on how they are applied.[80] A 'compelling' or 'important' public interest rationale for an acquisition does not necessarily require an acquiring body to establish that an acquisition is *actually* justified. It may suffice to show that the acquisition is *hypothetically* or *conceivably* justifiable given a particularly important public aim (which might be very broadly defined). Such 'conceivability review' is highly deferential to the judgments of the legislature and executive.[81] Tests of 'necessity' or 'least intrusive means' apparently require acquisition-specific justification. However, that justification may still be established by reference to a very broad objective, relative to which a wide range of means could reasonably be regarded as necessary. Where an objective is broadly stated, judges may infer an intention to pursue a more specific objective from the acquisition itself, which is likely to satisfy even a heightened scrutiny test. The Irish doctrine considered in this chapter shows that the adoption of a heightened standard of review does not necessarily correspond to strict scrutiny of the aims of deprivations.

However, the Supreme Court's decision in *Reid* suggests one way that constitutional property rights protection may constrain the purposes of deprivations, namely by mandating strict scrutiny of the scope of legislative deprivation powers. This approach does not require political judgment on the part of courts, or any second guessing of policy judgments, but encourages transparency and clarity on the part of legislators in enacting powers that can be exercised to deprive owners of their property. This in turn helps to ensure that owners are less likely in practice to be caught unaware by a disruptive deprivation, allowing for smoother transitions in owners' evolving expectations concerning security of possession.[82]

80 Stephen Jones notes the tendency for arguments for strict scrutiny in the expropriation to be vague as to the actual import of the test proposed: Jones, 'Trumping Eminent Domain Law' (n 77).

81 Nicole Stelle-Garnett uses the phrase 'conceivability review' in the US context and says '. . .so long as some conceivable purpose justifies the exercise of eminent domain, the means by which the government acquires land is essentially beyond scrutiny': N. Stelle-Garnett, 'Planning as Public Use?' (2007) 34 *Ecology Law Quarterly* 443, 452.

82 On this 'transition smoothing' function of constitutional property rights protection, see C. M. Rose, 'Property and Expropriation: Themes and Variations in American Law' (2000) *Utah Law Review* 1 and H. Doremus, 'Takings and Transitions' (2003) 19 *Journal of Land Use and Environmental Law* 1.

7.5 Competing Priorities in Progressive Approaches to Purpose-Constraint

7.5.1 Tensions in the Law and Theory of Deprivations

The judicial interpretation of the Irish constitutional property clauses demonstrates that in practice, even where they have an express mandate to do so, judges may be reluctant to develop contested concepts like social justice and the common good to scrutinise the aims of the political branches of government. This suggests that progressive approaches to property founded on ideas like social obligation or human flourishing are likely to prompt deferential judicial review rather than the explicit development of a progressive theory of the legitimate purposes of public law deprivations of property rights. Furthermore, the Irish experience demonstrates that judicial deference in respect of the *purposes* of deprivations cannot be overcome simply through tighter or stricter *means-ends* scrutiny. The Irish courts purport to apply a strict scrutiny standard in reviewing the constitutionality of decisions and/or laws that deprive owners of property rights, but in substance they have adopted a largely deferential approach on the question of purpose. In this respect, the case-law reveals a striking gap between judicial rhetoric, which robustly proclaims security of possession to be a core facet of ownership warranting strict scrutiny of interferences, and outcomes, which predominantly favour the public interest over individual property rights.

A similar tension is identifiable in progressive property theory on the public purpose question. On the one hand, progressive property scholars regard the existence of powers of compulsory acquisition as necessary to secure progressive ends, but on the other hand, they express concern about how such powers may be exercised, related to both the purpose and means of acquisitions. They wish to prevent unfair exercises of compulsory acquisition powers, while at the same time affirming the need for flexible acquisition powers.[83] To further explore the competing priorities of progressive property approaches to purpose-constraint, this section analyses two scholarly arguments on the issue in more detail. The aim is first, to give a flavour of the complexity of progressive property perspectives on the public purpose question; and second, to assess the

[83] For a succinct summary of this dilemma for progressive scholars, see G. S. Alexander, 'Eminent Domain and Secondary Rent Seeking' (n 71), 959. See also J. W. Singer, 'The Ownership Society and Takings of Property: Castles, Investments, and Just Obligations' (2006) 30 *Harvard Environmental Law Review* 309.

practicability of those approaches by analysing them in light of the case-law considered in this chapter. This analysis in turn helpfully illuminates aspects of the Irish doctrine considered in the previous part of this chapter.

7.5.2 *Security of Possession, Human Flourishing, and Personal Property*

Alexander advances one progressive perspective on deprivations (or, to use the terminology that he variously adopts, expropriations or exercises of the power of 'eminent domain').[84] As was seen in Chapter 2, Alexander argues that the core function of property is to secure human flourishing. Accordingly, he contends that judges should review expropriation powers and decisions to determine their consistency with that fundamental goal. This requires judges to adopt a purposive approach to constitutional interpretation. They must consider the competing property values implicated by a proposed acquisition, which Alexander contends include autonomy, personal security, self-determination, self-expression, and responsibility.[85] Such values must be balanced in light of the purpose of the public use requirement, which Alexander defines as being '. . .to prevent the state from forcing sales of land in circumstances which would sacrifice the values of property as a legally protected, especially a constitutionally protected, interest.'[86]

Such purposive analysis involves a largely contextual approach, subject to two presumptions that are suggested by Alexander as flowing from the 'human flourishing' justification of property: first, the power of the State to expropriate is, as a general matter, justified by the need to secure human flourishing; second, possession of property that secures personal autonomy and self-realisation (e.g., residential homes) should be strongly protected to facilitate human flourishing.[87] In respect of the first of these

[84] Alexander, 'The Public Use Requirement' (n 11). See also Alexander, *Property and Human Flourishing* (n 31), pp. 209–30.

[85] He identifies autonomy, personal security, self-determination, self-expression, and responsibility as values central to 'the instrumental fit between property and human flourishing'. Alexander, 'The Public Use Requirement' (n 11), pp. 124–26.

[86] Ibid., p. 123.

[87] Alexander is following the example of German law in this regard, which 'scales' claims to security of possession based on the importance of the held property to individual personal liberty and self-realisation on the one hand, and to other persons on the other hand: see ibid., pp. 127–28. This approach also echoes that advanced by Radin, providing

presumptions, Alexander argues that the capabilities required for individual human flourishing are dependent on the existence of necessary infrastructure, such as roads, utility lines, and parks. The need for that infrastructure in turn requires, and justifies, compulsory acquisition. Alexander argues that in cases where strong property values are identifiable on both 'sides' of an 'eminent domain' dispute, the proportionality principle should be employed, including a requirement that a court be satisfied that the collective goal(s) motivating an acquisition could not be achieved by less invasive means.[88]

The doctrine analysed in this chapter mirrors some features of this approach. In respect of *judicial reasoning*, Irish judges analyse compulsory acquisition powers and decisions on a case-by-case basis to determine whether they are justified by 'the exigencies of the common good' and 'the principles of social justice', which are expansive concepts capable of encompassing many of the 'property values' identified by Alexander, as well as non-property community interests. Proportionality analysis is used in some, but not all cases, to structure this holistic assessment. However, the Irish experience has been that judges do not articulate their understanding of social justice.[89] This is notwithstanding the fact that Article 43.2 provides an express mandate for judges to test the legitimacy of State interferences with the exercise of property rights by reference to 'the principles of social justice' and 'the exigencies of the common good'. In terms of *outcomes*, the Irish experience has been that the individual property values identified by Alexander (autonomy, personal security, self-expression, and responsibility) rarely win out over competing public interests that could be realised through compulsory acquisition.

A notable feature of Alexander's 'human flourishing' perspective on the question of public purpose is his contention that the nature of the property to be acquired and its significance for individual autonomy and

for differentiation in terms of constitutional protection between 'personal' and 'fungible' property: see Radin, 'Property and Personhood' (n 76).

88 Again, Alexander describes himself as borrowing from the German approach in this regard: 'The Public Use Requirement' (n 11), pp. 132–33. He has also argued that 'high scrutiny' of purpose may be warranted in cases involving the dispossession of an entire residential community. Alexander, 'Eminent Domain and Secondary Rent-seeking' (n 71), 965.

89 See, e.g., D. Barrington, 'Private Property Under the Irish Constitution' (1973) 8 *Irish Jurist* 1, 4, noting that Irish judges have instinctively avoided the questions of social and economic policy necessarily at issue in constitutional property law based on legitimacy and expertise concerns.

self-realisation should be considered by judges. As already noted, Radin proposed a differentiated approach to judicial review based on property's constitutive role in facilitating individual development and personhood. One criticism of this approach has been that assessing subjective connections to property is problematic because it requires judges to grapple with unfamiliar 'home' values.[90] Taking their lead from the fact that Article 40.5 of the Irish Constitution specifically protects the inviolability of the dwelling, Irish judges have begun in recent cases to differentiate between dwellings and other forms of real and personal property. This development has been controversial, not least because of disagreement amongst judges on whether inviolability of the dwelling should be understood as a guarantee of privacy within the physical space of a dwelling or as a guarantee of heightened security of possession of dwellings.[91] This supports the first criticism of Radin's thesis outlined above, namely the unfamiliarity of judges with 'home' values, which can present doctrinal challenges particularly in respect of securing predictability and consistency. Nonetheless, the Irish experience offers some insight into the doctrinal shape that differentiated legal protection for residential property may take. It supports Jones' contention that any such differentiation will in practice focus on bolstering valued socio-cultural meanings associated with object relations,[92] reflecting as it does Ireland's status as a home-ownership society.[93]

In *Wicklow County Council* v. *Fortune*,[94] Hogan J held that an injunction requiring the demolition of a dwelling built in contravention of planning laws had to be justified as the least invasive means of achieving relevant planning goals because of the importance of the inviolability of

[90] See, e.g., N. Hopkins, 'The Relevance of Context in Property Law: A Case of Judicial Restraint?' (2011) 31 *Legal Studies* 175, discussing the difficulties involved in distinguishing between domestic and commercial contexts in developing property law. See also L. Fox, *Conceptualising Home: Theories, Laws and Policies* (Oxford: Hart Publishing, 2007).

[91] For full discussion, see G. Hogan, G. Whyte, D. Kenny and R. Walsh, *Kelly: The Irish Constitution* (5th ed.) (Dublin: Bloomsbury, 2018), pp. 2042–55, R. Walsh, 'Reviewing Expropriations: Looking Beyond Constitutional Property Clauses' in B. Hoops, E. Marais, H. Mostert, J. A. M. A. Sluysmans, and L. C. A. Verstappen (eds.), *Rethinking Expropriation Law I: Public Interest in Expropriation* (The Hague: Eleven International Publishing, 2015), p. 125.

[92] Jones, 'Property and Personhood Revisited' (n 76).

[93] See M. Norris, 'Varieties of Home Ownership: Ireland's Transition from a Socialised to a Marketised Policy Regime' (2016) 31 *Housing Studies* 81, 81.

[94] [2012] IEHC 406.

the dwelling.[95] This approach entailed stricter scrutiny of deprivations of dwellings than other types of deprivations. However, Hogan J's approach was expressly rejected by another High Court judge in *Wicklow County Council* v. *Kinsella*,[96] primarily based on concerns about undermining planning law. In *Reid*, the Supreme Court expressed some support for *Fortune*, although it did not purport to rule on the standard of review to be applied to deprivations of property flowing from breaches of planning rules. However, McKechnie J suggested that the *impact* of compulsory acquisition could vary in different cases depending on the nature of the property taken and the extent of the taking involved.[97]

Most recently, in *Meath County Council* v. *Murray*,[98] the Supreme Court disagreed with *Fortune* insofar as it required strict scrutiny of orders seeking the demolition of unlawfully constructed property. It stressed the need to secure the public interest in the enforcement of planning control. However, it did not discount the potential relevance of the nature of property to a demolition decision. On this approach, the nature of the property that an individual will be deprived of is not an automatic trigger for heightened or strict scrutiny. Rather, it is a factor that is weighed in a broader proportionality analysis. *Murray* further suggests that strict scrutiny is appropriate where there is a deprivation involving no fault on the part of the dispossessed owner (as *per Clinton, Crosbie*, and *Reid*), but not where a deprivation is triggered by unlawful activity on the part of the dispossessed owner (as *per Murray*).[99] Accordingly, while the courts were motivated by the express recognition

[95] He said that Article 40.5 of the Constitution provided that 'the dwelling should enjoy the highest possible level of legal protection which might realistically be afforded in a modern society': Ibid. at [41]. On that basis, he required that in order to justify the proposed demolition, the council would have to show ' . . .that the continued occupation and retention of the dwelling would be so manifestly at odds with important public policy objectives that demolition was the only fair, realistic and proportionate response': Ibid. at [42].

[96] See [2015] IEHC 229.

[97] *Reid* (n 28) at 44. Article 40.5 of the Constitution, which specifically protects the inviolability of the dwelling, was referred to by the Supreme Court in *Reid* as a relevant constitutional right in that case, to be considered in conjunction with the property rights guarantees, but the Court did not confine its analysis concerning compulsory acquisition to dwellings.

[98] [2017] IESC 25.

[99] This distinction is further supported by the fact that the Irish courts have repeatedly upheld the constitutionality of statutory powers providing for the forfeiture of property, for example proceeds of crime legislation. See, e.g., *Clancy* v. *Ireland* [1988] IR 326; *Gilligan* v. *Criminal Assets Bureau* [1998] 3 IR 185; *Competition Authority* v. *Judge*

given to the dwelling in Article 40.5 of the Constitution to acknowledge its particular value, they continued to place considerable weight on the legal status of dwellings rather than focusing on the practical value of dwellings to occupants. While *Murray* opens the door to differentiated legal protection for various forms of property, it does not hold that the personhood function of legal protection for property rights necessarily outweighs countervailing collective concerns. Consistent with the overall approach of Irish constitutional property law, a holistic evaluation of the fairness of an interference with individual property rights is required.

7.5.3 Security of Possession, Political Participation, and Community Interests

Also writing from a progressive property perspective, Underkuffler[100] builds upon the work of Michelman[101] to argue that a key consideration for judges reviewing the constitutionality of compulsory acquisitions should be the impact on the 'material security' of adversely affected individuals, on their community networks, and on their ability to be effective participants in the political system.[102] Underkuffler's core argument is that the 'moral warrant' for such an interference with individual property rights is the consistency of that decision with equally respected participation.[103] She situates the exercise of compulsory acquisition powers in the context of overlapping, and at times competing, individual, community, and broader collective interests. Her approach focuses on the balance struck between the interests of the wider community in the benefits of a proposed redevelopment and the interests of the displaced

O'Donnell [2008] 2 IR 275; *Murphy* v. *GM* [2001] 4 IR 113; *Criminal Assets Bureau* v. *Kelly* [2012] IESC 64, and *Criminal Assets Bureau* v. *Murphy* [2017] IESC 64.

100 Underkuffler, 'Kelo's Moral Failure' (n 9).

101 F. I. Michelman, 'Mr. Justice Brennan: A Property Teacher's Appreciation' (1980) 15 *Harvard Civil Rights-Civil Liberties Law Review* 296.

102 Similarly, Peñalver focuses on the dignitary value of a person's home, including its importance for an individual's sense of self-worth, and contends that when the State exercises its power of eminent domain, it must show that such action was '. . .necessary to accomplish important public objectives' and must adequately compensate owners for their losses. E. M. Peñalver, 'Property Metaphors' (n 10), 2976.

103 Underkuffler, 'Kelo's Moral Failure' (n 9), 383. Others have approached this issue through calling for stricter compensation requirements: see, e.g., H. Dagan, 'Takings and Distributive Justice' (1999) 85 *Virginia Law Review* 741 (advocating a progressive compensation system that would award greater compensation to poor condemnees).

community.[104] In addition, she emphasises the value of community networks as an *individual* interest to be considered in assessing the constitutionality of compulsory acquisitions. Finally, Underkuffler raises a concern that 'eminent domain' is usually exercised in respect of communities with limited social, economic, and political power.[105]

It is likely to be the case that even within a community, individuals will have competing, and at times conflicting, views about the merits or demerits of a compulsory acquisition.[106] Some owners may not have deeply embedded community connections, depending, for example, on their location or their personal circumstances and preferences.[107] The complex participatory frameworks established by planning law regimes appear designed in part to provide a space for mediating between such competing views.[108] Accordingly, drawing reliable presumptions about the significance of community connections would likely prove challenging for judges.[109] Evidence of subjective connections to communities

[104] Underkuffler 'Kelo's Moral Failure' (n 9), 385. To those could be added the general societal (or 'community') interest in a flexible expropriation power that was highlighted by Alexander, 'The Public Use Requirement' (n 11).

[105] Wendell Pritchett raises similar concerns about the systemically targeted nature of eminent domain of blighted property, focusing in particular on its inequitable racial impact: '[t]he reality of urban renewal was that redevelopment was used to reshape the racial and economic geography of cities': W. Pritchett, 'The "Public Menace" of Blight: Urban Renewal and the Private Uses of Eminent Domain' (2003) 21 *Yale Law and Policy Review* 1, 46. See also P. Boudreaux, 'Eminent Domain' (n 71); Nader and Hirsh, 'Making Eminent Domain Humane' (n 72); A. Goodin, 'Rejecting the Return to Blight in Post-*Kelo* State Legislation' (2007) 82 *New York University Law Review* 177 and C. N. Brown, 'Justice Thomas' *Kelo* Dissent: The Perilous and Political Nature of Public Purpose' (2016) 23 *George Mason Law Review* 273.

[106] G. Parchomovksy and P. Siegelman, 'Selling Mayberry: Communities and Individuals in Law and Economics' (2004) 92 *California Law Review* 75, 144, note that communities are generally not conflict free, can support unattractive values, and '. . .can be stifling and can breed narrow-mindedness and conformity'.

[107] See E. M. Peñalver, 'Property as Entrance' (2005) 91 *Virginia Law Review* 1889 on the various types of community connections that individuals have, ranging from binds to tightly knit communities to looser networks, e.g., in urban environments.

[108] On the role of participatory frameworks in compulsory acquisition processes see, e.g., B. Slade and R. Walsh, 'The Marginality of Property in Expropriation Law: A Comparative Assessment' in G. Muller, G. J. Pienaar, R. Brits, B. V. Slade and J. Van Wyk (eds.), *Transformative Property Law* (Cape Town: Juta Publishing, 2018), p.21 and Stelle-Garnett, 'Planning as Public Use' (n 81).

[109] The need for contextual analysis is heightened by the fact that different types of compulsory acquisitions may have different community impacts. For example, Parchomovksy and Siegelman distinguish between three types of takings: isolated takings (with no or very limited community impact); tippings (involving the condemnation of multiple properties in a community); and clearings (involving the total

may also be difficult for judges to identify and assess. Inferences could perhaps be drawn from the nature of adversely affected communities (e.g., their physical infrastructure, evidence of community demographics, details of activities). However, such an approach would require judges to reach potentially controversial conclusions about the make-up and operation of 'good' communities and 'good' community actors. Alternatively, a principle could be established, in the manner suggested by many commentators in respect of residential property, that heightened scrutiny should apply in *all* cases of community disruption. This approach would overcome the problem concerning judicial assessment of community connections but would be engaged in almost all cases of compulsory acquisition.[110] Such uniformity seems inconsistent with the flexible compulsory acquisition power identified as necessary in progressive property theory.[111]

Underkuffler's concerns about the impact of eminent domain on material security, community connections, and political empowerment can perhaps be better understood as concerns about the social justice implications of the exercise of compulsory acquisition powers. Irish constitutional property law demonstrates one way that this concern could be addressed in legal doctrine. As was already seen, in *Re Article 26 and the Health (Amendment) (No 2) Bill, 2004*,[112] the Supreme Court held, '. . .the right to ownership of property has a moral quality which is intimately related to the humanity of each individual. It is also one of the pillars of the free and democratic society established under the Constitution.'[113] It stated that the Constitution protects property rights of both high and comparatively low economic value, affording particular protection '. . .where the persons affected are among the more vulnerable sections of society and might more readily be exposed to the risk of unjust attack.'[114] The Court argued that the individuals who were adversely affected by the Bill – who were mostly elderly – would have had limited ability to understand and question the legality of burdens imposed upon them. On this approach, the concern about expansive or

uprooting of communities): Parchomovsky and Siegelman, 'Selling Mayberry' (n 11), 137–38.

110 For criticism of such a general heightened scrutiny approach see, e.g., Blais, 'The Public Use Clause' (n 72).

111 See Alexander, 'The Public Use Requirement' (n 11).

112 *Re Article 26 and the Health (Amendment (No 2) Bill 2004* (n 19).

113 Ibid. at 201–02.

114 Ibid. at 208.

potentially exploitative use of deprivation powers is reflected not in constitutional constraints on the *purposes* of compulsory acquisitions, but rather in judicial review of the *impact* of such acquisitions.

In the Irish context, such a status-focused approach finds plausible textual support in Article 43.2's explicit reference to the regulation of the exercise of property rights by reference to 'the principles of social justice'.[115] For example, Boudreaux argues that a focus on the political status and power of dispossessed owners '. . .would allow eminent domain to play a role in helping, not hindering, the cause of social justice.'[116] As was noted in Chapter 2, Mulvaney argues for attention to 'identity' in property law, involving '. . .contextual concern for the current status – including the social, economic, and political needs – of the groups or individuals involved in particular resource conflicts.'[117] He contends that such an approach emphasises individuals' connections to their communities and their social obligations, which in turn inform the definition of property rights. At the heart of Mulvaney's focus on identity is consideration of the human stories that are implicated in property disputes.[118] Accordingly, Mulvaney argues that legal rules may apply differently depending on the circumstances of the adversely affected individuals. He argues for concentration:

> . . . not only on individuals' present status, established property holdings, and current wealth, but also on (i) individuals' and communities' personal, social, political, and economic identities that have impacted their life courses and relation to property law to date, and (ii) the overall effects of continuing to recognize those property holdings presently in place.[119]

[115] This interpretation of the meaning of 'the principles of social justice' is further supported by Article 45. 4. 1° of the Irish Constitution, which contains a 'Directive Principle of Social Policy' stating '. . .the State pledges itself to safeguard with especial care the economic interests of the weaker sections of the community, and, where necessary, to contribute to the support of the infirm, the widow, the orphan, and the aged.' While the Directive Principles are stated to be non-cognisable by the courts, they have had some limited impact on judicial interpretations of the meaning of the common good in Article 43.2.2°: see R. Walsh, 'Private Property Rights in the Drafting of the Irish Constitution: A Communitarian Compromise' (2011) 33 *Dublin University Law Journal* 86, 109–13.

[116] Boudreaux, 'Eminent Domain' (n 71), 55.

[117] T. M. Mulvaney, 'Progressive Property Moving Forward' (2014) 5 *California Law Review Circuit* 295, 366.

[118] See T. M. Mulvaney, 'Legislative Actions and Progressive Property' (2016) 40 *Harvard Environmental Law Review* 137, 159–60 for discussion of other progressive property approaches with a similar focus.

[119] Ibid., 161.

In relation to compulsory acquisition, he contends that the tendency to exercise those powers in respect of the property of less affluent communities signals the need to attend to the identities of those whose property is compulsorily acquired.[120] In many respects, the Supreme Court's decision in the *Health Bill case* illustrates this approach in action. However, the Court did not elaborate on its understanding of vulnerability, nor did it articulate a theory of social justice to ground its focus on 'identity'.

The idea of vulnerability has received extensive consideration in legal theory in recent years, rooted in the work of Fineman.[121] While a detailed exploration of this theory is beyond the scope of this book, it provides a useful basis for considering alternative directions that the approach adopted in the *Health Bill case* could potentially take. Most significantly, Fineman resists an identity focus, arguing that vulnerability is '. . .universal and constant, inherent in the human condition'.[122] According to this view, vulnerability should always be considered where the impact of a public action or decision on individual rights is in issue. Such an understanding of vulnerability rejects a comparative doctrinal test such as that adopted in the *Health Bill case*, which was focused on identifying 'the more vulnerable sections of society'. In adopting this approach, the Supreme Court assumed that as a category, the adversely affected owners in that case were vulnerable and lacking in political capacity. However, as Fox-O'Mahony points out, '. . .the heterogeneity of older owners as an "identity group" . . . threatens to render any broad use of an "at risk" label inherently suspect'.[123] The vulnerability of owners will vary – as Fineman puts it, '. . .our vulnerabilities range in magnitude and potential at the individual level',

[120] See Mulvaney, 'Progressive Property Moving Forward' (n 117), 371–73.

[121] See, e.g., M. A. Fineman, 'The Vulnerable Subject: Anchoring Equality in the Human Condition' (2008) 20 *Yale Journal of Law & Feminism* 1; M. A. Fineman, 'Equality, Autonomy, and the Vulnerable Subject in Law and Politics' in M. A. Fineman and A. Grear (eds.), *Vulnerability: Reflections on a New Ethical Foundation for Law and Politics* (Farnham: Ashgate, 2013), p. 13, and M. A. Fineman, 'The Vulnerable Subject and the Responsive State' (2010) 60 *Emory Law Journal* 251.

[122] Fineman, 'The Vulnerable Subject' (n 121), 24. Fineman's work has been applied by legal scholars in property law contexts: see, e.g., H. Carr, 'Housing the Vulnerable Subject: The English Context' in M. A. Fineman and A. Grear (eds.), *Vulnerability: Reflections on a New Ethical Foundation for Law and Politics* (Farnham: Ashgate, 2013), p. 107 and L. Fox-O'Mahony, 'Ageing, Difference and Discrimination: Property Transactions in the Crucible of Human Rights Norms' (2013) 24 *King's Law Journal* 202.

[123] L. Fox-O'Mahony, 'Ageing, Difference and Discrimination' (n 122), 211.

informed by the various contexts in which we are embedded.[124] Fineman's approach to vulnerability points to the need to consider the embedded social and economic situation of *all* adversely affected owners and their context-specific political power. Notwithstanding Mulvaney's use of the 'identity' label that Fineman resists, in fact the approach that he advocates closely resembles Fineman's argument for contextual attention to vulnerability.

Defining and identifying vulnerability in this context (indeed in any legal context) is a complex, contestable exercise. As Carr and Hunter put it, 'vulnerability is a particularly ambiguous and elusive requirement'.[125] A resolution of this conceptual ambiguity is beyond the scope of this chapter. However, it is possible to situate the Irish approach to vulnerability in terms of connections between the democratic process, independence and private ownership that were explored in Chapter 2. The decision in the *Health Bill case* points towards what Michelman terms a 'structural' understanding of constitutional property rights as entitling all individuals on an equal basis to '. . .the maintenance of the conditions of one's fair and effective participation in the constituted order', including in particular protection against '. . .sudden changes in the major elements and crucial determinants of one's established position in the world, as one has come reasonably to understand that position.'[126] In this approach, individual property rights that underpin and facilitate political participation are protected against abrupt, destabilising disruptions. It suggests that 'vulnerability' exists where the material security of adversely affected owners would be threatened in a manner that would undermine independence, prompting the need for heightened scrutiny. This approach does not provide an easy answer to the complex distributive dilemmas often raised in constitutional property rights adjudication. However, as a doctrinal strategy, it has the potential to clarify and focus the assessments of fairness undertaken by judges by highlighting the

124 Fineman, 'The Vulnerable Subject' (n 121), 10. However, Fineman's approach has been criticised as failing to provide a facility for prioritising amongst vulnerable individuals in making policy decisions, leading to the suggestion that vulnerability should be considered relative to a threat or problem. N. A. Kohn, 'Vulnerability Theory and the Role of Government' (2014) 26 *Yale Journal of Law and Feminism* 1.

125 H. Carr and C. Hunter, 'Managing Vulnerability: Homelessness Law and the Interplay of the Social, the Political and the Technical' (2008) 30 *Journal of Social Welfare and Family Law* 293, 304.

126 Michelman, 'Mr. Justice Brennan' (n 101), 306.

basic goal of facilitating equal, effective participation in a democratic society.

The *Health Bill case* signposts but does not develop any of these lines of thought. However, it signals that further exploration of vulnerability has a practical role to play in the development of constitutional property law in the Irish context. Future doctrinal developments will provide insights that will be of interest to the development and implementation of progressive property approaches in other jurisdictions.

7.6 Conclusions

Considered against the backdrop of the broader scholarly debate on the 'public purpose' or 'public use' question, the Irish experience shows that the adoption of stricter means-ends scrutiny will not necessarily result in a more interventionist approach on the part of judges. Once broad purposes for deprivations are accepted as constitutional, any means-ends scrutiny of such deprivations will necessarily be deferential given the very broad range of means that are conceivably or hypothetically necessary to secure goals such as redevelopment. From a progressive property perspective, the reluctance of Irish courts to place constraints on legislative freedom through purpose-limitations is positive in one sense, as it means that the constitutional protection of property rights does not impede the realisation of important collective goods through the exercise of compulsory acquisition powers. However, the progressive property perspectives considered in this chapter all place some weight on the value of security of possession, both for the individual and for society.

Irish constitutional property law demonstrates the practical challenges presented by this tension between competing progressive goals concerning property rights. The Irish courts have laid down two key requirements: that statutory powers that enable public authorities to deprive owners of their property must be strictly construed; and further, that where the legitimacy of specific *administrative* decisions resulting in deprivation is challenged, such decisions should be shown to be clearly justified by 'the exigencies of the common good'. While these features of Irish constitutional property law are rhetorically suggestive of strong protection for security of possession, property rights are in fact generally treated as fungible in nature. The progressively framed delimiting principles in Article 43.2 – 'the exigencies of the common good' and 'the principles of social justice' – have grounded the identification of a purpose-constraint. However, those delimiting principles have not been interpreted by the courts in a manner that clearly or consistently explains the nature and stringency of that purpose-constraint. This highlights the difficulties that judges experience in interpreting and implementing such concepts even where they are enshrined in the text of the Constitution.[127] Overall, in respect of security of possession, the progressively framed delimiting principles in the Constitution have prompted a pro-public interest approach rather than an approach reflecting the more 'full-blooded' liberal conception of ownership suggested in some of the Irish courts' rhetoric.[128]

The *Health Bill case* suggests a route for bridging this gap between rhetoric and outcomes through a focus on the social and economic situation of owners who are deprived of property through public law measures or decisions. It presents a potential doctrinal avenue for addressing progressive property concerns about deprivations, in particular about the impact on the political status and power of adversely affected individuals, the consequences for community integrity and connections, and the potential for disproportionate impact on particular groups. It marks a meaningful judicial attempt to address Mulvaney's progressive property theme of 'identity'. However, at present it stands alone in Irish constitutional property law. More needs to be done to analyse and explain how 'identity' is to be taken into account doctrinally, including the relevance of the idea of vulnerability, and how to accommodate Rule of Law considerations. These issues are considered further in Chapter 9.

The previous chapter, this chapter, and the next, all demonstrate that the Irish courts do not sharply distinguish between different types of interference with property rights (whether regulating the exercise of constitutionally protected property rights or depriving an owner of such rights), or between issues of justification (considered in this chapter) and remedy (considered in the next chapter). Rather, a contextual approach is adopted. This involves a holistic assessment of the fairness of an interference with property rights, taking account of a broad range of factors, including the purpose of the interference, the presence of fair procedures in the implementation of such an interference, its distributional implications, and any provision for compensation. Nonetheless, important differences between cases involving deprivation and cases involving

[127] See F. I. Michelman, 'Expropriation, Eviction, and the Gravity of the Common Law' (2013) 24 *Stellenbosch Law Review* 245, 248–49.

[128] J. W. Harris, *Property and Justice* (Oxford: Oxford University Press, 1996), p. 30.

restrictions on the exercise of property rights are identifiable. As was seen in this chapter, strict scrutiny is applied by the courts to the exercise of compulsory acquisition powers, albeit not robustly. The next chapter will analyse the different approaches to compensation taken in respect of both categories of cases, demonstrating that they are not sharply distinguished. Rather, they exist on a spectrum of more-to-less presumptively 'unjust attacks' on property rights.

8

Security of Value in a Progressive Constitutional Context

8.1 Introduction

Unlike most other fundamental rights, states can legitimise interferences with property rights by paying financial compensation to an adversely affected owner, subject to the weak purpose constraints considered in the previous chapter. In this way, property rights are treated as primarily fungible interests, with constitutional protection afforded to their *exchange* value rather than their *use* value. As Calabresi and Melamed famously described it, property rights are often protected by 'liability rules' rather than 'property rules'.[1] Liability rules allow for the non-consensual deprivation of property rights in return for payment of an objectively determined value (often, but not necessarily, market value). Under such rules, owners are entitled to monetary compensation for loss of entitlement but cannot veto such loss.[2] The presence or absence of compensation and the measure of any compensation payable are highly relevant factors in determining whether a regulation or deprivation of property rights is constitutionally permissible.[3] In addition, compensation requirements add a budgetary hurdle to the imposition of such measures.[4]

This chapter explores the degree of security of value that the Irish constitutional protection of property rights affords to owners. The Irish Constitution makes no express reference to compensation and it

[1] G. Calabresi and A.D. Melamed, 'Property Rules, Liability Rules and Inalienability: One View of the Cathedral' (1972) 85 *Harvard Law Review* 1089.

[2] As Carol Rose explains, this means that property protected by property rules and property protected by liability rules are not the same, with the latter in effect a type of option. C. M Rose, 'Property and Expropriation: Themes and Variations in American Law' (2000) *Utah Law Review* 1, 10.

[3] A. J. van der Walt and R. Walsh, 'Comparative Constitutional Property Law' in M. Graziadei and L. Smith, *Comparative Property Law* (Cheltenham: Edward Elgar, 2017) pp. 193, 213.

[4] H. Doremus, 'Takings and Transitions' (2003) 19 *Journal of Land Use* 1, 11.

explicitly recognises the State's power to regulate the exercise of property rights in accordance with 'the principles of social justice' to secure 'the exigencies of the common good'. This appears to provide an ideal constitutional environment for a progressive approach to compensation. That hypothesis will be tested in this chapter through an exploration of Irish compensation doctrine and relevant progressive property perspectives on compensation. Through such grounded doctrinal analysis, this chapter examines the complexity of progressive property approaches to security of value, which as with the public purpose requirement considered in the previous chapter, involve a tension between guarding against unfair exploitation and avoiding excessive constraint of legislative freedom.

Two views of compensation tend to be distinguished and framed in oppositional terms in constitutional property law and scholarship: one focused on full (usually market value) compensation through the enforcement of rules; the other focused on qualified compensation entitlements administered through contextual decision making (whether judicial or administrative). Allen terms these approaches the 'liberal' and 'social democrat' views of compensation respectively.[5] He characterises the liberal view as treating compensation as a matter of corrective justice, whereas the social democrat view associates it with distributive justice.[6] In a similar vein, Rose distinguishes between Lockean-inspired neo-classical economic approaches to property rights and civic republican conceptions of property, arguing that disagreements over the significance of these purposes of property '. . .are manifested in disagreements about the circumstances under which the public may regulate property without compensation.'[7] This chapter demonstrates that while 'liberal' and 'social democrat' views may be neatly distinguishable in theory, in practice, the irresolvable tension between them is at the heart of constitutional property law. This can be seen in Irish compensation doctrine, which moves

[5] T. Allen, 'Liberalism, Social Democracy, and the Value of Property under the European Convention on Human Rights' (2010) *International and Comparative Law Quarterly* 1055. See also J. Sluysmans, S. Verbist, and R. de Graaff, 'Compensation for Expropriation: How Compensation Reflects a Vision on Property' (2014) 3 *European Property Law Journal* 1.

[6] Allen, 'Liberalism, Social Democracy, and the Value of Property' (n 5), 1058, and Sluysmans, Verbist, and de Graaff, 'Compensation for Expropriation' (n 5), 29. See also G. S. Lunney Jr, 'Compensation for Takings: How Much Is Just?' (1993) 42 *Catholic University Law Review* 721, emphasising the differing levels of trust in the legislature that these two approaches reflect.

[7] C. M. Rose, '*Mahon* Reconstructed: Why the Takings Issue is Still a Muddle' (1984) 57 *Southern California Law Review* 561, 594.

between the 'liberal' and 'social democrat' views, between a rule-based and contextual approach, and between prioritising legislative and judicial decision making.

This chapter first analyses the broad structure of Irish compensation law, including the distinction drawn between deprivations of property and restrictions on the exercise of property rights. In Section 8.3, it considers the role of Article 43.2's reference to 'the principles of social justice' in shaping the role of distributive justice in Irish compensation doctrine. Section 8.4 addresses Irish compensation law's corrective justice focus. It analyses the constitutional principles that govern the value of the compensation that must be paid to owners where an entitlement to compensation is held to arise, which are largely generated in the context of deprivations of property, particularly the compulsory acquisition of land. This reflects the fact that where compensation is held to be required for a regulatory interference with property rights, the primary remedy in Irish law is invalidation of the empowering legislation, not an award of compensation.[8] Sections 8.5 and 8.6 analyse progressive property approaches to compensation in light of Irish compensation doctrine. They focus on two foundational issues in property theory that are raised by the compensation question: first, in Section 8.5, the *ends* of property, in particular whether those are primarily the protection of owners' interests, including the value of their holdings, or whether they are more socially oriented; second, in Section 8.6, the *means* of property, in particular whether it should consist primarily of rules or standards. Section 8.7 concludes.

8.2 'Unjust Attack' and the Deprivation/Restriction Spectrum

Although it is not mentioned in Article 40.3.2° or Article 43, compensation is a key factor that Irish judges consider when assessing whether a legislative scheme that restricts the exercise of property rights or deprives an owner of such rights is an 'unjust attack' on those rights in breach of

[8] There is provision in Irish constitutional law for an action to be taken for damages for breach of constitutional rights, which could potentially be influential in the property rights context. To date, that route has not generally been taken by aggrieved owners, reflecting the emergent nature of the Irish constitutional tort. For discussion of the development of constitutional torts in Irish law, see G. W. Hogan, G. Whyte, D. Kenny and R. Walsh, *Kelly: The Irish Constitution*, 5th ed. (Dublin: Bloomsbury Professional, 2018), pp. 1535–42.

the requirements of the Constitution.[9] The case-law establishes that compensation is much more likely to be constitutionally required where the State *deprives* an owner of his or her real or personal property than where it controls the *exercise* of property rights. In addition, it is important to distinguish between deprivation of all an owner's powers in respect of some 'thing', whether tangible or intangible – such as the right to control its use, to exclude others from it, and to sell or transfer it – and deprivation of one or more of those powers falling short of total deprivation. Finally, a deprivation may take only a part of some thing, for example where a section of a landholding is compulsorily acquired.

These much-debated distinctions between deprivation and restriction/regulation were addressed in the Irish context in *Central Dublin Development Association* v. *The Attorney General.*[10] It involved a wide-ranging constitutional challenge to the Local Government (Planning and Development) Act, 1963, which introduced planning control. Kenny J described the circumstances in which compensation was constitutionally required for interferences with property rights as follows: '[i]f any of the rights which together constitute our conception of ownership are abolished or restricted (as distinct from the abolition of all the rights), the absence of compensation for this restriction or abolition will make the Act which does this invalid if it is an unjust attack on property rights.'[11] This approach is circular, as the need for compensation is assessed by reference to the concept of 'unjust attack', but the presence or absence of compensation is itself relevant to that concept. As such, the broader question of what constitutes a fair burden re-surfaces when judges consider when compensation is due; justification and remedy are not sharply distinguished. To assist in answering that foundational question of fairness, Kenny J developed the distinction between deprivations of the whole 'bundle of rights' and more limited restrictions, saying: '. . .while

9 *J & J Haire & Co Ltd* v. *Minister for Health* [2009] IEHC 562, *Re Article 26 and the Health (Amendment) (No.2) Bill 2004* [2005] 1 IR 105.

10 (1975) 109 ILTR 69. For comparative discussion of the deprivation/regulation issue, see R. Walsh and A. J. van der Walt, 'Comparative Constitutional Property Law' in L. Smith and M. Graziadei (eds.), *Research Handbook on Comparative Property Law* (Cheltenham: Elgar Publishing, 2017), p. 193.

11 *Central Dublin Development Association* (n 10) at 86. In *M & F Quirke & Sons* v. *An Bord Pleanála*, O'Neill J re-stated Kenny J's approach in *Central Dublin Development Association* with approval, saying: '[c]ompensation will be required in circumstances where property is wholly expropriated or where the bundle of rights which constitute ownership are substantially taken away but lesser interferences with property rights would not require compensation': [2010] 2 ILRM 91 at 110.

some restrictions on the exercise of some of the rights which together constitute ownership do not call for compensation because the restriction is not an unjust attack, the acquisition by the State of all the rights which together make up ownership without compensation would in almost all cases be such an attack.'[12] The loss or restriction of one or more incidents of ownership is unlikely to require compensation, but where the State takes all those incidents, compensation will usually be required.

Applying this approach, Kenny J concluded that the 1963 Act was not an unjust attack on property rights. He held that the power for local authorities to make a development plan after hearing and considering objections was constitutional because development plans were necessary for the common good. Kenny J acknowledged that the making of such a plan would decrease the value of some real property. However, he held that there was no requirement of compensation for those devaluations.[13] Kenny J also rejected the argument that the requirement that owners apply for permission for the development of land or the retention of structures violated Articles 40.3.2° and 43 of the Constitution. He reasoned that such an interference was not an uncompensated acquisition, but rather was an adverse interference with only one incident of ownership.

Kenny J's analysis contains the two key distinctions noted at the outset of this section, between deprivations and restrictions on the one hand, and between total and partial deprivation on the other. It indicates that compensation may in theory be constitutionally required for both types of interference with property rights – in Irish law, the central question is always whether the interference, absent compensation, is an 'unjust attack' on property rights. The closer the interference comes to the deprivation end of the spectrum, the more likely it is that that question will be answered in the affirmative. In cases falling short of full deprivation, it is a question of degree, meaning for instance that the appropriation of the right to use one's land in a certain way, or of the right to

[12] *Central Dublin Development Association* (n 10) at 86.

[13] Kenny J noted that (at the time) the Rent Restrictions Acts and the Landlord and Tenant Acts made substantial inroads into the freedom of owners to use their property as they wished, and yet no suggestion had ever been made that those Acts were unconstitutional or that affected owners were entitled to compensation for losses suffered pursuant to the Acts: ibid. at 84. However, in the subsequent decision of the Supreme Court in *Blake v. The Attorney General* [1982] 1 IR 117, the Rent Restriction Acts were struck down as unconstitutional interferences with property rights, in part due to the lack of compensation for adversely affected owners.

alienate one's land under particular circumstances, is less likely to require compensation.[14] In this way, *Central Dublin Development Association* resists what Radin termed 'conceptual severance' – the discrete protection of each incident of ownership through compensation – even though as was discussed in Chapter 4 it characterises ownership as a disaggregated 'bundle of rights'.[15] Any interference with property rights must be assessed against the backdrop of the totality of the incidents of ownership. A deprivation of only one of those incidents will not usually require compensation, while depriving an owner of all those incidents will ordinarily require compensation. On the spectrum between these two extremes, compensation is constitutionally required if the extent of regulation or deprivation constitutes an 'unjust attack' absent compensation – in other words, if it imposes an unfair burden on the adversely affected owner.

The approach set out by Kenny J in *Central Dublin Development Association* has become the basis upon which Irish courts generally determine whether compensation should be paid by the State where it restricts property rights. They have usually upheld uncompensated restrictive measures, consistent with a rejection of 'conceptual severance'.[16] For example, in *PMPS Ltd* v. *The Attorney General*, the plaintiff industrial and provident society and one of its shareholders challenged the constitutionality of the Industrial and Provident Societies (Amendment) Act, 1978.[17] Section 5(2) of the Act provided that, subject to a possible extension, industrial and provident societies were not to accept or hold deposits after a transition period of five years. No compensation was payable to the societies for losses suffered because of this change in the law. In the Supreme Court, O'Higgins CJ rejected the plaintiffs' contention that the impugned provision constituted a deprivation of the society's business or the property rights of its shareholders. He held that it was a regulation and control of the society's business in the public interest and as such was not an 'unjust attack' on property

[14] *Central Dublin Development Association* (n 10) at 86.

[15] M. J. Radin, *Reinterpreting Property* (Chicago: University of Chicago Press, 1995), p. 129.

[16] See, e.g., *O'Callaghan* v. *Commissioner for Public Works* [1985] ILRM 364 (historic preservation legislation); *Pine Valley Developments* v. *Minister for the Environment* [1987] IR 23 (revocation of outline planning permission), and *Gorman* v. *Minister for the Environment* [2001] 2 IR 414 (devaluation of taxi licence through deregulation).

[17] [1983] 1 IR 339.

rights.[18] As both Rose and Doremus note, such interferences primarily involve questions of transition connected to changes in legal rules.[19] Where those transitions are not unduly abrupt and do not single out particular groups or individuals unfairly, restrictions imposed on the exercise of property rights will usually be constitutional without compensation.[20]

However, there are some decisions that demonstrate a marginal element of 'conceptual severance' in Irish constitutional property law. In *ESB v. Gormley*, discussed further below, a deprivation of the right to exclude was held to be invalid absent compensation in circumstances where a semi-state body was empowered to make a permanent physical imposition on privately owned land.[21] In *Blake* v. *Attorney General* and *Re Article 26 and the Housing (Private Rented Dwellings) Bill 1981*, the lack of compensation for adversely affected owners was cited as a factor weighing in favour of finding rent control measures unconstitutional.[22] In *Re Article 26 and the Employment Equality Bill 1996*, a requirement that employers bear the costs of ensuring workplace accessibility without compensation was found to be unconstitutional.[23] However, in a wide range of other decisions, the right to profit has not been protected in this way.[24] Overall, therefore, 'conceptual severance' is an outlier trend in Irish constitutional property law, which generally applies the 'whole bundle' approach articulated in *Central Dublin Development Association*.

[18] Ibid. at 361. A similar unwillingness to guarantee the profitability of commercial activities through compensation was evident in the Supreme Court's decision in *Pine Valley* (n 16), which held that compensation was not required where the applicants bought property based on its value with a grant of outline planning permission attached that was subsequently found to be void because its grant was *ultra vires* the Minister for the Environment's powers. In reaching this conclusion, the Court reasoned that a grant of outline planning permission was an enhancement of an owner's property rights, and further, that investment in land for development was 'a major example of a speculative or risk commercial practice': at 37. See also *M & F Quirke & Sons* (n 11) at 110, and *Liddy* v. *The Minister for Public Enterprise and the Irish Aviation Authority* [2003] 2 JIC 0401 (4 February 2003) (HC).

[19] Rose, 'Mahon Reconstructed' (n 7), 18 and Doremus, 'Takings and Transitions' (n 4).

[20] For discussion of these criteria see, e.g., Doremus, 'Takings and Transitions' (n 4), 34.

[21] [1985] 1 IR 129.

[22] See [1982] 1 IR 117; [1983] IR 181.

[23] [1997] IESC 6, [1997] 2 IR 321.

[24] See, e.g., *PMPS* v. *Attorney General* [1983] 1 IR 339; *Pine Valley* (n 16); *Gorman* (n 16); *M & F Quirke & Sons* (n 10), and *Liddy* (n 18).

8.3 The Distributive Justice Focus in Irish Compensation Law

8.3.1 Introduction

There is significant overlap in Irish compensation law between the judicial treatment of two distinct questions: whether compensation ought to be paid for a deprivation of property and the measure of such compensation. Both these issues are considered in this section. Article 43.2's reference to 'the principles of social justice' as a core delimiting principle influences judicial decisions about *when* compensation is required and *how much* it should be worth. Where the objective of an interference with property rights is deemed to be particularly consonant with 'the principles of social justice', the Irish courts recognise the possibility that compensation may not be constitutionally required or that less than full compensation may be permissible. In this way, there is a significant (although largely unacknowledged) distributive focus in Irish compensation law.

The case-law generating these principles illustrates how Article 43.2's reference to 'the principles of social justice' can be applied by courts to justify limitations on owners' rights, here, to security of value through compensation. The decisions show that even where there is express constitutional recognition of a 'progressive' delimiting principle such as social justice, common law conceptions of property can influence judicial approaches to compensation, resulting in presumptively strong compensation entitlements.[25] However, as will be seen, the Irish courts have tempered this tendency by holding that those presumptive entitlements can potentially be displaced where the public-regarding aims of deprivations are particularly important and where legislation expressly indicates how compensation should be addressed. This section analyses how the Irish courts reached this accommodation of property rights and social justice in relation to compensation.

8.3.2 The Doctrinal Root of the Distributive Justice Focus in Compensation Law

Dreher v. *Irish Land Commission* was the first decision in which the Irish courts expressly recognised a role for 'the principles of social justice' in

[25] For discussion of a similar pattern in South African law, see F. I. Michelman, 'Expropriation, Eviction, and the Gravity of the Common Law' (2013) 24 *Stellenbosch Law Review* 245, 248–49.

shaping owners' compensation entitlements. It concerned the compulsory acquisition of land by the Land Commission for redistribution from landlords to tenant farmers.[26] Under s. 2 of the Land Bond Act 1934, all money paid by the Commission was through an issue of land bonds 'equal in nominal amount to such purchase money.'[27] The plaintiff challenged s. 2 on the basis that the value of the bonds paid to him was less than the market value of his property. Walsh J developed the implications of Article 43's reference to 'the principles of social justice' for compensation as follows:

> The State in exercising its powers under Article 43 must act in accordance with the requirements of social justice but clearly what is social justice in any particular case must depend on the circumstances of the case... It does not necessarily follow that the market value of lands at any given time is the equivalent of just compensation as there may be circumstances where it could be considerably less than just compensation and others where it might in fact be greater than just compensation. The market value of any property whether it be land or chattels or bonds may be affected in one way or another by current economic trends or other transient conditions of society.[28]

This analysis contains three key points. First, it identifies contextual adjudication as necessary in this context. Second, it suggests that compensation may not be required in all cases where property is compulsorily acquired by the State in the interests of the common good. Walsh J drew an unarticulated distinction between public objectives advancing 'the principles of social justice' that could justify the exercise of the power of compulsory acquisition and objectives that were strong enough to also overcome the presumptive need for compensation. On the facts, Walsh J emphasised the legitimacy of the objectives of the Land Acts but concluded that compensation was necessary.[29] Given that land reform was consistently accepted as an important public objective in Ireland both before and after the adoption of the 1937 Constitution, the fact that it did not meet the threshold for no or reduced compensation in *Dreher* suggests that the bar is set high. Third, Walsh J distinguished between

[26] [1984] ILRM 94.

[27] The Land Commission could only pay cash where land was offered for sale under s. 27 of the Land Act 1950, which was not the case in *Dreher*.

[28] *Dreher* (n 26) at 96. The market value of land bonds fluctuated between the date of their issuance and the date of trial. However, Walsh J emphasised that the yield from the bonds was considerably better than that obtainable on deposits from banks: at 97.

[29] Ibid. at 96.

'just compensation' and the market value of lands, noting that in some cases market value could be considerably *less* than just compensation, and in other cases considerably *more*. However, again he did not set out any benchmark or test for determining 'just compensation'.[30]

Walsh J's actual holding on the facts in *Dreher* did not turn on these points – his focus was on whether the value of the compensation payable under the statutory scheme satisfied the Constitution's requirements in respect of property rights. He stressed that while the interest rate set for land bonds sought as far as possible to reflect the market value of acquired land, the value of land bonds was necessarily subject to market forces outside the control of the Minister.[31] Consequently he held that the impugned section went '. . .as far as is reasonably possible to take into account the results of inflation and fluctuating rates of interest so far as they are reasonably foreseeable.'[32] The other two judges in the case, Griffin J and Henchy J, agreed with Walsh J's judgment but limited it to the facts of the case.[33] Therefore, while certain *dicta* in Walsh J's judgment in *Dreher* undoubtedly express the view that compensation is not always necessary where private property is compulsorily acquired and that market value compensation may be less than or more than just compensation depending on the facts of the case, the actual basis for his decision was that the State cannot insulate the value of compensation from all market impacts. According to Walsh J, it was sufficient to satisfy the requirements of the Constitution that the compensation scheme was designed to reflect market value insofar as was practicable. In his subsequent judgment in *Webb* v. *Ireland*, Walsh J affirmed the view that he had articulated in *Dreher* concerning the impact of 'the principles of social justice' on compensation entitlements.[34] He stated that the State could compulsorily acquire historical treasure objects, '. . .in the interest of the common good, in accordance with Article 43, and subject to the payment of just compensation, *if in the circumstances justice required the*

[30] He could have been thinking along the lines of 'make-whole' compensation, whereby an owner would receive compensation to reflect the actual loss he suffered from the acquisition of his property, which could in some cases be more, and in some cases less, than the market value of the property. This approach was later adopted in *Gunning* v. *Dublin Corporation* [1983] ILRM 56 and *Dublin Corporation* v. *Underwood* [1997] 1 IR 69.

[31] *Dreher* (n 26) at 97–98.

[32] Ibid. at 97.

[33] Ibid. at 98–99.

[34] [1988] 1 IR 353.

payment of any compensation.'[35] In this way, he framed the entitlement to compensation as contingent on the demands of fairness.

8.3.3 *Dreher Applied*

Subsequent cases focused on Walsh J's *dicta* in *Dreher* as a basis for holding that the 'principles of social justice' may obviate the need for compensation or justify less than market value compensation. Significantly, the cases adopting this approach concerned restrictions on the exercise of property rights, not deprivations.

For example, in *O'Callaghan* v. *Commissioners for Public Works*, O'Higgins CJ rejected the contention that s. 8 of the National Monuments Act 1930 (as amended) was unconstitutional because it allowed preservation orders to be issued restricting the use of historically significant land without compensation.[36] He quoted Walsh J's *dicta* in *Dreher* approvingly without addressing the fact that *Dreher* concerned the compulsory acquisition of land whereas *O'Callaghan* involved a restriction on the use of land. He held that the uncompensated restriction on user suffered by the plaintiff was justified by 'the common duty of all citizens' to preserve monuments and by the fact that he had notice of the restriction prior to purchasing the land.[37] This reasoning suggests that where a person invests with knowledge of limitations on his rights over the relevant property, compensation is less likely to be required for such limitations, because they do not undermine any expectations legitimately formed in relation to the value of the land. Furthermore, it is assumed in these circumstances that the market will have adjusted prices to reflect restrictions on property rights.[38]

In *ESB* v. *Gormley*, *Dreher* was also interpreted as authority for the view that the principles of social justice could in some circumstances mean that the payment of compensation is not demanded by the

[35] Ibid. at 390 (emphasis added). In contrast, in *Tormey v. Commissioners for Public Works*, 21 December 1972 (SC), the Court clearly regarded the payment of generous compensation for the *acquisition* of land for preservation purposes as desirable in the interests of justice.

[36] *O'Callaghan* (n 16).

[37] Ibid. at 368.

[38] On this point, see also *Webb* (n 34) at 395–96. However, in *Brennan* v. *The Attorney General*, Barrington J said '. . .the concept of "horizontal equity" springs from the fact that the people adapt themselves to any legal system. It can hardly be used to defend the legal system.' [1983] ILRM 449 at 479.

constitutional protection of private property rights.[39] However, on the facts, compensation was held to be required for a limited physical interference with the relevant land. The case concerned the constitutionality of ss. 53 and 98 of the Electricity (Supply) Board Act, 1927. Section 53 (5) provided that where the Electricity Supply Board (ESB) served notice of its intention to place an electric line across a persons' land and it did not receive consent for entry onto the land within 14 days, it could place the line on the land against the landowner's wishes. Section 98 allowed the Board to lop or cut any trees, shrubs, or hedges obstructing or interfering with the laying of wires or with the surveying of routes. There was no statutory provision for compensation in respect of the exercise of either power.

Finlay CJ held that the exercise of the s. 53 power impeded the agricultural use of the land, prevented the owner from building on the land occupied by the mast, and damaged the amenity of the land around the owner's house, but that the power to lay the transmission line compulsorily was a requirement of the common good. He held that s. 53 did not come within the category of cases where 'the principles of social justice' indicated that compensation should not be paid, since compensation was clearly practicable in the circumstances. The ESB was already at the time of the judgment paying compensation on an *ex gratia* basis to farmers in line with guidelines agreed with the Irish Farmers' Association. Finlay CJ emphasised that fact in concluding that a compensation requirement would not impose an additional cost that would be '. . .inconsistent with social justice or the requirements of the common good'.[40] He also stressed that ESB had a statutory power under s. 45 of the 1927 Act to compulsorily acquire land, easements, or other rights over land *upon payment of compensation*, which it had not employed. Accordingly, s. 53 was held to be an unjust attack on property rights absent compensation. However, the restriction imposed by s. 98 was deemed to be sufficiently minimal in nature to be permissible without compensation.

Therefore, despite the rejection of 'conceptual severance' in *Central Dublin Development Association*, a permanent physical interference with land that is not held to be *de minimis* may require compensation. The owners' right to exclude others (including the State) from making any permanent physical imposition on its property is in this way treated as a

[39] *ESB* (n 21) at 150.
[40] Ibid., at 151.

particularly important incident of ownership.[41] However, insofar as it is afforded distinctive protection, the right to exclude is secured by liability rules rather than property rules, as demonstrated by the weak guarantee for security of possession considered in the previous chapter.

In *Gormley*, the Court's conclusion that paying compensation was possible without creating social justice or common good problems influenced its decision to invalidate the uncompensated interference with property rights. Concerns about the practicability of paying compensation for public law interferences with property rights resurfaced in the context of Ireland's financial crisis between 2008–2011, given the need for austerity measures. This time, practicability augured *against* invalidation, since compensation entitlements would in substance defeat the purpose of austerity measures.

In an important decision prior to the crisis, *Re Article 26 and the Health (Amendment) (No. 2) Bill 2004,*[42] the Supreme Court determined that individuals can only be deprived of their property by the State without compensation in very exceptional circumstances, whether through State acquisition or extinction of property rights. As already discussed, the case concerned the constitutionality of a Bill designed to retrospectively validate illegally imposed residential care charges by abrogating payees' rights of action to recover those charges. The Court referred to *O'Callaghan* and *Dreher*, but stressed the special factual circumstances involved in those cases and held:

> . . .it is clear that where an Act of the Oireachtas interferes with a property right, the presence or absence of compensation is generally a material consideration when deciding whether that interference is justified pursuant to Article 43 or whether it constitutes an 'unjust attack' on those rights. In practice, substantial encroachment on rights, without compensation, will rarely be justified.[43]

This largely echoes Kenny J's approach in *Central Dublin Development Association* in acknowledging the significance of compensation to the identification of 'unjust attacks' on property rights, as well as the fact that

[41] See also on this point the decision of the US Supreme Court in *Loretto* v. *Teleprompter Manhattan CATV Corp* 458 U.S. 419 (1982), and in the UK context, see R. Walsh, 'Belfast Corporation v O.D. Cars [1959]: Setting Parameters for Restricting Use' in S. Douglas, R. Hickey and E. Waring eds., *Landmark Cases in Property Law* (Oxford: Hart, 2015) p. 227, pp. 235–37.

[42] [2005] 1 IR 105.

[43] Ibid. at 201.

a restriction on property rights falling short of full deprivation can be unjust in the absence of compensation. The Bill had as one of its core *objectives* the denial of a legal entitlement to compensation for the abrogation of property rights.[44] Consequently, the Court held that it could not be characterised as regulating the exercise of property rights, or as seeking to balance the interests of different categories of individuals in society. It could only be justified if necessary to stave off '. . .an extreme financial crisis or a fundamental disequilibrium in public finances.'[45] On the facts, it determined that such a crisis did not exist, and the Bill was accordingly declared unconstitutional. In reaching this conclusion, it emphasised the vulnerable nature of the adversely affected group, which it held was relevant given Article 43.2's reference to 'the principles of social justice'.

Over the subsequent course of Ireland's economic crisis and in its aftermath, judges determined that the extreme circumstances referred to by the Supreme Court in the *Health Bill case* had in fact materialised, such that the abrogation of property rights for financial reasons without compensation could be constitutional. On this basis, they upheld the constitutionality of various austerity measures. Significantly, the cases were primarily concerned with reductions in the value of property rights rather than the kind of outright deprivation that was involved in the *Health Bill* case. In *obiter* comments in the High Court in *JJ Haire Ltd* v. *Minister for Finance*, McMahon J referred to the *dictum* concerning the abrogation of property rights for financial purposes in the *Health Bill case* and said, '[a]lthough a strict reading of this *dictum* does not unequivocally say that such a crisis will justify such abrogation, it could be argued that it strongly suggests it.'[46] The case concerned reductions in fees payable to pharmacists providing services on behalf of the State. Given the economic backdrop to these measures, McMahon J characterised them as regulating rather than abrogating property rights.[47] He concluded that they did so in a proportionate manner in light of the 'exceptional threat to the economic well-being of the State and to its people' caused by the economic crisis.[48]

44 However, the State had made *ex gratia* compensation payments to some 20,000 people.

45 *Re Article 26 and the Health (Amendment) (No. 2) Bill 2004* (n 42) at 206.

46 [2009] IEHC 562 at [124].

47 Ibid. at [122].

48 Ibid. at [116]. McMahon J in fact ruled on a different basis, which was that the pharmacists' property rights were reflected in the terms of their contracts with the State, which allowed for unilateral alteration of terms by the State. The High Court

In *Dowling* v. *Minister for Finance*,[49] where Hogan J suggested that the voice of the law could be 'fainter' in the context of an economic emergency, the Court of Appeal upheld the constitutionality of the price paid to shareholders of Irish Life and Permanent by the State for the compulsory acquisition of shares as part of a broader project of bank recapitalisation. That price had been challenged on the basis that a 10 per cent discount was imposed on market value, which shareholders argued was a disproportionate interference with their property rights. The Court of Appeal accepted that following the decision of the Supreme Court in *Rafferty* v. *Minister for Agriculture*[50] (considered further below), in principle the shareholders were entitled '. . .to something close to the full market value of their shares.'[51] However, Hogan J distinguished *Rafferty* on the basis that the adversely affected owners in that case were entirely innocent and were deprived of real property in the public interest. In contrast in *Dowling*, the bank was failing and would have collapsed within days without state intervention, resulting in the total loss of shareholder value. As Hogan J put it, 'in a market economy such as ours shareholders cannot realistically expect to be compensated by the State for what amounts, objectively, to a poor investment decision.'[52] Accordingly, the ministerial direction order that effected the devaluation was upheld. The economic context within which the devaluation occurred was critical to that decision.

8.3.4 *Assessing the Impact of 'The Principles of Social Justice'*

Overall, Article 43.2's reference to 'the principles of social justice' has formed the basis for fairness-based review that is weighted in favour of the public interest, with compensation generally *not* required. This is notwithstanding the fact that judges reason from a baseline that reflects an implicit liberal conception of ownership along the lines sketched by

subsequently upheld the constitutionality of a pension levy imposed upon all public sector workers as an austerity measure in *Unite the Union* v. *Minister for Finance* [2010] IEHC 354. See also *MacDonncha* v. *Minister for Education* [2013] IEHC 226.

49 [2018] IECA 300.

50 [2014] IESC 61.

51 *Dowling* (n 49) at [158].

52 Ibid. at [159]. See relatedly *Permanent TSB Group Holdings Plc* v. *Skoczylas* [2020] IECA 1.

Honoré.[53] They justify their pro-public interest decisions by reference to a variety of factors, including: the categorisation of an interference as either expropriatory or restrictive in nature,[54] the fact that an adversely affected owner had notice of the risk or likelihood of a particular restriction,[55] the identification of certain burdens as flowing from common responsibilities or limitations imposed on owners,[56] or the fact that the property or value interfered with is a product of regulation[57] or speculation.[58] However, the progressive tenor of Article 43.2 proves less influential when pitted against deprivation of real or personal property. There, as the next section explores further, judicial intuitions about the presumptive entitlements of owners lean strongly in favour of full compensation, with 'the principles of social justice' raising the possibility of *legislative* provision for reduced compensation.

8.4 The Corrective Justice Focus in Irish Compensation Law

8.4.1 The Challenges of 'Making Whole' through Compensation

Wyman describes takings as 'readily comprehensible' in corrective justice terms, according to which compensation returns the victim to a 'pre-wrong base-line', with courts generally leaving it to legislatures to consider and if necessary address the justice of that base-line.[59] Wyman's description accurately captures how compensation for deprivations is dealt with in Irish constitutional property law, namely through a default requirement for full compensation for deprivations of property rights. As Wyman points out, the meaning of 'making whole' is not self-evident.[60] 'Full' compensation is commonly based on market value, and some

[53] A. M. Honoré, 'Ownership' in A. G. Guest (ed.), *Oxford Essays in Jurisprudence* (Oxford: Oxford University Press, 1961), pp. 144–45.

[54] This distinction was emphasised by Kenny J in *Central Dublin Development Association* (n 10).

[55] See, e.g., *O'Callaghan* (n 16) and *Gorman* (n 16).

[56] See, e.g., *Re Article 26 and Part V of the Planning and Development Bill 1999* [2000] 2 IR 321 and *O'Callaghan* (n 16).

[57] See, e.g., *Maher* v. *Minister for Agriculture* [2001] 2 IR 139 and *Gorman* (n 16).

[58] See, e.g., *Pine Valley* (n 16) and *Re Article 26 and Part V of the Planning and Development Bill* 1999 (n 56).

[59] K. M. Wyman, 'The Measure of Just Compensation' (2008) 41 *University of California Davis Law Review* 239, 249.

[60] Ibid., 250.

scholars have endorsed this approach.[61] Others have argued that if the aim is to make owners 'whole', at least some attempt to capture subjective losses is appropriate.[62] For example, Lee identifies a number of types of subjective value that can arise in the context of compulsory acquisitions of homes, including sentimental value, the value of alterations to property, location benefits, out-of-pocket expenses, the information costs of adapting to a new neighbourhood, the potential gains from trade recouped by the acquiring authority/transferee, and the loss of a dispossessed owner's autonomy.[63] The Irish doctrine, as this part will show, is largely concerned with capturing readily quantifiable economic losses. It involves an element of subjective assessment as it recognises that different owners may incur different types of consequential economic losses depending on their circumstances, which should be compensated. However, it does not attempt to capture subjective considerations such as the degree of connection to an acquired property.

8.4.2 The Presumptive Entitlement to Market Value Compensation

The Supreme Court in *Re Article 26 and Part V of the Planning and Development Bill, 1999*, laid down a default, but non-absolute, requirement for market value compensation for deprivations of property, e.g.,

[61] See, e.g., B. A. Lee, 'Just Undercompensation: The Idiosyncratic Premium in Eminent Domain' (2013) 113 *Columbia Law Review* 593. Lee cautions against characterising market value as objective, noting,'. . .the extent to which property has any value independent of people's preferences is at best uncertain': 606. See also Y. C. Chang, 'Economic Value or Fair Market Value: What Form of Takings Compensation Is Efficient?' (2012) 20 *Supreme Court Economic Review* 35, supporting *ex post* fair market value assessment by owners of appropriated property with a schedule of bonus rates, for example for factors such as length of tenure.

[62] See, e.g., G. S. Lunney, Jr., 'Takings, Efficiency, and Distributive Justice: A Response to Professor Dagan' (2000) 99 *Michigan Law Review* 157, 168, defining 'just compensation' as 'that level of compensation that made the landowners indifferent between accepting the payment and the loss they experienced.' See also A. Bell and G. Parchomovsky, 'Taking Compensation Private' (2007) 59 *Stanford Law Review* 871, 890–95; M. A. Heller and R. M. Hills, 'LADS and the Art of Land Assembly' (2008) 121 *Harvard Law Review* 1465. Subjective assessment is often linked to proposals for an element of self-assessment in compensation law: see, e.g., A. Bell and G. Parchomovsky, 'Essay: Takings Reassessed' (2001) 87 *Virginia Law Review* 277, 316 and L. A. Fennell, 'Revealing Options' (2005) 118 *Harvard Law Review* 1399, 1406.

[63] Lee, 'Just Undercompensation' (n 61). He argues that many of these losses are in fact captured in market value compensation, but accepts that above market value may be appropriate in some circumstances to compensate for lost autonomy and sentimental value.

through compulsory acquisition of land, which has been affirmed in subsequent cases.[64] The Bill that the Supreme Court was asked by the President to review in that case created a legal basis for imposing conditions on grants of planning permission requiring a contribution to the provision of social and affordable housing, which could be in the form of a transfer of land, built units, or an equivalent financial contribution.[65] In return, developers received compensation reflecting the value of the land *before* the grant of planning permission.[66]

The Court acknowledged that the operation of Part V would result in significantly less than market value compensation. It stated that the appropriate test to apply in considering whether the provisions of the Bill were an unjust attack on property rights was the proportionality principle. It further held that in applying that test, it should be borne in mind that an owner was ordinarily entitled to at least the market value of any property compulsorily acquired by the State in the public interest. However, while it was 'unquestionably of importance', the Court said that this default rule was not absolute.[67] Drawing on this conclusion, the Court characterised land-use regulation as an exceptional case that did not require the payment of market value compensation.[68] The reasoning of the Supreme Court may have been that since an owner of land could *avoid* the compulsory transfer provided for in the Bill by choosing to use his/her land for purposes other than large-scale residential/mixed-use development requiring planning permission, the Bill was best categorised as a control of use provision rather than a compulsory acquisition law. However, the Court did not explicitly justify its characterisation of the Bill in these terms. Rather, the Court reasoned that a grant of planning permission enhanced the value of property and that the State was not required to compensate for the loss of such enhanced value that would be caused by the operation of the Bill's provisions.[69]

64 *Re Article 26 and Part V of the Planning and Development Bill* (n 56).

65 The obligation applied to developments (residential or mixed) of over four houses or exceeding 0.2 hectares. The percentage contribution was set by the relevant local authority, subject to an upper limit of 20 per cent of the overall development.

66 This was characterised as 'existing use' value compensation. There was provision for greater compensation for those who bought, inherited, or were gifted land prior to the commencement of the measure.

67 *Re Article 26 and Part V of the Planning and Development Bill* (n 56) at 351–52.

68 It invoked *Central Dublin Development Association* (n 9) to support this conclusion. Ibid. at 352–53. (Omission of 'on' in reported judgment.)

69 In support of this conclusion, the Court referred to the decision of the US Supreme Court in *United States* v. *Fuller*, where Rehnquist CJ held '. . .the Government as condemnor

The *Planning and Development Bill case* left the law on both the entitlement to compensation and the measure of compensation for deprivations of property rights in a confused state, since it indicated that market value compensation should usually be paid for deprivations but also allowed for exceptions, without specifying the nature and scope of such exceptions. Unhelpfully, it purported to both distinguish and apply *Dreher*.[70] Subsequently, the Supreme Court in the *Health Bill case* affirmed the view set out in *Central Dublin Development Association* that compensation is material to the assessment of 'unjust attack' and that substantial interferences with property rights without any compensation will normally be unjust.[71] However, it said nothing about the appropriate *measure* of any compensation to be paid by the State. The Supreme Court in *Rafferty* v. *Minister for Agriculture* affirmed the statement in *Dreher* that market value compensation could be less or more than just compensation, depending on the circumstances of the case.[72] Delivering the majority judgment, Denham CJ accepted *obiter* the possibility that there could be legitimate reasons for the legislature to curtail compensation entitlements, but suggested that the justification for any such restrictions would be reviewed by courts on the basis of strict scrutiny of the grounds for such exceptions, and based on the proportionality principle.

8.4.3 'Total Loss' Compensation

The Acquisition of Land (Assessment of Compensation) Act, 1919, sets out rules for the assessment of compensation for compulsory acquisition, which are applied and in some cases adapted in various statutory

may not be required to compensate a condemnee for elements of value that the Government has created, or that it might have destroyed under the exercise of government authority other than the power of eminent domain.' (1972) 409 US 488 at 492. The Court in the *Planning and Development Bill case* simply noted this view without expressly approving it or disapproving it: (n 56) at 353–52. However, it suggests that the Court may exclude all government-created value from assessments of compensation.

70 See D. O'Donnell, 'Property Rights in the Irish Constitution: Rights for Rich People, Or a Pillar of Free Society?' in E. Carolan and O. Doyle (eds.), *The Irish Constitution – Governance and Values* (Dublin: Round Hall, 2008), pp. 412, 425, arguing that the Supreme Court relegated *Dreher* to its own facts. O'Donnell points out that the Supreme Court reiterated *Dreher's* statement concerning the need for *more* than market value compensation in some cases, but did not reiterate its statement concerning less than market value compensation.

71 *Re Article 26 and the Health (Amendment) (No. 2) Bill 2004* (n 42).

72 *Rafferty* (n 50) at [44].

contexts.[73] In interpreting these rules in light of the Constitution, the Irish courts have generally attempted to put a dispossessed owner back in the position he or she would have been in were it not for the acquisition, which in some cases has necessitated *more than* market value compensation. This approach is rooted in the Supreme Court's decision in *Comyn v. Attorney General*, where Kingsmill Moore J stated that a compensation award should achieve equivalence from the perspective of the dispossessed owner.[74] He reasoned (as a matter of statutory, not constitutional, interpretation):

> . . .it seems to me that common law, common sense and common decency speak with one voice and lay down the overriding principle that when a man has been compulsorily dispossessed of his property, whether by individual, corporation, or State, he shall receive in exchange whatever the property was worth to him. He did not ask to have his property taken. If it is taken for the public weal he should not be a loser.[75]

Kingsmill Moore J said; 'every element of value to the owner must receive its proper compensation', including diminution in good will, future value (for example, potential value for building purposes), loss of profits, removal expenses etc.[76] He qualified this by holding that when assessing compensation, account should not be taken of the personal views or attachments of the owner concerning the property.

The High Court affirmed equivalence as the guiding principle in *Gunning* v. *Dublin Corporation*.[77] The plaintiff's business premises were compulsorily acquired and he successfully asserted an entitlement to compensation for relocation costs, temporary loss of business, double overheads, time spent seeking new premises, and miscellaneous disturbances. Carroll J held, '[t]he underlying principle is the principle of equivalence. The owner should be able to recover personal loss imposed on him by the forced sale – otherwise he will not be fully compensated – but he should recover neither more nor less than his total loss.'[78] Significantly, *Gunning* (like *Comyn)* was not based on the constitutional property clauses, but rather on an interpretation of the 1919 Act.

[73] For a comprehensive overview of Irish compulsory acquisition law, see R. Walsh, 'Expropriation in Ireland' in J. Sluysmans, S. Verbist, and E. Waring (eds.), *Expropriation in Europe* (Alphen aan den Rijn: Wolters Kluwer, 2015).

[74] [1950] IR 142 at 167.

[75] Ibid.

[76] Ibid. at 170–71.

[77] *Gunning* (n 30).

[78] Ibid. at 62.

However, in *Dublin Corporation* v. *Underwood*, the Supreme Court placed the equivalence principle on a clear constitutional footing.[79] The plaintiff had issued a compulsory acquisition order in respect of the respondent's two investment properties. In the Supreme Court, Keane J upheld the High Court decision that reinvestment costs should be compensated, saying:

> It would be patently unjust, in my view, for the dispossessed owner to receive less than the total loss which he has sustained as a result of the compulsory acquisition: such a construction of the relevant legislation would be almost impossible to reconcile with the constitutional prohibition of unjust attacks on the property rights of the citizens.[80]

Keane J accepted that the respondent would have continued to hold the relevant properties as investments but for the acquisition and would incur additional expenses in buying replacement investment properties.[81]

This 'make-whole' approach was affirmed by the Supreme Court in *Rafferty* v. *The Minister for Agriculture*, which arose out of an outbreak of foot and mouth disease in February 2001.[82] The Minister ordered the culling of the plaintiffs' sheep flocks, even though they were not actually infected with the disease. The plaintiffs contended that the compensation paid to them under the Diseases of Animals Act 1966 was inadequate because it did not capture all their consequential losses. They argued that the traits of their animals should have been considered in assessing their compensation. In the High Court, McGovern J rejected this argument, holding that they had in fact received significantly more than market value compensation. He suggested that a constitutional requirement of compensation for all consequential losses '…could have enormous implications for the Exchequer, and impose a serious and disproportionate burden on the taxpayer.'[83] However, on appeal, the Supreme Court concluded that the adversely affected owners were entitled to compensation for their total losses. Denham CJ held that the key question was

[79] *Underwood* (n 30).

[80] Ibid. at 129.

[81] Keane J did acknowledge that there might in some cases be very remote consequences for a property owner flowing from a compulsory acquisition order that would not be compensable, but he felt that the plaintiff's reinvestment costs were not too remote, and could be recovered under Rule 6 of the 1919 Act, either as compensation for disturbance, or as one of the 'other matter(s) not directly based on the value of land' for which compensation could be paid under the 1919 Act. Ibid. at 129–30.

[82] [2008] IEHC 344.

[83] Ibid. at [38].

the meaning of 'compensation' in s. 17 (2) of the Diseases of Animals Act. Since the statutory provision did not provide any definition or guidance, she held that the Court had to apply the 'ordinary meaning' of 'compensation', which she determined included consequential losses, in order to avoid an 'unjust attack' on property rights.[84] In reaching this conclusion, she approved the equivalence principle set out in *Underwood.* As already noted, Denham CJ suggested *obiter* that statutory exceptions to that principle would be subject to strict scrutiny as to their grounds and to proportionality review. In his concurring judgment, O'Donnell J stressed the need for statutory guidance on the principles for assessment of compensation. He agreed that compensation meant total loss, to be assessed by reference to market value, but reserved his position on the constitutionality of legislative exceptions to that principle.

The 'equivalence' cases indicate that where legislation provides for compensation for deprivation of property rights, the Irish courts will construe it as providing compensation for all consequential losses where that interpretation is open, whether because of ambiguity in the legislation or because it is deemed to be constitutionally required to secure fairness. The adequacy of market value compensation or less than market value compensation will be assessed contextually, with judges reserving the right to gap-fill through interpreting legislative rules considering the need to protect constitutional property rights. New disputes or controversies may cast the fairness of existing compensation principles into doubt or highlight gaps. For example, debate continues concerning the compulsory acquisition of land to facilitate the development of a road by-passing Galway city centre.[85] Under the 1919 Act, compensation for such compulsory acquisition would usually reflect the market value of the property that is taken, coupled with compensation for disturbance including relocation and/or reinvestment costs where appropriate. However, many owners in the by-pass pathway stand to suffer considerable under-compensation: first, following the Irish housing market crash in 2007, some properties are still in negative equity[86]; second, many owners stand to lose the significant financial benefit involved in tracker

[84] *Rafferty* (n 50) at [46].

[85] See M. Lyons, 'Galway Bypass Raises Concerns Among Residents', 12 February 2015, www.irishtimes.com/life-and-style/homes-and-property/galway-bypass-raises-concerns-among-residents-1.2099768 (last visited 17 August 2020).

[86] For helpful analysis of the causes and consequences of the housing market crash in Ireland, see M. Norris, *Property, Family and the Irish Welfare State* (Basingstoke: Palgrave Macmillan, 2016), pp. 206–28, 240–51.

mortgages if they are dispossessed, since those attractive mortgage terms will not transfer to a replacement property[87]. Based on the equivalence principle, a court faced with this issue might well interpret existing statutory compensation rules to capture these losses, e.g., through an expanded understanding of compensation for disturbance.

8.4.4 *The Impact of Context on 'Market Value'*

Generally, 'market value' is taken to mean the price that a willing vendor would accept and a willing purchaser would pay for something at a specific time. In the *Planning and Development Bill case*, the Supreme Court described the market value of residential land as the price that it might be expected to fetch on the open market considering any development rights.[88] However, the meaning of 'market value' is clearly context-dependent and subjective. As Lee puts it:

> [t]he assertion that a given sum is the 'fair market value' of an object is not a neutral starting point from which to begin further analysis, but rather is the conclusion of a (tacit) line of reasoning dependent on premises about what aspects of an object are salient for determining which other objects are similar enough that their transaction prices can indicate the fair market value of the object in question.[89]

Like the *entitlement* to compensation, the meaning of 'market value' is shaped by the specific context in which compensation falls to be determined, as well as by the constraining impact of compensation entitlements on legislative freedom.

In the context of discrete regulatory systems, 'market value' may not be discernible or may not provide a useful measure of compensation. For instance, in *Maher* v. *The Minister for Agriculture*[90], holders of EU milk-production quota who were not in fact producing milk objected to

[87] The Irish Central Bank defines a tracker mortgage as follows: '[a] tracker mortgage is a type of home loan where the interest rate charged on the loan tracks that of another publicly available rate, typically the interest rate set by the European Central Bank.' www.centralbank.ie/consumer-hub/explainers/what-is-the-tracker-mortgage-examination (last visited 27 March 2020).

[88] *Planning and Development Bill, 1999* (n 56) at 349. In the High Court in *Rafferty* v. *The Minister for Agriculture*, McGovern J held market value to mean the price payable to replace acquired property, rather than the price that the acquired property itself could have made on the open market: (n 82) at 14.

[89] Lee, 'Just Undercompensation' (n 61), 618.

[90] *Maher* (n 57).

regulations that in effect required them to either resume milk production or to sell their quota to the Minister for Agriculture at a price that they contended was below market value.[91] The Supreme Court rejected this challenge to the regulations. In his judgment, Murray J reasoned, '... "open market" is hardly an apt term since the market in milk, and hence its price, is a creature of the particular market conditions created by the regulatory regime itself.'[92] He held that the maximum price fixed by the Minister for quota struck a fair balance between the interests of existing quota-holders and those wishing to acquire quota, and further that the opportunity to sell at the prices created by the former regulatory regime surrounding milk quotas was not a property right protected by the Constitution. Similarly, in *Shirley* v. *AO Gorman*, the context in which compensation fell to be paid influenced the meaning of 'market value'.[93] Peart J held that normally a person who is compulsorily deprived of property in the public interest should receive at least market value compensation. However, he upheld s. 7 of the Landlord and Tenant (Amendment) Act, 1984, which fixed the price at which a landlord could be required under s. 8 of the Landlord and Tenant (Ground Rents) (No. 2) Act, 1978 to sell the fee simple in his property to a tenant at one-eighth of the amount that a willing purchaser would give and a willing vendor would accept for the property. Peart J felt that that value fairly and reasonably reflected the landlord's residual interest in the property, since in most cases where s. 7 applied, the landlord lacked the right to retake possession and was only entitled to receive a small rent.

The practicability of compensation payments and their potential to impede the realisation of the public interest can also inform judicial interpretations of 'market value'. Otherwise, the very purpose of compulsory acquisition powers could be defeated. In *Re Murphy*, Henchy J rejected the plaintiff's argument that the intended use of compulsorily acquired land for public housing should be taken into account in assessing compensation.[94] He noted that under the terms of the Acquisition of Land (Assessment of Compensation) Act 1919, '...while the basic rule is that the measure of compensation is to be the open market value of the land, the arbitrator must leave out of the reckoning of that value the

[91] The European Communities (Milk Quota) Regulations 2000 (S.I. No. 94 of 2000).
[92] *Maher* (n 57) at 232.
[93] [2006] IEHC 27.
[94] [1977] IR 243.

existence of the proposed local authority development.'[95] He reasoned that this exclusion was necessary to prevent the acquisition of land for socially desirable purposes from being impeded by prohibitively high prices triggered by publicity surrounding a proposed development.

8.5 Assessing Compensation's Ends through a Progressive Property Lens

Property law scholarship on compensation is vast and reflects a wide range of ends, ranging from perspectives that focus on the costs, incentive effects, and overall economic efficiency of different compensation rules,[96] to public choice arguments focused on protecting owners against political process breakdowns through compensation;[97] to arguments (considered in the previous chapter) for increased compensation for deprivations of certain types of property, particularly residential homes, based on personhood,[98] to understandings of compensation as a means of ensuring fairness in the distribution of social costs.[99] This part focuses on progressive property arguments that in various ways contend that distributive considerations should shape owners' compensation entitlements. By connecting progressive property theory on this issue to the Irish compensation doctrine considered in the previous parts, it seeks to illuminate how such theory can be implemented in constitutional property rights adjudication. The first section considers progressive property approaches to the question of compensation for interferences with property rights falling short of deprivation, while the second section focuses on deprivation.

95 Ibid. at 254.

96 See, e.g., L. Blume and D. L. Rubinfeld, 'Compensation for Takings: An Economic Analysis' (1984) 72 *California Law Review* 569, 616–17 (arguing that governmental risk aversion supports less-than-full compensation on efficiency grounds); W. A. Fischel and P. Shapiro, 'Takings, Insurance, and Michelman: Comments on Economic Interpretations of "Just Compensation" Law' (1988) 17 *Journal of Legal Studies* 269 (arguing that zero compensation will reduce the incentive for investment).

97 Again, the literature is vast: see, e.g., D. A. Farber, 'Public Choice and Just Compensation' (1992) 9 *Constitutional Comment* 279; S. Levmore, 'Just Compensation and Just Politics' (1990) 22 *Connecticut Law Review* 285, and W. A. Fischel, *Regulatory Takings: Law, Economics, and Politics* (Cambridge, MA: Harvard University Press 1995).

98 See, e.g., H. Dagan, 'Takings and Distributive Justice' (1999) 85 *Virginia Law Review* 741 (advocating a progressive compensation system that would award greater compensation to poor condemnees).

99 See, e.g., F. I. Michelman, 'Property, Utility, and Fairness: Comments on the Ethical Foundations of "Just Compensation" Law (1967) 80 *Harvard Law Review* 1165.

8.5.1 *Restricting the Exercise of Property Rights – Fairness, Flourishing, and Change*

Progressive property scholarship generally resists rigid or absolute compensation entitlements for interferences with property rights falling short of deprivation.[100] Regulatory freedom and flexibility is prioritised to secure the public interest.[101] Property rights are framed as dynamic and evolving, meaning that change does not necessarily destabilise expectations in a manner warranting compensation.[102] At the same time, disproportionate or exploitative burdening of individuals or groups in the public interest is resisted.[103] These core progressive property themes on compensation help to illuminate aspects of the Irish doctrine on compensation, which as was seen in the earlier parts of this chapter adopts a contextual, fairness-focused approach to determining when compensation is required to legitimise restrictions on the exercise of property rights.

Writing from a progressive property perspective on the question of 'regulatory takings' in the US context (interferences with property falling short of outright deprivation that may require compensation), Singer characterises the key question as being one of 'adequate justification'.[104]

[100] See, e.g., J. W. Singer, 'Justifying Regulatory Takings' (2015) *Ohio Northern University Law Review* 601 and T. M. Mulvaney, 'Progressive Property Moving Forward' (2014) 5 *California Law Review* 349, 364–66.

[101] See notably J. W. Singer, No Freedom Without Regulation: The Hidden Lesson of the Subprime Crisis (New Haven: Yale University Press, 2015); Entitlement: The Paradoxes of Property (New Haven: Yale University Press, 2000).

[102] See, e.g., G. S. Alexander, E. M. Peñalver, J. W. Singer, and L. S. Underkuffler, 'A Statement of Progressive Property' (2009) 94 *Cornell Law Review* 743; L. S. Underkuffler, *The Idea of Property: Its Meaning and Power* (Oxford: Oxford University Press, 2003); 'Property and Change: The Constitutional Conundrum' (2013) 91 *Texas Law Review* 2015, and G. S. Alexander, 'The Social-Obligation Norm in American Property Law' (2009) 94 *Cornell Law Review* 745.

[103] See, e.g., H. Dagan, *Property: Values and Institutions* (Oxford: Oxford University Press, 2011); 'Expropriatory Compensation, Distributive Justice, and the Rule of Law' in B. Hoops, E. Marais, H. Mostert, J. Sluysmans, and L. Verstappen (eds.), *Rethinking Expropriation Law I: Public Interest in Expropriation* (The Hague: Eleven International Publishing, 2015), p. 349; 'Reimagining Takings Law' in G. S. Alexander and E. M. Penalver (eds.), *Property and Community* (Oxford: Oxford University Press, 2009), p. 39; 'Takings and Distributive Justice' (n 98); G. S. Alexander and E. M. Peñalver, 'Properties of Community' (2009) 10 *Theoretical Inquiries in Law* 127; Alexander, 'The Social Obligation Norm' (n 102); L. S. Underkuffler, 'Kelo's Moral Failure'(2006) 15 *William & Mary Bill of Rights Journal* 377, and Singer, 'Justifying Regulatory Takings' (n 100).

[104] Singer, 'Justifying Regulatory Takings' (n 100).

He argues that regulations of use serving legitimate public purposes can normally be imposed without compensation, no matter how significant their economic impact on adversely affected owners. The question is whether when considered from a 'democratic' point of view concerned with human dignity and equal concern and respect, an uncompensated burden is justifiable. That assessment involves considering the appropriateness of imposing the costs of an impugned restriction on individual owners or particular groups of owners.

Relatedly, Alexander argues that owners can be required to suffer uncompensated losses in order to secure human flourishing for all within society.[105] As he puts it, 'an owner is morally obligated to provide to the society of which the individual is a member those benefits that the society reasonably regards as necessary for human flourishing'.[106] Owners' social obligations extend beyond reciprocity understood as the requirement to give in return for specific benefits, since owners can be required to give to persons other than those from whom they have received, and in different amounts. However, the extent of owners' obligations is not unlimited – account is required to be taken of fairness, individual respect, autonomy, and dignity.[107] Alexander characterises the tension between the goals of securing the human flourishing of all and respecting individual autonomy and dignity as '...an aspect of the irreducible tension that runs throughout all of the law of property', in particular constitutional property.[108] He contends that the scope of owners' obligations should be determined contextually, through both political and judicial 'practical judgment' and 'deliberative discussion'.[109]

The Irish courts focused on the question of 'unjust attack' posed by Article 40.3.2°, leading to circular analysis on the question of compensation; compensation is required if an interference with the exercise of property rights would be 'unjust' absent compensation. At the level of 'test', concepts such as 'adequate justification' and 'social obligation' are like 'unjust attack'. They re-pose the basic question of fairness in the distribution of collective burdens that was considered in the context of the 'discrimination' factor in Chapter 6. For clarity and guidance about

105 Alexander, 'The Social Obligation Norm' (n 102).
106 Ibid., 774.
107 See similarly, Alexander and Peñalver, 'Properties of Community' (n 103), 143.
108 Alexander, 'The Social Obligation Norm', (n 102) 772. He suggests that this tension at least in part explains why takings law is so muddy.
109 G. S. Alexander, 'Takings and the Post-Modern Dialectic of Property' (1992) 9 *Constitutional Commentary* 259, 276.

what fairness entails in practice, we must look to patterns identifiable in both outcomes and judicial reasoning in constitutional property rights adjudication.[110] In structuring and explaining their analysis, Irish judges tend not to frame their decisions directly in terms of fairness, or other 'progressive' ends such as human dignity, equal concern and respect, and human flourishing. Rather, judges use the proportionality principle and factors such as owners' reasonable expectations of value,[111] owners' notice of restrictions,[112] the regulatory context of activities on land,[113] owners' duties to the common good,[114] and the nature of the interference (in particular, whether it is expropriatory or regulatory and whether it affects real or personal property).[115] In this way, although Article 43 itself squarely addresses the tension between property rights and social justice, judges prove reluctant to explicitly engage with the basic 'fair-burdening' question posed by both Singer and Alexander. While Alexander acknowledges that the tension between individual and collective interests in property may not be capable of being *resolved*, the Irish experience further suggests that transparent 'practical judgment' and 'deliberative discussion' on this issue may not be forthcoming from judges.

In her progressive property approach to compensation, Underkuffler envisages a broad degree of legislative freedom to change property rights without paying compensation. She grounds this approach in an 'operative' conception of property, according to which susceptibility to change and compromise is inherent in the nature of property.[116] She contrasts this conception of property with what she terms the 'common' conception of property, according to which the rights of ownership are

[110] Singer, 'Justifying Regulatory Takings' (n 98).

[111] See, e.g., *Pine Valley* (n 16) on the lack of protection for economic value associated with speculative activities.

[112] See, e.g., *O'Callaghan* (n 15).

[113] See, e.g., *Maher* (n 57) and *Re Article 26 and Part V of the Planning and Development Bill* (n 56).

[114] *O'Callaghan* (n 15) and *Re Article 26 and Part V of the Planning and Development Bill 1999* (n 56).

[115] See, e.g., *Central Dublin Development Association* (n 10).

[116] As she puts it, '[t]he bottom line is that any property right, previously conferred, is at most a statement of the way that conflicting interests have been resolved at one particular moment. As understandings of consequences change, "rights" will change': L. S. Underkuffler, 'What Does the Constitutional Protection of Property Mean?' (2016) 5 *Brigham-Kanner Property Rights Conference Journal* 109, 117. See also Underkuffler, *The Idea of Property* (n 102), p. 48.

presumptively clear and static but are subject to public control.[117] She argues that the purpose of the constitutional protection of property is to protect individuals against radical, unjustified changes in the status quo. Underkuffler identifies a number of dimensions of property as particularly affecting compensation issues: the 'spatial dimension', since the definition of the 'property interest' involved in a case will fundamentally influence the 'impact' that an interference has and with it the strength of any claim for compensation;[118] the 'temporal dimension', which concerns the moment at which the content of rights in property are fixed, which in turn influences their susceptibility to change thereafter;[119] and the dimension of 'stringency', concerning the strength of protection for property rights in the face of competing collective demands.[120]

The Irish courts have not clearly articulated their understanding of the various 'dimensions' of property identified by Underkuffler in relation to compensation. For example, while *Central Dublin Development Association* indicates resistance to 'conceptual severance', it does not clarify whether the spatial baseline for assessing the fairness of uncompensated regulatory restrictions is the owner's property *as a whole* or the particular property or landholding. Although the matter has never been addressed explicitly, it seems clear from subsequent Irish cases that acquisition of any part of an owner's real property (e.g., part of a larger parcel of land) gives rise to a constitutional entitlement to compensation.[121] The constitutionality of temporary total deprivations of property or temporary physical interferences with land has not been directly addressed by the Irish courts.[122] Finally, the dimension of stringency has been somewhat clarified in respect of judicial review of

[117] Underkuffler suggests that comprised within this common conception of property is the protection of possessions, the protection of one's business, and the protection of 'expectations' of development of one's land. Underkuffler, *The Idea of Property*, (n 102), p. 39.

[118] Ibid., p. 23.

[119] Ibid., pp. 29–30.

[120] Ibid., p. 20 and p. 28.

[121] See, e.g., *Re Article 26 and Part V of the Planning and Development Bill 1999* (n 56), where owners were held to have a presumptive right to compensation where 20 per cent of a site was subject to compulsory acquisition. Similarly *Chadwick* v. *Fingal County Council* [2008] 3 IR 66 clearly proceeds on the basis that an owner is entitled to compensation where part of his land is the subject of outright expropriation by the State.

[122] Although in the pre-1937 case of *Rooney* v. *The Minister for Agriculture*, Powell J accepted that the temporary acquisition of property for public purposes could give rise to an entitlement to compensation: [1920] 1 IR 176.

legislative rules providing for less than full compensation for *deprivations* – Denham CJ in *Rafferty* suggests that such rules are subject to strict scrutiny as to their grounds, and to proportionality review.[123] However, her comments on this matter were *obiter*. The dimension of stringency is even less clear for restrictions on the exercise of property rights: judges generally defer to legislative decisions concerning the circumstances in which compensation should be paid, but in a small number of marginal cases have strongly asserted that compensation is required.[124]

As was seen in Chapter 4, where the property that is adversely affected by a regulatory control is *physical* in nature, that control is generally framed by judges as limiting clearly defined rights, reflecting a 'common conception' of property. In cases involving regulatory permissions, something akin to an 'operative' conception has been adopted, with uncompensated restrictions on the exercise of property rights accepted by courts on the basis that such permissions are inherently susceptible to change.[125] However, the latter category of cases is relatively narrow. Overall, the 'common conception' is dominant. That dominance is clearly reflected in the presumptive 'full compensation' entitlement for deprivations. Nonetheless, Irish constitutional property law shows that even where a 'common conception' of property is applied, social justice considerations can be accommodated in compensation doctrine. Denham CJ's approach in *Rafferty* signals to the legislature that it may be able to defend 'no-compensation' or less than full compensation rules by reference to the common good and social justice, indicating that such exceptions are not placed off-limits by the Constitution. Furthermore, compensation for interferences falling short of deprivations is considered as part of a multi-factorial fairness assessment, not treated by judges as a rule-based entitlement of owners.

8.5.2 Mediating Property Rights and Social Justice in Compensation

The Irish courts apply a corrective-justice approach through a presumptive make-whole compensation rule for deprivations that includes

123 *Rafferty* (n 50).

124 See, e.g., *ESB* (n 20). in respect of exclusion and *Blake* (n 22) and *Re Article 26 and the Housing (Private Rented Dwellings) Bill 1981* (n 22) in respect of use.

125 See, e.g., *Hempenstall* v. *Minister for the Environment* [1994] 2 IR 20, *Gorman* (n 16) (devaluation of taxi licence through deregulation).

consequential losses over and above market value but does not include subjective losses. However, layered over this default *judicial* rule, which the courts have held to be mandated by the Constitution, is scope for less generous *legislative* compensation rules based on social justice considerations. In this way, the primary role of compensation for deprivations is corrective, but it can be given a distributive function by the legislature, reflecting Article 43.2's statement of the power of the State to delimit the exercise of property rights to secure 'the principles of social justice' and 'the exigencies of the common good'.

Dagan advances a progressive vision for accommodating corrective and distributive justice in respect of compensation for expropriation, aspects of which are well illustrated by Irish compensation doctrine.[126] He contends that a uniform full compensation approach gives insufficient attention to the significance of community membership in shaping owners' obligations.[127] Accordingly, he argues for a differentiated compensation regime that identifies, based on the judicial and/or legislative application of predictable rules or informative standards rather than *ad hoc* judicial determinations of fairness, categories of cases within which partial compensation is justifiable. At the same time, he stresses the importance of protecting politically and/or socio-economically weak individuals. On this basis, Dagan argues that the *purpose* of an expropriation should not generally influence the compensation that is payable to a dispossessed owner.[128] Instead, Dagan endorses reduced compensation where justified by personhood and/or community considerations. First, Dagan contends, '. . .full compensation can apply to all (and only to) expropriations of constitutive property, while partial compensation applies only to expropriations of fungible property (and to all such

[126] See, e.g., H. Dagan, 'Expropriatory Compensation' (n 103); *Property: Values and Institutions* (n 103) pp. 87–151; 'Reimagining Takings Law' (n 103); 'Takings and Distributive Justice' (n 98).

[127] As Dagan puts it, '[I]t defines our obligations qua citizens and qua community members as exchanges for monetizable gains, and thereby commodifies both our citizenship and our membership in local communities': 'Expropriatory Compensation', (n 103), p. 358.

[128] For criticism of double counting of purpose, see also A. J. van der Walt, *Constitutional Property Law* (Cape Town: Juta, 3rd ed., 2011), pp. 515–18. Dagan acknowledges that sometimes redistribution is an intentional goal of a deprivation, citing land reform and measures designed to 'achieve greater social justice' as examples. In such circumstances, he accepts that where necessary to avoid the purpose of the measure being defeated, no or partial compensation should be permissible. Ibid., p. 349.

cases).'[129] Second, Dagan argues that reciprocity of advantage should inform compensation assessments:

> Long-term (and rough) reciprocity of advantage implies that a public authority need not pay compensation if, and only if, two conditions prevail. The first is that the disproportionate burden of the public action in question is not overly extreme. The second is that this burden is offset, or is highly likely to be so, by benefits accruing from other – past, present, or future – public actions that harm neighbouring properties similar in magnitude to the landowner's current injury.[130]

Relatedly, he argues that when an expropriation benefits the local community of which the owner is a member rather than the public at large, the compensation payable can be reduced by a fixed amount to capture the owner's heightened obligations to his/her local community.[131]

Irish compensation law on deprivations provides practical illustration of aspects of the model advocated by Dagan. *Ad hoc* judicial decision making has a very limited role: compensation is guaranteed *ex ante* through the pattern of judicial precedents identifying a constitutional entitlement to 'equivalent' compensation; exceptions to that principle may be permissible, but only if established through legislation, which given the resistance to retrospectivity considered in Chapter 6, will usually also be *ex ante*. The purpose of an interference with property rights, including how 'socially just' it is deemed to be by judges, influences the circumstances in which judges accept the legitimacy of partial or no-compensation. However, the strong presumption in favour of full compensation for deprivations coupled with the requirement of strict scrutiny of exceptions to that default principle means that the objective of a deprivation is only likely to be held to justify no, or reduced, compensation in compelling cases, most particularly those where the core objective is itself redistributive (e.g., austerity measures and land reform). Dagan resists 'double-counting' of the purpose of regulations or deprivations generally in respect of compensation, but accepts the legitimacy of

129 Dagan, 'Expropriatory Compensation', (n 103), p. 363.

130 Ibid., p. 364.

131 Dagan acknowledges that neither the distinction between constitutive and fungible property nor the distinction between local community and public benefits is clear cut, but he suggests that legislators and/or judges can use other law applying these distinctions to integrate them into compensation law. Ibid., p. 366.

such double-counting where the purpose of the legislation is redistributive.[132]

Dagan's notion of 'long-term reciprocity of advantage' is also identifiable in Irish compensation doctrine. For example, claims for compensation in the planning law context have generally been rejected on the basis of an understanding that reciprocal advantages offset losses suffered by owners.[133] This judicial interpretation has mirrored the progressive reduction in the range of statutory compensation entitlements in the Irish planning law regime over time, which allowed for gradual adjustments in owners' expectations concerning land-use.[134] The central role of proportionality analysis in Irish constitutional property law, considered in Chapter 5, provides an obvious vehicle for considering reciprocity of advantage and fairness in individual burdening, for example in applying the 'minimal impairment' and 'impact' limbs of the proportionality principle.

Other relevant factors identified by Dagan include the nature of the property taken (including whether it is constitutive or fungible);[135] the degree of diminution in value (i.e. where on the spectrum between financial wipeout and *de minimis* interference a given deprivation sits);[136] and contextual factors such as economic crisis and historical injustice raising distributive considerations. To date, the Irish courts have not specifically recognised the nature of the property taken as relevant to the measure of compensation. However, they have been reluctant to recognise compensation entitlements for mere loss of value, especially in regulatory contexts, suggesting an implicitly less protective attitude

132 Dagan, 'Expropriatory Compensation', (n 103), p. 349.

133 See, e.g., *Central Dublin Development Association* (n 10) and *Re Article 26 and Part V of the Planning and Development Bill 1999* (n 56).

134 Yvonne Scannell stresses that s. 190 of the Planning and Development Act 2000 does recognise an entitlement to compensation for loss of value resulting from a refusal of planning permission: Y. Scannell 'The Catastrophic Failure of the Planning System' (2011) 33 *Dublin University Law Journal* 393, 424–25. However, section 191 of the 2000 Act claws back that entitlement by establishing a wide range of reasons for refusal that defeat that entitlement to compensation and by providing that changes in zoning or the imposition of conditions on grants of planning permission do not trigger an entitlement to compensation. The range of 'non-compensatable' reasons has been progressively expanded over time.

135 On this, see also D. B. Barros, 'Home as a Legal Concept' (2006) 46 *Santa Clara Law Review* 255, 298.

136 For an argument in favour of giving primacy to this factor by compensating for unanticipated regulatory destruction of a significant proportion of an owner's assets, see W. M. Treanor, 'The Armstrong Principle, The Narratives of Takings, and Compensation Statutes' (1997) 38 *William & Mary Law Review* 1151.

towards fungible property.[137] They do distinguish between 'wipeout' and '*de minimis*' interferences, including through proportionality analysis.[138] The Irish courts have specifically pointed to contextual factors such as historic land reform projects and circumstances of economic crisis as relevant considerations that inform constitutional property rights adjudication.[139] Finally, the Supreme Court has identified the socio-economic and political status of the group adversely affected by an abrogation of property rights as a relevant consideration, which illustrates two strands of argument about compensation advanced by Dagan (and others): first, and most directly, the view that compensation should vindicate the rights of groups who are vulnerable (politically and/or socio-economically);[140] second, the view that the community impact of deprivations of property should in some circumstances prompt the award of more than market-value compensation.[141] However, the practical impact of these principles has not been developed in Irish constitutional property law outside the narrow circumstances of one case – the *Health Bill case*.[142]

8.6 Assessing Compensation's Means through a Progressive Property Lens

Debate continues concerning the appropriate *means* of compensation law, in particular whether it should be applied primarily through

137 See, e.g. *Hempenstall* (n 125) and *Gorman* (n 15).

138 See, e.g., *ESB* (n 21)

139 See e.g. *Fisher* v. *Irish Land Commission* [1948] IR 3; *Foley* v. *Irish Land Commission* [1952] 1 IR 118; *JJ Haire* (n 9), and *Dowling* (n 49).

140 See, e.g., Dagan, 'Expropriatory Compensation' (n 103); Treanor, 'The Armstrong Principle' (n 136); P. Boudreaux, 'Eminent Domain, Property Rights, and the Solution of Representation Reinforcement' (2006) 83 *Denver University Law Review* 1. However, Alexander objects to a process approach on the basis of the inherently contestable nature of its empirical foundations, since no clear answer is available to the question of whether a 'discrete and insular minority' is disadvantaged or uniquely advantaged within the political process by virtue of that status: Alexander, 'The Social-Obligation Norm', (n 102), 773–74.

141 See, e.g., Dagan, 'Expropriatory Compensation' (n 103); S. Stern, 'Takings, Community and Value: Reforming Takings Law to Fairly Compensate Common Interest Communities' (2015) 23 *Journal of Law and Policy* 141, and S. Stern, 'Remodeling Just Compensation Law: Applying Restorative Justice to Takings Law Doctrine' (2017) 30 *Canadian Journal of Law and Jurisprudence* 413.

142 The *Health Bill case* itself involved an unusual set of circumstances – an attempted retrospective abrogation of property rights as a legislative response to the State attempting to levy charges without a legal basis with knowledge of that lack of legal basis. Section 1 of the Bill amended s. 53 of the Health Act 1970 s (1)(b) by inserting sub-s. 5: '[s]ubject to subsection (6), it is hereby declared that the imposition and payment of a relevant charge is, and always has been, lawful.'

contextual judicial decision making or through rule-based decision making by legislatures and judges. On the one hand, scholars have argued that a strictly rule-based approach is impossible given the complex competing individual and social values implicated in constitutional property rights adjudication.[143] On the other hand, scholars have also highlighted significant downsides to *ad hoc* judicial decision making, including a loss of predictability for owners concerning their rights.[144]

As the analysis in this chapter has demonstrated, there is no blanket protection for security of value in Irish constitutional property law. Rather, there is *presumptive* liability rule protection for outright expropriations of land, and *potential* liability rule protection for all other interferences with property rights. Statutory deviations from market value compensation for deprivations may be permissible subject to strict scrutiny and proportionality review by the courts, although definitive clarity on this point from the Supreme Court is awaited.[145] As such, contextual judicial decision making has a relatively limited role in relation to compensation for deprivations. Judges will not of their own initiative carve out exceptions to the default full compensation rule, with Denham CJ's approach in *Rafferty* suggesting that the courts have the role of assessing the constitutionality of any *statutory* exceptions on a case-by-case basis. However, judicial decision making on the question of compensation for regulatory controls is wholly contextual, focused as it is on the question of 'unjust attack'. In this way, Irish compensation law employs a combination of a core liability rule and a peripheral 'governance rule', involving fine-grained contextual analysis.[146] This combination of legal techniques will result in the kind of predictable understanding of security of value sought by 'information' property theorists only if clear judicial reasoning is offered to support two aspects of compensation decisions: first, the movement from exclusion and

[143] See, e.g., A. Lehavi, 'The Dynamic Law of Property: Theorizing the Role of Legal Standards' (2011) 42 *Rutgers Law Journal* 81 and M. Porier, 'The Virtue of Vagueness in Takings Doctrine' (2002) 24 *Cardozo Law Review* 93.

[144] See, e.g., S. Rose-Ackerman, 'Against Ad Hocery: A Comment on Michelman' (1988) 88 *Columbia Law Review* 1697. See also Dagan, *Property: Values and Institutions* (n 102), pp. 148–49.

[145] *Rafferty* (n 50).

[146] On 'governance rules' see, e.g., H. E. Smith, 'Mind the Gap: The Indirect Relationship between Ends and Means in American Property Law' (2009) 94 *Cornell Law Review* 959 and H. E. Smith 'Exclusion versus Governance: Two Strategies for Delineating Property Rights' (2002) 31 *Journal of Legal Studies* S453.

liability rules to governance rules in particular cases; second, the application of governance rules and the resulting situated, contextual judgment.

Irish compensation law is relatively clear on the first question: in the deprivation context, the shift to governance rule assessment, if permissible, may be triggered by the *legislature*, not the courts. This approach guarantees some *ex ante* notice and predictability for owners, given the strong presumption against retrospective application considered in Chapter 6. In the restriction context, governance rule assessment predominates and compensation is a contingent entitlement. Overall, this structure is reasonably clear and comprehensible and allows for the development of settled expectations concerning security of value, although the types of legislative aims that might justify a 'no' or 'reduced' compensation regime for deprivations remain ambiguous.

On the second question of the application of governance rules, Irish compensation doctrine paints a less positive picture of a broadly progressive approach to compensation in action, as judges have tended to obfuscate their reasoning in applying the 'unjust attack' standard rather than squarely addressing the questions of fairness, or 'adequate justification', that are raised.[147] Outcomes generally favour the public interest, although as Chapter 6 showed, the factors articulated to support those outcomes are not always consistently invoked or applied. There are rare instances of stricter protection of security of value, for example discrete protection of the right to profit.[148] Accordingly, a degree of unpredictability surrounds the scope of constitutional protection for property rights, lending some support to criticisms levied against progressive property's support for contextual judicial decision making.[149] However, that unpredictability is largely at the margins of Irish compensation law, with the core of an owners' entitlements in respect of security of value relatively clear from the outcomes considered in this chapter: deprivation usually triggers full compensation; regulation does not usually trigger a compensation entitlement.

147 Singer, 'Justifying Regulatory Takings' (n 100).

148 *Blake* (n 22), *Re Article 26 and the Private Rented Dwellings Bill* (n 22), *Re Article 26 and the Employment Equality Bill* (n 23).

149 On this critique, see Smith, 'Mind the Gap' (n 146), and on the merits of a rule-based approach see, e.g., H., E. Smith, 'Property and Property Rules' (2004) 79 *New York University Law Review* 1719; H., E. Smith, 'Property as the Law of Things' (2012) 125 *Harvard Law Review* 1691, and T. W. Merrill and H. E. Smith, 'The Property/Contract Interface' (2001) 101 *Columbia Law Review* 773. The conflict between 'information' and 'progressive' theories on this point is well analysed by J. Baron, 'The Contested Commitments of Property' (2010) 61 *Hastings Law Journal* 917.

8.7 Conclusions

Although as argued by Sluysmans et al., compensation certainly does reflect a vision of property,[150] in legal doctrine that vision is not always coherent or easily definable as reflecting a 'liberal' or 'social democrat' view, or as focused on either an 'information' or a 'progressive' approach to protecting property rights. Rather, these visions may co-exist, interact, and compete for priority on an ongoing basis. The compensation doctrine considered in this chapter illustrates this well. Irish judges have drawn on both the 'liberal' and 'social democrat' views of compensation in an intuitive, *ad hoc*, and often unconscious manner to build a structure for compensation law centred around a presumptive rule in favour of full compensation for deprivations of property and a contextual fairness standard for restrictions on the exercise of property rights falling short of deprivation. Judges' (usually unarticulated) conceptions of private ownership and its merits influence the circumstances in which they find compensation to be constitutionally required.[151] As was already discussed, those conceptions are influenced by the common law tradition within which Irish constitutional property law operates, with judges tending to apply something similar to Honoré's liberal conception of ownership as their baseline in disputes about compensation.[152]

The default full compensation rule for deprivations indicates that even in a jurisdiction where social justice is expressly enshrined as a constitutional value that delimits individual property rights, common law conceptions of property remain influential in the public law context.[153] Although owners are not afforded a veto over acquisition or deprivation in the face of competing public interests (as seen in the previous chapter), they are afforded a strong guarantee of security of value in the event of deprivation. The demands of social justice and the common good are primarily accommodated through weak constitutional protection for security of value where public law interferences with property rights fall short of outright acquisition or deprivation. In this way, 'governance' rules are at the periphery of Irish compensation law in respect of

[150] Sluysmans, Verbist, and de Graaff, 'Compensation for Expropriation' (n 5).

[151] As Christopher Serkin notes, 'the scope of liability rule protection is determined by how courts actually value the right': C. Serkin, 'The Meaning of Value: Assessing Just Compensation for Regulatory Takings' (2005) 99 *North Western Law Review* 677, 680.

[152] Honoré, 'Ownership' (n 53), pp. 107–47.

[153] For criticism of this trend in the US context, see T. M. Mulvaney 'Foreground Principles' (2013) 20 *George Mason Law Review* 837.

deprivations, but they constitute its doctrinal core in respect of restrictions on the exercise of property rights. Compensation is required for such measures where it would be 'unjust' not to compensate. Questions of practicability, legitimacy of expectations, reciprocity, individual contribution to the creation of value, civic responsibility, and vulnerability, all surface in judicial determinations as relevant considerations, with some applied in a quasi-rule-like fashion by courts and others arising inconsistently and incompletely in judicial reasoning.

Overall, notwithstanding the implicit adoption of a 'common conception' of property, the compensation principles that have been developed in Irish constitutional property law allow significant scope for uncompensated restrictions on the exercise of property rights. Other identifiable progressive tendencies in the doctrine include judicial resistance to 'conceptual severance' in analysing compensation entitlements; the attention paid to the status of adversely affected owners; and the rejection of an entitlement to compensation for all losses in value due to regulatory changes. In these ways, Irish constitutional property law demonstrates that progressively framed property clauses can support a distributive focus in compensation law on the part of both legislatures and judges while at the same time guaranteeing a clear core of protection for security of value. While Irish compensation law gives some support to criticisms of the ends-focus and *ad hocery* of progressive property,[154] owners are guaranteed a *reasonable*, although not *absolute*, degree of certainty about security of value.

[154] See, e.g., Smith, 'Mind the Gap' (n 146).

9

Learning from Progressive Property in Action

Context, Complexity, and the Democratic Mediation of Property Rights and Social Justice

9.1 Introduction

Irish constitutional property law shows how judges may in practice 'maintain a constitutional tension' between the protection of individual property holdings and the limitation of such holdings in the public interest.[1] Michelman suggests that this tension is capable of 'partial resolutions', such that it is experienced as 'generative', not a 'dead end'.[2] The task of achieving productive 'partial resolutions', although described in different ways and operating at various levels, lies at the heart of much of the theoretical debate about property rights that has been considered in this book. It also captures the inescapably political nature of constitutional property law. As van der Walt puts it, constitutional property rights '…are characterised by a political and democratic struggle to find the proper balance between individual entitlements and the social restriction of property.'[3] Constitutionalising property

[1] A. J. van der Walt, 'The Constitutional Property Clause: Striking a Balance Between Guarantee and Limitation' in *Property and the Constitution*, Janet McLean ed., (Oxford: Hart Publishing, 1999), pp. 109, 128. See similarly Nestor Davidson arguing that in property law, '…any given form represents the resolution of the competition between the multiple and often clashing ends that property serves.' N. M. Davidson, 'Standardization and Pluralism in Property Law' (2008) 61 *Vanderbilt Law Review* 1597, 1601.

[2] F. I. Michelman, 'Property as a Constitutional Right', (1981) 38 *Washington & Lee Law Review* 1097, 1110. See similarly Marc Poirier, describing regulatory takings doctrine in the US context as '…fertile and generative precisely because it is inevitably, and perhaps quintessentially, vague and unresolvable.' M. Poirier, 'The Virtue of Vagueness in Takings Doctrine' (2003) 24 *Cardozo Law Review* 93, 190.

[3] A. J. van der Walt, 'The Modest Systemic Status of Property Rights' (2014) 1 *Journal of Law, Property and Society* 15, 96.

rights complicates matters by including judges in the array of actors involved in this struggle.[4]

In addressing this tension at the level of text, the Irish Constitution's property rights provisions adopt a qualified progressive approach: they protect property rights against 'unjust attack', subject to delimitation by the State to secure 'the exigencies of the common good' and 'the principles of social justice'. Van der Walt captures the tension embedded within Article 43.2, arguing, '[t]he social justice provisions reflect a seemingly contradictory effort, cast in the form of constitutional obligations, simultaneously to exclude others from our property and to care for others using our property.'[5] The central aim of this book was to assess if, and how, these qualified progressive property rights guarantees have translated into legal doctrine and outcomes and whether they provide useful insights about progressive property in action. This chapter considers the challenges and advantages of these broadly progressive constitutional provisions that emerge from their interpretation and application by judges, and the lessons suggested for progressive property theory.

Most fundamentally, Irish constitutional property law illustrates the primacy afforded by judges to political determinations of the appropriate mediation of property rights and social justice, whether through legislation or administrative decision-making. As Nedelsky puts it, 'property implicates the core issues of politics: distributive justice and the allocation of power', and this is reflected in a predominantly deferential judicial attitude towards the judgment of the elected branches of government.[6] The outcomes analysed in this book show that 'partial resolutions' of the tension between property rights and social justice embodied in legislation are given substantial weight, with *ex ante* adjustments of owners' rights rarely invalidated by judges.

Section 9.2 reassesses progressive property views about the impact of conceptions of property in light of the analysis of Irish constitutional property law in the preceding chapters. Section 9.3 reconsiders the complexity dispute between progressive property theorists and

[4] A. Alvaro, 'Why Property Rights Were Excluded from the Canadian Charter of Rights and Freedoms' (1991) 24 *Canadian Journal of Political Science* 309.

[5] A. J. van der Walt, 'The Protection of Property under the Irish Constitution' in E. Carolan and O. Doyle (eds.), *The Irish Constitution: Governance and Values* (Dublin: Thomson Roundhall, 2008) pp. 398, 400.

[6] J. Nedelsky, 'Should Property Be Constitutionalized? A Relational and Comparative Approach' in G. E. van Maanen and A. J. van der Walt (eds.), *Property Law on the Threshold of the Twenty-first Century* (Antwerp: Maklu, 1996), pp. 417, 427.

information property theorists through the Irish lens. Section 9.4 examines the related questions of deference to political judgment in the mediation of property rights and social justice and the respective roles of public and private law in advancing progressive property's agenda. Section 9.5 explores the intuitive, under-reasoned nature of judicial decision-making on constitutional property rights that emerges from the analysis in previous chapters, and the consequent need for attention to local factors in progressive property theory and in comparative constitutional property law. Section 9.6 assesses Irish constitutional property law through the prism of Mulvaney's 'progressive property themes', which were considered in Chapter 2. It argues for greater transparency from judges in constitutional property rights adjudication concerning the reasons for outcomes and considers potential doctrinal translations of progressive property approaches focused on the marginality, identity, and vulnerability of owners. Section 9.7 concludes.

9.2 Reassessing the Impact of Conceptions of Property

Van der Walt suggests, '[b]y adopting a mix of "liberal and communitarian elements", the Irish Constitution paradoxically positions itself squarely within both broad traditions.'[7] This approach in the text of the Constitution influences judicial interpretation, resulting in 'an interpretive attitude that reflects some classic liberal and some communitarian or social-responsibility elements.'[8] The 'liberal' element of that interpretive attitude primarily involves an intuitive acceptance by judges of a liberal conception of the incidents of ownership, embracing the exclusive rights to possession, use, and disposition of private property. This reflects the fact that transfer, bequest, and inheritance are specifically protected in Article 43.1.[9] The right to exclude has also been identified in a number

[7] van der Walt, 'The Protection of Private Property under the Irish Constitution' (n 5), p. 401.

[8] Ibid.

[9] Margaret-Jane Radin notes, '[t]he classical liberal conception of property embraces a number of broad aspects or indicia, often condensed to three: the exclusive rights to possession, use and disposition': M. J. Radin, *Reinterpreting Property* (Chicago: University of Chicago Press, 1993), p. 120. See also R. Epstein, *Takings: Private Property and the Power of Eminent Domain* (Cambridge, MA: Harvard University Press, 1985), p. 304. These incidents of ownership have been identified by the Irish courts as constitutionally protected: see *Fitzpatrick* v. *The Criminal Assets Bureau* [2000] 1 IR 217 and *Reid* v. *Industrial Development Agency* [2015] IESC 82.

of decisions as constitutionally protected, although not absolutely.[10] Beyond these incidents, the nature of the presumptive rights of ownership is not defined in Irish constitutional property law. Lockean inspired intuitions about ownership as a reward for individual effort have influenced the contexts in which the constitutional protection for property rights has been held to apply, albeit inconsistently and partially.[11] This 'core image' of property rights as rights over real and personal property recognised by law as a reward for productive activity has yet to be expressly acknowledged by judges, but its influence is clear in the case-law.

The intuitively identified rights of owners are balanced *against* the public interest, rather than being *defined by* collective goals. Alexander categorises this type of approach as 'limitational'. Following such an approach, the court asks '[w]hether the limitation that the state has imposed on the property is constitutionally justified', usually via 'a multi-step proportionality principle'.[12] In implementing such a 'limitational' approach, the Irish courts have variously relied on the text of the Constitution, a rationality standard, and proportionality analysis. The 'limitational' nature of Article 43 both rationalises and is reinforced by the tendency of the Irish courts to focus almost exclusively on analysing the constitutionality of restrictions on property rights, not on developing the meaning of property itself.[13]

Van der Walt characterises this tendency to treat property as a pre-political right embodied in private law and susceptible to *exceptional* restriction in the public interest as a feature of the 'rights paradigm' in

[10] *Ashbourne Holdings* v. *An Bord Pleanála* [2003] 2 IR 114 and *O'Sullivan* v. *Department of the Environment* [2010] IEHC 376.

[11] As Harris notes, '. . .social conventions commonly incorporate, and are shaped by reference to, the assumption that meritorious work should receive a reward in the form of property.' J. W. Harris, *Property and Justice* (Oxford: Oxford University Press, 2002), p. 229.

[12] G. S. Alexander, *The Global Debate Over Constitutional Property – Lessons for American Takings Jurisprudence* (Chicago: University of Chicago Press, 2006), p. 122.

[13] Van der Walt identified '. . .the almost complete lack of concern about the meaning or scope of the term "property"', as an interesting feature of Irish constitutional property doctrine, which he suggests may be 'a reflection of the fact that the Irish courts place heavy emphasis on the legitimacy and justice of every particular limitation of property rights, which means that it is less important to decide whether a particular right is property than to decide whether a specific limitation of that right is justified.' A. J. van der Walt, *Constitutional Property Clauses: A Comparative Analysis* (Cape Town: Juta, 1999), p. 231.

property law.[14] Underkuffler describes it in terms of the 'common conception' of property, according to which '[p]roperty is asserted, *as an entity*, against collective power. Collective forces, under this conception, are clearly external to the protection that property, as an entity, affords.'[15] The rights flowing from ownership are absolutely protected and are fixed in time.[16] They can only be overridden by compelling public interests.[17] Underkuffler argues, '[i]f we assume – *as a part of property's very nature* – a particular institutional understanding, or a particular (immutable) configuration of individual rights and collective powers, we have, in effect, gone very far toward predetermining the question of how much protection property does or should provide.'[18] On this basis, she contends that the adoption of a common conception of property necessarily leads to strict protection of property rights.[19] She sees the common conception as weighting the scales in favour of judicial invalidation; as she puts it, '[o]ne begins with the perception that individual use and individual control are *normatively* justified; as a necessary corollary of this presumption, collective use and collective control are *not*.'[20] From this perspective, the common conception poses the risk of privileging the status quo. As an alternative, she advances an 'operative conception' that views change as part of the meaning of property. This reflects a broader theme of progressive property: that ideas like social justice, equal respect, and human flourishing should shape the *meaning of*, and *recognition of*, property rights, rather than simply operating to justify *limits* on such rights.[21]

This strand of argument in the progressive property school of thought is challenged by Irish constitutional property law. Notwithstanding the 'common conception' of property identifiable in the judicial interpretation of the property rights provisions, outcomes in constitutional

[14] A. J. van der Walt, *Property in the Margins* (Oxford: Hart Publishing, 2008), p. 41.

[15] L. S. Underkuffler, *The Idea of Property: Its Meaning and Power* (Oxford: Oxford University Press, 2003), p. 40.

[16] Ibid., pp. 40–1.

[17] Ibid., p. 45.

[18] Ibid., p. 61.

[19] Ibid., p. 54.

[20] Ibid., p. 57.

[21] See, e.g., J. W. Singer, *Entitlement: The Paradoxes of Property* (New Haven: Yale University Press, 2000), p. 215, C. K. Odinet, 'Of Progressive Property and Public Debt' (2016) 51 *Wake Forest Law Review* 1101, 1104.

property disputes have generally favoured the public interest.[22] Invalidations on property rights grounds are rare overall.[23] Where they occur, they can often be explained as concerned with general constitutional principles like retrospectivity, fair procedures, or rationality. Cases where the courts strike down legislation because they disagree with the legislature's view on the substantive balance struck between property rights and the common good and/or social justice are very few in number.[24] Overall, Irish constitutional property law reflects what Alvaro identifies as a 'democratic-communitarian system', wherein '. . .property ownership does not disappear but is subordinated to the democratic will'.[25] This is a striking outcome given the natural law language used to express the individual right to private ownership in Article 43.1, which might raise concerns about strict rights protection. In fact, the Constitution's protection for property rights has rarely impeded reforms enacted through legislation. However, judicial interpretation of the property rights provisions has not independently driven progressive change.

In advocating a 'limitational' approach, Harris identified scope for uncompensated interferences with the exercise of property rights[26] and for owners' legitimate expectations to evolve over time in line with developing patterns of restriction.[27] Both these trends are identifiable in Irish constitutional property law. For example, planning control was originally interpreted as a restriction on property rights warranting compensation.[28] Over time political and judicial attitudes evolved, with

[22] For detailed analysis of this deferential approach, see R. Walsh, 'The Constitution, Property Rights and Proportionality: A Reappraisal' (2009) 31 *Dublin University Law Journal* 1.

[23] See G. W. Hogan, G. F. Whyte, D. Kenny and R. Walsh, *Kelly: The Irish Constitution*, 5th ed. (Dublin: Bloomsbury Professional, 2018), pp. 2420–22, for an enumeration of the wide range of cases in which restrictions have been upheld by the courts, including on grounds of the common good.

[24] The key outlier examples are: *Blake* v. *Attorney General* [1982] IR 117; *Re Article 26 and the Housing (Private Rented Dwellings) Bill 1989* [1983] 1 IR 181; and *Re Article 26 and the Employment Equality Bill 1996* [1997] 2 IR 321.

[25] Alvaro, (n 4), 310. Alvaro takes the term from P. Monahan, *Politics and the Constitution* (Toronto: Carswell Methuen, 1987), pp. 103–6 and applies it in the property rights context.

[26] Harris, *Property and Justice* (n 11), p. 97.

[27] Ibid., p. 77.

[28] See notably *In re Viscount Securities Ltd* (1978) 112 ILTR 17 at 20; *Grange Developments Ltd* v. *Dublin County Council* [1986] 1 IR 246 at 256; *Keane* v. *An Bord Pleanála* [1998] 2 ILRM 241 at 262, and *Butler* v. *Dublin Corporation* [1999] 1 IR 565.

planning restrictions now rarely triggering statutory compensation entitlements and the Supreme Court resisting recognising any uncontrolled 'right to develop' as a facet of owners' constitutionally protected property rights.[29] Furthermore, the Irish experience shows that a 'limitational' approach does not necessarily prevent restrictions on the exercise of property rights from being accepted as a matter of social practice.[30] As Waldron notes, 'people nowadays identify their property in a way that takes net account of actual and sometimes likely restrictions on use and development.'[31] Therefore, at least in the public law context that has been the focus of this book, the Irish experience shows that progressive property ideas can be given effect through a 'limitational' approach that supports the imposition of democratically determined constraints on ownership through deferential review.[32]

This feature of Irish constitutional property law shows that explicit textual recognition of the State's power to regulate the exercise of property rights can contribute to securing progressive outcomes through legislative and administrative action. Much ink has been spilled by progressive property scholars in establishing that uncompensated regulatory control of the exercise of property rights is in principle legitimate.[33] In the Irish context, the capacity of the State to regulate in the public interest, including through limiting the exercise of individual property rights, is expressly recognised in the text of the Constitution and readily accepted by judges. This highlights one potential benefit of embedding progressive ideas like social justice in the Constitution: it may help to ensure that constitutional property rights do not bar or impede

[29] *Tracey* v. *Ireland* [2019] IESC 70 at 26–27.

[30] On this see, e.g., Underkuffler, arguing that the reality of changing social needs means that a 'common conception' of property is problematic: Underkuffler, *The Idea of Property* (n 15), p. 43. See also L. S. Underkuffler, 'Property as Constitutional Myth: Utilities and Dangers' (2007) 92 *Cornell Law Review* 1239.

[31] J. Waldron, *The Rule of Law and the Measure of Property* (Cambridge: Cambridge University Press, 2012), p. 69.

[32] Where a 'limitational' approach may prove less helpful is where progressive property theory seeks to show that in the private law context, owners have obligations that are not dependent on implementation or enforcement through legislation. For further consideration of the potential differences in approach required in public and private law contexts, see R. Walsh, 'Property, Human Flourishing and St Thomas Aquinas: Assessing a Contemporary Revival' (2018) 31 *Canadian Journal of Law and Jurisprudence* 197, 216–19.

[33] See, e.g., J. W. Singer, *Entitlement* (n 21); *No Freedom Without Regulation: The Hidden Lesson of the Subprime Crisis* (New Haven: Yale University Press, 2015); 'Justifying Regulatory Takings' (2015) 41 *Ohio Northern University Law Review* 601, and Underkuffler, *The Idea of Property* (n 15).

the elected branches of government from introducing legal reforms with redistributive implications.[34] It does so in part by shifting the focus to the justifiability of particular regulations of the exercise of property rights rather than the *per se* permissibility of regulation.[35]

Irish constitutional property law suggests that at least in terms of outcomes in legal disputes resolved in the courts, relatively little may turn on whether the judicial focus is on redefining property rights in progressive terms or on justifying legislative limits on property rights based on progressive property concepts like fairness or social obligation. Both approaches are underpinned by an understanding of property rights as shaped by collective interests, and both are potentially compatible with progressive agendas. As Poirier puts it, the key shared insight is '. . .that property is a kind of social relation that is renegotiated over time as circumstances change', with the renegotiation capable of being directed either at limits on property rights or at property rights understood as *inherently* limited.[36] Irish constitutional property law shows that even where a 'limitational' approach is adopted and a 'common conception' of property is influential, constitutional property rights do not necessarily entrench the status quo *provided there is political support for change.*

The emphasis placed by progressive property theory on the question of the definition of property rights as opposed to their limitation may have been an important rhetorical move in creating a clear fault line between it and efficiency-based analysis in property law. It also reflects a desire to mark out a distributive justice function for property law while at the same time avoiding endorsing wide-scale redistribution of property rights or resources.[37] Finally, it is indicative of a lack of trust in the

[34] For discussion of this concern about constitutional property rights see, e.g., Nedelsky, 'Should Property be Constitutionalized?' (n 6); van der Walt, 'The Modest Systemic Status of Property Rights' (n 3), and F. I. Michelman, 'Possession v. Distribution in the Constitutional Idea of Property' (1987) 72 *Iowa Law Review* 1319, 1319–20.

[35] On this point, see Priviledge Dhliwayo and Rashmi Dyal-Chand, 'Property in Law' in G. Muller et al. (eds.), *Transformative Property Law* (Cape Town: Juta, 2018) p. 295, at p. 312, arguing in discussing South African constitutional property law, '[f]rom a constitutional perspective, limitations are from the beginning part of the system within which property functions. Consequently, justification refers to justifying the authority and reasons for and effect of a specific limitation imposed on the right to exclude, instead of justifying the very existence of a limitation'.

[36] Poirier, 'The Virtue of Vagueness' (n 2), 100.

[37] See, e.g., G. S. Alexander, *Property and Human Flourishing* (New York: Oxford University Press, 2018) p. 67, arguing that human flourishing property theory is 'not primarily redistributive' because '[m]ost of the obligations that property owners owe under the human flourishing theory result from ownership of property itself. That is, they are

ability of political processes to appropriately mediate property rights and social justice through legislative and administrative decision-making. As Katz puts it, '[o]ne objection (from a progressive outlook) is that looking to the state to solve the problems produced by ownership is a less reliable solution than directly tailoring the position of ownership to constrain the selfishness of owners.'[38] By treating the obligations of owners as inherent in property rights, progressive property ensures that the *principle* of owners' obligations, if not their content, is a fixed part of the legal landscape that is not dependent on shifting patterns of political support.

The Irish experience lends some support to the latter rationale for progressive property's definitional strategy. Notwithstanding the predominantly deferential judicial approach in constitutional property rights adjudication, Ireland has experienced consistently high levels of political conservativism in respect of property rights. Nedelsky's description of the US experience is equally applicable in the Irish context: '. . .judicial practice does not seem as yet to have shaken the popular force of the idea of property as a limit to the legitimate power of government.'[39] Whether this is because of the constitutional property rights guarantees cannot be definitively determined. However, it is consistently defended by politicians as required by the Constitution's property rights guarantees.[40] In fact, as the analysis in previous chapters showed, only a very small number of inconsistently applied decisions

inherent in what it means to own property and what ownership involves in a modern society.' He distinguishes between specific obligations, which are incidents of ownership, and general obligations like progressive taxation, which he characterises as redistributive. He also argues that his human flourishing theory is not primarily redistributive because it focuses on capabilities, with '. . . provision of resources' a 'derivative not primary task': p. xx. See also G. S. Alexander and E. M. Peñalver, *An Introduction to Property Theory* (Cambridge: Cambridge University Press, 2012), p. 124, where they argue, '[t]he human flourishing theory does not redistribute entitlements so much as it defines them'. However, at pp. 128–29, they argue '[r]edistribution of land rights via in-kind transfers of ownership or occupancy will at times be the only appropriate way of fostering flourishing.'

38 L. Katz, 'Ownership and Social Solidarity: A Kantian Alternative' (2011) 17 *Legal Theory* 119, 128. See also H. Dagan, *Property: Values and Institutions* (New York: Oxford University Press, 2011), pp. 63–67, on the problems with relying on public law to protect the property-less.

39 J. Nedelsky, 'American Constitutionalism and the Paradox of Private Property' in J. Elster and R. Slagstad (eds.), *Constitutionalism and Democracy* (Cambridge: Cambridge University Press, 1988), pp. 241, 263.

40 On the influence of the advice of the Attorney General on Irish constitutional law, see D. Kenny and C. Casey, 'Shadow Constitutional Review: The Dark Side of Pre-Enactment Political Review in Ireland and Japan' (2020) 18 *International Journal of Constitutional*

of the Irish Supreme Court support an interpretation of the Constitution as significantly constraining legislative freedom.[41] This fact is reflected in the more interventionist political approach that has been adopted on some distributive issues, for example the almost total removal of compensation entitlements for planning restrictions and the imposition of social housing obligations on developers. In crisis circumstances, political support for limiting property rights has also mobilised: during the economic crisis, through austerity measures; during the housing crisis, through measures like vacant site levies and enhanced security of tenure; and during the Covid-19 crisis, through temporary bans on evictions and rent increases, as well as far-reaching restrictions on trade. This suggests that political will, driven by the perceived importance of the objective of a restriction on property rights, can displace a generally conservative political culture linked to the Constitution's property rights provisions. The Irish experience has been that judges are willing to support such shifts in approach through deferential review.

This complex interaction between doctrine, outcomes, legal interpretation, and political decision-making highlights a risk posed by constitutional property rights guarantees from a progressive property perspective. Specifically, it demonstrates that even within a constitutional framework that in many respects fits the progressive property model, outlier decisions strictly protecting property rights can create, bolster, or justify political conservativism. Given the nature of legal advice, which tends to err on the side of caution, constitutional property rights create the potential for judicial decisions that may discourage the *introduction* of legislative reforms even where such decisions are not broadly reflective of the outcomes in constitutional property rights disputes. This chilling effect may be heightened in the Irish context by the existence of an institutional guarantee for private ownership, which has the effect of entrenching private ownership in the Irish legal, economic, and political order, although without rendering extant distributions of property immutable.

While, as this book illustrates, a wide range of restrictions on property rights have been enacted since the adoption of the Constitution in 1937, there is evidence of some political risk-adversity concerning the initiation

Law 51 and 'A One Person Supreme Court? The Attorney General, Constitutional Advice to Government, and the Case for Transparency' (2019) 42(1) 89.

[41] Most significantly, *Blake* (n 24), *Re Article 26 and the Housing (Private Rented Dwellings) Bill* 1981 (n 24) and *Re Article 26 and the Employment Equality Bill 1997* (n 24).

of new laws that restrict property rights, which has the effect of allying with property interests in privileging the status quo.[42] The courts have contributed to this dynamic, with doctrinal ambiguity fuelling political conservativism in relation to some important progressive reforms of the balance between property rights and social justice in Irish law, most controversially rent control.[43] In this respect, Irish constitutional property law supports Underkuffler's concern about the impact of 'mythical' understandings of property that deny its inherent contextuality in shaping social and economic debates, and laws.[44] It further demonstrates that coherence and transparency concerning the reasons for outcomes are important tools for progressive property theory in combatting political conservativism rooted in constitutional property rights guarantees. Finally, it highlights that by affirming private ownership as a constitutionally required public policy, institutional guarantees such as that contained in Article 43 may contribute to a political culture that is hesitant about imposing new limitations on property rights.

9.3 The Complexity Critique Considered through the Irish Lens

Information property theorists and progressive property theorists agree that both contextual judicial decision-making and rule-based decision-making should form part of any property system.[45] Where they disagree is on the appropriate frequency of contextual decision-making – on how often positions 'settled' by property rules should be reopened in the

[42] I am grateful to Oran Doyle for suggesting this understanding of the political impact of the Constitution on property issues in Ireland.

[43] See R. Walsh, 'Housing Crisis: There Is No Constitutional Block to Rent Freezes in Ireland' (*Irish Times*, 3 February 2020), available at www.irishtimes.com/opinion/housing-crisis-there-is-no-constitutional-block-to-rent-freezes-in-ireland-1.4159367?mode=sample&auth-failed=1&pw-origin=https%3A%2F%2Fwww.irishtimes.com%2Fopinion%2Fhousing-crisis-there-is-no-constitutional-block-to-rent-freezes-in-ireland-1.4159367 (last visited 11 August 2020), and 'What Would the 'Referendum on Housing' Be About and Do We Really Need One? (*Irish Times*, 22 July 2020), available at www.irishtimes.com/opinion/what-would-the-referendum-on-housing-be-about-and-do-we-really-need-one-1.4285592?mode=sample&auth-failed=1&pw-origin=https%3A%2F%2Fwww.irishtimes.com%2Fopinion%2Fwhat-would-the-referendum-on-housing-be-about-and-do-we-really-need-one-1.4285592 (last visited 11 August 2020).

[44] Underkuffler, 'Property as Constitutional Myth' (n 30), 1253.

[45] See H. E. Smith, 'Mind the Gap: The Indirect Relation between Ends and Means in American Property Law' (2009) 94 *Cornell Law Review* 959, 975 and J. W. Singer, 'Property as the Law of Democracy' (2014) 63 *Duke Law Journal* 1287, 1307.

interests of fairness.[46] Relatedly, they have different views on how much '. . .explicit consideration of social values' is appropriate.[47] In short, they diverge on what Baron terms the 'optimal level of complexity' in property law.[48] Excessive contextual decision-making is said by information property theorists to cause undue complexity, with resulting heightened information costs that impede the efficient functioning of property law as a system and pay insufficient attention to the 'architecture' of that system.[49] For example, Smith argues, '[p]romoting the promiscuous employment of contextual information in property is in keeping with ignoring the cost of delineation in the process of serving the purposes of property.'[50] Irish constitutional property law provides a useful test case for considering the degree to which contextual judicial decision-making is likely in fact to result in doctrinal incoherence and unpredictability, and what the nature and consequences of such unpredictability might be. The picture that emerges is more nuanced than the polarised academic debate on complexity would suggest.

In Irish constitutional property law, judges make determinations about 'unjust attacks' on property rights by reference to the State's power to delimit the exercise of property rights to secure 'the exigencies of the common good' and the 'principles of social justice'. Accordingly, the Irish Constitution's property rights provisions *require* judges to engage in 'situated judgment'.[51] In the application of this contextual approach to constitutional property rights adjudication, the public interest usually prevails over individual property rights. The reasons that motivate courts on rare occasions to strongly defend property rights are often not articulated, or if stated, are inconsistently applied. The doctrinal analysis

[46] J. B. Baron, 'The Contested Commitments of Property' (2009) 61 *Hastings Law Journal* 917.

[47] Ibid., 921.

[48] Ibid., 922.

[49] See, e.g., H. E. Smith, 'Restating the Architecture of Property' in B. McFarlane and S. Agnew (eds.), *Modern Studies in Property Law Vol. 10* (Oxford: Bloomsbury, 2019), p. 19; 'Complexity and the Cathedral: Making Law and Economics More Calabresian' (2019) 48 *European Journal of Law and Economics* 43; 'Property as the Law of Things' (2012) 125 *Harvard Law Review* 1691; 'Exclusion versus Governance: Two Strategies for Delineating Property Rights' (2002) 31 *Journal of Legal Studies* 453; T. W. Merrill and H. E. Smith, 'The Morality of Property' (2007) 48 *William & Mary Law Review* 1849; 'Optimal Standardization in the Law of Property: The Numerus Clausus Principle' (2000) 110 *Yale Law Journal* 1.

[50] H. E. Smith, 'Property is Not Just a Bundle of Rights' (2011) 8 (3) *Econ Journal Watch* 279, 283.

[51] F. I. Michelman, 'Takings, 1987' (1988) 88 *Columbia Law Review* 1600, 1629.

in earlier chapters extrapolated the patchwork of factors that are employed on an *ad hoc* basis by Irish judges to justify their decisions. Retrospectivity augurs against constitutionality, as does any procedural deficiency. Irrational or anomalous measures may be invalidated. Some targeted burdens may be found to be unconstitutional; others may be upheld, with the delineation between permissible and impermissible targeting unclear. Proportionality is a consideration, but one that largely re-poses in different language the core question of fairness posed by Articles 40.3.2° and 43. The usual outcome is that a restriction or deprivation of property rights is upheld against constitutional challenge, but neither the necessary combination of factors nor the threshold of 'unfairness' required to be reached to warrant invalidation is apparent from the case-law.

In this way, Irish constitutional property law shows that unpredictability is likely where progressive property ideas are implemented by judges concerning the *reasons* for decisions, but not necessarily concerning the *outcomes* themselves. That peripheral uncertainty can emerge as high-stakes, as with current doubts about the constitutionality of rent control as a means of responding to an ongoing housing crisis in Ireland.[52] However, for a number of reasons, its destabilising effects seem marginal: in most cases, the relative scope of the State's regulatory and expropriatory powers and an owner's property rights can be predicted with reasonable confidence.

First, as this book has shown, many of constitutional property's protective functions can be performed partially or wholly by other constitutional rights or values, such as fair procedures and equality. Its systemic implications in terms of the predictable protection of property rights may be less than the private law of property, since public law regulation of property rights can be narrower in its reach than the private law rules that govern day-to-day relations between individuals concerning property rights.[53] For example, most owners will never experience the exercise of compulsory acquisition powers in respect of their real property in Ireland, although all owners will be constrained in their use of real property by planning control.

Second, the balance of outcomes over time in Irish constitutional property rights adjudication has favoured the public interest, not

[52] See Walsh, 'Housing Crisis' and 'What Would the 'Referendum on Housing' Be About' (n 43). [1982] 1 IR 117.

[53] Walsh, 'Property, Human Flourishing, and St Thomas Aquinas' (n 32), 218.

property rights. This clear trend should cause owners to *anticipate* the likelihood of restriction rather than developing expectations of the continuation of the legal status quo. In turn, this should minimise destabilisation where new measures that restrict property rights are enacted.

Third, the comparatively high number of bills referred to the Supreme Court by the President on property rights grounds means that several contentious property rights restrictions were assessed for their constitutionality before they were enacted.[54] The simple fact of that high number of referrals reflects the consistently cautious political attitude towards property rights restrictions in Ireland.[55] The consequence of Article 26 referral in these cases was to avoid any destabilising impact on owners' expectations: the bills that were found to be unconstitutional were never enacted, and so never influenced owners' expectations, whether in respect of protection for their rights or the susceptibility of their rights to restriction; the bills that were found to be constitutional had any doubts about their permissibility permanently resolved prior to enactment, thereby resolving any uncertainty for owners concerning changes to their powers.

Fourth, Ireland has a global reputation as a jurisdiction wherein property rights are securely protected. For example, in 2020, Ireland was ranked the sixth freest economy globally in the Wall Street Journal/Heritage Foundation Index of Economic Freedom, second amongst 45 European states. It received a property rights index value of 86.6, against a global average value of 57.3.[56] Therefore, on the ground, any marginal uncertainty in constitutional property law is not having the effect of reducing real-world confidence in Ireland's ability to protect property rights. Article 43.1's institutional commitment to a private ownership system is clearly being implemented notwithstanding the

[54] Four out of a total of fifteen referrals have been decided on the basis of constitutional property rights issues, with a further referral also raising (but not being determined on the basis of) property rights.

[55] This author has argued with others elsewhere: '. . .the very fact that the President has seen fit to convene a Council of State meeting to consider a possible reference generally supposes that a significant doubt attaches to the constitutionality of the measure in the first place.' G. Hogan, D. Kenny and R. Walsh, 'An Anthology of Declarations of Unconstitutionality' (2015) 54 *Irish Jurist* 1, 16.

[56] www.heritage.org/index/country/ireland, last visited 3 September 2020. The Foundation assessed Ireland's property rights protection as follows: 'Property rights are well protected, and secured interests in property are recognized and enforced. Contracts are secure, and expropriation is rare.'

centrality of contextual judicial decision-making in Irish constitutional property law.

9.4 Deference to Democratic Decision-Making and the Public/Private Divide

Another important feature of Irish constitutional property law that minimises the destabilising effect of its contextual approach is the fact that judges largely defer to the balance struck in legislative or administrative decision-making between property rights and social justice. The 'social aspect' of property is regarded as appropriately negotiated on an evolving basis through democratically accountable political processes.[57] This is broadly consistent with the progressive property school of thought, with Macleod suggesting '[o]n all of these accounts, the rights and duties of property are products of, or accommodations reached through, political decision-making.'[58] As Mulvaney and Singer put it, '[d]emocracies do not serve property rights; property rights serve democratic values.'[59] Writing alone, Mulvaney refers to the process of state decision-making about property as '. . .a democratic one that requires accounting for the reality that social, economic, and moral perspectives on both the content of the values that property serves and what might harm these values evolve in the face of changing times and conditions.'[60] Similarly, van der Walt argues that property rights should be subject to democratic values,[61] while Michelman characterises the purpose of a 'takings' law regime as being to '. . .achieve some defensible reconciliation between democracy and private property.'[62] Constitutional property rights are in most cases in Irish law subordinated to democratic values as reflected in statutory and administrative limitations of those rights.

[57] A. M. Honoré, 'Ownership', in A. G. Guest (ed.), *Oxford Essays in Jurisprudence* (Oxford: Oxford University Press, 1961), p. 107, pp. 144–45.

[58] A. J. MacLeod, *Property and Practical Reason* (Cambridge: Cambridge University Press, 2015), p. 226.

[59] T. M. Mulvaney and J. W. Singer, 'Move Along to Where? Property in Service of Democracy' in G. Muller, R. Brits, B. V. Slade and J. van Wyk (eds.), *Transformative Property Law* (Cape Town: Juta, 2018), pp. 1, 20.

[60] T. M. Mulvaney, 'Property as Society' (2018) *Wisconsin Law Review* 911, 969–70.

[61] Van der Walt, 'The Modest Systemic Status of Property Rights' (n 34), 32–7. See also H. A. Overstreet, 'The Changing Conception of Property' (1915) 25 *International Journal of Ethics* 165, emphasising property's social purpose.

[62] F. I. Michelman, 'A Reply to Susan Rose-Ackerman' (1988) 88 *Columbia Law Review* 1712, 1713.

However, this aspect of Irish constitutional property law – the heavy weight accorded to 'partial resolutions' of the tension between property rights and social justice by the elected branches of government – casts into sharp relief an ambiguity in progressive property theory, namely whether it is predominantly concerned with clearing the way for *legislative* reform or whether its primary focus is on reshaping *private* law through judicial decision-making directed towards identifying and enforcing owners' obligations. Both are features of progressive property theory; the ambiguity concerns their relative priority.[63] While the focus of this book has been on public law, the Irish experience suggests that further clarification surrounding the respective roles of public and private law in advancing the progressive property agenda would assist in sharpening the response of progressive property to its critics on the issue of complexity. Information property theorists have long argued for innovation in property law to occur *ex ante* through legislative reform rather than through *ex post* intervention by judges, on the basis that the information costs generated by the latter are greater than the former.[64] Accordingly, to the extent that a progressive property strategy primarily focuses on owners' obligations as a justification for public law measures and decisions that control property rights, rather than as a basis for judicial reconfiguration of private law rights, information property theorists' concerns about destabilisation are reduced.

While there may well be correspondence between the normative values of property law in the public and private law contexts,[65] they involve different, albeit related and at times overlapping, legal means of achieving

[63] See, e.g., G. S. Alexander and E. M. Peñalver, 'Properties of Community' (2009) 10 *Theoretical Inquiries in Law* 127, 146–48 and *An Introduction to Property Theory* (n 37), pp. 86–7, arguing that owners' obligations justify action by the State to compel compliance, e.g. through redistributive legislation. Alexander's argument for a 'social obligation norm' in property contends that it provides an explanation for restrictions imposed on the rights of owners in both public and private law contexts: G. S. Alexander, 'The Social-Obligation Norm in American Property Law' (2009) 94 *Cornell Law Review* 745. A significant focus of Alexander's argument is on *judicial* interpretation and enforcement of such restrictions. Singer has applied his concept of an owner's 'duty of attentiveness' in both public and private law contexts, for example analysing 'minimum-standards regulations' in terms of owners' obligations: Singer, 'Property as the Law of Democracy' (n 45), 1302, and 'Democratic Estates: Property Law in a Free and Democratic Society' (2009) 94 *Cornell Law Review* 1009, 1052–53.

[64] See, e.g., Merrill and Smith 'Optimal Standardization' (n 49), 60–68; Smith, 'Property is Not Just a Bundle of Rights' (n 50), 287–88.

[65] G. S. Alexander, 'Property's Ends: The Publicness of Private Law Values' (2014) 99 *Iowa Law Review* 1257.

those values. The appropriate choice of legal means from a progressive property perspective will likely vary depending on the issue being addressed and the broader social, economic, and legal culture in which it arises.[66] A key consideration will be the degree to which legislative or judicial empowerment is preferable given local factors as a means of securing the 'ends' favoured by progressive property. Furthermore, the identification of owners' obligations has different effects in public and private law contexts. In the public law context, as illustrated by Irish constitutional property law, it primarily serves to justify legislative interferences with property rights, potentially influencing the judicial interpretation of such interferences in the event of constitutional challenge, for example by encouraging deference to political determinations. In the private law context, it imposes duties that must be fulfilled by owners directly, and in the event of dispute, enforced by judges. The Irish experience has been that judges treat progressively framed constitutional property rights as a prompt for judicial deference to democratic determinations of the appropriate balance between such rights and social justice rather than as an invitation for judicial innovation in interpreting and applying private law.

This shows that even where they are given an express constitutional mandate to do so, judges may be reluctant to engage in adjudication that requires them to openly state and justify their views on complex, contested concepts like fairness, the common good, and social justice. Barrington captures this dynamic well in analysing Article 43, saying: '...[j]udges have often been advised...to avoid involving the courts in questions of social or economic policy. But they have seldom needed this advice; their instinct is to avoid such involvement.'[67] The Irish courts have not articulated a theory of 'the principles of social justice' in Article 43.2, for example by identifying a 'social obligation norm' along the lines argued for by Alexander[68] or by emphasising the relational nature of

[66] Walsh, 'Property, Human Flourishing, and St Thomas Aquinas' (n 32), 218–19.

[67] D. Barrington, 'Private Property Under the Irish Constitution' (1973) 8 *Irish Jurist* 1, 4.

[68] Alexander, 'The Social Obligation Norm' (n 63). The Constitution Review Group in 1996 recommended the re-drafting of the property rights provisions of the Constitution to include, amongst other changes, a new qualifying clause providing '...property rights, since they carry with them duties and responsibilities, may be subject to legal restrictions, conditions, and formalities, provided these are duly required in the public interest and accord with the principles of social justice.' *Report of the Constitution Review Group* (Dublin: The Stationary Office, 1996), p. 366.

property law.[69] The early judicial understanding of the delimiting principles in Article 43.2 (the 'principles of social justice' and 'the exigencies of the common good') as '. . .political, economic or sociological tags, used in common language with different meanings by different people and devoid of any legal connotation whatever,'[70] continues to have influence notwithstanding the assertion of jurisdiction over those principles by the courts.[71] This doctrinal tendency is reflected in scholarship that discounts the imprint of Catholic social teaching on the text of the Constitution as anachronistic and irrelevant[72] and reads social justice out of Article 43.[73]

This tendency is not unique to Irish constitutional property law. Progressive property scholars have raised concerns that even where 'transformative' property rights guarantees are in place in the text of a constitution, judges may not give full effect to such guarantees.[74] Through their decisions in constitutional property law, judges must work out their relationship to the elected branches of government in striking the balance between overlapping individual and social values in the context of private ownership. As Alexander puts it, '[p]roperty clauses, like other constitutional provisions, are about who gets to decide what.'[75] Accordingly, in jurisdictions where the judiciary generally exercises a high level of self-restraint, in particular on distributive questions, 'progressive' aspects of constitutional property rights guarantees may be under-developed. A predominantly deferential approach has meant that

[69] See J. W. Singer and J. M. Beerman, 'The Social Origins of Property' (1993) 6 *Canadian Journal of Law & Jurisprudence* 217.

[70] Hanna J in *Pigs Marketing Board* v. *Donnelly* [1939] IR 413 at 421.

[71] See, e.g., *Re Article 26 and the Employment Equality Bill 1996* (n 24) at 367 and *Re Article 26 and Part V of the Planning and Development Bill 1999* [2000] 2 IR 321 at 357–58 for contemporary restatements of the primacy of the Oireachtas in this sphere.

[72] See, e.g., G. W. Hogan, 'The Constitution, Property Rights and Proportionality' (1997) 32 *Irish Jurist* 396 and G. W. Hogan, 'Foreword' in D. Keogh and A. McCarthy, *The Making of the Irish Constitution 1937: Bunreacht na hÉireann* (Cork: Mercier Press, 2007).

[73] D. O'Donnell, 'Property Rights in the Irish Constitution: Rights for Rich People, or a Pillar of Free Society?' in E. Carolan and O. Doyle (eds.), *The Irish Constitution: Governance and Values* (Dublin: Thomson Round Hall, 2008), p. 429; R. Keane, 'Land Use, Compensation and the Community' (1983) 18 *Irish Jurist* 23, 32; A. O'Neill, 'Property Rights and the Power of Eminent Domain' in Eoin Carolan and Oran Doyle (eds.), *The Irish Constitution: Governance and Values* (Dublin: Thomson Round Hall, 2008), p. 438.

[74] See, e.g., van der Walt, *Property in the Margins* (n 14) 26, 131, Alexander, *The Global Debate* (n 12), pp. 149–51, 182.

[75] Alexander, *The Global Debate* (n 12), p. 247.

the Irish property rights provisions have been implemented in a manner that broadly favours the public interest. This judicial attitude is most reliably attributed to the overall reluctance of Irish judges to second-guess the judgment of the elected branches of government on distributive issues, not to any worked out constitutional theory of 'social justice' and/or the 'common good'.[76]

However, the heavy weight accorded to legislative and administrative determinations of the appropriate balance between property rights and social justice is consistent with the Irish Constitution's drafting history. The exclusion of 'social obligation' language from the text of the constitutional property rights guarantees can be explained at least in part by the Catholic social policy that influenced the drafters, which emphasised individual rights rather than duties. At the same time, as was discussed in Chapter 3, Catholic teaching clearly did recognise that ownership has a 'social aspect'[77] or 'social function',[78] which the drafters attempted to capture in Article 43.2. The intention of the drafters was to enshrine in the Constitution a private ownership regime that would be socially adaptive and would take account of the needs of both owners and non-owners. Restrictions on the exercise of property rights were expressly authorised in the interests of social justice in Article 43.2. Article 45 specified objectives that the legislature should pursue in exercising that power, including widening the category of owners within the State. It sketched a vision for an institution of private ownership that would be firmly embedded in, and controlled by, Irish social and economic life. Taken together, Articles 43 and 45 put beyond doubt the power of the State to shape the institution of private ownership to attain progressive goals. The Constitution set the scene for a division of labour whereby the courts would secure the 'individual' aspect of private ownership and the legislature would implement its 'social' aspect guided by Article 45 and empowered by Article 43.2.

[76] The Irish courts have expressed the view that their functions are confined to the sphere of commutative, rather than distributive, justice: see, e.g., *O'Reilly* v. *Limerick Corporation* [1989] 1 ILRM 181 and *TD* v. *Minister for Education* [2001] 4 IR 259.

[77] Honoré, 'Ownership' (n 57), pp. 144–45.

[78] Léon Duguit, "Les Transformations générales du droit privé depuis le Code Napoléon" (1912, Paris, Félix Alcan), reproduced and translated in Various Authors, *Progress of Continental Law in the Nineteenth Century* (Little, Brown and Company, 1918) 65, 74. For a useful overview, see M. C. Mirow, 'The Social-Obligation Norm of Property: Duguit, Hayem, and Others' (2010) 22 *Fla J Int'l L* 191.

That has been largely reflected in Irish constitutional property doctrine, although the Directive Principles in Article 45 have had very little practical influence, either legally or politically.[79] This division of labour resonates in certain respects with Kantian approaches to property that distinguish sharply between 'private' and 'public' rights.[80] As Katz puts it, '[o]wners are not directly constrained by the needs of others, on this view, but the state is'.[81] Owners can be required to assist the state in meeting such needs. However, the nature of the 'social solidarity' that a Kantian approach requires – focused on avoiding individuals falling into a state of dependence – may not go far enough to capture the Irish Constitution's progressive concern with social justice and the common good, notwithstanding the fact that a wide range of interferences with property rights have been justified under a Kantian approach.[82] The Irish Constitution *requires* the State to secure alignment between the exercise of property rights and social justice in Article 43.2.1° as well as empowering it to regulate to secure the common good in Article 43.2.2°.

As Dagan argues, there is a risk that a Kantian understanding of property in the private law context could influence law-making in the public law context: as he puts it, '...private law should beware of entrenching attitudes that might hinder a just public order.'[83] The intuitive influence of the private law of property in shaping the conception of ownership that is applied in constitutional property law has been seen throughout the doctrinal analysis in this book, and a 'mythological' understanding of property as a robustly protected individual right that

[79] For analysis of Article 45's impact in the property context, see R. Walsh, 'Private Property Rights in the Drafting of the Irish Constitution: A Communitarian Compromise' (2011) 33 *Dublin University Law Journal* 86, 109–13.

[80] On Kantian property theory, see helpfully Katz, 'Ownership and Social Solidarity' (n 38), Dagan, *Property: Values and Institutions* (n 38), pp. 59–60, Alexander and Peñalver, *An Introduction to Property Theory* (n 37), pp. 70–79. For leading statements of the approach, see A. Ripstein, *Force and Freedom* (Boston: Harvard University Press, 2009), *Private Wrongs* (Boston: Harvard University Press, 2016), E. J. Weinrib, *Corrective Justice* (Oxford: Oxford University Press, 2012) and *The Idea of Private Law* (Oxford: Oxford University Press, 2012).

[81] Katz, ibid., 127.

[82] Ibid., 130.

[83] Dagan, *Property: Values and Institutions* (n 38), p. 65. He expands on this argument to justify internalising concerns about civic virtues and egalitarian distribution in the concept of ownership, arguing: '[t]he social meaning of the right to property – the common goods we believe this right is meant to realize – defines the realm of normatively powerful objects to government action, as well as the realm of objections that we tend to perceive as merely self-centered, and thus publicly inconsequential': pp. 132–33.

justifies political conservativism has been observed.[84] Accordingly, Dagan's concerns about the Kantian approach are relevant in the Irish context. While the 'limitational' approach adopted in Irish constitutional property law has not impeded progressive political reforms, its expressive effect may have contributed to a disconnect between the doctrinal reality of weak constitutional property rights protection and cultural perceptions of that protection as strong. Both these understandings of the Irish Constitution's protection for property rights can, and do, influence policy-making. Dagan helpfully highlights their interconnectedness – judicial decisions can have an expressive effect that impacts on the persuasiveness of owners' claims more broadly. The influence is mutual, since judicial decisions will be influenced by wider societal assumptions about the scope of owners' rights.

As Purdy says, '[s]ocieties are built on stories and unspoken presuppositions that detail why and how their practices are legitimate, beneficial, or natural: these lend shape to the practices of everyday life and help define the purposes and limits of power.'[85] Those stories and unspoken presuppositions influence, and are influenced by, judicial decisions in ways that do not necessarily correspond to the strict legal effect of such decisions. In this way, a complex symbiosis exists between the interpretation of property rights in legal doctrine and broader cultural assumptions and intuitions about the strength of those rights. As Underkuffler puts it; the meaning of property '. . .is more than what a court might decree it to be in a particular case'.[86] At the same time, such decrees are influential beyond the particular decisions in which they are articulated.

9.5 Intuitions and Localism in Constitutional Property Law

The doctrinal analysis in previous chapters showed that Irish judges largely reason in an intuitive, *ad hoc*, manner to reach 'partial resolutions' of the tension between property rights and social justice that is captured in Article 43 of the Constitution. The rhetoric of property is buried below the surface of the doctrine and is variable rather than stable. Judges select the images and ideas that best support their intuitive view of the

84 Underkuffler, 'Property as Constitutional Myth' (n 30).

85 J. Purdy, *The Meaning of Property: Freedom, Community, and the Legal Imagination* (New Haven: Yale University Press, 2010) p. 160.

86 L. S. Underkuffler, 'What Does the Constitutional Protection of Property Mean?' (2016) 5 *Brigham-Kanner Prop. Rts. Conf. J.* 109, 123.

requirements of fairness in a particular case and determine the scope of protection afforded to property rights on that basis. Following this intuitive approach, '. . .theory is immanent and evolving; its development is interdependent with practice.'[87]

While a number of the overlapping individual and social property values analysed in Chapter 2 are latent in constitutional property doctrine, the ideas and commitments that those values entail are observed obliquely, occasionally at the level of *dicta*, but more usually at the level of unarticulated judicial assumption. As Harris explains:

> Our perceptions are coloured by a host of value-laden assumptions. Some of these assumptions are local and passing, others are more pervasive and permanent facets of human association. Any of them may, one way or another, be raised to the level of conscious apprehension and then, perhaps, challenged. The bulk of them, however, provide a taken-for-granted background for all that we think and say.[88]

The intuitive approach that is evident in Irish constitutional property rights adjudication supports Gerhart's contention that social recognition, centred on '. . .social values that develop over time from countless interactions of individuals over claims about how resources ought to be used and over the equitable division of burdens and benefits within the society', is highly significant in both public and private property law.[89] In enforcing the institution of private ownership and in determining its scope, judges are influenced by their intuitive perceptions of its value, which feed back into the doctrine. However, the logical implications of the relevant theories of property are not usually carried through in decisions. Strong statements of principle can appear in isolated cases and remain undeveloped thereafter, as has been the position so far with the identity-focused decision of the Supreme Court in the *Health Bill case*,[90] considered further below. Property theory both feeds into, and is sporadically articulated to defend, the balance between individual and social values that is struck by judges in individual cases.

[87] M. J. Radin, 'Lacking a Transformative Social Theory: A Response' (1993) 45 *Stanford Law Review* 409, 413.

[88] Ibid., p. 63. See also Purdy, (n 85), p. 160.

[89] P. M. Gerhart, *Property Law and Social Morality* (New York: Cambridge University Press, 2013), p. 251. See relatedly Harris's discussion of social convention, *Property and Justice* (n 11), pp. 330–31.

[90] [2005] 1 IR 105.

From a comparative constitutional property law perspective, and from the perspective of the development of progressive property theory, the centrality of culturally embedded, intuitive judicial reasoning raises the further issue of localism. As the previous section showed, aspects of political culture such as the degree of trust between, and in, branches of government influence constitutional property rights adjudication, often unconsciously and almost always inexplicitly.[91] Cultural attitudes towards private ownership, both amongst politicians and in wider society, are also influential. This means that comparative constitutional property law must attend carefully to differences in political and legal culture and in broader societal attitudes towards private ownership.[92] As Singer puts it, 'unconscious presumptions' about ownership, rooted in 'culture, history, and law' are important factors in the analysis of property rights.[93] Furthermore, it means that the instantiation and practical implementation of progressive property theory will inevitably vary across jurisdictions and over time. While the core values and tenets of a progressive property approach may be clear, how those are implemented will depend on local factors, including the relative roles and powers of courts, legislatures and executives and the wider culture in respect of private ownership.

Therefore, a future focus of both comparative constitutional property scholarship and progressive property theory should be deeper analysis of the nature and effects of culturally embedded assumptions about ownership in different jurisdictions. This approach would allow for progressive property approaches to particular property problems to be more targeted through tailoring to local factors and needs, thereby better enabling progressive property to realise its aim of improving the law for those on the margins.[94] These priorities are already reflected in two emerging trends in progressive property theory: first, greater attention is being

[91] As Alexander notes, '[p]reexisting legal and political traditions and culture continue strongly to influence the stability and security of property rights even where those traditions and culture seemingly conflict with or are in tension with constitutional expressions.' Alexander, *The Global Debate* (n 10), p. 405.

[92] On this point, see also R. Walsh and L. Fox-O'Mahony, 'Land Law, Property Ideologies and the British Irish Relationship' (2018) 47 *Common Law World Review* 7, A. J. van der Walt and R. Walsh, 'Comparative Constitutional Property Law' in L. Smith and M. Graziadei (eds.), *Comparative Property Law: Global Perspectives* (Cheltenham: Edward Elgar, 2017), p. 193.

[93] Singer, *Entitlement* (n 21), p. 10. See also Harris, *Property and Justice* (n 11), pp. 64, 86.

[94] Alexander, *Property and Human Flourishing* (n 37), p. 320.

given to the usefulness of comparative analysis by US progressive property scholars[95]; second, distinctive 'progressive' approaches to property are developing in other jurisdictions.[96]

This book has contributed to this new direction in progressive property theory by unearthing and analysing some of the assumptions driving Irish constitutional property law. On the one hand, the influence of the common law and the associated liberal conception of ownership remains strong notwithstanding the distinctive, progressively framed treatment of property rights in the Constitution. On the other hand, the historic experience of land redistribution, coupled with the Catholic social teaching that influenced the drafting of the Constitution, established an acceptance of ownership as a *limited* right from the outset of the current constitutional regime. This is reflected in the outcomes in constitutional property rights adjudication, which are heavily influenced by judicial assumptions about the primacy of the elected branches of government in determining the appropriate distribution of resources. In rare cases, diverging judicial intuitions about the fairness of such political judgments overcome that general attitude of deference, resulting in invalidations that can be difficult to reconcile with previous decisions and are not always followed in subsequent cases.

9.6 Progressive Property's 'Themes' in Action

9.6.1 Humility and Transparency

Considered through the lens of Mulvaney's 'progressive property themes' of humility and transparency,[97] Irish constitutional property doctrine performs better on some fronts than others. The theme of 'humility' is reflected in a flexible judicial approach that recognises that the evolving

[95] Notably, Alexander, *The Global Debate* (n 12).

[96] See, e.g., van der Walt, 'The Modest Systemic Status of Property Rights' (n 3); E. van der Sijde, *Reconsidering the Relationship between Property and Regulation: a Systemic Constitutional Approach* (PhD thesis, University of Stellenbosch, 2015, on file with author) (South Africa); S. Blandy, S. Bright and S. Nield, 'The Dynamics of Enduring Property Relationships in Land' (2018) 81 *Modern Law Review* 85, 'Real Property on the Ground: The Law of People and Place' in H. Dagan and B. Zipursky (eds.), *Research Handbook on Private Law Theory* (Cheltenham: Edward Elgar, 2020), p. 237, and L. Fox-O'Mahony, 'Property Outsiders and the Hidden Politics of Doctrinalism' (2014) 67 *Current Legal Problems* 409.

[97] T. M. Mulvaney, 'Progressive Property Moving Forward' (2014) 5 *California Law Review Circuit* 349.

demands of the public interest can change the kinds of burdens that it is legitimate to place on owners. Outcomes generally favour the public interest, with very few categories of cases triggering stronger protection of property rights, most significantly the presumptive entitlement to compensation for deprivations. At the margins are cases where the courts rarely or inconsistently adopt a more protective approach. Examples include isolated discrete protection of the right to exclude as an 'incident of ownership'[98] and sporadic rejection of the imposition of targeted burdens on owners.[99] Transparency as to the *reasons* for such outlier decisions has not been forthcoming, with rationales variously unarticulated, incoherently explained, or inconsistently applied. A new judicial methodology focused on frankly explaining decisions rather than on obscuring the fact of judicial choice is required to bring the intuitions concerning the meaning and value of private ownership that currently animate judicial decision-making to the surface.

In this way, Irish constitutional property law shows that Mulvaney's theme of 'transparency' should be high on the list of priorities for progressive property. Such transparency would not resolve the tension between individual and collective interests in the protection of property rights. However, it would expose what is at stake in the ongoing, dynamic process of partially resolving that tension through legislative and executive decision-making and constitutional property rights adjudication. Clarity could emerge over time from the pattern of 'partial resolutions'[100] revealed in the outcomes of constitutional property rights disputes.[101] Irish constitutional property law should provide some comfort for progressive property theorists who advocate contextual, fairness-focused adjudication in respect of property rights, since it shows that such an approach can be adopted without fundamental destabilising effects. However, progressive property will struggle to comprehensively counter critiques grounded in the unpredictability and related inefficient information costs of contextual judicial decision-making if in practice judges

98 *ESB* v. *Gormley* [1985] 1 IR 129.

99 *Blake* (n 24), *Re Article 26 and the Housing (Private Rented Dwellings) Bill 1981* (n 24), *Re Article 26 and the Employment Equality Bill 1997* (n 24).

100 On this point, see J. W. Singer, 'The Rule of Reason in Property Law' (2013) 46 *UC Davis Law Review* 1369, 1389.

101 On the role of outcomes in clarifying the meaning of standards like fairness, see Singer, 'Justifying Regulatory Takings' (n 33).

resist confronting the core distributive justice questions that constitutional property rights raise.[102]

Requiring judicial frankness on this issue is not an easy ask. As the previous sections in this chapter highlighted, there are institutional reasons that compel judges to avoid or conceal the core function that they perform in constitutional property law in determining 'fairness'. As Lehavi argues, '[t]he judicial enterprise of filling norms with content on a dynamic basis touches on broad questions of legitimacy, division of powers, and other considerations that act as external constraints on such institutions.'[103] Beerman and Singer contend that requiring an honest and explicit engagement with the value choices involved in property law '. . .contradicts the judicial philosophy of "leaving lawmaking to the legislature" and keeping (or, rather, pretending to keep) the Court out of the business of making law.'[104] Furthermore, the gut-driven nature of decisions about fairness means that such decisions can be genuinely unconscious and not easy to pin down in terms that comfortably fit the style and scope of judicial decisions.[105] However, the judicial inclination for deference conflicts with the reality that judges must, and do, review distributional decisions in adjudicating constitutional property rights claims.[106] As Michelman puts it, acceptance is required of '. . .some greater degree of politicization of our ideal understanding of adjudication, and particularly constitutional adjudication, than we have yet learned to find comfortable'.[107]

102 On the distributive nature of constitutional property law, see F. I. Michelman, 'Liberties, Fair Values, and Constitutional Method' (1992) 59 *University of Chicago Law Review* 91, 99. For a good example of criticism of *ad hoc* adjudication in this context, see S. Rose-Ackerman, 'Against Ad-Hocery: A Comment on Michelman' (1988) 88 *Columbia Law Review* 1697.

103 A. Lehavi, 'The Dynamic Law of Property: Theorizing the Role of Legal Standards' (2011) 42 *Rutgers Law Journal* 81, 126. See also Singer and Beerman, 'The Social Origins of Property' (n 69), 22.

104 See also Singer and Beerman, 'The Social Origins of Property' (n 69), 22.

105 F. I. Michelman, 'Property, Utility, and Fairness: Comments on the Ethical Foundations of 'Just Compensation' Law' (1967) 80 *Harvard Law Review* 1165, 1249. See also Harris, *Property and Justice* (n 11), p. 368, and Audrey G. McFarlane, 'Rebuilding the Public-Private City: Regulatory Taking's Anti-Subordination Insights for Eminent Domain and Redevelopment' (2009) 42 *Indiana Law Review* 97, 137.

106 Michelman accurately captures the nature of the distributional decision entailed: '[a] court assigned to differentiate among impacts which are and are not "takings" is essentially engaged in deciding when government may execute public programs while leaving associated costs disproportionately concentrated upon one or a few persons.' Michelman, 'Property, Utility, and Fairness', (n 105), 1165.

107 Michelman, 'Possession v Distribution', (n 34), 1320–21.

Irish constitutional property law is currently wedged in an unsatisfactory space between 'a Cartesian constitutional jurisprudence of rules' and 'a pragmatic constitutional jurisprudence of values'.[108] Few rules are applied that might provide *definitive* guidance to either the State or private property owners on the scope of their respective powers and rights. For example, no 'stick' in the bundle of property is 'essentialised' and placed off limits to restrictions. There is no absolute requirement of compensation for either expropriation of property or regulation of the use of property. Redistributive laws are not absolutely ruled in or ruled out. The public interest *usually* prevails over individual property rights, but not always. The result is doctrinal ambiguity at the margins of Irish constitutional property law. This has been relatively insignificant in terms of the reality of legal property rights protection – there is a high degree of clarity and consistency concerning the qualified nature of the Constitution's property rights guarantees. However, that marginal uncertainty appears to have fostered or bolstered a political perception of property rights as strongly protected by the Constitution. As such, Irish constitutional property law should serve as a cautionary tale for progressive property theory, demonstrating that transparency may not be readily forthcoming from judges in constitutional property rights adjudication and that a cost of such a lack of transparency may be an inability to decisively rebut legal and political misapprehensions about the strength of constitutional protection for property rights.

9.6.2 Marginality, Identity, and Vulnerability in Constitutional Property Law

Van der Walt argues for more marginality thinking in property law, involving paying greater attention to '. . .the social position, economic status and personal circumstances of the parties involved in property relations or disputes'.[109] He contends:

> [a] focus on the margins . . .should involve more than just having sympathy or greater understanding for those in the margins because of their social context; it should include developing an eye for the power and

[108] F. I. Michelman, 'Tutelary Jurisprudence and Constitutional Property' in E. Paul and H. Dickman (eds.), *Liberty, Property and the Future of Constitutional Development* (New York: New York University Press, 1990), pp. 127, 154.

[109] van der Walt, *Property in the Margins*, (n 14), p. 245.

> status of their position in the margins and the reasons for their challenge to the regime.[110]

Relatedly, Mulvaney argues for a focus on identity involving capturing and considering the status of those affected by the operation of property law, if necessary through differential application of legal rules.[111] Applying this approach to so-called legislative exactions (burdens attached to regulatory permissions), Mulvaney argues for concentration:

> . . . not only on individuals' present status, established property holdings, and current wealth, but also on (i) individuals' and communities' personal, social, political, and economic identities that have impacted their life courses and relation to property law to date, and (ii) the overall effects of continuing to recognize those property holdings presently in place.[112]

Davidson emphasises the significance of vulnerability flowing from the link between identity and personal property, which he contends ought to be factored in when calibrating legal protection for property rights and when considering how ownership is incentivised and prioritised.[113] These progressive property approaches focused on marginality, identity, and vulnerability can be connected to republican approaches to property and the related idea of 'property as propriety', explored in Chapter 2.

Similar connections between property rights on the one hand, and democracy, marginality, identity, and vulnerability on the other hand, can be identified in the decision of the Irish Supreme Court in the *Health Bill case*.[114] There, the Court recognised the right to private ownership of external goods as a 'pillar' of the democratic system and held that the property rights of vulnerable individuals are particularly deserving of judicial protection.[115] As was discussed in Chapter 7, the Court did not develop its understanding of 'vulnerability', but rather proceeded on the basis that the group of owners that would have been adversely affected by the Bill lacked the political awareness and power to effectively protect their interests. In this way, the decision suggests the possible emergence of an approach to constitutional property rights adjudication that is

110 Ibid., pp. 245–46.

111 Mulvaney, 'Progressive Property Moving Forward' (n 97).

112 T. M. Mulvaney, 'Legislative Exactions and Progressive Property' (2016) 40 *Harvard Environmental Law Review* 137, 161.

113 N. M. Davidson, 'Property and Identity: Vulnerability and Insecurity in the Housing Crisis' (2012) 47 *Harvard Civil Rights and Civil Liberties Law Review* 119.

114 *Re Article 26 and the Health (Amendment) (No. 2) Bill 2004* (n 90) at 201–2.

115 Ibid. at 202.

'participation-oriented' and 'representation-reinforcing', to borrow from Ely.[116] Ely famously argued that judicial intervention was appropriate where the 'channels of political change' might be closed to some individuals or groups in society. He characterised the Takings Clause of the Fifth Amendment to the US Constitution as having the function of protecting minorities against unfair exploitation.[117] Similarly, Treanor argues that in takings cases, courts should focus on identifying and resolving instances of process failure, such as minority exploitation.[118]

Applying these approaches, judicial intervention to protect private property rights is warranted where the group targeted by a restriction is socially and politically weak and unable to defend its interests through the political system.[119] Generalised judgment is required in identifying 'discrete and insular minorities' or 'marginal' groups deserving of particular protection. Group definition raises scope for contestation, with divergences in views on this issue in scholarship likely to be reflected in divergences in approach in legal doctrine.[120] For example, in the *Health Bill case*, the Supreme Court acknowledged that some elderly people who were adversely affected by the referred bill did not fit the image of a vulnerable, politically disempowered group, but held that most of those

[116] J. H. Ely, *Democracy and Distrust – A Theory of Judicial Review* (Cambridge, MA: Harvard University Press, 1980), p. 87.

[117] The Takings Clause provides '…nor shall private property be taken for public use, without just compensation.' Ely characterises this clause as providing '…yet another protection of the few against the many.' Ibid., p. 97. He notes that it means '[i]f we want a highway or a park we can have it, but we're all going to have to share the cost rather than imposing it on some isolated individual or group.' Ibid., pp. 97–98.

[118] Treanor contends that 'compensation is due when a governmental action affects only the property interests of an individual or a small group of people and when, in the absence of compensation, there would be a lack of horizontal equity (i.e., when compensation is the norm in similar circumstances).' W. Treanor, 'The Original Understanding of the Takings Clause and the Political Process' (1995) 95 *Columbia Law Review* 782, 872.

[119] Ely describes how political processes can fail minority groups as follows: '[m]alfunction occurs when the *process* is undeserving of trust, when (1) the ins are choking off the channels of political change to ensure that they will stay in and the outs will stay out, or (2) though no one is actually denied a voice or a vote, representatives beholden to an effective majority are systematically disadvantaging some minority out of simple hostility or a prejudiced refusal to recognize commonalities of interest, and thereby denying that minority the protection afforded other groups by a representative system.' *Democracy and Distrust* (n 116), p. 103.

[120] For scholarly approaches to the question of group definition see, e.g., Treanor, 'The Original Understanding' (n 118) and J. E. Fee, 'The Takings Clause as a Comparative Right' (2003) *Southern California Law Review* 1003, 1003.

targeted did come within that category.[121] In contrast, Ely suggested that legislative targeting of the elderly should not be regarded as inherently suspect since political representatives can be presumed to understand the relevant differences that old age entails.[122]

This potential for disagreement demonstrates that concepts like marginality, identity, and vulnerability will not generate clear-cut, value-neutral standards or rules for constitutional property rights adjudication that can dispense with the need for judgment – far from it. The distinctions and delineations that such an approach requires judges to draw may generate their own doctrinal inconsistencies. For example, prior to the *Health Bill case*, targeted measures were struck down by the Supreme Court in *Blake* v. *Attorney General*[123] and *Re Article 26 and the Employment Equality Bill 1996*,[124] despite the fact that the groups affected by the impugned measures in those cases (landlords and employers) did not appear to be politically weak. Furthermore, the Irish courts have in subsequent decisions upheld restrictions that impose onerous burdens on discrete groups of owners.[125]

Such doctrinal incoherence, when coupled with the isolated nature of the statements in the *Health Bill case*, makes it hard to predict the likely impact of the decision. It may prove to be an inadvertent experiment with an identity focus motivated by the particularly sympathetic facts of the case, or it may mark the beginning of a new doctrinal direction that could involve a group-based identity focus or could be influenced by the emerging vulnerability theory considered in Chapter 7.[126] Both

[121] *Re Article 26 and the Health (Amendment) (No. 2) Bill 2004* (n 90) at 203.

[122] Ely, *Democracy and Distrust* (n 116), p. 160. He further argued that classifications targeting the poor should only be rarely regarded as suspect, because the unwillingness of government to give benefits to the poor stems from a reluctance to raise taxes, not from any unfair targeting: p. 162.

[123] *Blake* (n 24). McCormack criticises *Blake* on this basis, saying '. . .property owners do not usually constitute a "discrete and insular minority" who are unable to obtain accommodation within the political process.' G. McCormack, '*Blake-Madigan* and its Aftermath' (1983) 5 *Dublin University Law Journal* 205, 218.

[124] *Re Article 26 and the Employment Equality Bill 1996* (n 24).

[125] See, e.g., *JJ Haire & Co Ltd* v. *Minister for Health* [2009] IEHC 562, *Unite the Union* v. *Minister for Finance* [2010] IEHC 354, and *Dowling* v. *Minister for Finance* [2018] IECA 300.

[126] As was discussed in Chapter 6, the retrospective nature of the Bill was a key factor in the Supreme Court's finding, as was the fact that the State had imposed charges on the vulnerable individuals impacted by the Bill since 1976 with knowledge that it lacked a legal basis to do so following the decision of the Supreme Court in *In re Maud McInerney* [1976–77] ILRM 229.

approaches reflect Mulvaney's 'identity' theme and provide options for judges seeking to implement Article 43.2's commitment to social justice through legal doctrine in a way that pays particular attention to those on the margins. They are supported by the strength with which the participation rights of owners and their entitlements to fair procedures have been enforced by the Irish courts.[127] If developed, the *Health Bill case* could mark a significant change in approach by putting an adversely affected owner's personal circumstances, in particular their social and political status, at the centre of constitutional property rights adjudication.[128] In doing so, it would foreground the importance of social justice in Irish constitutional property law and provide an important practical exemplar for the future development of progressive property theories focused on ideas like marginality, identity, and vulnerability.

9.7 Conclusions

This book has advocated greater transparency in constitutional property law concerning the reasons for judicial decisions. However, transparency will not generate easy answers or monolithic explanations of the relationship between property rights and social justice in jurisdictions like Ireland that protect both values at a constitutional level. Nor will greater frankness from judges necessarily generate consensus or diminish contestation. As Michelman says, constitutional property clauses are 'radically ambivalent' and capable of supporting 'both left-leaning and right-leaning constitutional-legal applications'.[129] The doctrine analysed in this book shows that the dual protection of property rights and social justice in the Irish Constitution's property rights provisions is capable of being interpreted and applied in ways that variously prioritise the 'individual' and 'social' aspects of ownership, with oscillation between these priorities identifiable over time and in different contexts. Greater transparency would better enable critical debate about those shifts by clarifying the various 'partial resolutions' of the tension between property rights and social justice achieved by judges. However, transparency will not permanently or comprehensively resolve that tension.

[127] See the discussion of fair procedures in Chapter 6.

[128] As van der Walt notes, considerations such as poverty and social vulnerability are not usually relevant to a property regime: *Property in the Margins*, (n 14), 213–14.

[129] F. I. Michelman, 'The Property Clause Question' (2012) 19 *Constellations* 152, 157.

As well as advocating greater frankness from judges *in* doctrine, this book has sought to highlight the rewards of paying greater attention to legal doctrine and outcomes in theorising about constitutional property law.[130] It has adopted and advocated a 'mid-range' approach to analysing constitutional property law, attending to both theory and practice.[131] By analysing the partial and inconsistent manifestations of theory in legal doctrine, constitutional property scholarship can identify spaces within existing legal frameworks where there is potential to generate greater 'progressive' dividends. Doctrinal analysis does not need to be, and in this context should not be, focused on rationalising judicial decisions or presenting them as coherent or clear. Rather, valuable insights can be gained from exploring how 'the paradox and the contradiction' that is embedded in constitutional property rights guarantees is tackled by judges.[132] Accordingly, as well as continuing to make the case that predictability *can* emerge from contextual judicial decision-making,[133] progressive property scholarship should investigate unpredictability and incoherence where it does emerge. In addition, the progressive property school of thought should widen its lens by paying greater attention to the insights to be gained from progressive property in action in jurisdictions other than the US, and to the distinctive features of local applications of progressive property ideas.

In turn, constitutional property law in various jurisdictions could be illuminated and developed by being analysed through a progressive property lens, thereby helping to clarify the function and impact of

[130] On this point, see S. Blandy, S. Nield and S. Bright, 'Real Property on the Ground: the Law of People and Place' Theory' in H. Dagan and B.Zipursky (eds.), *Research Handbook on Private Law Theory* (Cheltenham: Edward Elgar, 2020), p. 237, arguing '. . .building an understanding of property in land from resources such as judgments and empirical data results in law that can be better designed to reflect property as it is understood and practiced, composed of complex, contextual relationships between people and place.' (p. 253).

[131] Harris advocates 'middle-range theorizing about property', rejecting both assertions about the justification of property institutions and high abstraction, which he characterizes as 'intuitionistic': Harris, *Property and Justice* (n 11), 166–67. On the benefits of a mid-range approach, see also Walsh and Fox O'Mahony, 'Land Law, Property Ideologies' (n 92).

[132] Van der Walt, *Property in the Margins* (n 14), p. 245.

[133] See, e.g., Singer, 'The Rule of Reason' (n 100) 1389, arguing '[a] large amount of predictability comes from stories that form exemplars that tell us what is inside and what is outside the standard'.

constitutional property rights.[134] Irish constitutional property law, often criticised as a muddle, was in many respects clarified by being analysed in this book in light of progressive property's core themes. Far from being 'a classic example of giving a right with one hand and taking it back with the other',[135] when viewed from a progressive property perspective, Irish constitutional property law represents a broadly coherent and effective attempt to implement a progressive structure for 'partial resolutions' of the tension between property rights and social justice. It shows that social justice is not a straightforward delimiting principle in the constitutional property context: judges may be reluctant to develop it due to its ambiguity, or may use it in an *ad hoc*, unpredictable manner. At the same time, it demonstrates that recognising social justice as a delimiting principle can help to prevent constitutional property rights guarantees blocking political reforms. Furthermore, at least in terms of outcomes, unpredictability stemming from contextual adjudication rooted in concepts like fairness and social justice may be a marginal rather than a systemic problem.

In these ways, both at a national and an international level, a full understanding of Irish constitutional property law provides important corrections to misapprehensions about the effect of constitutionalising property rights. Perhaps most fundamentally, it shows that constitutional protection is potentially compatible with progressive political agendas for the mediation of property rights and social justice, but that it can influence political attitudes towards that mediation in ways that do not always reflect the strict legal effect of constitutional property doctrine. Constitutional property rights can have influence that tends to protect the status quo even where they are not interpreted by judges in strict or absolutist terms. More generally, Irish constitutional property law

[134] On the contested function of constitutional property clauses see, e.g., F. I. Michelman, 'The Property Clause Question' (2012) 19 *Constellations* 152; T. Allen, 'The Right to Property', in T. Ginsburg and R. Dixon (eds.), *Comparative Constitutional Law* (Oxford: Elgar Publishing, 2011), p. 504; J. Nedelsky, 'Should Property be Constitutionalized? A Relational and Comparative Approach' in G. E. van Maanen and A. J. van der Walt (eds.), *Property Law on the Threshold of the Twenty-first Century* (Antwerp: Maklu, 1996), p. 417; B. Bryce, 'Property as a Natural Right and as a Conventional Right in Constitutional Law' (2007) 29 *Loyola of Los Angeles International and Comparative Law Review* 201; G. S. Alexander, 'Constitutionalising Property: Two Experiences, Two Dilemmas' in J. McLean (ed.), *Property and the Constitution* (Oxford: Hart Publishing, 1999), p. 88.

[135] K. C. Wheare, *Modern Constitutions* (Oxford: Oxford University Press, 1966), p. 43.

provides scholars with an array of fresh examples through which to ground and test theories and ideas about the complex relationship between property rights and social justice, which this book has sought to bring to the fore. The hope is that this contribution will enliven and enrich fundamental debates about that relationship that continue to drive progressive property theory and comparative constitutional property law.

BIBLIOGRAPHY

Books

Ackerman, B. A. *Private Property and the Constitution* (New Haven: Yale University Press, 1977).

Alexander, G. S. *The Global Debate over Constitutional Property* (Chicago: University of Chicago Press, 2006).

Property and Human Flourishing (Oxford: Oxford University Press, 2018).

Alexander, G. S. and Peñalver, E. M. *An Introduction to Property Theory* (Cambridge: Cambridge University Press, 2012).

Property and Community (Oxford: Oxford University Press, 2010).

Allen, C. *Housing Market Renewal and Social Class* (London: Routledge, 2008).

Allen, T. *Property and the Human Rights Act* (Oxford: Hart Publishing, 2005).

The Right to Property in Commonwealth Constitutions (Cambridge: Cambridge University Press, 2000).

Barak, A. *Proportionality: Constitutional Rights and the Limitations* (Cambridge: Cambridge University Press, 2012).

Brady, A. *Proportionality and Deference under the UK Human Rights Act: An Institutionally Sensitive Approach* (Cambridge: Cambridge University Press, 2012).

Bull, P. *Land, Politics and Nationalism: A Study of the Irish Land Question* (Dublin: Gill & Macmillan, 1996).

Cahillane, L. *Drafting the Irish Free State Constitution* (Manchester: Manchester University Press, 2016).

Casey, J. *Constitutional Law in Ireland*, 3rd ed. (Dublin: Round Hall, 2000).

Chubb, B. *The Government and Politics of Ireland*, 2nd ed. (London: Longman, 1970).

Clark, S. *Social Origins of the Irish Land War* (Princeton: Princeton University Press, 1979).

Coffey, D. K. *Drafting the 1937 Irish Constitution: Transnational Influences in Interwar Europe* (London: Palgrave Macmillan, 2018).

Cohen-Eliya, M. and Porat, I. *Proportionality and Constitutional Culture* (Cambridge: Cambridge University Press, 2013).

Cullen, L. M. *An Economic History of Ireland since 1660* (London: Batsford, 1987).

Curran, J. M. *The Birth of the Irish Free State 1921–1923* (Tuscalosa: University of Alabama Press, 1980).

Dagan, H. *Property: Values and Institutions* (New York: Oxford University Press, 2011).
A Liberal Theory of Property (Cambridge: Cambridge University Press, forthcoming, 2021).
Daly, M. *The Famine in Ireland* (Dundalk: Dundalgan Press, 1986).
Dicey, A. V. *Introduction to the Study of the Law of the Constitution*, 8th ed. (Indianapolis: Liberty Classics, 1982).
Dooley, T. A. M. *The Land for the People: The Land Question in Independent Ireland* (Dublin: University College Dublin Press, 2004).
Doyle, O. *Constitutional Equality Law* (Dublin: Thomson Round Hall, 2004).
The Constitution of Ireland: A Contextual Analysis (Oxford: Hart, 2018).
Dryzek, J. *Deliberative Democracy and Beyond: Liberals, Critics, Contestations* (Oxford: Oxford University Press, 2000).
Ely, J. H. *Democracy and Distrust – A Theory of Judicial Review* (Cambridge, MA: Harvard University Press, 1980).
Epstein, R. *Supreme Neglect* (New York: Oxford University Press, 2008).
Takings: Private Property and the Power of Eminent Domain (Cambridge, MA: Harvard University Press, 1985).
Ferriter, D. *The Transformation of Ireland, 1900–2000* (London: Profile Books, 2004).
Fischel, W. A. *Regulatory Takings: Law, Economics, and Politics* (Cambridge, MA: Harvard University Press, 1995).
Foley, B. *Deference and the Presumption of Constitutionality* (Dublin: Institute of Public Administration, 2008).
Fox, L. *Conceptualising Home: Theories, Laws and Policies* (Oxford: Hart Publishing, 2007).
Fuller, L. *The Morality of Law* (New Haven: Yale University Press, 1964).
Garvin, T. *The Evolution of Irish Nationalist Politics* (Dublin: Gill & Macmillan, 1981).
Gerhart, P. *Property Law and Social Morality* (Cambridge: Cambridge University Press, 2013).
Guinnane, T. *The Vanishing Irish: Households, Migration, and the Rural Economy in Ireland* (Princeton: Princeton University Press, 1997).
Harris, J. W. *Property and Justice* (Oxford: Oxford University Press, 1996).
Hayek, F. *The Constitution of Liberty* (Chicago: University of Chicago Press, 1960).
Hirschl, R. *Comparative Matters: The Renassiance of Comparative Constitutional Law* (Oxford: OUP, 2014).
Hogan, G. W. *Origins of the Irish Constitution 1928–1941* (Dublin: Royal Irish Academy, 2012).
Hogan, G. W. and Whyte, G. F. *Kelly: The Irish Constitution*, 4th ed. (Dublin: LexisNexis Butterworths, 2003).
Hogan, G. W., Whyte, G. F., Kenny, D. and Walsh, R. *Kelly: The Irish Constitution*, 5th ed. (Dublin: Bloomsbury Professional, 2018).
Kavanagh, A. *Constitutional Review under the UK Human Rights Act* (Cambridge: Cambridge University Press, 2009).

Kelly, J. M. *Fundamental Rights in the Irish Law and Constitution* (Dublin: Allen Figgis and Co Ltd, 1967).

A Short History of Western Legal Theory (Oxford: Clarendon Press, 1992).

Kelly, J. M., Hogan, G. W. and Whyte, G. F. *The Irish Constitution (Supplement to the Second Edition)* (Dublin: Jurist Publishing, 1987).

Keogh, D. and McCarthy, A. *The Making of the Irish Constitution 1937* (Cork: Mercier Press, 2008).

Kinealy, C. *A Death-Dealing Famine: The Great Hunger in Ireland* (London and Chicago: Pluto Press, 1997).

Kissane, B. *New Beginnings: Constitutionalism and Democracy in Modern Ireland* (Dublin: University College Dublin Press, 2011).

Knowles, D. *Hegel and the Philosophy of Right* (London: Routledge, 2002).

Kohn, L. *The Constitution of the Irish Free State* (London: George Allen & Unwin Ltd, 1932).

Laslett, P. (ed.). *John Locke, Two Treatises of Government* (Cambridge: Cambridge University Press, 1988).

Lee, J. J. *Ireland 1912–1985* (Cambridge: Cambridge University Press, 1989).

MacLean, J. (ed.). *Property and the Constitution* (Oxford: Hart Publishing, 1999).

Macleod, A. J. *Property and Practical Reason* (Cambridge: Cambridge University Press, 2015).

MacPherson, C. B. (ed.). *Property: Mainstream and Critical Positions* (Oxford: Blackwell, 1978).

McCoy, D. R. *The Elusive Republic: Political Economy in Jeffersonian America* (Chapel Hill, NC: University of North Carolina Press, 1980).

McGinnis, J. O. and Rappaport, M. B. *Originalism and the Good Constitution* (Cambridge, MA: Harvard University Press, 2013).

Merton, R. K. *Social Theory and Social Structure* (New York: Simon & Schuster, The Free Press, 1949).

Monahan, P. *Politics and the Constitution* (Toronto: Carswell Methuen, 1987).

Muller G., Pienaar G. J., Brits R., Slade B. V., Van Wyk J. (eds.), *Transformative Property Law* (Cape Town: Juta, 2018).

Munzer, S. R. *A Theory of Property* (New York: Cambridge University Press, 1990).

Nedelsky, J. *Private Property and the Limits of American Constitutionalism: The Madisoninan Framework and its Legacy* (Chicago: University of Chicago Press, 1990).

Norris, M. *Property, Family and the Irish Welfare State* (London: Palgrave Macmillan, 2016).

Nozick, R. *Anarchy, State and Utopia* (Oxford: Blackwell, 1974).

Ó Cearúil, M. *Bunreacht na hEireann – A Study of the Irish Text* (Dublin: Stationery Office, 1999).

Ó Gráda, C. *A Rocky Road: The Irish Economy Since the 1920's* (Manchester: Manchester University Press, 1997).

Pateman, C. *Participation and Democratic Theory* (Cambridge: Cambridge University Press, 1970).

Patten, A. *Hegel's Idea of Freedom* (Oxford: Oxford University Press, 1999).

Penner, J. E. *The Idea of Property in Law* (Oxford: Oxford University Press, 1997).

Plant, R. *Hegel* (Oxford: Unwin Brothers Ltd., 1973).

Portier, C. (ed.), *The Great Irish Famine* (Cork: Mercier Press, 1995).

Purdy, J. *The Meaning of Property: Freedom, Community and the Legal Imagination* (New Haven: Yale University Press, 2010).

Radin, M. J. *Reinterpreting Property* (Chicago: University of Chicago Press, 1993).

Raz, J. *The Authority of Law* (Oxford: Clarendon Press, 1979).

Ripstein, A. *Private Wrongs* (Cambridge, MA: Harvard University Press, 2016).

Rose, C. M. *Property and Persuasion: Essays on the History, Theory, and Rhetoric of Ownership* (Boulder, CO: Westview Press, 1994).

Ryan, A. *Property and Political Theory* (Oxford: Basil Blackwell, 1984).

Scalia, A. *A Matter of Interpretation: Federal Courts and the Law* (Princeton: Princeton University Press, 1997).

Shiva Rao, B. *Select Constitutions of the World* (Madras: Madras Law Journal Press, 1934).

Singer, J. W. *Entitlement: The Paradoxes of Property* (New Haven: Yale University Press, 2000).

No Freedom Without Regulation: The Hidden Lesson of the Subprime Crisis (New Haven: Yale University Press, 2015).

Sunstein, C. *Designing Democracy – What Constitutions Do* (Oxford: Oxford University Press, 2001).

Tully, J. *A Discourse on Property: John Locke and His Adversaries* (New York: Cambridge University Press, 1980).

Underkuffler, L. S. *The Idea of Property: Its Meaning and Power* (Oxford: Oxford University Press 2003).

Van der Walt, A. J. *Constitutional Property Clauses: A Comparative Analysis* (Cape Town: Juta, 1999).

Constitutional Property Law (Cape Town: Juta Publishing, 2005).

Constitutional Property Law, 3rd edn, (Cape Town: Juta Law, 2011).

Property in the Margins (Oxford: Hart, 2009).

Waldron, J. *The Right to Private Property* (Oxford: Oxford University Press, 1988).

The Rule of Law and the Measure of Property (Cambridge: Cambridge University Press, 2012).

Wall, M. *The Penal Laws, 1691–1760* (Dublin, 1961/1967).

Weinrib, E. J. *The Idea of Private Law* (Oxford: Oxford University Press, 2012).

Wheare, K. C. *Modern Constitutions* (Oxford: Oxford University Press, 1966).

Wigmore, J. H. Borchard, E. Pollock, F. Register, L. B. and Bruncken, E. *Progress of Continental Law in the Nineteenth Century* (Boston: Little, Brown and Company, 1918), p. 65.

Book Chapters

Alexander, G. S. 'Constitutionalising Property: Two Experiences, Two Dilemmas' in J. McLean (ed.), *Property and the Constitution* (Oxford: Hart Publishing, 1999), pp. 93–108.

'Critical Land Law' in S. Bright & J. Dewar (eds.) *Land Law: Themes and Perspectives* (Oxford: Oxford University Press, 1998), pp. 52–78.

'The Public Use Requirement and the Character of Consequentialist Reasoning' in B. Hoops, E. Marais, H. Mostert, J.A.M.A. Sluysmans, and L.C.A. Verstappen (eds.), *Rethinking Expropriation Law II: Public Interest in Expropriation* (The Hague: Eleven International Publishing, 2015), pp. 113–36.

'The Human Flourishing Theory' in H. Dagan and B. Zipursky (eds.), *Research Handbook on Private Law Theory* (Cheltenham: Edward Elgar, 2020), pp. 203–219.

Allen, T. 'The Right to Property' in T. Ginsburg and R. Dixon (eds.), *Comparative Constitutional Law* (Oxford: Elgar Publishing, 2011), pp. 504–18.

Blandy S., Nield S., and Bright S., 'Real Property on the Ground: The Law of People and Place' in H. Dagan and B. Zipursky (eds.), *Research Handbook on Private Law Theory* (Cheltenham: Edward Elgar, 2020), pp. 237–253.

Carr, H. 'Housing the Vulnerable Subject: the English Context' in M. A. Fineman and A. Grear (eds.), *Vulnerability: Reflections on a New Ethical Foundation for Law and Politics* (Farnham: Ashgate, 2013), pp. 107–23.

Dagan, H. 'Expropriatory Compensation, Distributive Justice, and the Rule of Law' in B. Hoops, E. Marais, H. Mostert, J. Sluysmans and L. Verstappen (eds.), *Rethinking Expropriation Law I: Public Interest in Expropriation* (The Hague: Eleven International Publishing, 2015), pp. 349–68.

'Reimagining Takings Law' in G.S. Alexander and E.M. Penalver (eds.), *Property and Community* (Oxford: Oxford University Press, 2009), pp. 39–56.

'Autonomy and Property' in H. Dagan and B. Zipursky (eds.), *Research Handbook on Private Law Theory* (Cheltenham: Edward Elgar, 2020), pp. 185–202.

Douglas, S. and MacFarlane, B. 'Defining Property Rights' in J.E. Penner and H.E. Smith (eds.), *Philosophical Foundations of Property Law* (Oxford: Oxford University Press, 2013), pp. 219.

Doyle, O. and Whyte, G. F. 'The Separation of Powers and Constitutional Egalitarianism after the *Health (Amendment) (No. 2) Bill Reference*', in E. O'Dell (ed.), *Older People in Modern Ireland – Essays on Law and Policy* (Dublin: First Law, 2006), pp. 393–426.

English, R. 'Socialist Republicanism in Independent Ireland 1922–1949', in M. Cronin and J. M. Regan (eds.), *Ireland: The Politics of Independence, 1922–1949* (Basingstoke: MacMillan, 2000), pp. 84–97.

Fineman, M. A. 'Equality, Autonomy, and the Vulnerable Subject in Law and Politics' in M. A. Fineman and A. Grear (eds.), *Vulnerability: Reflections on a New Ethical Foundation for Law and Politics* (Farnham: Ashgate, 2013), p.13.

Gray, K. 'Land Law and Human Rights' in L. Tee (ed.), *Land Law: Issues, Debates, Policy* (Devon: Willan Publishing, 2002), pp. 211–45.

Gray, K. and Gray, S. F. 'The Idea of Property in Land' in S. Bright and J. Dewar (eds.), *Land Law Themes and Perspectives* (Oxford: Oxford University Press, 1998), pp. 15–51.

Grey, T. C. 'The Disintegration of Property', in J. R. Pennock and J. W. Chapman (eds.), *Property: Nomos XXII* (New York: New York University Press, 1980), pp. 69–85.

Hart, H.L.A. 'Are There Any Natural Rights' in J. Waldron (ed.), *Theories of Rights* (Oxford: Oxford University Press, 1984), pp. 77–90.

Hogan, G. W. 'Foreword' in D. Keogh and A. McCarthy, *The Making of the Irish Constitution 1937: Bunreacht na hÉireann* (Cork: Mercier Press, 2007).

Honoré, A. M. 'Ownership', in A.G. Guest (ed.), *Oxford Essays in Jurisprudence* (First Series) (Oxford: Oxford University Press, 1961), pp. 104–147.

Kavanagh, A. 'Deference or Defiance? The Limits of the Judicial Role in Constitutional Adjudication' in G. Huscroft (ed.), *Expounding the Constitution – Essays in Constitutional Theory* (Cambridge: Cambridge University Press, 2008), pp. 184–218.

Keane, R. 'Property in the Constitution and in the Courts', in Brian Farrell (ed.), *De Valera's Constitution and Ours* (Dublin: Gill & MacMillan, 1988), pp.137–51.

Kenny, D. 'Merit, Diversity, and Interpretive Communities: The (Non-Party) Politics of Judicial Appointments And Constitutional Adjudication' in L. Cahillane, T. Hickey and J. Gallen (eds.), *Politics, Judges, and the Irish Constitution* (Manchester: Manchester University Press, 2017), pp. 136–49.

Lee, B. A. 'Average Reciprocity of Advantage', in J. E. Penner and H. E. Smith (eds.) *Philosophical Foundations of Property Law* (Oxford: Oxford University Press, 2013), pp. 99–128.

McDonagh, E. 'Philosophical-Theological Reflections on the Constitution' in F. Litton (ed.), *The Constitution of Ireland 1937–1987* (Dublin: Institute of Public Administration, 1988), pp. 192.

Merrill, T. W. and Smith, H. E. 'The Architecture of Property' in H. Dagan and B. Zipursky (eds.), *Research Handbook on Private Law Theory* (Cheltenham: Edward Elgar, 2020), pp. 134–154.

Michelman, F. I. 'Proportionality Outside the Courts (with Special Reference to Popular and Political Constitutionalism)' in V. Jackson and M. Tushnet (eds.), *Proportionality: New Frontiers, New Challenges* (Cambridge: Cambridge University Press, 2018) pp. 30–50.

'Tutelary Jurisprudence and Constitutional Property' in E. Paul and H. Dickman (eds.), *Liberty, Property and the Future of Constitutional Development* (New York: New York University Press, 1990), pp. 127.

Mulvaney, T. M. and Singer, J. W. 'Move Along to Where? Property in Service of Democracy' in Muller G., Pienaar G. J., Brits R., Slade B. V., Van Wyk J. (eds.), *Transformative Property Law* (Cape Town: Juta, 2018) pp. 1–20.

Nedelsky, J. 'American Constitutionalism and the Paradox of Private Property' in J. Elster and R. Slagstad (eds.), *Constitutionalism and Democracy* (Cambridge: Cambridge University Press, 1988), pp. 241–74.

'Should Property Be Constitutionalized? A Relational and Comparative Approach' in G. E. van Maanen and A. J. van der Walt (eds.), *Property Law on the Threshold of the Twenty-first Century* (Antwerp: Maklu, 1996), pp. 417–32.

Newman, C. M. 'Using Things, Defining Property' in J. Penner and M. Otsuka (eds.), *Property Theory: Legal and Political Perspectives* (Cambridge: Cambridge University Press, 2018), pp. 69–98.

O'Donnell, D. 'Property Rights in the Irish Constitution: Rights for Rich People, or a Pillar of Free Society?' in E. Carolan and O. Doyle (eds.), *The Irish Constitution - Governance and Values* (Dublin: Thompson Round Hall, 2008), pp. 412–30.

O'Neill, A. 'Property Rights and the Power of Eminent Domain' in E. Carolan and O. Doyle (eds.), *The Irish Constitution: Governance and Values* (Dublin: Thomson Round Hall, 2008), pp. 431–45.

Passaglia, P. 'Irish Judicial Review of Legislation: A Comparative Perspective' in G. F. Ferrari and J. O'Dowd (eds.), *75 Years of the Constitution of Ireland* (Dublin: Clarus Press, 2014), pp. 17–35.

Singer, J. W. 'Property and Social Relations: From Title to Entitlement' in C. Geisler and G. Daneker (eds.), *Property and Values: Alternatives to Public and Private Ownership* (Washington, DC: Island Press, 2000), pp. 69–90.

'Democratic Property: Things We Should Not Have to Bargain For' in H. Dagan and B. Zipursky (eds.), *Research Handbook on Private Law Theory* (Cheltenham: Edward Elgar, 2020) pp. 220–236.

Slade, B. and Walsh, R. 'The Marginality of Property in Expropriation Law: A Comparative Assessment' in G. Muller, G. J. Pienaar, R. Brits, B. V. Slade, and J. Van Wyk (eds.), *Transformative Property Law* (Cape Town: Juta Publishing, 2018), pp. 21–51.

Smith, H. E. 'Restating the Architecture of Property' in B. McFarlane and S. Agnew (eds.), *Modern Studies in Property Law Vol. 10* (Oxford: Bloomsbury, 2019), pp. 19.

Van der Walt, A. J. 'Housing Rights in the Intersection between Expropriation and Eviction Law' in L. Fox O'Mahony and J. A. Sweeney (eds.), *The Idea of Home in Law: Displacement and Dispossession* (Farnham: Ashgate, 2011), pp. 55–100.

'The Constitutional Property Clause: Striking a Balance between Guarantee and Limitation' in J. McLean (ed.), *Property and the Constitution* (Oxford: Hart, 1999), pp.109-46.

'The Protection of Private Property Under the Irish Constitution: A Comparative and Theoretical Perspective' in E. Carolan and O. Doyle (eds.), *The Irish Constitution: Governance and Values* (Dublin: Thomson Roundhall, 2008), pp. 398–411.

Van der Walt, A. J. and Walsh, R. 'Comparative Constitutional Conceptions of Property', in M. Graziadei and L. Smith (eds.), *Comparative Property Law: A Research Handbook* (Cheltenham: Edward Elgar Publishing, 2017), pp. 193–215.

Verstappen, L. 'Rethinking Public Interest in Expropriation Law: Introductory Observations' in B. Hoops, E. Marais, H. Mostert, J.A.M.A. Sluysmans, and L.C.A. Verstappen (eds.), *Rethinking Expropriation Law I: Public Interest in Expropriation* (The Hague: Eleven International Publishing, 2015), pp. 15–36.

Walsh, B. 'Foreword' in J. O'Reilly and M. Redmond, *Cases and Materials on the Irish Constitution* (Dublin: Incorporated Law Society of Ireland, 1980).

'The Judicial Power, Justice and the Constitution of Ireland' in D. Curtin and D. O'Keeffe (eds.), *Constitutional Adjudication in European Community and National Law – Essays in Honour of Justice T. F. O'Higgins* (Dublin: Butterworths, 1992), p 145.

Walsh, R. 'Expropriation in Ireland' in J. Sluysmans, S. Verbist, and E. Waring (eds.), *Expropriation in Europe* (Alphen aan den Rijn: Wolters Kluwer, 2015).

'Reviewing Expropriations: Looking Beyond Constitutional Property Clauses' in B. Hoops, E. J. Marais, H. Mostert, J.A.M.A. Sluysmans and L.C.A. Verstappen (eds.), *Rethinking Public Interest in Expropriation Law I* (The Hague: Eleven International Publishing, 2015), pp.125–52.

'The Evolving Relationship between Property and Participation in English Planning Law' in N. Hopkins (ed.), *Modern Studies in Property Law - Volume 7* (Oxford: Hart Publishing, 2013), pp. 263–90.

Articles

Aalen, F. 'Constructive Unionism and the Shaping of Rural Ireland, c 1880–1921' (1993) 4(2) *Rural History* 137–64.

Abraham, D. 'Liberty without Equality: The Property-Rights Connection in a 'Negative Citizenship' Regime' (1996) 21 *Law and Social Inquiry* 1–65.

Alexander, G. S. 'Pluralism and Property' (2012) 80 *Fordham Law Review* 1017–52.

Alexander, G. S. 'Eminent Domain and Secondary Rent-Seeking' (2005) 1 *New York University Journal of Law and Liberty* 958–66.

'Governance Property' (2012) 160 *University of Pennsylvania Law Review* 1853–87.
'Intergenerational Communities' (2014) 8 *Law Ethics Human Rights* 21–57.
'Ownership and Obligations: The Human Flourishing Theory of Property' (2013) 43 *Hong Kong Law Journal* 451–62.
'Property as a Fundamental Right? – The German Example' (2003) 88 *Cornell Law Review* 733–78.
'Property's Ends: The Publicness of Private Law Values' (2014) 99 *Iowa Law Review* 1257–96.
'Takings and the Post-Modern Dialectic of Property' (1992) 9 *Constitutional Commentary* 259–77.
'The Social-Obligation Norm in American Property Law' (2009) 94 *Cornell Law Review* 745–820.
'Time and Property in the American Republican Legal Culture' (1991) 66 *New York University Law Review* 273–85.
Alexander, G. S. and Peñalver, E. M. 'Properties of Community' (2009) 10 *Theoretical Inquiries in Law* 127–60.
Alexander, G. S., Peñalver, E. M., Singer, J. W. and Underkuffler, L. S. 'A Statement of Progressive Property' (2009) 94 *Cornell Law Review* 743–44.
Allan, T. R. S. 'Human Rights and Judicial Review: A Critique of Due Deference' (2006) 65 *Cambridge Law Journal* 671–95.
Allen, T. 'Liberalism, Social Democracy and the Value of Property under the European Convention on Human Rights' (2010) 59 *International and Comparative Law Quarterly* 1055–78.
'Property as a Fundamental Right in India, Europe and South Africa' (2007) 15 *Asia Pacific Law Review* 193–218.
Alvaro, A. 'Why Property Rights Were Excluded From the Canadian Charter of Rights and Freedoms' (1991) 24 *Canadian Journal of Political Science* 309–29.
Ankerson, T. T. and Ruppert, T. 'Tierra y Libertad: The Social Function Doctrine and Land Reform in Latin America' (2006) 19 *Tulane Environmental Law Journal* 69–120.
Arnstein, S. R. 'A Ladder of Citizen Participation' (1969) 35 *Journal of American Planners* 216–24.
Baker, C. E. 'Property and its Relation to Constitutionally Protected Liberty' (1986) 134 *University Pennsylvania Law Review* 741–816.
Baron, J. B. 'Rescuing the Bundle-of-Rights Metaphor in Property Law' (2013) 82 *University of Cincinnati Law Review* 57–101.
'The Contested Commitments of Property' (2010) 61 *Hastings Law Journal* 917–68.
Barrington, D. 'Private Property Under the Irish Constitution' (1973) 8 *Irish Jurist* 1–17.

Barros, B. 'Home as a Legal Concept' (2006) 46 *Santa Clara Law Review*, 255–306.

'Legal Questions for the Psychology of Home' (2009) 83 *Tulane Law Review* 645–60.

'Property and Freedom' (2009) 4 *New York University Journal of Law & Liberty* 36–69.

Bartie, S. 'The Lingering Core of Legal Scholarship' (2010) 30 *Legal Studies* 345–369.

Becker, L.C. 'Too Much Property' (1992) 21 *Philosophy and Public Affairs* 196–206.

Beitz, C. R. 'Property and Time' (2018) 27 *Journal of Political Philosophy* 419–40.

Bell, A. and Parchomovsky, G. 'Pliability Rules' (2002) 101 *Michigan Law Review* 1–79.

'A Theory of Property' (2005) 90 *Cornell Law Review* 531–616.

'Essay: Takings Reassessed' (2001) 87 *Virginia Law Review* 277–318.

'Taking Compensation Private' (2007) 59 *Stanford Law Review* 871–906.

Bettman, A. 'Constitutionality of Zoning' (1923) 37 *Harvard Law Review* 834–59.

Blackstone, W. *Commentaries on the Laws of England* *2 (1765–69). A Facsimile of the First Edition (with an introduction by Brian Simpson) (Chicago: University of Chicago Press, 1979).

Blais, L. E. 'The Public Use Clause and Heightened Rational Basis Review' (2016) 48 *Connecticut Law Review* 1497–516.

Blandy, S. Bright, S. and Nield, S. 'The Dynamics of Enduring Property Relationships in Land' (2018) 81 *Modern Law Review* 85–113.

Blume, L. and Rubinfeld, D. L. 'Compensation for Takings: An Economic Analysis' (1984) 72 *California Law Review* 569–624.

Blumenthal, J. A. ' "To Be Human": A Psychological Perspective on Property" (2009) 83 *Tulane Law Review* 609–44.

Bonilla, D. 'Liberalism and Property in Colombia: Property as a Right and Property as a Social Function' (2011) 80 *Fordham Law Review* 1135–70.

Boudreaux, P. 'Eminent Domain, Property Rights, and the Solution of Representation Reinforcement', (2005) 83 *Denver University Law Review* 1–56.

Bray, Z. 'The New Progressive Property and the Low-Income Housing Conflict' (2012) 4 *Brigham Young University Law Review* 1109–68.

Bryce, B. 'Property as a Natural Right and as a Conventional Right in Constitutional Law' (2007) 29 *Loyola of Los Angeles International and Comparative Law Review* 201–90.

Cahillane, L. 'An Insight into the Irish Free State Constitution' (2014) 54 *American Journal of Legal History* 1–38.

'Why Judicial Appointments Reform is Necessary', Constitution Project @UCC, 16 December 2019.

Calabresi, G. and Melamed, A.D. 'Property Rules, Liability Rules, and Inalienability: One View of the Cathedral' (1972) 85 *Harvard Law Review* 1089–128.

Calfee, C. '*Kelo* v. *City of New London:* The More Things Stay the Same, the More They Change' (2006) 33 *Ecology Law Quarterly* 545–82.

Carr, H. and Hunter, C. 'Managing Vulnerability: Homelessness Law and the Interplay of the Social, the Political and the Technical' (2008) 30 *Journal of Social Welfare and Family Law* 293–307.

Chang, Y. C. 'Economic Value or Fair Market Value: What Form of Takings Compensation Is Efficient?' (2012) 20 *Supreme Court Economic Review* 35–88.

Claeys, E. R. 'Property 101: Is Property a Thing or a Bundle?' (2009) 32 *Seattle University Law Review* 617–50.

'The *Penn Central* Test and Tensions in Liberal Property Theory' (2006) 30 *Harvard Environmental Law Review* 339–69.

Cohen, C. E. 'Eminent Domain after *Kelo* v. *City of New London:* An Argument for Banning Economic Development Takings' (2006) 29 *Harvard Journal of Law and Public Policy* 491–568.

Colby, T. B. 'Originalism and Structural Argument' (2019) 113 *Northwestern University Law Review* 1297–334.

Coletta, R. 'Reciprocity of Advantage and Regulatory Takings: Toward a New Theory of Takings Jurisprudence' (1990) 40 *American University Law Review* 297–366.

Crawford, C. 'The Social Function of Property and the Human Capacity to Flourish' (2011) 80 *Fordham Law Review* 1089–134.

Cribbet, J. E. 'Concepts in Transition: The Search for a New Definition of Property' (1986) 1 *University of Illinois Law Review* 1–42.

Cruft, R. 'Are Property Rights Ever Basic Human Rights?' (2010) 12 *British Journal of Politics and International Relations* 142–54.

Dagan, H. 'Takings and Distributive Justice' (1999) 85 *Virginia Law Review* 741–804.

'The Craft of Property' (2003) 91 *California Law Review* 1517–72.

'The Public Dimension of Private Property' (2013) *King's Law Journal* 260–88.

'The Social Responsibility of Ownership' (2007) 92 *Cornell Law Review* 1125–74.

Davidson, N. M. 'Standardization and Pluralism in Property Law' (2008) 61 *Vanderbilt Law Review* 1597–663.

Davidson, N. M. 'Property and Identity: Vulnerability and Insecurity in the Housing Crisis' (2012) 47 *Harvard Civil Rights and Civil Liberties Law Review* 119–40.

'Sketches for a Hamiltonian Vernacular as a Social Function of Property' (2011) 80 *Fordham Law Review* 1053–70.

Davidson, N. M. and Dyal-Chand, R. 'Property in Crisis' (2010) 78 *Fordham Law Review* 1607–60.

Davies, G. 'The Relationship between Empirical Legal Studies and Doctrinal Legal Studies' (2020) *Erasmus Law Review*, https://doi.org/10.5553/ELR.000141.

Delaney, V.T.H. 'Irish and Scottish Land Resettlement Legislation' (1959) 8 *International and Comparative Law Quarterly* 299–319.

Diamond, M. 'The Meaning and Nature of Property: Homeownership and Shared Equity in the Context of Poverty' (2009) 29 *St. Louis University Public Law Review* 85–112.

Doremus, H. 'Takings and Transitions' (2003) 19 *Journal of Land Use and* Environmental Law 1–211.

Dorfman, A. 'Private Ownership and the Standing to Say So' (2014) 64 *University of Toronto Law Journal* 402–41.

'Private Ownership' (2010) 16 *Legal Theory* 1–35.

'The Normativity of the Private Ownership Form' (2012) 75 *Modern Law Review* 981–1009.

Dos Santos Cunha, A. 'The Social Function of Property in Brazilian Law' (2011) 80 *Fordham Law Review* 1171–81.

Dunning, W. A. 'Irish Land Legislation since 1845 I' (1892) 7 *Political Science Quarterly* 57–79.

Dyal-Chand, R. 'Sharing the Cathedral' (2013) 46 *Connecticut Law Review* 647–723.

Edgeworth, B. 'Rural Radicalism Restrained: The Irish Land Commission and the Courts (1933–1939)' (2007) 42 *Irish Jurist* 1–28.

Epstein, R. A. 'A Clear View of the Cathedral: The Dominance of Property Rules' (1997) 106 *Yale Law Journal* 2091–120.

Farber, D. A. 'Public Choice and Just Compensation' (1992) 9 *Constitutional Comment* 279–308.

Farrell, B. 'The Drafting of the Irish Free State Constitution: III' (1971) 6 *Irish Jurist* 110–35.

Faughnan, S. 'The Jesuits and the Drafting of the Irish Constitution of 1937' (1988) 26 *Irish Historical Studies* 79–102.

Fee, J. E. 'The Takings Clause As A Comparative Right' (2003) 76 *South California Law Review* 1003–66.

Fennell, L. A. 'Picturing Takings' (2012) 88 *Notre Dame Law Review* 57–114.

'Revealing Options' (2005) 118 *Harvard Law Review* 1399–1488.

'Taking Eminent Domain Apart' (2004) *Michigan State Law Review* 957–1004.

Fineman, M. A. 'The Vulnerable Subject and the Responsive State' (2010) 60 *Emory Law Journal* 251–75.

'The Vulnerable Subject: Anchoring Equality in the Human Condition' (2008) 20 *Yale Journal of Law & Feminism* 1–23.

Fischel, W. A. and Shapiro, P. 'Takings, Insurance, and Michelman: Comments on Economic Interpretations of "Just Compensation" Law' (1988) 17 *Journal of Legal Studies* 269–93.

Fox-O'Mahony, L. 'Ageing, Difference and Discrimination: Property Transactions in the Crucible of Human Rights Norms' (2013) 24 *King's Law Journal* 202–36.

'Property Outsiders and the Hidden Politics of Doctrinalism' (2014) 67 *Current Legal Problems* 409–45.

Gallagher, E. F. 'Breaking New Ground: Using Eminent Domain for Economic Development' (2005) 73 *Fordham Law Review* 1837–73.

Garvin, T. 'The Anatomy of a Nationalist Revolution. Ireland, 1858–1928' (1986) 28 *Comparative Studies in Society and History* 468–501.

Glackin, S. 'Back to Bundles: Deflating Property Rights, Again' (2014) 20 *Legal Theory* 1–24.

Godsil, R. D. 'Viewing the Cathedral from Behind the Color Line; Property Rules, Liability Rules, and Environmental Racism' (2004) 53 *Emory Law Journal* 1807–86.

Gold, A. S. and Smith, H. E. 'Sizing Up Private Law' (August 9, 2016), available at https://papers.ssrn.com/sol3/papers.cfm?abstract_id=2821354.

Goodin, A. 'Rejecting the Return to Blight in Post-Kelo State Legislation' (2007) 82 *New York University Law Review* 177–208.

Gray, K. 'Can Environmental Regulation Constitute a Taking of Property at Common Law?' (2007) 24 *Environmental and Planning Law Journal* 161–81.

'Equitable Property' (1994) 47 *Current Legal Problems* 157–214.

'Human Property Rights: The Politics of Expropriation' (2005) 16 *Stellenbosch Law Review* 398–412.

Hamill, S. 'Community, Property, and Human Rights: The Failure of Property-as-Respect' (2017) 27 *Journal of Law and Social Policy* 7–27.

'Restricting Access to Property: Citizens, Owners, Residents, and Claims to Property' (unpublished manuscript, on file with author).

Heller, M. A. 'The Tragedy of the Anticommons: Property in the Transition from Marx to Markets' (1998) 111 *Harvard Law Review* 621–88.

Heller, M. A. and Hills, R. M. 'LADS and the Art of Land Assembly' (2008) 121 *Harvard Law Review* 1465–527.

Hickman, T. 'The Substance and Structure of Proportionality' (2008) *Public Law* 694–716.

Hogan, G. W. 'The Constitution, Property Rights and Proportionality' (1997) 32 *Irish Jurist* 373–97.

Hogan, G. W., Kenny, D. and Walsh, R. 'An Anthology of Declarations of Unconstitutionality' (2015) 54 *Irish Jurist* 1–30.

Hogan, H. and Keyes, F., The Housing Crisis and the Constitution' (November 16, 2020), available at https://ssrn.com/abstract=3731506.

Hohfeld, W. N. 'Fundamental Legal Conceptions as Applied in Judicial Reasoning' (1917) 26 *Yale Law Journal* 710–70.

'Some Fundamental Legal Conceptions as Applied in Judicial Reasoning' (1913) 23 *Yale Law Journal* 16–59.

Hopkins, N. 'The Relevance of Context in Property Law: A Case of Judicial Restraint?' (2011) 31 *Legal Studies* 175–98.

Hutchinson, T. and Duncan, N. 'Defining and Describing What We Do: Doctrinal Legal Research' (2012) *Deakin Law Review* 83–119.

Jackson, V. 'Constitutional Law in an Age of Proportionality' (2015) 125 *Yale Law Journal* 3095–196.

Jones, J. D. 'Property and Personhood Revisited'(2011) 1 *Wake Forest Journal of Law & Policy* 93–136.

Jones, S. J. 'Trumping Eminent Domain Law: An Argument for Strict Scrutiny Analysis Under the Public Use Requirement of the Fifth Amendment' (2000) 50 *Syracuse Law Review* 306–14.

Katz, L. 'Exclusion and Exclusivity in Property Law' (2008) 58 *University of Toronto Law Journal* 275–315.

Keane, R. 'Land Use, Compensation and the Community' (1983) 18 *Irish Jurist* 23–33.

Kelly, D. B. 'Pretextual Takings: Of Private Developers, Local Governments, and Impermissible Favoritism' (2009) 17 *Supreme Court Economic Review* 173–235.

'The Right to Include' (2014) 63 *Emory Law Journal* 857–924.

Kelly, H. *Private Property Rights Under the Irish Constitution* (PhD thesis, University College Dublin, 2010).

Kenny, D. 'Proportionality and the Inevitability of the Local: a Comparative Localist Analysis of Canada and Ireland' (2018) 66 *American Journal of Comparative Law* 537–78.

Kenny, D. and Casey, C. 'A One Person Supreme Court? The Attorney General, Constitutional Advice to Government, and the Case for Transparency' (2019) 42(1) *Dublin University Law Journal* 89–118.

'Shadow Constitutional Review: The Dark Side of Pre-Enactment Political Review in Ireland and Japan' (2020) 18 *International Journal of Constitutional Law* 51–77.

Keogh, D. and McCarthy, A. 'The Catholic Church and the Writing of the 1937 Constitution' (2005) 13 *History Ireland* 36–41.

Keyes, F., 'Property Rights and Housing Legislation' (19 June 2019) Oireachtas Library and Research Centre Briefing Paper, Keyes, F. and Hogan, H., The Housing Crisis and the Constitution' (November 16, 2020), available at https://ssrn.com/abstract=3731506.

Kleyn, D. 'The Constitutional Protection of Property: A Comparison Between the German and the South African Approach' (1996) 11 *South African Publiekreg/Public Law* 402–45.

Knowles, D. 'Hegel on Property and Personality' (1983) 33 *The Philosophical Quarterly* 45–62.

Kochan, D.J. '"Public Use" and the Independent Judiciary: Condemnation in an Interest-Group Perspective' (1998) 3 *Texas Review of Law and Politics* 49–116.

'Keepings' (2015) 23 *New York University Environmental Law Journal* 355–89.
'The [Takings] Keepings Clause: An Analysis of Framing Effects from Labelling Constitutional Rights' (2018) 45 *Florida State University Law Review* 1021–106.

Kocourek, A. 'The Hohfeld System of Fundamental Legal Concepts' (1920) 15 *Illinois Law Review* 24–39.

Krier, J. E. and Serkin, C. 'Public Ruses' (2004) *Michigan State Law Review* 859–75.

Lametti, D. 'The Concept of Property: Relations through Objects of Social Wealth' (2003) 53 *University of Toronto Law Journal* 325–78.

Lazzarotti, J. J. 'Public Use or Public Abuse' (2000) 49 *University of Missouri-Kansas City Law Review* 49–75.

Lee, B. A. 'Just Undercompensation: The Idiosyncratic Premium in Eminent Domain' (2013) 113 *Columbia Law Review* 593–655.

Lehavi, A. 'The Dynamic Law of Property: Theorizing the Role of Legal Standards' (2011) 42 *Rutgers Law Journal* 81–140.

Lewinsohn-Zamir, D. 'Compensation for Injuries to Land Caused by Planning Authorities: Towards a Comprehensive Theory' (1996) 46 *University of Toronto Law Journal* 47–127.

Lopez, A. B. 'Weighing and Reweighing Eminent Domain's Political Philosophies Post-Kelo' (2006) 41 *Wake Forest Law Review* 237–301.

Lovett, J. A. 'Progressive Property in Action: The Land Reform (Scotland) Act 2003' (2011) 89 *Nebraska Law Review* 739–818.

Lubens, R. 'The Social Obligation of Property Ownership: A Comparison of German and US Law' (2007) 24 *Arizona Journal of International and Comparative Law* 389–449.

Lunney Jr., G. S. 'Compensation for Takings: How Much Is Just?' (1993) 42 *Catholic University Law Review* 721–70.

Lunney, G. S. 'Responsibility, Causation and the Harm-Benefit Line in Takings Jurisprudence' (1995) 6 *Fordham Environmental Law Journal* 433–521.

Lunney, Jr., G. S. 'Takings, Efficiency, and Distributive Justice: A Response to Professor Dagan' (2000) 99 *Michigan Law Review* 157–82.

Mac Niocaill, G. 'The Contact of Irish and Common Law' (1972) 23 *Northern Ireland Legal Quarterly* 16–23.

Macleod, G. and Johnstone, C. 'Stretching Urban Renaissance: Privatizing Space, Civilizing Place, Summoning "Community"' (2012) 36 *International Journal of Urban and Regional Research* 1–28.

Mahoney, J. D. 'Kelo's Legacy: Eminent Domain and the Future of Property Rights' (2005) *Supreme Court Review* 103–33.

Mansnerus, L. 'Public Use, Private Use, and Judicial Review in Eminent Domain', (1983) 58 *New York University Law Review* 409–56.

McCormack, G. 'Contractual Entitlements and the Constitution' (1982) 17 *Irish Jurist* 340–46.

'*Blake-Madigan* and Its Aftermath' (1983) 5 *Dublin University Law Journal* 205–24.

McCrudden, C. 'Legal Research and the Social Sciences' (2006) 122 *Law Quarterly Review* 632–50.

McFarlane, A. G. 'Properties of Instability: Markets, Predation, Racialized Georgraphy, and Property Law' (2011) 5 *Wisconsin Law Review* 855–928.

'Rebuilding the Public-Private City: Regulatory Taking's Anti-Subordination Insights for Eminent Domain and Redevelopment' (2009) 42 *Indiana Law Review* 97–163.

Meidinger, E. E. 'The "Public Uses" of Eminent Domain: History and Policy' (1981) 11 *Environmental Law Journal* 1–66.

Merriam, D. 'Time to Make Lemonade from the Lemons of the *Kelo* Case' (2016) 48 *Connecticut Law Review* 1569–91.

Merrill, T.W. 'Property and the Right to Exclude' (1998) 77 *Nebraska Law Review* 730–55.

'The Economics of Public Use' (1986) 72 *Cornell Law Review* 61–116.

'The Landscape of Constitutional Property' (2000) 86 *Virginia Law Review* 885–1000.

Merrill, T. W. and Smith, H. E. 'Optimal Standardization in the Law of Property: The Numerus Clausus Principle' (2000) 110 *Yale Law Journal* 1–70.

'The Morality of Property' (2007) 48 *William and Mary Law Review* 1849–95.

'The Property/Contract Interface' (2001) 101 *Columbia Law Review* 773–852.

Michelman, F. I. 'Possession vs. Distribution in the Constitutional Idea of Property' (1987) 72 *Iowa Law Review* 1319–50.

'Takings, 1987' (1988) 88 *Columbia Law Review* 1600–29.

'A Reply to Susan Rose-Ackerman' (1988) 88 *Columbia Law Review* 1712–13.

'Constitutional Protection for Property Rights and the Reasons Why: Distrust Revisited' (2012) 1 *Brigham Kanner Property Rights Journal* 217–38.

'Expropriation, Eviction and the Gravity of the Common Law' (2013) 24 *Stellenbosch Law Review* 245–63.

'Good Government, Core Liberties, and Constitutional Property: An Essay for Joe Singer' (2016) 5 *Brigham-Kanner Property Rights Conference Journal* 27–44.

'Liberties, Fair Values, and Constitutional Method' (1992) 59 *University of Chicago Law Review* 91–114.

'Mr. Justice Brennan: A Property Teacher's Appreciation' (1980) 15 *Harvard Civil Rights-Civil Liberties Law Review* 296–308.

'Property as a Constitutional Right' (1981) 38 *Washington & Lee Law Review* 1097–114.

'Property, Federalism and Jurisprudence: A Comment on *Lucas* and Judicial Conservatism' (1993) 35 *William and Mary Law Review* 301–28.

'Property, Utility, and Fairness: Comments on the Ethical Foundations of "Just Compensation" Law' (1967) 80 *Harvard Law Review* 1165–258.

'The Property Clause Question' (2012) 19 Constellations 152–63.

Mirow, M.C. 'Origins of the Social Function of Property in Chile' (2011) 80 *Fordham Law Review* 1183–217.

'The Social-Obligation Norm of Property: Duguit, Hayem, and Others' (2010) 22 *Florida Journal of International Law* 191–26.

Mohr, T. 'British Involvement in the Creation of the First Irish Constitution' (2008) 30 *Dublin University Law Journal* 166–86.

Mossoff, A. 'What Is Property? Putting the Pieces Back Together' (2003) 45 *Arizona Law Review* 371–444.

Moyn, S. 'The Secret History of Constitutional Dignity' (2014) 17 *Yale Human Rights and Development Journal* 39–73.

Mulvaney, T. M. 'Progressive Property Moving Forward' (2014) 102 *California Law Review* 349–73.

Mulvaney, T. M. 'Foreground Principles' (2013) 20 *George Mason Law Review* 837–77.

'Legislative Exactions and Progressive Property' (2016) 40 *Harvard Environmental Law Review* 137–71.

'Property as Society' (2018) *Wisconsin Law Review* 911–70.

Nader, R. and Hirsh, A. 'Making Eminent Domain Humane' (2004) 49 *Villanova Law Review* 207–32.

Nakamura, M. 'Freedom of Economic Activities and the Right to Property' (1990) 53 *Law and Contemporary Problems* 1–12.

Nash, J. R. 'Packaging Property: The Effect of Paradigmatic Framing of Property Rights' (2009) 83 *Tulane Law Review* 691–734.

Nash, J. R. and Stern, S. M. 'Property Frames' (2010) 87 *Washington University Law Review* 449–504.

Neary, P. and O'Grada, C. 'Economic War and Structural Change: The 1930s in Ireland' (1991) *Irish Historical Studies* 27 (10) 250–66.

Nevin, B. 'Housing Market Renewal in Liverpool: Locating the Gentrification Debate in History, Context and Evidence' (2010) 25 *Housing Studies* 715–33.

Norris, M. 'Varieties of Home Ownership: Ireland's Transition from a Socialised to a Marketised Policy Regime' (2016) 31 *Housing Studies* 81–101.

O'Dell, E. and Whyte, G. F. 'Is This a Country for Old Men and Women? – *In re Article 26 and the Health (Amendment) (No. 2) Bill 2004*' (2005) 27 *Dublin University Law Journal* 368–92.

Odinet, C. K. 'Of Progressive Property and Public Debt' (2016) 51 *Wake Forest Law Review* 1101–62.

Olivecrona, K. 'Locke's Theory of Appropriation' (1974) 24 *Philosophical Quarterly* 220–34.

Oswald, L. S. 'The Role of "Harm/Benefit" and "Average Reciprocity of Advantage" Rules in a Comprehensive Takings Analysis' (1997) 50 *Vanderbilt Law Review* 1447–524.

Overstreet, H. A. 'The Changing Conception of Property' (1915) 25 *International Journal of Ethics* 165–78.

Parchomovksy, G. and Siegelman, P. 'Selling Mayberry: Communities and Individuals in Law and Economics' (2004) 92 *California Law Review* 75–146.

Paul, J. 'The Hidden Structure of Takings Law' (1991) 63 *South California Law Review* 1393–548.

Peñalver, E. M. 'Property as Entrance' (2005) 91 *Virginia Law Review* 1889–972.

'Is Land Special?' (2004) 31 *Ecology Law Quarterly* 227–88.

'Land Virtues' (2009) 94 *Cornell Law Review* 821–88.

'Property Metaphors and Kelo v New London: Two Views of the Castle' (2006) 74 *Fordham Law Review* 2971–6.

Penner, J. E. 'The "Bundle of Rights" Picture of Property' (1996) 43 *UCLA Law Review* 711–820.

Peterson, A. L. 'The Takings Clause: In Search of Underlying Principles, Part II – Takings as Intentional Deprivations of Property Without Moral Justification', (1990) 78 *California Law Review* 55–162.

Poirier, M. 'The Virtue of Vagueness in Takings Doctrine' (2003) 24 *Cardozo Law Review* 93–192.

Pritchett, W. 'The "Public Menace" of Blight: Urban Renewal and the Private Uses of Eminent Domain' (2003) 21 *Yale Law and Policy Review* 1–52.

Purdy, J. 'A Few Questions about the Social Obligation Norm' (2009) 94 *Cornell Law Review* 949–58.

'A Freedom-Promoting Approach to Property: A Renewed Tradition for New Debates' (2005) 72 *University of Chicago Law Review* 1237–98.

'People as Resources: Recruitment and Reciprocity in the Freedom-Promoting Approach to Property' (2007) 56 *Duke Law Journal* 1047–117.

Radin, M. J. 'Lacking a Transformative Social Theory: A Response' (1993) 45 *Stanford Law Review* 409–24.

'Market-Inalienability' (1986–1987) 100 *Harvard Law Review* 1849–937.

'Property and Personhood', (1982) 34 *Stanford Law Review* 957–1016.

'The Colin Ruagh Thomas O'Fallon Memorial Lecture on Reconsidering Personhood' (1995) 74 *Oregon Law Review* 423–48.

Reich, C. 'The New Property' (1964) 73 *Yale Law Journal* 733–87.

Report of the Constitution Review Group (Dublin: The Stationary Office, 1996).

Rivers, J. 'Proportionality and Variable Intensity of Review' (2006) 65 *Cambridge Law Journal* 174–207.

Roark, M. L. 'Under-Propertied Persons' (2017) 27 *Cornell Journal of Law and Public Policy* 1–64.

Rodgers, C. 'Nature's Place? Property Rights, Property Rules and Environmental Stewardship' (2009) 68 *Cambridge Law Journal* 550–74.

Rose-Ackerman, S. 'Against Ad Hocery: A Comment on Michelman' (1988) 88 *Columbia Law Review* 1697–711.

Rose, C. M. 'Canons of Property Talk, or, Blackstone's Anxiety' (1998) 108 *Yale Law Journal* 601–32.

'Crystals and Mud in Property Law' (1988) 40 *Stanford Law Review* 577–610.

'*Mahon* Reconstructed: Why the Takings Issue is Still a Muddle' (1984) 57 *Southern California Law Review* 561–99.

'Property and Expropriation: Themes and Variations in American Law' (2000) *Utah Law Review* 1–38.

'Property as the Keystone Right?' (1996) 71 *Notre Dame Law Review* 329–70.

Rosser, E. 'Destablizing Property' (2015) 48 *Connecticut Law Review* 397–472.

'The Ambition and Transformative Potential of Progressive Property' (2013) 101 *California Law Review* 107–71.

Rossi, J. 'Participation Run Amok: The Costs of Mass Participation for Deliberative Agency Decisionmaking' (1997) 92 *Northwestern University Law Review* 173–250.

Sales, N. A. 'Classical Republicanism and the Fifth Amendment's "Public Use" Requirement' (2000) 49 *Duke Law Journal* 339–382.

Sax, J. L. 'Takings and the Police Power', (1964) 74 *Yale Law Journal* 36–76.

Schnalby, S. J. 'Property and Pragmatism: A Critique of Radin's Theory of Personhood and Property' (1993) 45 *Stanford Law Review* 347–407.

Scotford, E. and Walsh, R. 'The Symbiosis of Property and English Environmental Law – Property Rights in a Public Law Context' (2013) 76 *Modern Law Review* 1010–45.

Scott, J. W. 'Public Use and Private Profit: When Should Heightened Scrutiny be Applied to "Public-Private" Takings?' (2003) 12 *Journal of Affordable Housing and Community Development Law* 466–90.

Serkin, C. 'The Meaning of Value: Assessing Just Compensation for Regulatory Takings' (2005) 99 *North Western Law Review* 677–742.

Serkin, S. '*Penn Central* Take Two' (2016) 92 *Notre Dame Law Review* 913–42.

Shapiro, F. R. 'The Most-Cited Law Review Articles Revisited' (1996) 71 *Chicago-Kent Law Review* 751–79.

Sharfstein, D. J. 'Atrocity, Entitlement, and Personhood in Property' (2012) 98 *Virginia Law Review* 635–90.

Siems, M. M. 'Legal Originality' (2008) 28 *Oxford Journal of Legal Studies* 147–64.

Simon, W. H. 'Social-Republican Property' (1991) 38 *UCLA Law Review* 1335–414.

Singer, J. W. 'Democratic Estates: Property Law in a Free and Democratic Society' (2009) 94 *Cornell Law Review* 1009–62.

'Justifying Regulatory Takings' (2015) 41 *Ohio Northern University Law Review* 601–70.

'Property as the Law of Democracy' (2014) 63 *Duke Law Journal* 1287–335.

'The Legal Rights Debate in Analytical Jurisprudence' (1982) 6 *Wisconsin Law Review* 975–1060.

'The Reliance Interest in Property Revisited' (2011) 7 *Harvard Journal of the Legal Left* 79–82.

Singer, J. W. 'The Rule of Reason in Property Law' (2013) 46 *UC Davis Law Review* 1369–1434.

Singer, J. W. and Beerman, J. M. 'The Social Origins of Property' (1993) 6 *Canadian Journal of Law & Jurisprudence* 217–48.

Sluysmans, J., Verbist, S. and de Graaff, R. 'Compensation for Expropriation: How Compensation Reflects a Vision on Property' (2014) 3 *European Property Law Journal* 1–33.

Smith, H. E. 'Complexity and the Cathedral: Making Law and Economics More Calabresian' (2019) 48 *European Journal of Law and Economics* 43–63.

'Exclusion and Property Rules in the Law of Property' (2004) 90 *Virginia Law Review* 965–1049.

'Exclusion versus Governance: Two Strategies for Delineating Property Rights' (2002) 31 *Journal of Legal Studies* 453–87.

'Mind the Gap: The Indirect Relation between Ends and Means in American Property Law' (2009) 94 *Cornell Law Review* 959–90.

'Property and Property Rules' (2004) 79 *New York University Law Review* 1719–98.

'Property as the Law of Things' (2012) 125 *Harvard Law Review* 1691–726.

'Property Is Not Just a Bundle of Rights' (2011) 8 *Econ Journal Watch* 279–91.

'The Persistence of System in Property Law' (2015) 163 *University of Pennsylvania Law Review* 2055–84.

Snare, F. 'The Concept of Property' (1972) 9 *American Philosophical Quarterly* 200–6.

Solum, L. B. 'Originalism and the Unwritten Constitution' (2013) *University Illinois Law Review* 1935–84.

Somin, I. 'Controlling the Grasping Hand: Economic Development Takings After *Kelo*' (2007) 15 *Supreme Court Economic Review* 183–271.

Steele, J. 'Participation and Deliberation in Environmental Law: Exploring a Problem-Solving Approach' (2001) 21 *Oxford Journal of Legal Studies* 415–42.

Stelle-Garnett, N. 'Planning as Public Use?' (2007) 34 *Ecology Law Quarterly* 443–470.

'The Neglected Political Economy of Eminent Domain' (2006) 105 *Michigan Law Review* 115–50.

'The Public Use Question as a Takings Problem', (2003) 71 *George Washington Law Review* 934–82.

Stern, J. Y. 'Property's Constitution' (2013) 101 *California Law Review* 277–326.

Stern, S. 'Remodeling Just Compensation Law: Applying Restorative Justice to Takings Law Doctrine' (2017) 30 *Canadian Journal of Law and Jurisprudence* 413–42.

'Takings, Community and Value: Reforming Takings Law to Fairly Compensate Common Interest Communities' (2015) 23 *Journal of Law and Policy* 141–202.

Stern, S. M. 'Residential Protectionism and the Legal Mythology of Home' (2009) 107 *Michigan Law Review* 1093 144.

'The Inviolate Home: Housing Exceptionalism in the Fourth Amendment' (2009) 95 *Cornell Law Review* 101–48.

Teichgraeber, R. 'Hegel on Property and Poverty' (1977) 38 *Journal of the History of Ideas* 47–64.

Thomas, P. 'Property's Properties: From Hegel to Locke' (2003) 84 *Representations* 30–43.

Treanor, W. 'The Original Understanding of the Takings Clause and the Political Process' (1995) 95 *Columbia Law Review* 782–887.

Treanor, W. M. 'The Armstrong Principle, The Narratives of Takings, and Compensation Statutes' (1997) 38 *William & Mary Law Review* 1151–76.

Underkuffler, L.S. 'Property and Change: The Constitutional Conundrum' (2013) 91 *Texas Law Review* 2015–37.

'Kelo's Moral Failure' (2006) 15 *William & Mary Bill of Rights Journal* 377–87.

'Property as Constitutional Myth: Utilities and Dangers' (2007) 92 *Cornell Law Review* 1239–54.

'Property, Sovereignty, and the Public Trust' (2017) 18 *Theoretical Inquiries in Law* 329–53.

'What Does the Constitutional Protection of Property Mean?' (2016) 5 *Brigham-Kanner Property Rights Conference Journal* 109–24.

van der Sijde, E. *Reconsidering the Relationship between Property and Regulation: A Systemic Constitutional Approach* (PhD thesis, University of Stellenbosch, 2015, on file with author).

van der Walt, A. J. 'Comparative Notes on the Constitutional Protection of Property Rights' (1993) 19 *Recht en kritiek* 39.

van der Walt, A. J. 'Double Property Guarantees: A Structural and Comparative Analysis' (1998) 14 *South African Journal of Human Rights* 560–86.

'The Modest Systemic Status of Property Rights' (2014) 1 *Journal of Law, Property and Society* 15–106.

van Gestel, R. and Micklitz, H. W. 'Why Methods Matter in European Legal Scholarship' (2014) 20 *European Law Journal* 292–316.

Vandevelde, K.J. 'The New Property of the Nineteenth Century: The Development of the Modern Concept of Property' (1980) 29 *Buffalo Law Review* 325–67.

Walsh, R. '"The Principles of Social Justice": The Compulsory Acquisition of Private Property for Redevelopment in the US and Ireland' (2010) 32 *Dublin University Law Journal* 1–23.

'Private Property Rights in the Drafting of the Irish Constitution: A Communitarian Compromise' (2011) 33 *Dublin University Law Journal* 86–115.

'Property, Human Flourishing, and St Thomas Aquinas: Assessing a Contemporary Revival' (2018) 31 *Canadian Journal of Law and Jurisprudence* 197–222.

'The Constitution, Property Rights and Proportionality: A Reappraisal' (2009) 31 *Dublin University Law Journal* 1–34.

'"The Principles of Social Justice" and the Compulsory Acquisition of Private Property for Redevelopment in the United States and Ireland' (2010) 32 *Dublin University Law Journal* 1–24.

'Securing Possession of the Home in the COVID-19 Context: the Irish Experience' forthcoming in Boggenpoel et al (eds), Property Responses to a Global Pandemic (forthcoming, Cape Town: Juta, 2021).

'COVID-19's Silver Lining - Housing, the Constitution, and the Scope for Post-Crisis Reform' COVID-19 Law and Human Rights Blog (19 June 2020) http://tcdlaw.blogspot.com/2020/06/covid-19s-silver-lining-housing.html

'COVID-19, Powers of Entry, and the Constitutional Protection for the Dwelling' COVID-19 Law and Human Rights Observatory Blog (8 September 2020) https://tcdlaw.blogspot.com/2020/09/covid-19-powers-of-entry-and.html

' Legislative Coupling in the COVID-19 Crisis - Disentangling the 5km Travel Restriction and the Eviction Ban' (2 March 2021) https://tcdlaw.blogspot.com/2021/03/legislative-coupling-in-covid-19-crisis.html

Walsh, R. and Fox-O'Mahony, L. 'Land Law, Property Ideologies and the British-Irish Relationship' (2018) 47 *Common Law World Law Review* 7–34.

Weiss, B. M. 'Progressive Property Theory and Housing Justice Campaigns' (2019) 10 *UC Irvine Law Review* 251–85.

Williams, J. 'The Rhetoric of Property' (1997) 83 *Iowa Law Review* 277–361.

Wyman, K. M. 'The Measure of Just Compensation' (2008) 41 *University of California Davis Law Review* 239–87.

Wyman, K. M. 'The New Essentialism in Property' (2017) 9 *Journal of Legal Analysis* 183–246.

Others

Newspaper Articles

Clarke, J. 'Taoiseach Welcomes Cut to Ex-AIB Chief's Pension', *Journal.ie*, 7 November 2012.

Dalton, E. 'Right to Property Adding to Housing Crisis, Says Council Chief', *Irish Times*, 17 September 2018.

Fitzgerald, G. 'Time to Exorcise the Ghosts of Past British Concerns', *Irish Times*, July 27 1996.

Grogan, D. 'Property Rights Too Strong – Taoiseach', *Irish Times*, September 5 1985.

Jones, J. H. 'Right to a Secure Home Must Be Added to Constitution, Say Advocates' *Irish Times*, 28 February 2019.

Linnane, D. 'Labour Party Want Right to Home Put Into the Constitution', *Evening Echo*, 6 November 2018.

Lyons, M. 'Galway Bypass Raises Concerns Among Residents', *Irish Times*, 12 February 2015.

Melia, P. and Treacy, C. 'Constitution Blocked Me in Bid to Supply Homes – Kelly', *Irish Independent*, 1 April 2016.

Walsh, R. 'Housing Crisis: There Is No Constitutional Block to Rent Freezes in Ireland', *Irish Times*, 3 February 2020.

'What Would the 'Referendum on Housing' Be About and Do We Really Need One? *Irish Times*, 22 June 2020.

University College Dublin Archive Papers

UCDAD/P4/362
UCDAD/P4/363.
UCDAD/P150/2371
UCDAD/P150/2385
UCDAD/P150/2387
UCDAD/P150/2393
UCDAD/P150/2395
UCDAD/P150/2401
UCDAD/P150/2416
UCDAD/P150/2429

Irish National Archive Papers

National Archives Boxes on the Constitution Committee 1922, at M1, T1 and S2
National Archives of Ireland, Department of an Taoiseach File S/8953
National Archives of Ireland, Department of an Taoiseach File S/9715 A.

CASES

America

Armstrong v. *United States*, 364 U.S. 40, 49 (U.S. 1960).
Berman v. *Parker* 348 U.S. 26 (1954).
Hawaii Housing Authority v. *Midkiff* 467 US 229 (1984).
Hodel v. *Irving* 481 U.S. 704 (1987).
Jacque v. *Steenberg Homes, Inc.* 563 N.W.2d 154 (Wis. 1997).
Kelo v. *City of New London* 545 U.S. 469 (2005).
Loretto v. *Teleprompter Manhattan Corporation* 458 U.S. 419 (U.S. 1982).
Lucas v. *South Carolina Coastal Commission* (1992) 505 US 1003
Matthews v. *Bay Head Improvement Ass'n* 471 A.2d 355 (N.J. 1984).
Preseault v. *United States*, 100 F.3d 1525 (Fed. Cir. 1996).
Raleigh Ave. Beach Ass'n v. *Atlantis Beach Club*, 879 A.2d 112 (N.J. 2005).
State v. *Shack* 58 N.J. 297, 277 A.2d 369 (1971).
United States v. *Fuller* (1972) 409 US 488

Germany

Groundwater case (1981) 58 BverfGE 300
Hamburg Flood Control case (1968) 24 BverfGE 36
The Co-Determination Case (1979) BVerfGE 50
The Small Garden Plot Case (1979) BVerfGE 52

South Africa

Modderklip East Squatters v. *Modderkilp Boerdery (Pty) Ltd* 2004 3 All SA 169 (SCA), 2005 5 SA 3 (CC).

Ireland

Aer Lingus Ltd v. *Minister for Finance* [2018] IEHC 198
Albatros Feeds Ltd v. *Minister for Agriculture* [2007] 1 IR 221
An Blascaod Mor Teoranta v. *Commissioners for Public Works* [1998] IEHC 38; [2000] 1 IR 6

Ashbourne Holdings v. *An Bord Pleanála* [2003] 2 IR 114
Attorney General v. *Hamilton* [1993] 2 IR 250
Attorney General v. *Paperlink* [1984] ILRM 373
Attorney General v. *Southern Industrial Trust* (1960) 94 ILTR 161
Aurelius Capital Master Ltd v. *Minister for Finance* [2011] IEHC 267
Blake v. *The Attorney General* [1982] 1 IR 117
Blehein v. *Minister for Health* [2009] 1 IR 275
Brady v. *Donegal County Council* [1989] ILRM 282
Brendan Dunne Ltd v. *Fitzpatrick* [1958] 1 IR 29
Brennan v. *Attorney General* [1983] ILRM 449 [1984] ILRM 355
Browne v. *Attorney General* [1991] 2 IR 58
Buckley v. *Attorney General* [1950] IR 67
BUPA Ireland Ltd v. *Health Insurance Authority* [2006] IEHC 431
Butler v. *Dublin Corporation* [1999] 1 IR 565
Byrne v. *Fingal County Council* [2001] 4 IR 565
Cafolla v. *O'Malley* [1985] IR 486
Carrigaline Community Television Broadcasting Co Ltd v. *Minister for Transport* [1997] 1 ILRM 241
Casey v. *Minister for the Environment* [2004] 1 IR 402
Cassels v. *Dublin Corporation* [1963] 1 IR 193
Central Dublin Development Association v. *Attorney General* (1975) 109 ILTR 69
Chadwick v. *Fingal County Council* [2008] 3 IR 66
Chaulk v. *R* [1990] 3 SCR 1303
Chestvale Properties Ltd v. *Glackin* [1993] 3 IR 35
Child v. *Wicklow County Council* [1995] 2 IR 447
Clancy v. *Ireland* [1988] IR 326
Clinton v. *An Bord Pleaná*la [2005] IEHC 84, [2007] 4 IR 701
Clinton v. *Quirke* [2005] IEHC 84; [2007] 4 IR 701
Competition Authority v. *Judge O'Donnell* [2008] 2 IR 275
Comyn v. *Attorney General* [1950] IR 142
Condon v. *Minister for Labour* (11 June 1980) (HC) [1981] IR 62
Cork Institute of Technology v. *Minister for Transport* [2017] IEHC 762
County Council of Meath v. *Murray* [2017] IESC 25
Cox v. *Ireland* [1992] 2 IR 503
Criminal Assets Bureau v. *Kelly* [2012] IESC 64
Criminal Assets Bureau v. *Murphy* [2017] IESC 64
Crosbie v. *Custom House Dock Development Authority* [1996] 2 IR 531
Daly v. *Revenue Commissioners* [1995] 3 IR 1
Deighan v. *Heirne* [1986] 1 IR 603 (HC) [1990] 1 IR 499 (SC).
Dellway Investment Ltd v. *National Asset Management Agency* [2010] IEHC 364 [2011] IESC 13, [2011] 4 IR 1
District Judge McMenamin v. *Ireland* [1996] 3 IR 100

Dowling v. *Minister for Finance* [2012] IEHC 436
Dowling v. *Minister for Finance* [2018] IECA 300
DPP (Long) v. *McDonald* [1983] ILRM 223
DPP v. *G(G)(A Minor)* [2010] 1 ILRM 93
Dreher v. *Irish Land Commission* [1984] ILRM 94
Dublin Corporation v. *Underwood* [1997] 1 IR 69
Dublin County Council v. *Grealy* [1990] 1 IR 77
Dunne v. *Hamilton* [1982] ILRM 290
East Donegal Co-Operative Livestock Market v. *Attorney General* [1970] IR 317
Egan v. *An Bord Pleanála* [2011] IEHC 44
Eircell Ltd v. *Leitrim County Council* [2000] 1 IR 479
EMI Records (Ireland) Ltd v. *UPC Communications Ireland Ltd* [2007] IEHC 377
ESB v. *Cork County Council* 28 June 2000 (HC).
ESB v. *Gormley* [1985] 1 IR 129
Falcon Travel Ltd v. *Owners Abroad Group plc* [1999] 1 IR 175
Finn v. *Bray UDC* [1969] IR 169
Fisher v. *Irish Land Commission* [1948] IR 3
Fitzpatrick v. *The Criminal Assets Bureau* [2000] 1 IR 217
Foley v. *The Irish Land Commission* [1952] IR 118
Frescati Estates v. *Walker* [1975] IR 177
Gilligan v. *The Criminal Assets Bureau* [1998] 3 IR 185
Gorman v. *The Minister for the Environment* [2001] 2 IR 414
Grange Developments Ltd v. *Dublin County Council* [1986] 1 IR 246
Grant v. *Roche Products (Ireland) Ltd* [2008] 4 IR 679
Greene v. *Minister for Agriculture* [1990] 2 IR 1
Guinness & Co v. *Commissioners of Inland Revenue* [1923] 2 IR 186
Gunning v. *Dublin Corporation* [1983] ILRM 56
Hamilton v. *Hamilton* [1982] IR 466
Hand v. *Dublin Corporation* [1989] IR 26
Hanrahan v. *Merck, Sharpe and Dohme* [1988] ILRM 629
Hanrahan v. *The Environmental Protection Agency* [2005] IEHC 5867, [2006] 1 ILRM 275
Heaney v. *Ireland* [1994] 3 IR 593
Hempenstall v. *Minister for the Environment* [1994] 2 IR 2
Hygeia Chemicals Ltd v. *Irish Medicines Board* [2005] IEHC 226
Hygeia Chemicals Ltd v. *Irish Medicines Board* [2005] IEHC 226 [2010] IESC 4
In re Deansrath Investments [1974] IR 228
In re Eylewood Ltd [2010] IEHC 57 [2011] 1 ILRM 5
In re Linen Supply of Ireland Ltd [2010] IEHC 28
In re Maud McInerney [1976–77] ILRM 229
In re Viscount Securities Ltd (1978) 112 ILTR 17

Island Ferries Teoranta v. *Galway County Council* [2013] IEHC 587
J & J Haire & Company Ltd v. *Minister for Health* [2009] IEHC 562
Keane v. *An Bord Pleanála* [1998] 2 ILRM 241
Landers v. *The Attorney General* (1975) 109 ILTR 1
Lawlor v. *Minister for Agriculture* [1990] 1 IR 356
Liddy v. *The Minister for Public Enterprise and the Irish Aviation Authority* [2003] 2 JIC 0401 (4 February 2003) (HC).
Limerick Corporation v. *Sheridan* (1956) 90 ILTR 50
Lough Swilly Shellfish Growers Co-Operative Society Ltd v. *Bradley* (29 June, 2010) (HC).
Lovett v. *The Minister for Education* [1997] 1 ILRM 89
M & F Quirke & Sons v. *An Bord Pleanála* [2010] 2 ILRM 91
MacDonncha v. *Minister for Education* [2013] IEHC 226
Macklin v. *Greacen & Co Ltd* [1983] IR 61
MacPharthalain v. *The Commissioners of Public Works* [1992] 1 IR 111 (HC), [1994] 3 IR 353 (SC).
Madigan v. *Attorney General* [1986] 1 ILRM 136
Maher v. *Minister for Agriculture* [2001] 2 IR 139
McDonagh & Sons Ltd v. *Galway Corporation* [1995] 1 IR 191
McGrath v. *Limestone* [2014] IEHC 382
Moynihan v. *Greensmyth* [1977] 1 IR 55
Muldoon v. *Minister for the Environment* [2015] IEHC 649
Murphy v. *GM* [2001] 4 IR 113
Murphy v. *Stewart.* [1973] 1 IR 97
Murtagh Properties Ltd v. *Cleary* [1972] 1 IR 330
National Asset Loan Management Ltd v. *Breslin* [2017] IECA 283
National Asset Loan Management Ltd v. *McMahon, National Asset Loan Management* v. *Downes* [2014] IEHC 71
Neurendale Ltd v. *Dublin City Council* [2009] IEHC 588
North Wall Quay Property Holding Company Ltd v. *Dublin Docklands Authority* [2008] IEHC 305
Nottinghamshire County Council v. *B* [2013] 4 IR 622
NVH v. *Minister for Justice* [2017] IESC 35
O'Brien v. *Keogh* [1972] IR 144
O'Brien v. *Manufacturing Engineering Company Ltd* [1973] IR 334
O'Brien v. *The Personal Injuries Assessment Board* [2005] IEHC 100 [2008] IESC 71
O'Callaghan v. *Commissioners for Public Works* [1983] ILRM 391 [1985] ILRM 364
O'Connell v. *BATU* [2016] IECA 86
O'Neill v. *Minister for Agriculture* [1998] 1 IR 539
O'Reilly v. *Limerick Corporation* [1989] 1 ILRM 181
O'Sullivan v. *Department of the Environment* [2010] IEHC 376

PC v. *Minister for Social Protection* [2017] IESC 63
Permanent TSB Group Holdings Plc v. *Skoczylas* [2020] IECA 1
Phonographic Performance (Ireland) Ltd v. *Cody* [1998] 4 IR 504
Pigs Marketing Board v. *Donnelly* [1939] IR 413
Pine Valley Developments v. *Minister for the Environment* [1987] IR 23
PMPS v. *Attorney General* [1983] 1 IR 339
Rafferty v. *Minister for Agriculture* [2008] IEHC 344; [2014] IESC 61
Re Article 26 and Part V of the Planning and Development Bill, 1999 [2000] 2 IR 321
Re Article 26 and the Employment Equality Bill, 1996 [1997] IESC 6; [1997] 2 IR 321
Re Article 26 and the Health (Amendment (No 2) Bill 2004 [2005] 1 IR 105
Re Article 26 and the Housing (Private Rented Dwellings) Bill, 1981 [1983] IR 181
Re Article 26 and the Offences Against the State (Amendment) Bill 1940 [1940] IR 470
Re Murphy [1977] IR 243
Re Ranks (Ireland) Ltd [1989] 1 IR 1
Re Sugar Distributors Ltd [1995] 2 IR 194
Reid v. *IDA* [2013] IEHC 433 (HC); [2015] IESC 82 (SC).
Rodgers v. *Irish Transport and General Workers' Union* [1978] ILRM 51
Rooney v. *The Minister for Agriculture*[1920] 1 IR 176
Sherry v. *Brennan* [1979] ILRM 113
Shirley v. *AO Gorman & Company Ltd* [2006] IEHC 27
Simmonds v. *Ennis Town Council* [2012] IEHC 281
Sinnott v. *Minister for Education* [2001] 2 IR 545
Sister Mary Christian v. *Dublin City Council* [2012] IEHC 163 [2012] 2 IR 506
Smyth v. *Railway Procurement Agency* (5 March 2010) (HC).
Sony Music Entertainment (Ireland) Ltd v. *UP Communications Ireland Ltd (No 1)* [2015] IEHC 317, [2016] IECA 231
TD v. *Minister for Education* [2001] 4 IR 259
The Dunraven Limerick Estates Company v. *The Commissioners of Public Works* [1974] 1 IR 113
The State (Keegan) v. *The Stardust Victims Compensation Tribunal* [1986] 1 IR 642
The State (Pheasantry) v. *District Judge Donnelly* [1982] ILRM 512
Tormey v. *Commissioners for Public Works* (21 December 1972) (SC).
Tracey v. *Ireland* [2019] IESC 70
Tuffy v. *O'Neill* [2013] IEHC 231
Tuohy v. *Courtney* [1994] 3 IR 1
Unite the Union v. *Minister for Finance* [2010] IEHC 354
Vone Securities v. *Cooke* [1979] IR 59
Waterford County Council v. *John A Wood* [1999] 1 IR 556
Webb v. *Ireland* [1988] 1 IR 353
Whelan v. *Cork Corporation* [1991] ILRM 19

White v. *Bar Council of Ireland* [2016] IEHC 406 [2016] IECA 363
White v. *Dublin City Council* [2004] 1 IR 545
Wicklow Company Council v. *Kinsella* [2015] IEHC 229
Wicklow County Council v. *Fortune (no. 1)* [2012] IEHC 406

INDEX

CAMBRIDGE STUDIES IN CONSTITUTIONAL LAW

(continued from page ii)

A.W. Dicey and the Common Law Constitutional Tradition Mark D. Walters

Europe's Second Constitution: Crisis, Courts and Community Markus W. Gehring

A.V. Dicey and the Common Law Constitutional Tradition: A Legal Turn of Mind Mark D. Walters

Administrative Competence: Reimagining Administrative Law Elizabeth Fisher and Sidney A. Shapiro

Legal Sabotage: Ernst Fraenkel in Hitler's Germany Douglas Morris

Proportionality in Action: Comparative and Empirical Perspectives on the Judicial Practice Edited by Mordechai Kremnitzer, Tayla Steiner and Andrej Lang

Constitutional Dialogue: Democracy, Rights, Institutions Edited by Geoffrey Sigalet, Grégoire Webber and Rosalind Dixon

The Veiled Sceptre: Reserve Powers of Heads of State in Westminster Systems Anne Twomey

Vigilance and Restraint in the Common Law of Judicial Review Dean Knight

The Alchemists: Questioning Our Faith in Courts as Democracy-Builders Tom Gerald Daly

Australia's Constitution after Whitlam Brendan Lim

Building the Constitution: The Practice of Constitutional Interpretation in Post-Apartheid South Africa James Fowkes

Dimensions of Dignity: The Theory and Practice of Modern Constitutional Law Jacob Weinrib

Reason of State: Law, Prerogative, Empire Thomas Poole

Bills of Rights in the Common Law Robert Leckey

The Guardian of the Constitution: Hans Kelsen and Carl Schmitt on the Limits of Constitutional Law Translated by Lars Vinx, with an introduction and notes by Lars Vinx

Parliamentary Bills of Rights: The Experiences of New Zealand and the United Kingdom Janet L. Hiebert and James B. Kelly

Lawyering for the Rule of Law: Government Lawyers and the Rise of Judicial Power in Israel Yoav Dotan

Balancing Constitutional Rights: The Origins and Meanings of Postwar Legal Discourse Jacco Bomhoff

Judges on Trial: The Independence and Accountability of the English Judiciary Shimon Shetreet and Sophie Turenne

Proportionality and Constitutional Culture Moshe Cohen-Eliya and Iddo Porat

The Politics of Principle: The First South African Constitutional Court, 1995–2005 Theunis Roux

The New Commonwealth Model of Constitutionalism: Theory and Practice Stephen Gardbaum

Searching for the State in British Legal Thought: Competing Conceptions of the Public Sphere Janet McLean

Judging Social Rights Jeff King

Proportionality: Constitutional Rights and Their Limitations Aharon Barak

Parliamentary Sovereignty: Contemporary Debates Jeffrey Goldsworthy